The Ocean, the Bird, and the Scholar

HELEN VENDLER

The Ocean, the Bird, and the Scholar

Essays on Poets and Poetry

HARVARD UNIVERSITY PRESS

Cambridge, Massachusetts
London, England
2015

Pages 431–433 constitute an extension of the copyright page

Library of Congress Cataloging-in-Publication Data

Vendler, Helen, 1933–

    The ocean, the bird, and the scholar : essays on poets and poetry / Helen Vendler.

      pages   cm

    Includes bibliographical references and index.

    ISBN 978-0-674-73656-6 (hardcover : alk. paper)

1. Poetry.   2. Poetics.   I. Title.

    PN1031.V365   2015

    818.1—dc23

                                    2014040692

For Killian and Céline, bearing the future

Contents

The Ocean, the Bird, and the Scholar

Introduction

Intensities

In giving an account of my life as a critic, I want to begin with the three most intense episodes of my own learning: the most decisive one, the eeriest one, and the most anguishing one.[1]

The most decisive intensity accompanied my instinctive conviction that I should write solely on poetry. When I was in graduate school, one had to classify oneself as a scholar of a certain historical period in England or America. I called myself, when forced to do so, "a Victorian." Yet I had seen that many of my teachers, though officially scholars of a given period, were internally something else. These were the poetry people—Rosemond Tuve, Douglas Bush—who, no matter what their period, taught chiefly poetry rather than plays or novels. I sensed that I too belonged to that crypto-group of poetry people, and it gave me a ratifying satisfaction to vow that whatever "the profession" might think of me, I would always write only about poetry, without confining myself to a single century or a single country. (Some years ago, in the papers of a close friend who had died, I came across a letter I had written to her when I was in my early twenties, describing the poets I wanted to write about: they came from several different periods and from both England and America, so my resolve was firm even then.)

The eeriest intensity of my history was aroused by my discovery, at twenty-three, of the poetry of Wallace Stevens. It was as if my own naked spirit spoke to me from the page. I'd read dozens of poets by the time I came across Stevens, and I'd memorized scores of poems, but it was through him that I understood style as personality, style as the actual material body of inner being. Before

I could make out, in any paraphrasable way, Stevens's poems, I knew, as by telepathy, what they meant emotionally. This experience was so peculiar that I was overcome by a desire to know how that perfusion, which somehow bypassed intellectual translation, was accomplished. All my later work has stemmed from the compulsion to explain the direct power of idiosyncratic style in conveying the import of poetry.

If the discovery of lyric as a field was the most decisive episode of my life as a critic, and the impact of Stevens, revealing to me my consuming interest in linguistic and structural idiosyncrasy, the eeriest one, the most anguishing episode came when I was thirty-four, in 1967. I was divorced, raising my son, David, receiving minimal child support ($90 per month), and working very hard teaching ten courses a year—four each term (of which one was night-school overload) and two each summer. I'd published my dissertation on Yeats in 1963, but I hadn't been able to write in a continuous fashion since then. I'd failed to make progress with a book on George Herbert, realizing that I'd have to train myself further in Renaissance poetry, a task I didn't then have time for. Instead, I had begun a book on Stevens, but my energy was flagging, and I had no money for child care or household help. One night, exhausted, I tried to think how to make my life easier. I obviously had to continue teaching and keeping house and taking care of my young son. The only way I could make my life easier was to give up writing. "They can't make me," I said to myself in panic and fear and rage. "They can't make me do that." I suppose "They" were the Fates, or the Stars, but I knew that to stop writing would be a form of self-murder. I decided to apply for a Fulbright Professorship to obtain a respite. After a year of mandarin leisure in Bordeaux in 1968–1969, teaching three hours a week, everything improved: I was tenured and had a lighter teaching load; David was a little older.

Because my son was an only child, and I thought he needed an available companion in the house, I had resolved never to work when he was at home and awake. Such as it was, my life of learning and teaching—indistinguishable to me from my life of writing—was a patchy, often fatigued, and always anxious one. As my son got older, the precious nighttime hours after he went to sleep shrank in extent; soon, like any adolescent, he was staying up later than I was. My life of studying and writing then began to take place, contrary to my circadian rhythm, in the early hours of the morning. I envied my male colleagues, who, in those days, seemed to have everything done for them by their spouses. Marjorie Nicolson's essay saying that what a woman scholar needed was a wife never seemed truer.

Being a Critic

Over time, I've written books on poets from Shakespeare to Seamus Heaney, with Herbert and Keats and Yeats and Stevens and Dickinson in between. The choice of a single genre as a field of expertise is still hardly acknowledged in job advertisements, yet how many scholars or critics can teach—or write about—all the genres equally well? The fundamentally different structures of literature—linear in narrative, dialectic in drama, and concentric in lyric—and the historical failures (except in unusual cases) of great poets to write workable plays or novels (or great novelists to write memorable lyrics) suggest basic incompatibilities among the genres. I only once, in want of money, agreed to review a novel (Mary McCarthy's *Birds of America* for the *New York Times Book Review*), and although I don't think the review was mistaken, I felt such guilt at falsifying my competence that I never again consented to write on fiction.

I must say something about the vocation that separates me from the "scholar"—at least from what the typical scholar is thought to be. I'm a critic rather than a scholar, a reader and writer more taken by texts than by contexts. From the time I was very young I continually asked myself, as I read through the works of poets, why some texts seemed so much more accomplished and moving than others. Why was Milton's "L'Allegro" more satisfactory than his "On the Death of a Fair Infant Dying of a Cough"? I believed, and still do, that anyone literate in poetry could see that the one was superior to the other. (Those who suppose there are no criteria for such judgments merely expose their own incapacity.) Still, to clarify to oneself and then to others, in a reasonable and explicit way, the imaginative individuality of a poem and to give evidence of its architectural and technical skill isn't an easy task. I've been brought to mute frustration by it when I know intuitively that something is present in the poem that I haven't yet been able to isolate or name or describe or solve. In chapter 12 of *Lord Jim*, Joseph Conrad remarks on "that mysterious, almost miraculous, power of producing striking effects by means impossible of detection which is the last word of the highest art." I wanted, hardly knowing how, to detect the means of that power.

A critic of my sort is, I suppose, "learned" in a way—that is, she has a memory for stories, styles, and structures she has seen before, and she understands the expressive possibilities latent in writing (from the larger forms of myth and narrative to the almost invisible arrangements of prepositions and articles). She remembers the combinations and permutations of words and syntax that she has come across, and is curious about the power of new assemblages. Against the background of known structures, she recognizes and defines original ones, finding names for them and inventing taxonomies in which they might be arranged. Her "learning" resembles the "learning" of poets, which, though deeply etymological and architectonic, is often unsystematic and idiosyncratic. She often fails at the most elementary undertakings of "scholarly" life, such as remembering facts, entering polemical debates, and relating works to the political or philosophical history of their era. She has—at least I have—no capacity for broad synthetic statements.

Since every generalization needs an anecdote, I recall here the time I was hastily asked to substitute for a colleague in a term course in Romantic Poetry. I knew and loved the work of the six poets that I was to teach, but I felt some obligation, since I was preparing a "period course," to make some general re-marks, to evoke some synthetic connections among the poets. I mentally tried out every sentence I could think of beginning "The Romantic poets are" or "The Romantic poets do" and, finding none of them true, descended to looking for smaller sentences that began, "Wordsworth and Coleridge both" or "Byron and Keats equally," and so on. Any completion I could think of was either otiose ("wrote blank verse") or thematic ("responded to the French Revolution"). Looking into scholarly books didn't help me. I told the students that I would teach them about the poetry of each poet individually, but that poets are en-tirely too idiosyncratic to be compared with each other, and when poems are considered under gross thematic rubrics, all generic and linguistic originality vanishes from sight. My end-of-term evaluations came back saying, "She was fine on individual poets, but she didn't tell us anything about Romanticism." (I learned not to apologize to students beforehand.)

Like all writers, I've had to accept the limits of my own capacities: the intri-cacies of poetic style and imagination are to me as compelling as the labyrinths of ideology or history to others. And just as I would be incompetent as a theo-rist or a new historicist, I've seen that many scholars are incompetent as inter-preters of poetry. To understand a poem it's necessary above all to understand its functional stylistic elements; when a scholar—without a profound knowl-edge of the poet's work—swoops in on a single poem to illustrate an ideolog-ical point, he or she tends to falsify both the poem and the poet in question. There is no ready and easy way to take the measure of a lyric: it must be seen in itself and as part of an individual oeuvre and as part of a literary tradition before it can be used to support any scholarly point at all.

Beginnings

What makes a critic? Parental legends of my childhood all had to do with words: that I began to talk at nine months; that by the time I was one, I knew a hundred words (that story is true; we found, after my parents' death, a list in the desk headed "Words Sister knew at one"); that at two, hearing my four-year-old sister say the "Our Father" in Latin, I asked from my crib, "Daddy, can I say it too?" and did. (Why any father would *want* to teach his four-year-old to recite the *Pater Noster* is another question.) My mother (who by the rules of the Boston school system had to relinquish at marriage her work as a primary-school teacher) was the fount of poetry in the house, quoting it frequently in conversation; my father was the (often unreasonable) pedagogical experimenter, seeing how far he could press us to learn new languages. From working as a paymaster for the United Fruit Company in Cuba and later teaching English in Puerto Rico, my father was fluent in Spanish; he added French and Italian during postgraduate study to qualify as a high-school teacher of Romance languages. So we children too (my sister and I, that is; my brother, refusing, simply fled the house after school) were to learn first Spanish, and then French, and then Italian at home. At the same time, Latin was being purveyed to us at church and at my Catholic elementary school (we sang high and low Mass, the standard Latin hymns, and such "extras" as the Holy Week *Tenebrae,* as well as the Psalms in antiphonal chorus). Classical Latin—Caesar and Virgil—was added in high school. Language took on, under these many forms, a strange and inexplicable shimmer, and I soon saw the disparate poetic effects possible in different linguistic and prosodic systems. My father gave us simple poems in Spanish— Bécquer, Darío—and I added them to the store of English poems I was finding in the anthologies in the house. In high school it was French poets that drew me, especially Ronsard (because I had discovered Shakespeare's sonnets) and Baudelaire (because I had discovered T. S. Eliot). The natural act of a critic is to compare, and I was always comparing.

I was always writing, too. When I wrote my first "poem" at six, I thought that a poem was something that scanned and rhymed. It wasn't until I was fifteen, when I read and memorized a whole batch of Shakespeare's sonnets, that I saw that a poem could tell the truth about one's inner being. In a night of what then seemed visionary insight, I wrote, at one sitting, five Shakespearean sonnets, and launched myself into a steady and secret writing of verse. It was for the following ten years the only honest part of my life.

Impediments

Most of my life was not honest. I was raised in an exaggeratedly observant Catholic household; my mother took us with her to daily Mass. From the time I went to school at four, my every day except Sunday began with a sung Requiem Mass, since in a large parish every day was necessarily the monthly or yearly anniversary of someone's death. With the Mass and the *Dies Irae* as daily bread, my imagination was never deprived. Against the disappointments and losses of her life, my mother shored the comforts of religion, which included writing conventional devotional verse that was faultless in prosody if in nothing else; it was occasionally published in Catholic journals. (My mother's mother, whose North Carolinian father had been a public scribe in Boston, had written verse, too, my mother told me.) As soon as I began, at eleven, to ask questions of my mother about matters of doctrine that I found incredible—from the Virgin Birth to the Resurrection—or matters of practice that I found intolerable—such as the prohibitions on birth control and divorce—she simply reiterated her belief in the Church as guide in matters of faith and morals, and closed off discussion. I began to feel both heretical and isolated.

I pleaded to be allowed to go to the Boston Girls' Latin School, as I was later to plead to be allowed to go to Radcliffe, but in both cases my parents denied me my wish. (In the second case, they were obeying Cardinal Cushing's forbidding from the pulpit, under pain of mortal sin, education at godless, atheistic, secular universities—it was the era of McCarthy.) In Roman Catholic elementary school, high school, and college, I couldn't ever publicly reveal what I was thinking. In college, two friends and I heard that certain nuns had warned other girls against us as a "bad element." We were innocent virgins, living soberly at home with our parents and getting A's; and we didn't understand. Much later, when I told this story to Czesław Miłosz, he laughed and said that one of the Jesuits in his high school had said to him at fifteen, "Miłosz, you have a criminal face." They knew us before we knew ourselves.

I'd expected to concentrate in English literature in college, but literature, I discovered with disgust, was taught as a branch of faith and morals. (This experience inoculated me forever against adopting any "ism" as a single lens through which to interpret literature.) I thought perhaps the French Department would be different, but there the study of French literature jumped more or less from Molière to Péguy, because Diderot, Pascal, Voltaire, Flaubert, Zola, Proust, and so on, were all on the Index of Forbidden Books and could not be assigned for reading. In desperation, I turned to the sciences, where faith and morals could not corrupt intellectual life. In my classes in chemistry, biology, physics, and mathematics, not only did I come upon a new way of looking at the world but I also learned the useful logic of sequential and evidential exposition, which helped form the way I write. Unsure of what I should do with my major in chemistry, I took the Medical College Admission Test and applied for a Fulbright in mathematics. I was awarded the Fulbright, shelved the idea of applying to medical school, and went to Belgium. On realizing that I was for the first time in my life out of my parents' power, I changed from mathematics back to literature (with the permission of the Fulbright authorities), and wrote to Harvard requesting admission to the PhD program in English.

During all this time of unwilling incarceration in religious environments, my poems were the only place I met myself. I submitted one to the college poetry contest; it won but wasn't allowed to be printed in the college magazine, because it was thought by the nun-advisor to be indecent. It began:

> The mind's a prostitute at heart,
> Knows no joy until the hour
> The innocent curtains are blown apart,
> Olympus presses a golden shower.
>
> Nor fastidious, either—as welcome is
> A bull as swan, if Jove's beneath.
> The willing girl is first to kiss
> The milky horn, the orange beak.

I meant every word of it; the only simile I could find for the appetitiveness and promiscuity of the mind in the presence of whatever would carry it off to a new place was a sexual one. It was longing and then elation that I felt when hunting down truth and having it burst upon me, but I was too ignorant at that time to know that prostitution had no longing or elation in it.

My verse writing continued sporadically in graduate school. I felt, though, that there was something my poems didn't have, though I tried to make them both emotionally accurate and formally competent. At last, as I happily wrote my dissertation, I found my true genre, the more prosaic one of criticism, and my desire to write poetry slipped away. (I much later realized that I don't possess the Coleridgean "continual reverie" of imagination; I don't live life on two planes at once as imaginative people do.) I felt some guilt about ceasing to write poetry, and wondered whether I had betrayed a vocation. In my thirties, I was at a party where Robert Lowell, Anne Sexton, and Elizabeth Bishop were present, and one of them asked me if I wrote poetry. I confessed to my lingering guilt and self-questioning about stopping. They laughed me to scorn, telling me that if I'd been meant to be a poet and had tried to stop, I'd immediately have found myself prey to migraines, indigestion, insomnia, or something worse, that the Muse will not be balked of her own. I felt much better.

The familial and educational impediments I've described helped, I suppose, to make me a critic. I was always having, as an adolescent, to inquire into what I *did* think if I didn't think what everyone without exception around me did; and then I had to ask *why* I thought such things; and then I had to look for verification in other sources (operas, poems, autobiographies, never novels) of the attitudes I'd adopted. My first external action stemming from independence of thinking came when I was fifteen. It was customary, once a year at Sunday Mass, for the congregation to stand en masse and "take the pledge of the Legion of Decency," promising publicly not to attend any movies rated C ("objectionable") or D ("condemned"). My family—along with everyone else in the parish church—stood up to take the pledge. I remained grimly, obstinately, and conspicuously seated. Of course nobody said a word to me about it: the practice of the house was never to air anything. But from then on my parents knew that I had set my will against theirs, powerless though I was in every practical way. After I left my parents' house, I never again went to church. In spite of the grandeur and pathos of the Christian myths, I couldn't square them with my young and fierce worship of truth. Writing, I think, became in my adult life a compensation for all the years of mutinous silence at home and at school.

Furtherings

The first sustained and positive experience that helped make me a critic was a year spent at Boston University as a special student when I was twenty-two. Harvard, in the person of the chairman of the English Department, had replied, when I wrote from Belgium wanting to apply to the PhD program, that I had no qualifications. I wrote back, asking what I would have to do to be qualified. An equally dismissive letter said, "Well, you could take English courses, and then apply." I came back from my Fulbright, lived uneasily at home, went to Boston University, enrolled in six English courses each semester, took the Graduate Record Examination, and applied to Harvard, which admitted me. At BU, my teachers led me from my literally medieval upbringing into the expansive precincts of secular thought. (I recall a teacher in a Renaissance course beginning his opening lecture by explaining that once upon a time people actually believed in such things as Heaven, Purgatory, and Hell; I felt like gesturing in the general direction of my parents' house.) One of my teachers at BU, Morton Berman, gave me my first permanent model of delightful and thought-provoking teaching. In his quick-witted, vivid, and penetrating lectures, he entered with entire sympathy into the minds of the writers he taught, from Carlyle to Hopkins, from Newman to Tennyson. And he took his students seriously. To write about literature for such a teacher was to feel all the old constricting bonds unloosed, to see vistas of possible Elysian fields of the mind. (I dedicated my third book to him.) And Boston University—after my sequestration and confinement in all-female religious schools—seemed an intellectual Utopia, proving that students of all ages, races, sexes, classes, and religions could learn together. I had at last found a world I could live in, and I've never regretted the world I left.

The hatred, frustration, and fear that had dominated my emotions in adolescence gradually drained away as I experienced two of the great blessings of adult life, friendship and motherhood. These new dimensions made me conscious of what I'd found lacking in most of the scholarly and critical prose to which I'd been exposed: that is, a rich sense of the passions underlying and motivating literary expression. The base of poetry in the emotions was tacitly ignored in scholarship and criticism, and yet I felt one couldn't understand the way a poem evolves stylistically without acknowledging that base. If there was any conscious drive in me to alter the field of criticism as I encountered it, it was to insert into the analysis of lyric an analysis of its motivating emotions and convictions, and to demonstrate their stylistic results.

By thirty I had found, finally, freedom and affection, and had left what I saw as falsehood and repression in a search for truth and expressiveness. When I dedicated my first book of essays to my son, I did it with a quotation from Ben Jonson which expressed at its close the qualities I wanted both for us as a family and for my work: "Freedom and truth; with love from those begot."

The Profession

My first professional experience as a graduate student was to hear the chairman of the English Department of Harvard say to me warningly, as he signed my program card during the opening week of classes, "You know we don't want you here, Miss Hennessy: we don't want any women here." I left his office trembling. (Thirteen years later, he apologized.) There were still professors in 1956 who would not admit women to their seminars. Almost all of the women admitted to the English PhD program at Harvard left. In those days, the structural difficulties in the way of women's success were hardly understood: women PhD's followed their nonacademic husbands to towns where there was no university or college; or to colleges where rules concerning nepotism prohibited their working where their husband worked; or to colleges restricted to male teachers and students; or to universities unwilling to hire a woman who was a wife and mother. The social pressure to have the "normal" number of children, and to stop working after children were born, was strongly felt. Doubts about women's intellectual powers were still widespread. And as women PhD's, defeated by these factors, fell by the wayside, the professors who had trained them became increasingly skeptical of the worth of investing in students who would probably never practice their profession. Women entering the Graduate School at Harvard felt their secondary status.

On the other hand, there were several professors in the department of English who were as eager to support women as men, and I had the luck to be taught by some of these. One (John Kelleher, who, as a literary historian and poet, never forgot the link of literature to life) recommended my thesis on Yeats to the Harvard University Press; another (Douglas Bush, who, like John Kelleher, knew the poems he taught by heart) sent my name the year after I earned my PhD to the Guggenheim Foundation; and a third (Reuben Brower) later invited me to co-publish with him. Perhaps the most important influence on me at Harvard was I. A. Richards. I had wanted to take his course (I already knew his work), but the chairman, with a scornful remark in that first interview ("He's not even a member of the department!"), forbade it, scratching out the course number himself on my program card and writing in a course in Chaucer. But he couldn't prevent me from auditing Richards's course, and I found in his lectures how meditation on a poem could open into further and further depths of perception. Rosemond Tuve came to Harvard for a year as a sabbatical replacement for Harry Levin; her seminar on Spenser taught me to think of poems in terms of genre, and we became lifelong friends. Northrop Frye visited, too; I was one of the crowd that had the thrilling experience of hearing *The Anatomy of Criticism* delivered orally before it saw publication. When I came to write my dissertation, I asked myself whose prose style I admired, and (knowing myself incapable of Douglas Bush's wit) turned to Frye as a model. Because I admired clarity, and Frye was always clear, I studied his sentences and his paragraphs, and learned from his example how to write a chapter. (I learned, later, much more about writing a book from my brilliant editor at the Harvard University Press, Margaretta Fulton.)

Though the profession as a whole was not friendly to women, stubborn persistence, at least in some cases, could carry the day. My first job was at Cornell, and when at midyear I had a baby, the chairman deprived me of teaching, declaring that those who had had babies knew that people with babies couldn't teach. At last, through the kind intervention of my colleague Stephen Parrish, the chairman relented and gave me a single spring-term 8 A.M. section of Freshman English. (Nobody but graduate students taught at 8 A.M.; I got up at six o'clock, readied myself and the baby, drove the baby three houses down the street to the babysitter, drove around the lake to class from eight to nine o'clock, drove back and picked up the baby at nine thirty, and felt I didn't have a job at all except when I was grading papers at night.) The following year the chairman gave me my job back full time and, deciding I was serious, began to ask me to substitute in courses above the freshman level as colleagues went on leave; in my third year he asked me to give a course of my own. A striking advance in my literary learning came at Cornell when I audited Paul de Man's course in Valéry, Rilke, and Stevens; I encountered deconstruction (in which I had already been implicitly tutored by Stevens's poetry) and found it useful in its salutary countering of unity, coherence, and emphasis with dispersal, contradiction, and disjunction.

The profession, when I entered it, was not unfriendly to literary criticism, though many colleagues considered criticism lightweight by comparison to "real" scholarship. What the field *was* unfriendly to was reviewing, which was referred to as "mere journalism." I, on the other hand, took reviewing as the occasion for serious thought, and didn't see why it should be looked down on. Because of my slender means, I took every reviewing job I could get; reviewing was an agreeable and intellectual way to earn money, and it became for me a self-seminar in the new. To be asked to write on a new book by John Berryman or James Merrill or Elizabeth Bishop was already a joy; and reviewing to a word limit for the general public taught me to aim in my prose for concision and a personal voice. After I had been writing for some years for the *New York Times Book Review* and the *New York Review of Books,* I had a call from William Shawn of the *New Yorker,* asking me to be their poetry critic. To me as to everyone writing for him, Mr. Shawn gave free rein, unlimited space, and genial encouragement.

I should tell the tale of my very first *New Yorker* review, because it sheds light on Mr. Shawn's character. I was asked to review the collected poems of an author who had recently died. I wrote truthfully on the scope and limits of the author's work, and sent off the review. Then came a phone call from Mr. Shawn: "Mrs. Vendler, I very much liked your review; it was interesting and well done. But I wanted to explain that I don't feel I can print it." (My heart sank.) "You see, there are things in it that I believe might hurt the feelings of the poet's widow, and I wouldn't want to be responsible for that." (I hadn't reckoned on live people being connected with a dead poet.) But Mr. Shawn kindly went on to add, "I'm sure there will be something else very soon that we'll want you to do for us"—and he kept his word. I wrote for the magazine for many years, until a new editor changed its character. Luckily, other editors continued to give me space, especially Robert Silvers of the *New York Review of Books,* and some new editors took me on (among them Leon Wieseltier of the *New Republic* and Mary-Kay Wilmers of the *London Review of Books*).

Along with reviewing, I continued to write books on individual poets. To me the most extraordinary drama in literature—and the best context in which to investigate stylistics—is the development of a poet from callow imitation into full lyric mastery. I was helped in thinking about that process of development by two resources. In reflecting on its emotional and intellectual factors, I was influenced by Freud, as was natural to a member of my generation, and especially to one reading poets who had undergone psychotherapy: Lowell, Bishop, Berryman, Plath, Sexton. The husband of my close friend Marguerite Stewart owned the complete Freud, and I often browsed in those volumes when I was in their house. I learned from Freud's seductive expository style as well as his provocative content. The second resource that influenced me in studying the poets' development and the consequent changes in their style was the discipline of linguistics. My then husband, Zeno Vendler, was a linguist as well as a philosopher, and his library of books on linguistics gave me, when we were first married, a new way into the minutiae of style. Stylistics is a relatively undefined field, sometimes practiced by linguists, sometimes by critics; it has had a more continuous tradition in European than in Anglo-American criticism. However, linguists and stylisticians too often separate the elements of style from the total imaginative practice of a poet and from the psychological and intellectual motivations of verse. In writing on poets, I have wanted to connect inseparably—as they are connected in the fluent progress of a poem—imagination, feeling, and stylistic originality. Each poet presents a new stylistic field; and one must perceive, in each case, a map by which one can draw a path from stylistic result back to imaginative and emotional cause. My life as a critic has really been a life of coming to understand the expressive powers of the English language over several centuries as they are idiosyncratically invented and modulated by lyric poets.

Each of my books on a single author has had a polemical purpose as well as a descriptive one. These were, in sequence: to interpret Yeats's *Vision* as less a book of occult doctrine than as a thesis on poetics; to rehabilitate Stevens's longer poems in objecting to the view (most vividly expressed by Randall Jarrell) that they were elephantine and ponderous; to show (*contra* Coleridge and others) that an atheist's reading of Herbert could reveal the power and fineness of his poetry to those who didn't share his religious beliefs; to argue that Keats's odes exist not only as detached poems but also as a purposive sequence working out reflections on poetics that rebut associationist and sensationalist theories of the arts; to insist, in my second book on Stevens, that he was far from being the cold and solely intellectual writer represented by his conventional reputation; to consider Shakespeare's sonnets as individual experiments in lyric language and structure rather than as narrative sites of thematic expression; and to represent Seamus Heaney, whose poetry had so often been treated exclusively within political or national frameworks, as a writer who made original interventions in almost all the lyric genres. In commenting on Dickinson, I wanted to show her blasphemous and harsher moments as much as her well-known charm and despair.

I've sometimes been characterized as a "formalist" critic: indeed, Frank Lentricchia (before his apostasy from his earlier positions) once called me the "Queen of Formalism"—two neo-Marxist denunciations in one. The label "formalist," it should be recalled, was in the earlier part of this century a term of abuse bestowed on their enemies by Marxist theorists of literature. To call someone a formalist is to accuse that person of being an elitist concerned with the technical carapace of art to the exclusion of its intellectual, human, and material significance. "Formalist" is always, even now, a term used pejoratively. I prefer, for what I do, the classical label of "commentary" or Pater's label, "aesthetic criticism." The presumption of commentary, from the first classical commentaries down to our own day, is that literary works are complex enough in thought and style to solicit detailed intellectual and critical reflection; the presumption of aesthetic criticism is that artworks have not been seen accurately until the intrinsic relations governing the structural and formal shapes they assume are perceived and accounted for. An aesthetic critic is naturally concerned with the generic and formal aspects of an artwork, its implicit poetics, its internal structures of relation, its intellectual argument, and its expressive means, but such a critic wants also to deduce and describe the internal factors motivating the invention of such idiosyncratic forms. Form is content as deployed. Content is form as imagined.

During my years of teaching, some members of the profession became unfriendly to aesthetic criticism, finding it either "naive" or "essentialist." They also became unfriendly to lyric poetry itself: lyrics were too short to be good texts for deconstructive purposes, and novels and plays appeared to be more suitable sites for the information retrieval about social conditions on which a politicized criticism depends. An agonized article in *PMLA* asked why the study of poetry had gone under. But in spite of such transient professional attitudes, the appetite of the young for the study of poetry hasn't abated. When scholars in English departments haven't provided it, the young have infiltrated programs in creative writing or in foreign languages to find it. The young respond to poetry for the same reason I did at their age: poems, as histories of human consciousness, describe complex truths of human response, and they structure words with particular force, wit, charm, intellectual responsibility, and plangency. In fact, when a life experience arrives that is as yet unrepresented in lyrics, the young person accustomed to being accompanied in life by poems feels desperately at a loss, as I did when I encountered the absence of significant poems on that mysterious emotional upheaval known as motherhood. We still lack a great poet writing great poems on that subject, although Sylvia Plath made a beginning.

The larger problem for critics, professionally speaking, is that American culture is as yet too young to prize poetry—or, for that matter, any complex form of intellectuality except perhaps science (because science "works," and our New World history has made us pragmatists). America, having sloughed off Europe, is still too raw and ignorant to be proud of its own native achievements in art and poetry and music. A student can graduate from high school in the United States without knowing that there ever was an American architect or composer or painter or sculptor or philosopher, and without reading any of the more complex poems written by our American authors. That, I think, will change as we eventually become proud of the significant artworks composed on our own soil, and incorporate them, as part of the patrimony of our patriotism, into the general education of the young. Meanwhile, those of us living within what Stevens called "the radiant and productive atmosphere" of poetry transmit as far as we can, in books and in the classroom, the beautiful, subversive, sustaining, bracing, and demanding legacy of the poets. The pieces of writing in this collection were written in the belief that poetry belongs to all, but that its audience often needs—as I do still—paths into its inexhaustible precincts.

1

The Ocean, the Bird, and the Scholar

How the Arts Help Us to Live

When it became useful in educational circles in the United States to group various university disciplines under the name "The Humanities," it seems to have been tacitly decided that philosophy and history would be cast as the core of this grouping, and that other forms of learning—the study of languages, literatures, religion, and the arts—would be relegated to subordinate positions. Philosophy, conceived of as embodying truth, and history, conceived of as a factual record of the past, were proposed as the principal embodiments of Western culture, and given pride of place in general education programs.

But this confidence in a reliable factual record, not to speak of faith in a reliable philosophical synthesis, has undergone considerable erosion. Historical and philosophical assertions issue, it seems, from particular vantage points, and are no less contestable than the assertions of other disciplines. The day of limiting cultural education to Western culture alone is over. There are losses here, of course—losses in depth of learning, losses in coherence—but these very changes have thrown open the question of how the humanities should now be conceived, and how the study of the humanities should, in this moment, be encouraged.

I want to propose that the humanities should take, as their central objects of study, not the texts of historians or philosophers, but the products of aesthetic endeavor: art, dance, music, literature, theater, architecture, and so on. After all, it is by their arts that cultures are principally remembered. For every person who has read a Platonic dialogue, there are probably ten who have seen a Greek marble in a museum; or if not a Greek marble, at least a Roman copy; or if not a Roman copy, at least a photograph. Around the arts there exist, in orbit, the commentaries on art produced by scholars: musicology and music criticism, art history and art criticism, literary and linguistic studies. At the periphery we might set the other humanistic disciplines—philosophy, history, the study of religion. The arts would justify a broad philosophical interest in ontology, phenomenology, and ethics; they would bring in their train a richer history than one which, in its treatment of mass phenomena, can lose sight of individual human uniqueness—the quality most prized in artists, and most salient, and most valued, in the arts.

What would be the advantage of centering humanistic study on the arts? The arts present the whole uncensored human person—in emotional, physical, and intellectual being, and in single and collective form—as no other branch of human accomplishment does. In the arts we see both the nature of human predicaments—in Job, in Lear, in Isabel Archer—and the evolution of representation over long spans of time (as the taste for the Gothic replaces the taste for the Romanesque, as the composition of opera replaces the composition of plain-chant). The arts bring into play historical and philosophical questions without implying the prevalence of a single system or of universal solutions. Artworks embody the individuality that fades into insignificance in the massive canvas of history and is suppressed in philosophy by the desire for impersonal assertion. The arts are true to the way we are and were, to the way we actually live and have lived—as singular persons swept by drives and affections, not as collective entities or sociological paradigms. The case histories developed within the arts are in part idiosyncratic, but in part they are applicable by analogy to a class larger than the individual entities they depict. Hamlet is a very specific figure—a Danish prince who has been to school in Germany—but when Prufrock says, "I am not Prince Hamlet," he is in a way testifying to the fact that Hamlet means something to everyone who knows about the play.

If the arts are so satisfactory an embodiment of human experience, why do we need studies commenting on them? Why not merely take our young people to museums, to concerts, to libraries? There is certainly no substitute for hearing Mozart, reading Dickinson, or looking at the boxes of Joseph Cornell. Why should we support a brokering of the arts? Why not rely on their direct impact? The simplest answer is that reminders of art's presence are constantly necessary. As art goes in and out of fashion, some scholar is always necessarily reviving Melville, or editing Monteverdi, or recommending Jane Austen. Critics and scholars are evangelists, plucking the public by the sleeve, saying, "Look at this," or "Listen to this," or "See how this works." It may seem hard to believe, but there was a time when almost no one valued Gothic art or, to come closer to our own time, *Moby-Dick* and *Billy Budd*.

A second reason to encourage scholarly studies of the arts is that such studies establish in human beings a sense of cultural patrimony. We in the United States are the heirs of several cultural patrimonies: a world patrimony (of which we are becoming increasingly conscious); a Western patrimony (from which we derive our institutions, civic and aesthetic); and a specifically American patrimony (which, though great and influential, has, bafflingly, yet to be established securely in our schools). In Europe, although the specifically national patrimony was likely to be urged as preeminent—Italian pupils studied Dante, French pupils studied Racine—most nations felt obliged to give their students an idea of the Western inheritance extending beyond native production. As time passed, colonized nations, although instructed in the culture of the colonizer, found great energy in creating a national literature and culture of their own with and against the colonial model. (We can see this, for instance, in the example of nineteenth- and twentieth-century Ireland.) For a long time, American schooling paid homage, culturally speaking, to Europe and to England; but increasingly we began to cast off European and English influence in arts and letters without, unfortunately, filling the consequent cultural gap in the schools with our own worthy creations in art and literature. Our students leave high school knowing almost nothing about American art, music, architecture, and sculpture, and having only a superficial acquaintance with a few American writers.

We will ultimately want to teach, with justifiable pride, our national patrimony in arts and letters—by which, if by anything, we will be remembered—and we hope, of course, to foster young readers and writers, artists and museum-goers, composers and music enthusiasts. But these patriotic and cultural aims alone are not enough to justify putting the arts and the studies of the arts at the center of our humanistic and educational enterprise. What, then, might lead us to recommend the arts and their commentaries as the center of the humanities? Art, said Wallace Stevens, helps us to live our lives. I'm not sure we are greatly helped to live our lives by history (since, whether or not we remember it, we seem doomed to repeat it) or by philosophy (the consolations of philosophy have never been very widely received). Stevens's assertion is a large one, and we have a right to ask how he would defend it. How do the arts, and the scholarly studies attendant on them, help us to live our lives?

Stevens was a democratic author, and he expected his experience, and his reflections on it, to apply widely. For him, as for any other artist, "to live our lives" means to live in the body as well as in the mind, on the sensual Earth as well as in the celestial clouds. The arts exist to relocate us in the body by means

of the work of the mind in aesthetic creation; they situate us on the Earth, paradoxically, by means of a mental paradigm of experience embodied, with symbolic concision, in a physical medium. It distressed Stevens that most of the
human beings he saw walked about blankly, scarcely seeing the Earth on which
they lived, filtering it out from their pragmatic urban consciousness. Even when
he was only in his twenties, Stevens was perplexed by the narrowness of the
way in which people inhabit the Earth:

> I thought, on the train, how utterly we have forsaken the Earth, in the
> sense of excluding it from our thoughts. There are but few who consider
> its physical hugeness, its rough enormity. It is still a disparate monstrosity,
> full of solitudes & barrens & wilds. It still dwarfs & terrifies & crushes.
> The rivers still roar, the mountains still crash, the winds still shatter. Man
> is an affair of cities. His gardens & orchards & fields are mere scrapings.
> Somehow, however, he has managed to shut out the face of the giant from
> his windows. But the giant is there, nevertheless.[1]

The arts and their attendant disciplines restore human awareness by releasing
it into the ambience of the felt world, giving a habitation to the tongue in newly
coined language, to the eyes and ears in remarkable re-creations of the physical
world, to the animal body in the kinesthetic flex and resistance of the artistic
medium. Without an alert sense of such things, one is only half alive. Stevens
reflected on this function of the arts—and on the results of its absence—in
three poems that I will take up as proof-texts for what follows. Although
Stevens speaks in particular about poetry, he extends the concept to *poesis*—
the Greek term for making, widely applicable to all creative effort.

Like geography and history, the arts confer a patina on the natural world. A
vacant stretch of grass becomes humanly important when one reads the sign
"Gettysburg." Over the grass hangs an extended canopy of meaning—struggle,
corpses, tears, glory—shadowed by a canopy of American words and works,
from the Gettysburg Address to the Shaw Memorial. The vacant plain of the
sea becomes human when it is populated by the ghosts of Ahab and Moby-Dick.
An unremarkable town becomes "Winesburg, Ohio"; a rustic bridge becomes
"the rude bridge that arched the flood," where Minutemen fired "the shot heard
round the world." One after the other, cultural images suspend themselves,
invisibly, in the American air, as—when we extend our glance—the Elgin
marbles, wherever they may be housed, hover over the Parthenon, once their
home; as Michelangelo's Adam has become, to the Western eye, the Adam of

Genesis. The patina of culture has been laid down over centuries, so that in an English field one can find a Roman coin, in an Asian excavation an emperor's stone army, in our Western desert the signs of the mound builders. Over Stevens's giant earth, with its tumultuous motions, there floats every myth, every text, every picture, every system, that creators—artistic, religious, philosophical—have conferred upon it. The Delphic oracle hovers there next to Sappho, Luther's theses hang next to the Grünewald altar, China's Cold Mountain neighbors Sinai, Bach's Mass in B Minor shares space with Rabelais.

If there did not exist, floating over us, all the symbolic representations that art and music, religion, philosophy, and history, have invented, and all the interpretations and explanations of them that scholarly effort has produced, what sort of people would we be? We would, says Stevens, be sleepwalkers, going about like automata, unconscious of the very life we were living: this is the import of Stevens's 1943 poem "Somnambulisma." The poem rests on three images, of which the first is the incessantly variable sea, the vulgar reservoir from which the vulgate—the common discourse of language and art alike—is drawn. The second image is that of a mortal bird, whose motions resemble those of the water but who is ultimately washed away by the ocean. The subsequent generations of the bird, too, are always washed away. The third image is that of a scholar, without whom ocean and bird alike would be incomplete.

> On an old shore, the vulgar ocean rolls
> Noiselessly, noiselessly, resembling a thin bird,
> That thinks of settling, yet never settles, on a nest.
>
> The wings keep spreading and yet are never wings.
> The claws keep scratching on the shale, the shallow shale,
> The sounding shallow, until by water washed away.
>
> The generations of the bird are all
> By water washed away. They follow after.
> They follow, follow, follow, in water washed away.
>
> Without this bird that never settles, without
> Its generations that follow in their universe,
> The ocean, falling and falling on the hollow shore,
>
> Would be a geography of the dead: not of that land
> To which they may have gone, but of the place in which
> They lived, in which they lacked a pervasive being,

In which no scholar, separately dwelling,
Poured forth the fine fins, the gawky beaks, the personalia,
Which, as a man feeling everything, were his.[2]

Without the bird and its generations, the ocean, says the poet, would be
"a geography of the dead"—not in the sense of the dead having gone to some
other world, but in the sense of their being persons who were emotionally and
intellectually sleepwalking, dead while alive, who lacked "a pervasive being."
To lack a pervasive being is to fail to live fully. A pervasive being is one that
extends through the brain, the body, the senses, and the will, a being that
spreads to every moment, so that one not only feels what Keats called "the
poetry of earth" but responds to it with creative motions of one's own.

Unlike Keats's nightingale, Stevens's bird does not sing; its chief functions
are to generate generations of birds, to attempt to sprout wings, and to try to
leave behind some painstakingly scratched record of its presence. The water
restlessly moves, sometimes noiselessly, sometimes in "sounding shallow[s]";
the bird "never settles." The bird tries to generate wings, but never quite succeeds; it tries to inscribe itself on the shale, but its scratchings are washed
away. The ocean is "falling and falling"; the mortal generations are following
and following. Time obliterates birds and inscriptions alike.

Imagine being psychically dead during the very life you have lived. That,
says Stevens, would be the fate of the generations were it not for the scholar.
Stevens does not locate his scholar in the ocean or on the shale, the haunts of
the bird; the scholar, says the poet, dwells separately. But he dwells in immense
fertility: things pour forth from him. He makes up for the wings that are never
wings, for the impotent claws; he generates "fine fins," the essence of the ocean's
fish; he creates "gawky beaks," opening in fledglings waiting to be fed so that
they may rise into their element, the air; and he reproduces new garments for
the Earth, called not regalia (suitable for a monarchy) but "personalia," suitable for the members of a democracy. How is the scholar capable of such pro-
fusion? He is fertile both because he is a man who "feel[s] everything," and
because every thing that he feels reifies itself in a creation. He gives form and
definition both to the physical world (as its scientific observer) and to the in-
choate aesthetic world (as the quickened responder to the bird's incomplete natural song). He is analogous to the God of Genesis; as he observes and feels
finniness, he says, "Let there be fine fins," and fine fins appear.

Why does Stevens name this indispensable figure a "scholar"? (Elsewhere
he calls him a "rabbi"—each is a word connoting learning.) What does learning

have to do with creation? Why are study and learning indispensable in reifying and systematizing the world of phenomena and their aesthetic representations? Just as the soldier is poor without the poet's lines (as Stevens says elsewhere), so the poet is poor without the scholar's cultural memory, his taxonomies and his histories. Our systems of thought—legal, philosophical, scientific, religious—have all been devised by "scholars" without whose aid widespread complex thinking could not take place and be debated, intricate texts and scores could not be accurately established and interpreted. The restless emotions of aesthetic desire, the wing-wish and inscription-yearning of the bird, perish without the arranging and creative powers of intellectual endeavor. The arts and the studies of the arts are for Stevens a symbiotic pair, each dependent on the other. Nobody is born understanding string quartets or reading Latin or creating poems; without the scholar and his libraries, there would be no per-petuation and transmission of culture. The mutual support of art and learning, the mutual delight each ideally takes in each, can be taken as a paradigm of how the humanities might be integrally conceived and educationally conveyed as inextricably linked to the arts.

"Somnambulisma" is the illustration of Stevens's adage "Poetry is the scholar's art." What is necessary, asks "Somnambulisma," for creative effort? Emotion, desire, generative energy, and learned invention—these, replies the poem, are indispensable in the artist. But there is another way of thinking about art, fo-cusing less on the creator of art than on those of us who make up art's audi-ence. What do we gain in being the audience for the arts and their attendant disciplines? Let us, says Stevens, imagine ourselves deprived of all the products of aesthetic and humanistic effort, living in a world with no music, no art, no architecture, no books, no films, no choreography, no theater, no histories, no songs, no prayers, no images floating above the Earth to keep it from being a geography of the dead. Stevens creates the desolation of that deprivation in a poem—the second of my three texts—called "Large Red Man Reading." The poem is like a painting by Matisse, showing us an earthly giant the color of the sun, reading aloud from great sky-sized tabulae which, as the day de-clines, darken from blue to purple. The poem also summons up the people of the giant's audience: they are ghosts, no longer alive, who now inhabit unhappily (having expected more from the afterlife) the remote "wilderness of stars." What does the giant describe to the ghosts as he reads from his blue tabulae? Nothing extraordinary—merely the normal furniture of life, the common and the beautiful, the banal, the ugly, and even the painful. But to the ghosts these are things achingly familiar from life and yet disregarded during it. Now they are achingly lost, things that they never sufficiently prized when alive, but that they miss devastatingly in the vacancy of space among the foreign stars.

> There were ghosts that returned to earth to hear his phrases,
> As he sat there reading, aloud, the great blue tabulae.
> They were those from the wilderness of stars that had expected more.
>
> There were those that returned to hear him read from the poem of life,
> Of the pans above the stove, the pots on the table, the tulips among
>   them.
> They were those that would have wept to step barefoot into reality,
>
> They would have wept and been happy, have shivered in the frost
> And cried out to feel it again, have run fingers over leaves
> And against the most coiled thorn, have seized on what was ugly
>
> And laughed, as he sat there reading, from out of the purple tabulae,
> The outlines of being and its expressings, the syllables of its law:
> *Poesis, poesis,* the literal characters, the vatic lines,
>
> Which in those ears and in those thin, those spended hearts,
> Took on color, took on shape and the size of things as they are
> And spoke the feeling for them, which was what they had lacked.
> (365)

The ghosts, while they were alive, had lacked feeling, because they had not registered in their memory "the outlines of being and its expressings, the syllables of its law." It is a triple assertion that Stevens makes here: that being possesses not only outlines (as all bodies do) and expressings (in all languages) but also a law, which is stricter than mere "expressings." Expressings by themselves cannot exemplify the law of being: only *poesis*—the creator's act of replicating in symbolic form the structures of life—pervades being sufficiently to intuit and to embody its law. *Poesis* not only reproduces the content of life (its daily phenomena) but finds a manner (inspired, "vatic") for that content, and in the means of its medium—here, the literal characters of its language—embodies the structural laws that shape being to our understanding.

Stevens's anecdote-of-audience in "Large Red Man Reading" suggests how ardently we would want to come back, as ghosts, in order to recognize and relish the parts of life we had insufficiently noticed and hardly valued when alive. But we cannot—according to the poem—accomplish this by ourselves: it is only when the earthly giant of vital being begins to read, using poetic and prophetic syllables to express the reality, and the law, of being, that the experiences of life can be reconstituted and made available as beauty and solace, to help us live our lives.

How could our lives be different if we reconstituted the humanities around the arts and the studies of the arts? Past civilizations are recalled in part, of course, for their philosophy and their history, but for most of us it is the arts of the past that preserve Egypt and Greece and Rome, India and Africa and Japan. The names of the artists may be lost, the arts themselves in fragments, the scrolls incomplete, the manuscripts partial—but Anubis and the Buddha and *The Canterbury Tales* still populate our imaginative world. They come trailing their interpretations, which follow them and are like water washed away. Scholarly and critical interpretations may not outlast the generation to which they are relevant; as intellectual concepts flourish and wither, so interpretations are proposed and discarded. But we would not achieve our own grasp on Vermeer or Horace, generation after generation, without the scholars' outpourings.

If we are prepared to recognize the centrality of artists and their interpreters to every past culture, we might begin to reflect on what our own American culture has produced that will be held dear centuries from now. Which are the paintings, the buildings, the novels, the musical compositions, the poems, through which we will be remembered? What set of representations of life will float above the American soil, rendering each part of it as memorable as Marin's Maine or Langston Hughes's Harlem, as Cather's Nebraska or Lincoln's Gettysburg? How will the outlines and the expressings and the syllables of American being glow above our vast geography? How will our citizens be made aware of their cultural inheritance, and become proud of their patrimony? How will they pass it on to their children as their own generation is by water washed away? How will their children become capable of "feeling everything," of gaining "a pervasive being," capable of helping the bird to spread its wings and the fish to grow their "fine fins" and the scholar to pour forth his "personalia"?

To link, by language, feeling to phenomena has always been the poet's aim. "Poetry," said Wordsworth in his 1798 Preface to *Lyrical Ballads,* "is the breath and finer spirit of all knowledge; it is the impassioned expression which is in the countenance of all science." Our culture cannot afford to neglect the thirst of human beings for the representations of life offered by the arts, the hunger of human beings for commentary on those arts as they appear on the cultural stage. The training in subtlety of response (which used to be accomplished in large part by religion and the arts) cannot be responsibly left to commercial movies and television. Within education, scientific training, which necessarily brackets emotion, needs to be complemented by the direct mediation—through the arts and their interpretations—of feeling, vicarious experience, and interpersonal imagination. Art can often be trusted—once it is unobtrusively but ubiquitously present—to make its own impact felt. A set of Rembrandt self-portraits in a shopping mall, a group of still lifes in a subway, sonatas played in the lunchroom, spirituals sung chorally from kindergarten on—all such things, appearing entirely without commentary, can be offered in the community and the schools as a natural part of living. Students can be gently led, by teachers and books, from passive reception to active reflection. The arts are too profound and far-reaching to be left out of our children's patrimony: the arts have a right, within our schools, to be as serious an object of study as molecular biology or mathematics. Like other complex products of the mind, they ask for reiterated exposure, sympathetic exposition, and sustained attention.

The arts have the advantage, once presented, of making people curious not only about aesthetic matters, but also about history, philosophy, and other cultures. How is it that pre-Columbian statues look so different from Roman ones? Why do some painters concentrate on portraits and others on landscapes? Why did great ages of drama arise in England and Spain and then collapse? Who first found a place for jazz in classical music, and why? Why do some writers become national heroes, and others do not? Who evaluates art, and how? Are we to believe what a piece of art says? Why does Picasso represent a full face and a profile at the same time? How small can art be and still be art? Why have we needed to invent so many subsets within each art—within literature the epic, drama, lyric, novel, dialogue, essay; within music everything from the solo partita to the chorales of Bach? Why do cultures use different musical instruments and scales? Who has the right to be an artist? How does one claim that right? The questions are endless, and the answers provocative; and both questions and answers require, and indeed generate, sensuous responsiveness, a trained eye, fine discrimination, and a hunger for learning, all qualities we would like to see in ourselves and in our children.

Best of all, the arts are enjoyable. The "grand elementary principle of pleasure" (as Wordsworth called it) might be invoked more urgently than it now is to make the humanities, both past and present, mean something relevant to Americans. Once the appetite for an art has been awakened by pleasure, the nursery rhyme and the cartoon lead by degrees to Stevens and Eakins. A curriculum relying on the ocean, the bird, and the scholar, on the red man and his blue tabulae, would produce a love of the arts and humanities that we have not yet succeeded in generating in the population at large. When reality is freshly seen, through the artists and their commentators, something happens to the felt essence of life. As Stevens wrote in the third of my texts, "Angel Surrounded by Paysans," the angel of reality then briefly appears at our door, saying:

> . . . I am the necessary angel of earth,
> Since, in my sight, you see the earth again,
>
> Cleared of its stiff and stubborn, man-locked set,
> And, in my hearing, you hear its tragic drone
>
> Rise liquidly in liquid lingerings,
> Like watery words awash; like meanings said
>
> By repetitions of half meanings. Am I not,
> Myself, only half of a figure of a sort,
>
> A figure half seen, or seen for a moment, a man
> Of the mind, an apparition apparelled in
>
> Apparels of such lightest look that a turn
> Of my shoulder and quickly, too quickly, I am gone?
> (423)

That art-angel of the earth, renewing our sense of life and of ourselves, repeats only half meanings, because we provide the other half. Among us are the scholars who interpret those half-meanings into full ones, apparelling us anew in their personalia. In the apparels of his messenger, Stevens is recalling these lines from Wordsworth's great ode:

> There was a time when meadow, grove, and stream,
> The earth, and every common sight
> To me did seem
> Apparelled in celestial light,
> The glory and the freshness of a dream.

The secular angel refreshing our sense of the world, apparelled in Wordsworthian light, stays only for a moment, our moment of attention. But that moment of mental acuity recalls us to being, the body, and the emotions, which are, peculiarly, so easy for us to put to one side as we engage in purely intellectual or physical work. Just as art is only half itself without us—its audience, its analysts, its scholars—so we are only half ourselves without it. When, in this country, we become fully ourselves, we will have balanced our great accomplishments in progressive abstraction—in mathematics and the natural sciences—with an equally great absorption in art, and in the disciplines ancillary to art. The arts, though not progressive, aim to be eternal, and sometimes are. And why should the United States not have as much eternity as any other nation? As Marianne Moore said (in "England") of excellence, "It has never been confined to one locality."

2

Fin-de-Siècle Lyric

W. B. Yeats and Jorie Graham

The recent past always presents itself as if destroyed by catastrophe.
—Theodor Adorno, *Minima Moralia*, "Dwarf Fruit"

Except for us,
The total past felt nothing when destroyed.
—Wallace Stevens, *Esthétique du Mal*

Egypt and Greece, good-bye, and good-bye Rome!
—W. B. Yeats, "Meru"

She's deep into the lateness now.
—Jorie Graham, "History"

Fin-de-siècle writing suggests seriousness and flamboyance, hyperbole and arbitrariness. The notion of fin de siècle presents itself to reflection as unsuitable for lyric, since it derives from the time span of epic narration, and lyric generically prefers the brief moment to the narrative span. The primary formal problem for the writer of lyric who wishes to invoke the notion of history is how to tuck such a panoramic concept into a short-breathed poem. The fin-de-siècle poem is a subgenre within a lyric genre we could call the history poem, and in this chapter I have a few words to say about the way Yeats and Graham work toward solutions of the formal problem of reconciling the epic subject of history with the lyric moment.

But first I want to mention the literary-historical problem of the fin de siècle as a descriptive phrase. The phrase *fin de siècle,* as we have inherited it today, carries a nineteenth-century tonality, embracing a group of etiolated or exaggerated images and an associated aura of exhausted male sexuality, a sexuality dominated by the aggression of femmes fatales and a congeries of "perversions"—sadomasochism, suicide, homosexuality, incest, and so on. It would be a mistake, surely, to transfer this literary description, deriving from the nineteenth century, to the twentieth-century fin de siècle, which has acquired a different, if equally disturbing, sense of itself while not distancing itself altogether from the melodrama of the nineteenth-century phase.

Even in a turn-of-the-century predecessor, the nineteenth-century sense of the fin de siècle can suffer revision, and I therefore begin with Yeats, who produced classic fin-de-siècle poems in the nineties and then rewrote them vigorously in works composed later, during the interwar period, when he saw approaching what he regarded as the end of the European cultural synthesis.

Yeats thought about the fin de siècle in four ways, derived from various theories of history—classical, Christian, Celtic, and Nietzschean—available to him. Between 1889 and 1899, he saw the end of the century principally, as I've mentioned, in terms we are accustomed to think characteristic of the nineteenth-century fin de siècle—weariness, exhaustion, enervation. These are qualities a young man delights to express as, for the first time, he represents experience to himself as repetitive, too thoroughly known, too exhaustively foreseeable. In *The Wanderings of Oisin* (1889), Yeats's account of the kidnapping of the passive hero by a fairy femme fatale, the decadent tones that we associate with the French and British fin de siècle are thoroughly explored, and the subsequent volume *The Wind among the Reeds* (1899), with its poems of hopeless yearning, expressed in the dying fall of uncertain and quavering rhythms, is the fin-de-siècle book par excellence. It is in *The Wind among the Reeds* that we can begin to chart Yeats's conceptual models of the fin de siècle.

The Christian apocalyptic tradition is visible in the 1899 poem "The Secret Rose":

> When shall the stars be blown about the sky
> Like the sparks blown out of a smithy, and die?
> Surely thine hour has come, thy great wind blows,
> Far-off, most secret, and inviolate Rose?[1]

Considered formally, "The Secret Rose" acts to compress epic time into lyric time by allusion to events assumed to be well known; these take us from the archaic period through to the present. But Yeats is already drawn to another model of the end, a more political one, as he writes a poem about the Celtic Armageddon, the battle in the Valley of the Black Pig, on which his note reads: "All over Ireland there are prophecies of the coming rout of the enemies of Ireland, in a certain Valley of the Black Pig, and these prophecies are, no doubt, now, as they were in the Fenian days, a political force" (449). The entropic model of weariness unto death, the Blake-derived model of the Christian Apocalypse, and the political model of the great battle all present themselves to Yeats as plausible imaginative schemes for lyric at the turn of the century. But at this time, his tone does not change perceptibly from one model to the other. His tone does finally change in the twenties once he has encountered the ideas of Nietzsche and Spengler; he now begins to rewrite his earlier poems, as he takes on his favorite model by far of the fin de siècle, that of the repetitive but innovative spiral or gyre or vortex.

As "gyres run on" (343), subjective and objective eras succeed each other; Yeats's model for these is the classical era succeeded by the Christian era. At the end of the Christian era, expected in the year A.D. 2000, a new subjective era will, he announces, arrive; it will have as its dominating symbol not Helen of Troy, the child who inaugurated the two-thousand-year classical era before Christ, but the Rough Beast, who now replaces Jesus in the manger:

> Now I know
> That twenty centuries of stony sleep
> Were vexed to nightmare by a rocking cradle,
> And what rough beast, its hour come round at last,
> Slouches towards Bethlehem to be born?
> (185)

Though "The Second Coming" was not written at a calendric fin de siècle, it was written at the end of an era, when the First World War had destroyed Europe's peace and the Easter Rising, followed by the Troubles and a civil war, had changed the governance of Ireland. Yeats certainly believed that he was witnessing the breakup of the Christian historical era, as he says in *A Vision* (his conspectus of "history"); and in such poems as "The Second Coming" and "Leda and the Swan" he was in fact rewriting his early 1899 fin-de-siècle poems in a new imaginative form, as anticipatory fin-de-siècle poems characterizing the year 1999.

Yeats had also come to realize the inutility of statement in verse without a corresponding authenticating form, and both "The Second Coming" and "Leda and the Swan" find new formal models for the fin de siècle. "The Second Coming"—to resume it briefly in formal terms—is written in two unrhymed parts. The first contains eight lines and is written in an impersonal mode— "Things fall apart, the centre cannot hold"; the second contains fourteen lines and is written in the first person—"The darkness drops again, but now *I know*." We may interpret this doubled form as an attempt, in the first eight lines, to write an octave of impersonal "public" political discourse which has aspirations—visible in its eight-line exposition of a "problem"—toward the sonnet form. But the generalizing octave fails and cannot find its sestet. The writer then decides to rewrite his public and impersonal octave in a personal and lyric voice and is rewarded for his turn to lyric authenticity by a "vision out of Spiritus Mundi" in which he sees the awakening of the Rough Beast. His second attempt at a sonnet succeeds in providing both a consolidating image (in its Rough Beast "octave," which actually spills over, in a Miltonic *volta,* into the ninth line) and an intellectual conclusion: "Now I know." However, this successful "sonnet" still retains the blank-verse form as a signal of its wish to speak in the unrhymed lines of the initial failed octave. Blank verse is the lyric convention for speech or public oratory, whereas rhymed lines are the lyric convention for song. The originary failed speech of the first octave—which yet has aspirations toward lyric vision—is "replaced" by a personal sonnet, which yet, by keeping its oratorical aim (as shown by its unrhymed lines), deflects sonnet writing away from private song.

Similarly, in "Leda and the Swan," the formal model for "the cycle of the solid having turned"—Wallace Stevens's phrase—is the gradual metamorphosis of Zeus from pure bird (wings, bill, dark webs) to God (a glory and a rush) to human lover (a breast, a beating heart) to a synthesis of all three ("the brute [bird] blood [lover] of the air [sky-god]") before he returns to being pure bird (an "indifferent beak," 212). In these two poems, "The Second Coming" and "Leda and the Swan," Yeats folds epic into lyric by forcing the fin-de-siècle double moment—which combines cultural catastrophe with inception—to stand, by synecdoche, for the whole epic and dramatic narration it engenders:

> A shudder in the loins engenders there
> The burning wall, the broken roof and tower
> And Agamemnon dead.
> (212)

However, Yeats was too shrewd a poet not to suspect that beyond those models of time which he used to posit a sharp breaking point—the Apocalypse, the battle in the Valley of the Black Pig, the impregnation of Leda by Zeus—there might be another model of history, a model of "plus ça change," or (as Shakespeare said in sonnet 59) "whether revolution be the same." What if one stood outside the turns of history and merely watched, instead of being a participant? In certain poems written just before the outbreak of World War II, such as "Meru" and "Lapis Lazuli," Yeats imagines detached spectators (they are always Asian—Himalayan monks in "Meru," "three Chinamen" in "Lapis Lazuli") who can watch the decay of the West without chagrin.

These Asian contemplatives have now succeeded their "Christian" predecessors the Magi, who, in Yeats's World War I poem called "The Magi," have watched without contentment or satisfaction the historical panorama of Christ's life. Unsatisfied by the ignominy and mystery of Bethlehem, the Magi remain to watch for the outcome they expect, the triumphant coming of the Messiah; instead they find the greater fin-de-siècle confusion of Calvary. The Magi remain, therefore, in Yeats's imagination, figures for those who know that every worked-up emotion welcoming a fin de siècle is a fraud, that repetitiveness is the only truth:

> Now as at all times I can see in the mind's eye,
> In their stiff, painted clothes, the pale unsatisfied ones
> Appear and disappear in the blue depth of the sky
> With all their ancient faces like rain-beaten stones,
> And all their helms of silver hovering side by side,
> And all their eyes still fixed, hoping to find once more,
> Being by Calvary's turbulence unsatisfied,
> The uncontrollable mystery on the bestial floor.
>
> (124)

Unlike Yeats's later hermits and Chinese sages, the Magi have no capacity for tragic joy: they follow the gyres perpetually unsatisfied. They stand for the participant in history who is convinced that history is repetition without any ultimate meaning. Yeats emphasizes in this poem not simply inception but *both* poles, inception and conclusion. By writing "The Magi" in the hexameters that are the formal sign of epic, he gestures toward the whole Christian epic, which is contained in the Magi's ceaseless circling. In this bleak picture of history— especially bleak because it is predicated of the Magian witnesses to Christian incarnation and redemption—Yeats indulges his suspicion that the Magi can put no construction on divine history that will satisfy their quest for epic intelligibility.

Nonetheless, in spite of its cognitive dismay, "The Magi" is written with a formal repetitiveness that stands in for meaning. Repetitiveness itself becomes meaning because it is predictable: it precludes the random. The story of Jesus has only two poles, Bethlehem and Calvary, and we see their inexorable and predictable return—or rather the Magi's return to each of them in succession. If history is meaningless, it is at least predictable. In his later suspicion that his desired "tragic joy" was available only to nonparticipants in a given cycle, Yeats concedes the power, for participants in history, of any model of meaning—the circular classical passage from Golden Age to Iron Age and back, the linear Christian passage from Creation to Apocalypse, or the political rise from defeat to victory in the Valley of the Black Pig. These models, as I have said, like the model of repetitiveness, all find formal equivalents in Yeats's poetry. What does not find a formal equivalent in his practice, because Yeats did not entertain it conceptually, is randomness. He could tolerate the cognitive dissonance among his models of history because all of them rested on a notion of the predictable—demonstrated, in all his models, thematic and formal, by his patterned dynamic and his metrical order.

What interests me in Jorie Graham's work on models of history is that she avoids not only the classical and Christian models invoked by Yeats and others but also the Utopian models invoked by socialist and feminist poets. Instead, like Ashbery, whose favorite image of life is a ride on a circling carrousel with no destination, Graham attempts to be in the flow before analyzing it, though she also ponders demarcation. The continuum of history—rather than the events that demarcate and thereby organize time—is her subject. The continuum resists being called the *fin* of anything. And yet ends—or at least significant events—keep happening in Graham's poems; this is not usually the case in Ashbery, who tends, with his theoretical commitment to irony, to will "events" as such into a single level of pleasant insignificance.

The absence in Graham's work of the world-weariness of Yeats's poetry in the nineties suggests that what we are accustomed to call a fin-de-siècle tone—blanched, pale, sighing—is a limited phenomenon derived from certain poems of Swinburne, the Rossettis, and Yeats, themselves reacting against strenuous and even bombastic romantic and Victorian tonalities of revolution and moral endeavor. This reaction against revolutionary bombast and Utopian conviction (with their concurrent preachiness) may have only coincidentally arrived at the end of the last century, and our fin de siècle has had, whether in novels such as Don DeLillo's *Mao II* or in poetry such as Graham's, a tone of its own—confused rather than weary, screen-mobile rather than painting-static, jump-cut rather than continuous, interrogative rather than declarative, and ambiguous rather than conclusive. The conviction that one can speak authentically only of personal experience (in *Mao II*, that of the writer and photographer, for instance) and an equal conviction that one must speak also of incomprehensible mass events (in *Mao II*, the Moonie mass marriage) have struggled for dominance in the twentieth century. Mass synecdoche, if one may call it that, is the substitute for the late Victorian synecdoche of the detail. And yet the falsification of anything in representing it as a group phenomenon causes the compensatory insistence on the private. The formal incoherence caused in *Mao II* by authorial insistence—without nineteenth-century ligatures of plot coherence—on a simultaneity of mass and private phenomena offers textual evidence of the imaginative strain underlying such witnessing.

Graham's preoccupation with history and the end of history appears in marked form in several poems found in her 1991 book *Region of Unlikeness*.[2] The poems I have in mind reveal, even in their titles, Graham's intent to reflect on significant event, the temporal continuum, the forms of narrative, and the competitive roles of participant and watcher. The poems in question have as titles "History" (two poems are given that title), "Act III, Sc. 2," "Who Watches from the Dark Porch," and "The Phase after History." Graham's foreword to *Region of Unlikeness* quotes Augustine in the *Confessions*, as he broods on language as successivity and the human wish to spatialize that successivity: "You hear what we speak . . . and you do not want the syllables to stand where they are; rather you want them to fly away so that others may come and you may hear a whole sentence. So it is with all things that make up a whole by the succession of parts; such a whole would please us much more if all the parts could be perceived at once rather than in succession" (xi). In the poem called "Act II, Sc. 2," Graham spatializes her own life into textual form, significantly not choosing, as Yeats would have done, the moment of inception or conclusion but rather borrowing from Stevens an intermediate moment in the epic drama. (The poem of Stevens from which she borrows is one called "Chaos in Motion and Not in Motion," in which Stevens first names the moment in personal time, "Chaos in Motion," and then in textual space, "and not in Motion." In it, he announces that at this late moment "Scene 10 becomes 11, / In Series X, Act IV, et cetera.")[3] Graham's theme in "Act II, Sc. 2" is the problem of representing accurately one's position in participatory terms once one has begun, in middle life, to be a watcher of one's own history even as one enacts it:

> Look she said this is not the distance
> we wanted to stay at—We wanted to get
> close, very close. But what
> is the way in again? And is it

too late? She could hear the actions
rushing past—but they are on
another track.

(66)

Many of Graham's poems enact a rapid zooming, in alternate short and long
lines, between getting close and gaining distance; this poses at all times a problem
of historical representation. But a preoccupation with the degree to which the
events of history are mentally and textually constructed into acts and scenes
rather than "objectively" recorded is the stance that differentiates contemporary historiographers and poets of the fin de siècle from those who, like Spengler
and Yeats, tended to accept constructions already invented, even if such
schemes—linear, circular, spiral-shaped—were inconsistent with one another.
As Stevens said of the mind in "Of Modern Poetry":

> It has not always had
> To find: the scene was set; it repeated what
> Was in the script. Then the theatre was changed
> To something else. Its past was a souvenir.[4]

In Graham's poetry, time itself and the recorder of time are intimately linked,
cannot be conceptually separated, in that it is only the recorder who demarcates
time, points out moments worth remembrance. All the other moments in the
continuum will sink unnoticed. How do we explain what gets recorded? Perhaps attention is random: people might record what they happened to witness
or happened to come across. But Graham will not entertain that possibility: it is,
for her, the sacred obligation of the recorder to pay attention at the precisely
fated moment:

> the only
> right time, the intended time,
> punctual,
> the millisecond I was bred to look up into, click, no
> half-tone, no orchard of
> possibilities,
>
> up into the eyes of my own
> fate not the world's.

(93)

Graham's formulation here reflects the biblical idea of *kairos,* the time intended by God—usually a brief time—for some aspect of his will to become fulfilled (see, e.g., Romans 13:11, "Knowing the time . . . now it is high time to awake out of sleep"; or I Corinthians 4:5, "Therefore judge nothing before the time, until the Lord come, who both will bring to light the hidden things of darkness, and will make manifest the counsels of the hearts").

As she says in this passage, Graham also believes, in opposition to many historical poets, that it is only by chronicling accurately and punctually one's individual fate that one can, in lyric, "do" history. Against Yeats's prophetic wish to describe the world's fate as well as his own, Graham records the world's fate through her own. She can write about the epic of the Holocaust only by filtering it through the memory of a childhood visit to her Jewish grandmother confined to a nursing home. In this way, Graham sets herself against the purely spectatorial perspective of Yeats's Chinamen or Himalayan hermits and against the conventionally generalized prophetic position of poets such as Adrienne Rich, who have written about broad social conditions without explicit autobiographical reference to their own motivation within, or limits with respect to, the social problem at hand.

Attention, says Graham in the second poem she entitles "History," is always processing time; but Attention, gnawing the minutes like Ovid's *tempus edax* (Shakespeare's "Devouring Time"), is not, she argues, as we might think, free ranging, but chained. Historical attention, which Graham in the following passage calls "x," is always chained, at least for the poet, by private vocation:

Listen:

the x gnaws, making stories like small smacking

sounds,
    whole long stories which are its gentle gnawing.
. . . . .
    If the x is on a chain, licking its bone,

making the sounds now of monks
    copying the texts out,
muttering to themselves,
    if it is on a chain
. . . . .
that hisses as it moves with the moving x,
    link by link with the turning x

(the gnawing now Europe burning)
   (the delicate chewing where the atom splits),
if it is on a chain—
   even this beast—even this the favorite beast—
then this is the chain, the gleaming

   chain: that what I wanted was to have looked up at the right
time,
   to see what I was meant to see,
to be pried up out of my immortal soul,
   up, into the sizzling quick—

That what I wanted was to have looked up at the only
   right time, the intended time,
punctual,
   the millisecond I was bred to look up into.
   (92–93)

Reflection on history is peculiarly intensified by the arrival of the fin de siècle—"she's deep into the lateness now" (35), says Graham's first "History"—because of the arbitrary nature of temporal demarcation by century. One wants to characterize the departing century and to anticipate the new one, while conscious of the fictional and ultimately textual nature of such characterizations. The worst—or best—fin-de-siècle speculation is the apocalyptic one: that this is the absolute end of time, that there will be no more history. If the Christian Apocalypse, where all shall be revealed and justice shall be made manifest, is the sublimely comic version of the end of history, for Graham, Shakespearean tragedy, with its final obliteration of the central dramatis personae, is the atheist and materialist version of the end of history. In her extraordinary poem "The Phase after History," Graham brings together, in her characteristic way of coping with simultaneity, three narratives—linked as natural event, autobiographical experience, and literary archetype. The first narrative, of natural event, is that of an incident in which a bird has become lost in Graham's house and is about to batter itself to death against a windowpane unless she can find it and release it. The second narrative, that of autobiographical experience, retells the attempted suicide (followed by a successful suicide) of one of Graham's young students, who attempted with a knife to carve his face away from his body. The third narrative, representing the archetype behind both anterior narratives, is drawn from *Macbeth,* in which an old order, represented by Duncan, is brought to an end by Lady Macbeth in order to begin, as she hopes, a new phase of history, the dynastic reign of the Macbeths over Scotland. In the person of Lady Macbeth, Graham represents the fin de siècle as an active moment of assassination, in which the poet must kill the old century and the future it envisioned—Duncan and Duncan's sons—in order to begin a new era. The guilt and self-murder entailed are fully acted out in Graham's horrifying "phase after history."

For Graham, the human face symbolizes the forward-pointing, future-envisioning part of the self. One's normal tenderness toward one's own envisaged future is sharply checked by a self-hatred that causes either suicide or self-revision. One is convinced that for oneself there must come a moment of decisive change, a fin de siècle, that whatever follows must be different. An attempt to hear in one's inner being the rustle of a hitherto unenvisaged future—the bird's attempt to find a way out of the house—produces whatever meaning can be extracted from the fin de siècle:

> Which America is it in?
> Which America are we in here?
>   Is there an America comprised wholly
> of its waiting and my waiting and all forms of the thing
>   . . . . .
> a place of *attention?*
> (114)

Most of the notions of the future which first occur to the mind are false, trivial, wrong, incomplete, exhausted, inadequate. The Muse, rejecting these, tells the poet to wait until the right sentence of art, Keats's unheard melody, Graham's "inaudible . . . utterance," formulates itself:

> The voice says wait. Taking a lot of words.
> The voice always says wait.
>   The sentence like a tongue
> in a higher mouth
>
>   to make the other utterance, the inaudible one,
> possible,
>   the sentence in its hole, its cavity
> of listening,
>   flapping, half dead on the wing, through the

hollow indoors,
    the house like a head
with nothing inside
    except this breeze—
shall we keep going?
    Where is it, in the century clicking by?
Where, in the America that *exists?*

(114–115)

It is at this point in "The Phase after History" that Shakespeare enters: we hear a version of the voice of Duncan in *Macbeth,* wholly wrong about the future, as he says, arriving at the castle where he will be murdered, "This castle hath a pleasant seat, . . . the air nimbly recommends itself." The play makes it clear that Duncan's subsequent use of the word *guest* refers to "the temple-haunting martlet"; Graham, trusting us to remember the baffled bird flying crazily through her house, continues in an ironic misquotation, thinking of both the deceived Duncan and the endangered bird, "the guest approves / by his beloved mansionry [in place of Shakespeare's "loved masonry"] / that heaven's breath smells wooingly here" (115).

Thus ends part 1 of "The Phase after History." Part 2 begins, "The police came and got Stuart, brought him to / Psych Hospital. / The face on him the face he'd tried to cut off" (116). The voice of Shakespeare, now as Lady Macbeth, reenters, saying in altered words, of the student, not of Duncan, "Who would have imagined a face / could be so full of blood" (116). Stuart's future suicide is seen as a flash-forward in the past tense: "Later he had to take the whole body off // to get the face" (118). Stuart in the hospital, between his attempted suicide and his subsequent successful suicide, becomes the terrified bird unable to imagine its own future, as the poet waits

        to hear something rustle
  and get to it
before it rammed its lights out
  aiming for the brightest spot, the only clue.

(118)

The end of this fin-de-siècle poem comes in a flutter of inability to kill the old order or, if the old is killed, to bring to birth the new. We cannot truly see "the phase after history." The poet becomes Lady Macbeth, not knowing whether

the bird/sentence/face/old order is alive or dead and, if dead, how to cleanse
one's hands of the deed of murder:

> (make my keen knife see not the
> wound it makes)—
> . . . . .
> Is the house empty?
> Is the emptiness housed?
>   Where is America here from the landing, my face on
>
> my knees, eyes closed to hear
>   further?
> Lady M. is the intermediary phase.
>   God help us.
> Unsexed unmanned.
>   Her open hand like a verb slowly descending onto
>   the free,
> her open hand fluttering all round her face now,
>   trying to still her gaze, to snag it on
>
> those white hands waving and diving
>   in the water that is not there.

(120–121)

It is the most hopeless ending in Graham, in effect ending the tragedy with the
suicidal Lady Macbeth. It refuses the Shakespearean pseudoconsolation of the
restoration of the anterior old order in the crowning of Duncan's son Malcolm.
In this way, Graham remains faithful to the imaginative truth of Shakespeare's
play, which is interested in the fate of the Macbeths rather than in the Duncan
dynasty. For Graham here, the fin de siècle lies suspended in Lady Macbeth's
fluttering hand, unable to still her dreaming gaze, helpless to find the absolving
water. If history is a construction, then nothing guarantees its future except
the restless and unstillable flux of the human gaze, suicidal in its metaphysical
uncertainty and in its determination to annihilate its own past.

We may pause a moment to deduce, from this poem, that Graham thinks
any account of "the phase after history" incomplete without some reference to
her three simultaneities—natural event, personal complicity, and archetypal
literary patterning. Her jump cuts among these, and especially her concern with
middleness rather than with inception, conclusion, or repetition, suggest that

the fin de siècle, as we now imagine it, is something we actively will—as Graham's student willed his suicide—in an attempt to shake off an irredeemable past; or that it is something we hesitate over—like Lady Macbeth in her dream-reprise of the murder—as we seek to find something to justify our murder of the past, as we try to coordinate our executive hand and our intentional gaze; or that it is something that we head blindly into—like the bird crashing into the invisible windowpane. The indeterminacy of these possibilities, and the poet's incapacity to decide among them, leave Graham as watcher but also, in the end (in the person of Lady Macbeth), as participant in a history she does not understand.

A nother poem from *Region of Unlikeness,* one explicitly about the construction of historical event, is called "Who Watches from the Dark Porch." The watcher hears a nearby ambiguous child-cry—is it laughter? is it pain?—and must try to interpret it as a signal of the nature of being. Is Nature—or, as Graham calls it in this poem, "Matter"—inherently comic or tragic? Interpretation, appearing here allegorically personified as the consort of Matter, is necessarily tragic because it is mortal. Here is the beginning of "Who Watches," asking why we feel sure that our previous attempts to codify our history were lies:

> Is it because of history or is it because of matter,
>   mother Matter—the opposite of In-
>   terpretation: his consort: (his purple body lies
>   shattered against terrible
>   reefs)—matter, (in it
> a shriek or is it
>   laughter)
> (a mist or is it an angel they strangle)—
>   that we feel so sure we lied?
>
> (97)

The "instant replay" of interpretation arouses a nostalgia for presence:

> Said Moses show me Your face.
>   Not the voice-over, not
> the sound track (thou shalt not thou
>   shalt not), not the interpretation—buzz—
> the face.
>   But what can we do?
>
> (106)

Graham ends this typical flurry of injunctions, questions, and parenthetical interjections—so different from Yeats's agitated but dominating
declarativeness—with the injunction to sit still, a command borrowed from
Eliot's "Ash Wednesday" but lacking Eliot's Christian implication. Both the
writer's desire for revelation (which can lead to a false willed meaning) and
the nostalgia for presence (which can lead to religious sentimentality) threaten
the artist of the fin de siècle. Yielding to the first will create another abstract
Utopia of the sort we have already seen too many of; yielding to the second
will offer a premature ontology and a premature sentimental ethics.

> . . . sit still sit still the lively understandable
> spirit said,
> still, still,
> so that it can be completely the
>
> now.
> (108)

If this sitting—"don't wait, just sit, sit" (108)—reveals only that one is at *"the
scene of the accident"* (107) facing the "pileup of erasures—play, reverse play"
(107) in the scene of writing, then this will have to be the poetics exacted by
Graham's disbelief in predetermined schemes of history, those schemes that
have given us, in fact, the very model of the fin de siècle that Graham refuses. The Yeatsian curtain is not lifted, but then the Yeatsian darkness does not
drop, either. Play, reverse play, instant replay, erase, play again—this Becket-
tian model makes every moment both a beginning and an end. The tape runs
both ways and is always provisional, always expressed, formally speaking, in
the cresting and troughing irregularities of Graham's prosody. Or, in another
of Graham's metaphors (from Yeats, from Mallarmé), the dice are "being
incessantly retossed" (107).

Where, then, does the poet obtain confidence in representation? Her confidence, expressed in the poem "Soul Says," lies finally in the idiom of presentness itself, in the simplicity with which we say, without thinking, "The river
glints," or "The mother *opens the tablecloth up into the wind.*" These sentences
make a text, or fabric, which descends over the earth for a moment in an
"alphabet of ripenesses, / what is, what could have been." Graham concludes, as
Wordsworth concluded long ago, that the verbal object, insofar as it persists,
becomes a natural part of the material world: "(This is a form of matter of matter
she sang)" (125). As history becomes text, it is spatialized into fabric, a tarpaulin

(as Ashbery called it in the poem of that name) spread to cover the perceptual field. This is, in the end, a comic resolution, by which the temporal wave of presentness causes the hilarity of articulated expression in song. The last words in *Region of Unlikeness,* closing "Soul Says," are to be thought of, we are told, as words spoken by Prospero as he lays down his art:

> Now then, I said, I go to meet that which I liken to
> (even though the wave break and drown me in laughter)
> the wave breaking, the wave drowning me in laughter—
> (125)

Questions of such gravity as how to demarcate time are not solved, of course, in lyric; they are merely reimagined. Graham's drowning wave (tragedy) cannot be demarcated, as in Yeats, into epical inception, event, conclusion, or even into repetition; it can only be redescribed as comedy—generating an annihilating cosmic laughter. *The Tempest,* the single Shakespearean play that observes the unities of time, space, and action, chooses to describe the coextension of space, time, and human will as, finally, a comic form. Each ends only when all are ended, and the end of textuality and the end of history become, in *The Tempest* and "Soul Says," the comic ending of the dramatized world. While present event and textuality—the forms of lyric—persist, there can be, Graham's work suggests, no conclusive fin de siècle; but the intellectual strain of remaining in the now of the song cannot be entirely obliterated. The song is the place, Graham writes in "Soul Says," "(Where the hurry [of time] is stopped) (and held) (but not extinguished) (no)" (125). Each of these parentheses inserted in the soul's claim is a small fin de siècle in itself.

3

The Unweary Blues

The Collected Poems of Langston Hughes

The available poetry of Langston Hughes (1902–1967) used to be the *Selected Poems*, a collection that Hughes himself made for Knopf in 1959, reissued in 1990 as a Vintage Classic. It contained, naturally, no poems from Hughes's last two volumes of verse, *Ask Your Mama* (1961) and *The Panther and the Lash* (1967), nor from the earlier *The Dream Keeper* (1932). Hughes had censored out his most controversial poems, omitting, for instance, his allegorical comment on the Scottsboro case, "Christ in Alabama," which begins by addressing the oppressed blacks of the Southern states, modulates into a prayer to God (the "White Master above"), and ends with a description of Christ crucified by a racist South:

> Christ is a nigger,
> Beaten and black:
> Oh, bare your back!
>
> Mary is His mother:
> Mammy of the South,
> Silence your mouth.
>
> God is His father:
> White Master above
> Grant Him your love.
>
> Most holy bastard
> Of the bleeding mouth,
>   Nigger Christ
>   On the cross
>   Of the South.[1]

When you consider the genial, resolutely optimistic and humorously ironic character of Hughes's temperament, it is a mark of how desperate he felt that he should write such a poem. Yes, the magazine *Contempo* had solicited from him a comment on the Scottsboro boys (whom Hughes had visited in prison in 1931). Still, nothing but his own judgment made him throw back in the face of the South its own ostentatious "Christianity," a form of that religion which had not heard that God is love. In 1959, without any pressure from Knopf, he soft-pedaled, in his *Selected Poems,* the wild Hughes, the angry Hughes, the convert to Communist beliefs who wrote "Good Morning Revolution" and "Goodbye Christ":

> Goodbye,
> Christ Jesus Lord God Jehova,
> Beat it on away from here now.
> Make way for a new guy with no religion at all—
> A real guy named
> Marx Communist Lenin Peasant Stalin Worker ME—
> (166)

Maybe Hughes no longer believed in these suppressed poems; they are certainly not representative of his best work. Still, it is hard to describe his best work without these poems as foil. In *The Collected Poems of Langston Hughes,* edited by Arnold Rampersad and David Roessel, it is possible to see, without laborious work in a major library, just what the career of Langston Hughes, poet, produced.

The *Poems* completes Rampersad's long service to Hughes's memory. Rampersad's earlier splendid two-volume biography, *The Life of Langston Hughes,* virtually necessitated a coherent collection of the poetry. What is missing in the chronologically arranged *Poems,* however, is a listing of the table of contents of each of the separate volumes of Hughes's poetry. Since books such as *The Weary Blues* or *Fine Clothes to the Jew* represent historically important moments in literary history, it is necessary to know just what poems people had read when they bought or reviewed such volumes.

Hughes was by no means only a poet. The list of his works prefaced to this volume is divided into Poetry, Fiction, Drama, Humor, Biography, Autobiography, History, and For Young People, and he should be regarded first and foremost as a multigeneric writer, the sum of his various parts. He is not a major poet, but he is a fascinating, original, and disturbing one. He found, early on, a style that served him until the end of his life. His career lacks, therefore, that tenacious struggle to expand expression within poetic genres and poetic language that marks the work of the most ambitious poets.

Yet he wrote scores of genuine poems, and if his pen sometimes descended to propaganda, he was a propagandist who did not produce his work cynically. His idealistic belief in the power of the word to convince others, his faith in the poem as a "proletarian weapon," made Hughes sometimes forget that his own convictions had to be digested poetically before they could do poetic work. Or perhaps he did not forget at all: in his hurried life he may have believed the cause was so urgent that it did not leave him the time for that digestion of thought into style that alone allows poetically successful representation of belief.

Hack propagandists do not know how to write genuine poems; but a genuine poet who writes propaganda (as many have done) engages in a conscious faithlessness to art. Whether that faithlessness is justified by a "higher" or "greater" faith in human rights is a matter for the writer's conscience. Hughes represents the interesting case of a poet who did both sorts of verse concurrently, as though he could justify his hack work by continuing to practice his art at the same time. It is depressing to see a writer turn out boilerplate, but it would be more depressing to see him turn out nothing but boilerplate. During the years in which he was doing his most pedestrian Soviet flag-waving, Hughes also wrote gnomic poems like the famous one called "Personal":

> In an envelope marked:
> *Personal*
> God addressed me a letter.
> In an envelope marked:
> *Personal*
> I have given my answer.
> (173)

Rampersad's biography of Hughes struggles with these issues. The second volume is prefaced by a statement that Hughes himself made in 1964: "Politics can be the graveyard of the poet. And only poetry can be his resurrection." Rampersad speaks of Hughes's "compromises," and he does not hesitate to criticize them. Hughes wrote, for instance, a collection of biographical essays called *Famous American Negroes* that left out W. E. B. Du Bois, and Rampersad comments:

> The unkindest cut in his book, and one about which he should have
> felt a degree of agony, although he never referred to it publicly, was the

omission altogether of any reference to the greatest of black intellectuals, W. E. B. Du Bois. In fact, Langston managed to write a chapter about the accommodationist Booker T. Washington without once mentioning his most celebrated antagonist.

Yet Rampersad hastens to add: "Undoubtedly, it was taken for granted by his various publishers that even brief references to Du Bois and other radicals were out of the question in a text aimed at children."

Each such "compromise" has to be weighed in the context of its historical moment. The summer of 1953, when Hughes was putting together those biographical essays, followed Hughes's March appearance under subpoena before Senator McCarthy's committee, where Hughes refused to implicate others and was himself "exonerated." Rampersad criticizes Hughes's actions at the McCarthy hearing, contrasting his "largely passive, perhaps supine" behavior to the "spirited resistance" of Paul Robeson and others. And yet he recognizes that Hughes's evasive response was characteristic of his temperament: "As in the case of his sexuality, he had allowed the expression of his radical political zeal to wither, to atrophy, to evaporate."

No one of us is in a position to say, with moral hindsight, how we would have acted in Hughes's situation. We, too, might have written poems that are, by the standards of art, ignoble. But the appearance of a *Collected Poems* warrants the judging of the poetry as art. Bracketing the conditions of production of the poems, so amply retold in the *Life*—the hateful father, the incompetent mother, the patronizing white "Godmother," the abortive schooling at Columbia, the seafaring years, the graduation from Lincoln University, the conversion to Communism, the travels in the Soviet Union and China and Civil War Spain, the scriptwriting in Hollywood, the FBI attacks, the Harlem years, the McCarthy subpoena, the work in journalism, opera, and theater, the eventual heap of honors, the death from prostate cancer—we are entitled to ask what sort of poetry Hughes gave us and what lyric became, in his hands, that it was not before.

It is easy to name the literary and musical traditions inspiring Hughes's work. They include Whitman's democratic free verse, the dialect poems of Paul Laurence Dunbar, Sandburg's updating of Whitman, Amy Lowell's imagism, Negro spirituals, the blues, and jazz. Rampersad's biography not only traces most of these but also weighs their importance. There is less room in the biography for consideration of individual poems, or even for an account of Hughes's poetics. What sort of poetics, for instance, generates a poem such as "Personal"?

It is a poetics of announced reciprocity. It always takes two to make a Hughes poem (in this case, God and the poet). But it is a cryptic reciprocity, exchanged in private messages within envelopes marked "Personal." That label means "not to be read by anyone else." The message that God sends Hughes may not be the same message he sends to another American, or another black, or another poet, or another person; and the message Hughes sends back to God may not be the same message he would send to his mother, or to Senator McCarthy, or to the NAACP. Lyric, in this construction, is the message you send to God; and it is your answer to God's message to you—the idiosyncratic fate God has dealt you. If Dickinson said of her poetry, "This is my letter to the world / That never wrote to me," Hughes says, "This is my answer to the God / Who once addressed a destiny to me."

The first reciprocity, then, is the one between personal fate and the personal lyrics responding to that fate. Even the loneliest moment of all in Hughes, the moment of suicide, is represented as a moment of reciprocity:

Suicide's Note

The calm,
Cool face of the river
Asked me for a kiss.
(55)

The second characteristic of Hughes's verse is the idiosyncrasy of personal identity. The letter from God gave a personal fate, the fate of a single soul; and the fate is the fate of birth, not of current events. To be born a black American male in Kansas is not the same—as Hughes increasingly realized—as to be born a black American female in Harlem, or a black African in Nigeria. Hughes's letter from God was personal to him; and his watchful curiosity about the nature of other, equally personal, fates informs all his best writing. A black writer with a less fluid and multiple conception of identity would not have been able to do such lively social portraiture, would not have been so interested in the Harlem street scene. Someone with a more stereotypical sense of himself as black would not have gotten along so well, or experienced such genuine fellow feeling, as Hughes did in the multiracial cabins of the trading ships he worked on.

Reciprocity and idiosyncrasy could exist in a poetry of only two persons, as they do in the lyrics of George Herbert. But Hughes's poetry—to name a third characteristic of his writing—is inveterately social. There is always an explicit or implicit social (more often than erotic) other. It may be a landlord, or a set of fellow workers, or the nameless "they" of a racist society, or merely an old mule. But the lyric speaker, because he is so conscious of his own separate and idiosyncratic identity, is always aware of the bonds of social relation, happy or unhappy.

The fourth characteristic of the Hughes poem (at its normative best) is irony. Though irony is always, for the best of reasons, frequent in colloquial talk among the oppressed, it is oddly infrequent in the "high" literature of oppression, which tends toward the melodramatic and the tragic (Stowe, Zola, Hood). Du Bois's famous "double consciousness" of the "souls of black folk" does not necessarily produce irony, though it may produce the doubleness—watching oneself as if one were another—that can become a root of writerly irony. But the sort of humorous irony found everywhere in Hughes depends on the conscious diminution of self, which is precisely the sort of diminution that the role of tragic victim cannot tolerate. When someone else is diminishing you, it is hard to diminish yourself at the same time. Yet true moral defiance lies in refusing the very role of victim, which is always a role conferred by others rather than one self-invented. The invention of a new role, appropriate to one's lowly place in (actual) society but one not determined by society, is an act that Hughes is particularly good at:

Me and the Mule

My old mule,
He's got a grin on his face.
He's been a mule so long
He's forgot about his race.

I'm like that old mule—
Black—and don't give a damn!
You got to take me
Like I am.

(239)

The wry humor of this makes one forget, for a beat, the oddity of the mule's having a "race" at all. On reflection, we see that the mule is a product of miscegenation between horse and donkey, yet by now he has become just who he is. His black master does not think himself better than the mule, and he isn't,

socially speaking. But neither of them is going to disappear, and sooner or later
the world will get used to them. The truth of a humiliated position is not denied. On the contrary, the shot of energy that comes from truth-telling gives
the poem its kick.

When Hughes is at his best, irony pokes in to rebuke even denunciation. In his
"Memo to Non-White Peoples," he begins in what one might call the paranoid
position:

> They will let you have dope
> Because they are quite willing
> To drug you or kill you. . . .
>
> They will let you have alcohol
> To make you sodden and drunk
> And foolish.
> (456)

But the truth is that dope and alcohol need some cooperation, and the poem
veers from accusation of whites to accusation of blacks:

> They will gleefully let you
> Kill your damn self any way you choose
> With liquor, drugs, or whatever.
> (456)

Hughes's second thoughts of this sort transform many poems that would otherwise be predictable into wayward human documents. Irony is anathema, of
course, to all the true believers Hughes encountered—whether in the KKK,
the NAACP, the USSR, the FBI, or the police—and Hughes gently distanced
himself, in the long run, from all comprehensive belief systems, though he was,
by nature, a believer. Even when he is writing about being (in his imagination)
captured by the Klan, in a poem called "Ku Klux," he shows himself answering
questions ironically:

> They took me out
> To some lonesome place.
> They said, "Do you believe
> In the great white race?"

> I said, "Mister,
> To tell you the truth,
> I'd believe in anything
> If you'd just turn me loose."
>
> The white man said, "Boy,
> Can it be
> You're a-standin' there
> A-sassin' me?"
>
> (252)

Sooner or later, Hughes got around to "a-sassin'" every solemnity, especially the solemnity of coerced "belief" common to all religious and political organizations:

> They hit me in the head
> And knocked me down.
> And then they kicked me
> On the ground.
>
> A klansman said, "Nigger,
> Look me in the face—
> And tell me you believe in
> The great white race."
>
> (253)

Other forms of social coercion are less blatant than the kicks and punches of the Klan, but Hughes's irony in "Café: 3 A.M." mockingly registers them all, together with the hypocrisy underlying them:

> Detectives from the vice squad
> with weary sadistic eyes
> spotting fairies.
>> *Degenerates*
> some folks say.
>
> But God, Nature,
> or somebody
> made them that way.

Police lady or Lesbian
over there?
    Where?
(406)

It seems that the largely asexual Hughes may have had, besides the double consciousness of the black, the double consciousness of the homosexual (though he resisted the pressure of homosexuals such as Alain Locke and Countee Cullen, who tried to bring him out). The irony of existing in one otherness that was unconcealable—blackness—and one otherness that was hidden—homosexuality—made Hughes ultimately suspicious of all visible social surfaces. His lifelong loneliness made him a watcher of that vivid Harlem life in which he could not fully participate, whether as a member of the moralistic churchgoing set or as a participant in the far more careless street culture. What he could do was feel the feelings of both, and represent life having its way with both, as in his poem about "illegitimacy" called "S-sss-ss-sh!":

Nature has a way
Of not caring much
About marriage
Licenses and such.

    But the neighbors
    And her mother
    Cared very much!

The baby came one morning,
Almost with the sun.

    The neighbors—
    And its grandma—
    Were outdone!

But mother and child
Thought it fun.
(357)

It is evident from all these poems that Hughes's poetics is a poetics of the common tongue. Most of his poems are accessible to anyone who can read, and even the more allusive ones generally mention events that were, at the time, in the daily newspapers. Needless to say, Hughes was superbly literate, and had sailed with ease through university humanities courses (including the famous Contemporary Civilization course at Columbia). In choosing to write "simple" poems he excused himself from mastering complex traditional forms and proclaimed himself a follower of those oral traditions that had produced black folk songs and the blues. He even rewrote some of his quatrain-poems into the six-line blues form; and his first book declared, by calling itself *The Weary Blues*, that it was a book of songs as much as a book of poems. The divided self that is evident in the poem "Conservatory Student Struggles with Higher Instrumentation" was perhaps his own:

> The saxophone
> Has a vulgar tone.
> I wish it would
> Let me alone.
>
> The saxophone
> Is ordinary.
> More than that,
> It's mercenary!
>
> The saxophone's
> An instrument
> By which I wish
> I'd never been
> Sent!
>
> (319)

Whatever "sends" you as a writer is the language you have to write with; Hughes, with his strong musical sense, "felt" language in short rhythmic pulses. The pentameter appears very rarely in his work, and even the tetrameter is usually, as in the poem above, cut into dimeters. How, we might ask, would the saxophone poem be different if written out as a single six-line stanza in more "normal" English tetrameters?

> The saxophone has a vulgar tone.
> I wish it would let me alone.
> The saxophone is ordinary.
> More than that, it's mercenary!

> The saxophone's an instrument
> By which I wish I'd never been sent!

Such a "rewrite" destroys the poem as a representation of reluctant thinking by fits and starts. If we read the original poem properly, the line breaks and the stanza breaks have to be taken into account as we listen to what the conservatory student is "really" saying:

> The saxophone (which I wish I were playing now)
> Has a vulgar tone. (at least according to the standards of the
>   conservatory)
> I wish it would (at least while I'm here taking my lesson)
> Let me alone. (*it* is pursuing me, I'm not pursuing it)
>
> The saxophone (let me sternly remind myself)
> Is ordinary. (a euphemism; translation: "lower class")
> More than that, (and even worse)
> It's mercenary! (and the conservatory is "above" such things)
>
> The saxophone's (about which I can't stop thinking)
> An instrument (so why isn't it taught here at the conservatory?)
> By which I wish (but my wish doesn't amount to will)
> I'd never been (been what? attracted? degraded?)
> Sent! (ecstasy, aesthetic transport, the "wrong" sort of pleasure)

Hughes's poems are, as this example shows, poems of implication. For all their apparent "simplicity," they bear rereading. It is a rare one, among his better poems, that does not carry a scorpion sting in its tail or a spiritual insight in its epigrammatic close. If we do not "fill in the blanks," we miss the point. We are used to filling in the blanks in poems that announce themselves as complex, but in poems that resemble song lyrics we tend to think that what we see at the beginning is what we get, that the impression given by the first stanza will do for the whole. Hughes is quite likely to trip up such an assumption. Here are the first three stanzas of his four-stanza poem "Island" (376):

> Wave of sorrow,
> Do not drown me now:
>
> I see the island
> Still ahead somehow.

> I see the island
> And its sands are fair:

So far, so good. The speaker is almost drowning in an ocean of sorrow; opposed to this dark medium is an island with fair sands, the land of stability and happiness. We expect the poem to close with another repudiatory address to the threatening wave of sorrow:

> Do not drown me now:
> I am swimming there.

Instead, Hughes sees that the only way to a new stability is to trust oneself to the overwhelming wave of sorrow. And here is the whole poem:

> Wave of sorrow,
> Do not drown me now:
>
> I see the island
> Still ahead somehow.
>
> I see the island
> And its sands are fair:
>
> Wave of sorrow,
> Take me there.

Such a poem is like a *pensée*, with a coiled spring inside its heartfelt self. Its *dédoublement* in the last stanza shows that its first thought—"Do not drown me"—has turned into a truer second thought, "Take me there."

Everyone writing on Hughes has emphasized what he owes to the jazz of the Harlem clubs. There is not only the syncopated rhythm that he made his own, but also the demotic language that he introduced into his lyrics, summed up in the little poem "Advice":

> Folks, I'm telling you,
> birthing is hard
> and dying is mean—
> so get yourself
> a little loving
> in between.
>
> (400)

That "little loving" is a constant theme in Hughes, and so is the brevity of the "in between." The *carpe diem* of the Harlem slums is the theme of his greatest suite, "Montage of a Dream Deferred" (1951), which he prefaced with a deeply thought-out note:

> In terms of current Afro-American popular music and the sources from which it has progressed—jazz, ragtime, swing, blues, boogie-woogie, and be-bop—this poem on contemporary Harlem, like be-bop, is marked by conflicting changes, sudden nuances, sharp and impudent interjections, broken rhythms, and passages sometimes in the manner of the jam session, sometimes the popular song, punctuated by the riffs, runs, breaks and disc-tortions of the music of a community in transition. (387)

It is the word "impudent" that distinguishes Hughes's version of Harlem. The impudent voice in the sequence is often his own, throwing a skeptical query at the easier Harlem self-deceptions:

What? So Soon!

I believe my old lady's
pregnant again!
Fate must have
some kind of trickeration
to populate the
cullud nation!

    Comment against Lamp Post
You call it fate?
(398)

The antithetical positions exposed in such poems are reminiscent of Hughes's stories of Jesse B. Semple, otherwise known as "Simple." In those pieces, Simple tells an anecdote concerning racism to a black friend. The friend, taking a "larger" view, tries to put a better construction on the anecdote, or tries to convince Simple that things aren't so bad as they seem. Simple and his friend are both "right": Simple is right about the incident, and his friend is right about there being larger social truths than those available from a single person's experience. These contrasting points of view animate Hughes's poems as well as his prose; Hughes can see both the individual dream and the larger structural causes of the dream's defeat.

It is for this reason that Hughes needs to be a choral writer, casting many of his poems as a melange of voices. A typical choir of voices can be heard in the theme poem of his sequence, called "Deferred." The very multiplicity of wishes rising from the tenements of Harlem exposes the hopelessness of wishing: How many of these wishes will come true?

> *This year, maybe, do you think I can graduate?*
> . . . . .
> *To get through high at twenty's kind of late—*
> *But maybe this year I can graduate.*
>
> Maybe now I can have that white enamel stove
> . . . . .
>
> *Me, I always did want to study French.*
> . . . . .
>
> Someday,
> I'm gonna buy two new suits
> at once!
>
> *All I want is*
> *one more bottle of gin.*
>
> All I want is to see
> my furniture paid for.
> . . . . .
>
> *I want to pass the civil service.*
>
> I want a television set.
>
> *You know, as old as I am,*
> *I ain't never*
> *owned a decent radio yet?*
>
> I'd like to take up Bach.
>
> > *Montage*
> > *of a dream*
> > *deferred.*
>
> Buddy, have you heard?
>
> (413–414)

Hughes makes cunning juxtapositions. It is no accident, I think, that the voice of the person who minds never having had a decent radio precedes the voice of the person who knows of the existence of Bach. Only someone who wants to hear music wants a decent audio system; any radio will do for listening to the news. Though the untutored person who wants a better radio has probably (unlike the church organist) never heard of Bach, the musical talent may be the same. The person who wants two new suits at once is one of those restless souls who thirst for variety in life; to have one's choice absolutely circumscribed by the one wearable suit in the house bothers a certain temperament. These modest wishes—"one more bottle of gin" is not, after all, a sign of depravity—are the songs of America singing that Hughes, like Whitman, hears. They are signs of intellectual and aesthetic and erotic desire, and they are going to expire unsatisfied but not unheard, if Hughes has anything to say about it.

Hughes's choral poetics is one of universal desires. They are not unsatisfiable desires, they are not expensive desires, they are not evil desires. A society in which such simple and decent dreams are frustrated is the morally unjust society glimpsed through the interstices of *Montage of a Dream Deferred.* Hughes's Harlem has pimps and number-runners and illegitimate babies and alcohol and marijuana—but none of these things, *mutatis mutandis,* is unknown in "polite society," as both Hughes and his readers are well aware. Hughes dares to imply that Harlem life is universal life. At the same time, he avers that it is a special species of human life that its inhabitants would be sorry to lose. The speaker of "Nightmare Boogie" imagines a world in which the million black faces of America turn "dead white":

> I had a dream
> and I could see
> a million faces
> black as me!
> A nightmare dream:
> *Quicker than light*
> *All them faces*
> *Turned dead white!*
> (418)

No Harlem resident wants a world in which the blues, jazz, folk songs, folktales, black jokes, black dances, and everything else that the culture has thought up has vanished. The fiction that blacks wish that they were white explodes in the presence of such a nightmare. Hughes's belief in the authenticity and the beauty of black culture made him write his poems from within that culture, which he saw as a culture "in transition." His poetry was one of the agents of the transition—not to whiteness, but to a fuller set of possibilities for blackness, for ordinary dreams that would no longer find themselves deferred.

Hughes's Platonic drive toward perfection led him to an optimism that was the obverse of a lurking despair. Did he really believe that the erotic United Nations of his "Little Song" would come to pass?

> Carmencita loves Patrick.
> Patrick loves Si Lan Chen.
> Xenophon loves Mary Jane.
> Hildegarde loves Ben.
>
> Lucienne loves Eric.
> Giovanni loves Emma Lee.
> Natasha loves Miguelito—
> And Miguelito loves me.
>
> (609)

Maybe he was wise enough to speculate that since we are a single species, the universality of erotic attraction will finally defeat ethnic and racial tribalism. There is always a process of thinking behind Hughes's simplest poems. A lyric such as "Little Song" implicitly pits the erotic against the combined forces of nationalism, tradition, and language, and puts its bets on the erotic.

It is the intellectuality in Hughes's work that a cursory reading is likely to underestimate. Much has been said about how the blood of martyrs is the seed of the Church, and how evil destroys the souls of those who practice it, rather than the souls of their victims. But here is Hughes's version of these truisms, turned into a "Lynching Song":

> Pull at the rope!
> O, pull it high!
> Let the white folks live
> And the black boy die.
>
> Pull it, boys,
> With a bloody cry.

Let the black boy spin
While the white folks die.

The white folks die?
What do you mean—
The white folks die?

That black boy's
Still body
Says:
NOT I.
(214)

Hughes's poems, when they are good, show this concentration of exposition and this gift for alert reversal. They address primary human wishes and actions through the quick sketch, a form of social synecdoche. When Hughes is preaching or sloganeering, he is no more interesting, poetically speaking, than any other propagandist. But even his slackest poems are of interest as documents in an American life lived with great optimism in great loneliness, under conditions often demeaning to dignity.

There was, there is, no country in which everyone starts off equal, but the America that Hughes was born into was still the America of Jim Crow and laws against "miscegenation." He simply wouldn't have it that America could so betray itself, and so he called America to order over and over again, reminding it of its own founding principles. Like all reformers, he often looks foolish, especially in retrospect. And yet his taunts had the power to corrode the hypocrisy they exposed. When the Red Cross segregated blood donations, he fired off a squib:

The Angel of Mercy's
Got her wings in the mud,
And all because of
Negro blood.
(290)

If this 1943 poem were not firmly in place in Hughes's *Collected Poems*, who would now remember that the Red Cross practiced Jim Crow on blood? Rampersad's brief notes clear up such topical references, and make us see

Hughes's poems as documents of black life, in its personal and historical dimensions.

The black American intellectual's search for a viable life has taken many forms, and Hughes explored most of them—the white university, the black university, the return to Africa, European expatriation, internationalism via the Communist Party, life in Harlem, mixed-race life among bohemians. Almost the only option not open to Hughes was "passing." The "options," while seemingly voluntary, are all coerced by the ever-renewed experience of racist prejudice. Hughes's final option was to claim that freedom would have the last word. Racists, says Hughes in "Freedom," may think to burn or imprison or kill freedom by burning churches or imprisoning blacks or killing men:

> But Freedom
> Stands up and laughs
> In their faces
> And says,
> *No*—
> *Not so!*
> *No!*
> (562)

An unprovable statement, even an impotent negation. The belief in Platonic absolutes such as Freedom dies hard in Hughes, but the belief in the power of art dies even harder. The last lyric in the *Collected Poems*, "Flotsam," represents his body and his song cast up as flotsam after his death. The "yet" in the poem derives from the wind of the brave spirit still present in this book:

> On the shoals of Nowhere,
> Cast up—my boat,
> Bow all broken,
> No longer afloat.
>
> On the shoals of Nowhere,
> Wasted—my song—
> Yet taken by the sea wind
> And blown along.
> (562)

Unlike most of his own contemporaries, and unlike many of ours, Hughes was truthful enough to say that after death one is nowhere. Yet he remained

sanguine about the persistence of his song, even though he knew that the topical and propagandistic side of it would be wasted by time. True poems, on the
other hand, withstand historical vicissitude and are "blown along." It is a pity
that the dreary censorship inflicted on public school textbooks will prevent many
of Hughes's most powerful poems from reaching the very audience that would
respond to them most ardently.

4

The Nothing That Is

Chickamauga, *by Charles Wright*

The title poem of Charles Wright's *Chickamauga* doesn't mention the Civil War battle of Chickamauga or the soldiers who died in it, and in this it is typical of Wright's practice. The poem climbs to a vantage point where the anonymity of history has blanked out the details. What is left is the distillate: that something happened at this place, that its legacy of uneasiness inhabits the collective psyche (Wright was born in Tennessee), that it will not let us go and demands a response. A confessional poet might write about his own family's legacy from the war. A socially minded poet might recount the havoc of battle. A moral poet might debate what Melville called "the conflict of convictions." A landscape poet might describe the vacant battlefield as it is now. Wright is none of these, does none of these things.

What can a lyric poetry be that sidelines the confessional, the social, the moral, the panoramic? It can be—and in Wright's case, it is—eschatological. Eschatology sees the world under the sign of the last things: Death, Judgment, Heaven, Hell. Wright redefines these in his own way: Annihilation, History, Light, Disappearance. If we face annihilation as persons, and we do; if history judges us and disposes of us, and it does; if mass is clarified into energy, and it is; if every object vanishes, and it will—then what kind of language can we use of life that will be true of these processes and true of us?

Wright's earliest manifesto of the lyric that he wanted to write was phrased in negation, in 1971:

The New Poem

It will not resemble the sea.
It will not have dirt on its thick hands.
It will not be part of the weather.

It will not reveal its name.
It will not have dreams you can count on.
It will not be photogenic.

It will not attend our sorrow.
It will not console our children.
It will not be able to help us.[1]

How was Wright to find a set of positives to accompany these negatives? The three stanzas of "The New Poem" refuse mimesis of the external world (sea, dirt, weather); mimesis of the psychological world (name, dreams, face); and mimesis of the religious world (attendance, consolation, help). No objects, then; and no self; and no God. Has there ever been a more stringent set of requirements for poetry?

If the object of art is not mimesis and not self-identification and not consolation, many of the tones that we associate with poetry must also be forgone. The strict discipline that Wright imposes on himself is visible in all he writes. If an item from the world is mentioned, it must always be remembered that it has been selected and is not simply "there." The word used to mention it, once it has been settled on, has its own history, its own weight and color. If the self is mentioned, it must always be remembered that what has been invoked is merely one aspect of the self, one that fits the purposes of this particular poem and is constructed by the instruments available to this poem—its images, its location, its syntax. If sorrows or needs or desires appear, nobody grander than ourselves can be there to attend to them, help us with them or console our afflictions.

Thus, when we come to the poem "Chickamauga," none of the "warmer" tones of lyric are permitted to attend on the scene. No Civil War color and drama, no embattled Southern polemics, no grief even. There are five stanzas, arranged in Chinese-box fashion. In the middle is the peregrine face of the poet, to whom Chickamauga is a place of haunting significance. Readers cannot know the poet's human face; it lies under the mask of the poem. The masked face is bracketed, fore and aft, by history—first, by history in its cold indifference (discarding all of us "like spoiled fruit"), and second, by history as the trawling force that will haul us up, like fish, into its clarifying light and air where we cannot but suffocate. But this apparently omnipotent history, too, is bracketed fore and aft: by landscape, which banally outlives the history of the battle, and by language, the other enduring, transhistorical force.

Wright's structure—face enclosed by poem, face and poem enclosed by history, history enclosed by landscape and language—is in itself a powerful truth-telling geometry of destiny:

Chickamauga

Dove-twirl in the tall grass.
End-of-summer glaze next door
On the gloves and split ends of the conked magnolia tree.
Work sounds: truck back-up-beep, wood tin-hammer, cicada, fire
horn.

History handles our past like spoiled fruit.
Mid-morning, late-century light
calicoed under the peach trees.
Fingers us here. Fingers us here and here.

The poem is a code with no message:
The point of the mask is not the mask but the face underneath,
Absolute, incommunicado,
unhoused and peregrine.

The gill net of history will pluck us soon enough
From the cold waters of self-contentment we drift in
One by one
into its suffocating light and air.

Structure becomes an element of belief, syntax
And grammar a catechist,
Their words what the beads say,
words thumbed to our discontent.[2]

Such a poem will not be your choice if you are set on lyric that maintains the illusion of a direct mimetic personal speech by "suppressing" its status as composed and measured language. It will also not be your choice if you prefer "language poetry," which dispenses with structure, syntax, and grammar as authoritarian hegemonic structures that limit what can be said within them.

Wright offers the interesting example of a poet who wants to acknowledge in each of his poems that a poem is a coded piece of language and yet wants also to express, by that very code, the certainty that a piece of language exhibiting structure, grammar, and syntax is not "found art," but has been arranged by a questing human consciousness forever incommunicado beneath its achieved mask. He is not alone in his double desire. The foregrounding of the artifactual status of the lyric is common coin these days. What makes Wright unusual is his ascetic practice, his insistence on holding the rest of the poem to account under this double truth of incommunicado humanity and admitted inhumanness: nothing in the poem is allowed to ignore the strict metaphysics of its conception.

The "warm" tones of polemic, confession, startle, and fear—all those "immediacies" of direct expression—are forbidden him by his distanced and meditated stance. His poems, looked at from one perspective, lie about us like the life-masks they are: immobile, "placed," shaped, blanched. And yet, from another perspective, his poems are alive, as they struggle toward the transfiguration of still life that they will, at their end, achieve. There are two signs of livingness in Wright, one proper to individual poems, the other proper to his total oeuvre: there is temporality, as the present tense of any given poem slowly modulates into its dead future, and there is the change that takes place in the "objective" world, as different poems call into being varying perceptions, often stimulated by seasonal change.

After writing for a long time about the landscape of California, Wright moved to Virginia, and Charlottesville replaced Laguna Beach as the source of his images. Wright's usual "rule" of composition is that one or more images drawn from the landscape must set the musical tone of the poem. In "Lines after Rereading T. S. Eliot," the tone is set by Wright's own "wasteland between the brown / Apricot leaf and the hedge":

> The orchard is fading out.
> All nine of the fruit trees
> Diminish and dull back in the late Sunday sunlight.
>
> The dead script of vines
> scrawls unintelligibly
> Over the arbor vitae.
> (4)

As the season changes, we see the same orchard transformed, no longer a "wasteland," in "Still Life with Spring and Time to Burn," which begins:

> Warm day, early March. The buds preen, busting their shirtwaists
> All over the plum trees. Blue moan of the mourning dove.
> It's that time again,
>   time of relief, time of sorrow
> The earth is afflicted by.
> We feel it ourselves, a bright uncertainty of what's to come
>
> Swelling our own skins with sweet renewal, a kind of disease
> That holds our affections dear
>   and asks us to love it.
> And so we do, supposing
> That time and affection is all we need answer to.

For some, Wright says, time and affection may be the sole standards. But like Hopkins, who, after crying out "Nothing is so beautiful as Spring," had to answer to his own awareness of the eschatological ("Have, get, before it cloy, / Before it cloud, Christ, Lord, and sour with sinning"), Wright cannot rest in the sensuous moment. He "spoils" every such moment with his Eliot-like vision of "the skull beneath the skin." I pick up the spring poem where I cut it off:

> But we guess wrong:
>
> Time will append us like suit coats left out overnight
> On a deck chair, loose change dead weight in the right pocket,
> Silk handkerchief limp with dew,
>   sleeves in a slow dance with the wind.
> And love will kill us—
> Love, and the winds from under the earth
>   that grind us to grain-out.
>
> (66)

"But we guess wrong." The guess that hazards everything on time and affection omits too much for Wright, whose mind is saturated with death and the chilling Midas-petrifaction of words. His "But we guess wrong" is a close cousin of Milton's remark on pagan mythographers: "So they relate, erring." Milton could not lightly employ Greek mythology, because he considered it an imaginative fiction that belied the Christian truth to which he was obliged to adhere. Wright, bound no less straitly by the truths of death and arranged language, sees the immediate sensuous life (when offered in language) as no less a mythological fiction than the gods on Parnassus.

Wright has investigated many ways of folding death into life, absence into presence, deconstruction into construction. He has tried abstract titles; poems with notes attached so that details could be left out; titles specifying the occasion so that the following poem could be general; white space; desiccation of means; remoteness of stance; atemporality of narration. He has invoked a cluster of authenticating poets, artists, and musicians for his aesthetic practice—Dante, Hopkins, Dickinson, Hart Crane, Pound, Eliot, Tu Fu, Trakl, Montale, Piero della Francesca, Cézanne, Morandi—and here in *Chickamauga* there appear, among others, Elizabeth Bishop, Lao Tzu, Wang Wei, Paul Celan, Miles Davis, and Mondrian. More than most poets, Wright has owned up to being a site traversed by the languages, images, and tones of others, from Christian mystics to composers of country music. The religious yearning that used to find a home in doctrine is now, in that sense, homeless; but in Wright it persists in an urgent form, demanding to be housed somewhere, anywhere—in image, in landscape, in allusion, in geometry, in structure.

Piero's monumental figures with their glance fixed on something beyond the canvas; Cézanne's patches of color on white canvas; Morandi's ghostly bottles; Mondrian's repetitive figuration: all are symbols, to Wright, of the austerity of construction that satisfies his sense of lightness. These painters reprove the voluptuousness of the flesh, the heedlessness of the passing moment, the domesticities of contentment. The Chinese poets stand, in Wright, for the observer lost in the observation, for Buddhist emptiness, and for the stringencies of classic form. And the religious poets authenticate, for Wright, what used to be called the analogical level of experience—that which is not literal, nor figurative, nor emblematic, but which escapes direct representation by fact, or image, or emblem, and which drives poets to hints, intimations, and expressions of the ineffable. Country music and jazz are symbols of indigenous rhythms known to Wright since his youth.

This, more or less, is the map of Wright's poetics. Since his readers do not share all of Wright's talismanic obsessions, it has been his task to take us under the tent of his poems and make us care, not so much for his fetishes as for the harmonies that they create when they are assembled together. "This is a lip of snow and a lip of blood," says a 1981 poem called "Childhood's Body": those who want lips of blood will be put off by the chill of snow, those who want lips of snow will be put off by the stain of blood. Readers of poetry are well aware of the voice of the body ("Dance, and Provençal song, and sunburnt mirth") and the voice of the mind ("Nothing that is not there and the nothing that is"), but it is rarer to find the voice of the soul, especially the soul in its still-embodied state, conscious of its lip of snow meeting the body's lip of blood.

None of these voices is interesting to poetry, of course, unless the heart is present, too. It is in the junction of feeling heart and embodied soul that Wright locates his poetry. "This is too *hard*," protests the unwilling reader: "let me subside into blood or snow, one or the other." The Wright poem creates an anxiety that is very difficult to live within, since its constantly ticking clock adds certain loss to each daily gain:

> The subject of all poems is the clock,
> I think, those tiny, untouchable hands that fold across our chests
> Each night and unfold each morning, finger by finger,
> Under the new weight of the sun.
> One day more is one day less.[3]

What, then, are the rewards for subjecting oneself to the severity of Wright's pages, for living on his dissolving interface of feeling, between life and death? For a start, the brilliance of his images. His images, changing with the seasons, set the musical tone for each poem, and they are conceived in a manner that never ceases to astonish. One can never guess what word will come next on the page in a poem by Wright. Here is Venice, brilliant at night, dwindled at dawn, from *Chickamauga*'s "Venexia I":

> Too much at first, too lavish—full moon
> Jackhammering light-splints along the canal, gondola beaks
> Blading the half-dark;
> Moon-spar; backwash backlit with moon-spark . . .
>
> Next morning, all's otherwise
> With a slow, chill rainfall like ragweed
>   electric against the launch lights.
> Then grim-grained, then grey.
> This is the water-watch landscape, the auto-da-fé.
>
> (89)

In this sequence of images, sexual and visual energy shrivels, as a torture of exhausted observation succeeds the Hopkinsian intoxication. That is one reason to live in the poem with Wright: that emotional accuracy and verbal plenitude. Another is the floating tide of his musical line, which lifts the reader along its irregular cadence, as in "Easter 1989":

> Instinct will end us.
> The force that measles the peach tree
> > > will divest and undo us.
> The power that kicks on
> > > the cells in the lilac bush
> Will tumble us down and down.
> Under the quince tree, purple cross points, and that's all right
>
> For the time being,
> > > the willow across the back fence
> Menacing in its green caul.
> (10)

Anyone can hear, in this music, the perceptible turn between the first three sentences (variants on a single tune) and the fourth sentence, with its reticent irony at "For the time being." Just when Wright is being most biblical, the colloquial thrusts itself into the lines ("kicks on," "tumble us down," "and that's all right," "for the time being") and then something altogether unforeseeable—the "green caul" of the new—casts a ghastly light on the whole landscape.

If a reader wants more than the emotionally freighted image, more than the lift of a line, more than the heart's predicament between the snowy soul and the blooded body, then the poems by Wright that will linger most may be those that repeat religious promise in undoctrinal form. Here is the conclusion of Wright's Easter poem, at once biological and incandescent, borrowing its language from his earliest vocabulary for marvel, the Gospel resurrection:

> Nubbly with enzymes,
> The hardwoods gurgle and boil in their leathery sheaths.
> Flame flicks the peony's fuse.
> Out of the caves of their locked beings,
> > > fluorescent shapes
> Roll the darkness aside as they rise to enter the real world.
> (11)

"We get no closer than next-to-it," Wright concedes, but he won't abandon the hope of propinquity to the invisible, the "definer of all things":

> Something surrounds us we can't exemplify, something
> Mindless and motherless,
>   dark as diction and twice told.
> We hear it at night.
> Flake by flake,
>   we taste it like tinfoil between our teeth.
>
> (33)

Such an intuition is unprovable. Do we really hear it softly burying us, and taste it setting our teeth on edge, that unintelligible and aboriginal darkness? For those who do—who sense an enveloping and ethically burdening perplexity that is quite independent of personal tragedy, political evil, or scientific ignorance—Wright's poems will appear as attempts to lift a curtain, to enlighten memory, to name the abandoned, to pierce into "the horned heart of the labyrinth," where "the unsayable has its say." Wright's Minotaur—more sinister than the original, because it is shapeless—awaits the reader.

In his generation, the generation of Ashbery, Rich, Ammons, Ginsberg, Plath, and Merrill, Wright is perhaps closest to Plath in his intensity of the image, closest to Ammons in his sense of the sidereal. But he sounds like nobody else, and he has remained faithful to insights and intuitions—of darkness as of light—less than common in contemporary America.

5

American X-Rays

Forty Years of Allen Ginsberg's Poetry

In his poem "To Allen Ginsberg," Czesław Miłosz wrote:

> I envy your courage of absolute defiance, words inflamed, the fierce maledictions of a prophet.
>
> . . . . .
>
> Your blasphemous howl still resounds in a neon desert where the human tribe wanders, sentenced to unreality.
>
> . . . . .
>
> And your journalistic clichés, your beard and beads and your dress of a rebel of another epoch are forgiven.[1]

Allen Ginsberg, at the beginning of his *Selected Poems, 1947–1995*, gives his own definition of his "absolute defiance": "I imagined a force field of language counter to the hypnotic force-field control apparatus of media Government secret police & military with their Dollar billions of inertia, disinformation, brainwash, mass hallucination."

Ginsberg's "force field" came to public notice with the publication of *Howl and Other Poems*, in 1956, when Ginsberg was thirty years old. The title poem of the volume cried out against an America that devoured its young as the pagan god Moloch had devoured the children sacrificed to him. Ginsberg had seen his mother, Naomi—an immigrant from Russia—decline into persecution mania and eventual institutionalization; he himself, after an apparently successful transition from Paterson, New Jersey, to Columbia University, fell in with the petty criminality of friends, was briefly hospitalized in lieu of serving a prison sentence, and eventually left New York for San Francisco. Like his father, Louis, who was a high-school English teacher, Ginsberg wrote verse; but, while Louis's poetry was conventional and high-minded, his son's was tormented and ecstatic. In San Francisco, Ginsberg and others (Kenneth Rexroth, Jack Kerouac, Gary Snyder, Robert Duncan) emerged as the Beat movement, which in its frankness and its commitment to social and erotic reform provoked a storm in the world of writing. United States customs impounded as obscene copies of *Howl* printed in England, and the San Francisco police sent two officers to the City Lights bookshop, where the first edition was for sale, and arrested the publisher, the poet Lawrence Ferlinghetti. At the subsequent trial, the judge pronounced *Howl* not obscene and declared Ferlinghetti not guilty; the attendant publicity made both *Howl* and Ginsberg famous.

Howl was followed by other remarkable books, of which the most notable was *Kaddish and Other Poems*, in which the title poem, a long elegy for Ginsberg's mother, widened the sympathies of the American lyric by incorporating into it the vernacular anguish of the Jewish immigrant experience. Ginsberg later, with some grandeur, called two of his volumes *Planet News* and *The Fall of America*. William Carlos Williams had written, "It is difficult to get the news from poems," but Ginsberg put the news of the day into poetry in a bold and irreverent way. The FBI, the CIA, the Vietnam War, gay life, urban decay—all appeared regularly in Ginsberg's bulletins. Yet Ginsberg's remarkable poetic powers have been less extensively commented on than his many charities, his indefatigable political investigations, his support of other writers, his thronged readings (accompanied by finger cymbals, harmonium, chants), his world travel, his theatrical protests, his moral injunctions (against the hydrogen bomb, against political lies, against eco-destruction). These actions make him a significant cultural figure, but it is the poetry that makes him a significant literary figure.

Against the high odds of fame, overoccupation, and aging, Ginsberg continued to write poetry, and every one of his books had its memorable pieces. But that success was perennially threatened, and at times undone, by his two opposing neurotic temptations—paranoia and emotional withdrawal—and by his two poetic temptations—populism and "spontaneity." In his best poems, the ever-flickering paranoia is tempered by self-irony, humor, wisdom, or sheer curiosity about being; and the Buddhist quietism that would turn every phenomenon into illusion is revoked, just in time, by an eddy of feeling. If Ginsberg's populism craves a platinum record, it is checked by a scruple of art; and the spontaneity that records bus voice-overs on his travels is corralled by a sense of shapeliness. (When the balance of powers fails, the poems become either rant or sermon, rock lyric or journal notes.) Taken all together, Ginsberg's poems are X-rays of a considerable part of American society.

Ginsberg's dark sense of social evil must stem in part from his imaginative symbiosis with his paranoid mother, "from whose pained head," he says in "Kaddish," "I first took Vision." On the other hand, the America in which he came of age defined homosexual acts as crimes, pursued undeclared wars in Korea and Vietnam, ran puppet governments in South America and elsewhere, was undisguisedly racist, had unsavory dealings with the drug trade, and spied shamelessly on its citizens through the FBI. Ginsberg differed from his apolitical contemporaries not only in that his political education had begun early (through his mother) but in that his own marginality as a homosexual made resistance to the status quo necessary for self-respect. He differed from many activist poets in eventually coming to recognize that all bureaucracies are much the same: he was as unwelcome in Communist police states (Czechoslovakia and Cuba both threw him out) as he was in the United States. And he was aware (as most reformers are not) that the underlying cause of his zeal was aggression within himself, which was projected outward as suspected aggression in others. The rage and despair in Ginsberg's early poems were as much a product of self-loathing as of objective criticism of the world. Yet his own crises of feeling enabled his violent insights into the suffering inflicted by a repressive society on its young,

> who were expelled from the academies for crazy & publishing obscene odes
>   on the windows of the skull,
> . . . . .
> who got busted in their pubic beards returning through Laredo with a belt
>   of marijuana for New York,
> . . . . .
> who howled on their knees in the subway and were dragged off the roof
>   waving genitals and manuscripts . . . [2]

Ginsberg was saved from suicidal depression by what he called an "auditory vision," in which he heard a voice—he took it to be that of William Blake— reciting poetry. Since Ginsberg's own poetry has always been scored for the audible voice—endorsing orality over the inhibitions of literacy—it is no surprise that the vision was an auditory one. And, since Blake is the greatest English poet of disinhibition—as Whitman is its greatest American poet—it was Blake who would be the instigator and Whitman the guru of Ginsberg's early verse. Whitman's "Unscrew the locks from the doors! / Unscrew the doors themselves from their jambs!" was the epigraph for *Howl;* and—to complete the revolutionary triad of precursors—Shelley's "Die, / If thou wouldst be with that which thou dost seek!" was the epigraph for *Kaddish.*

Blake and Shelley and Whitman were, on the whole, better poetic models for Ginsberg's verse than Buddhist sutras. Ginsberg's path resembles that of T. S. Eliot: both possessed exceptionally high-strung sensibilities, which when exacerbated plunged them into states alarmingly close to madness; both had breakdowns; both sought some form of wisdom that could ameliorate, guide, or correct the excesses of their reactions; and what Eliot found in Dr. Vittoz's Lausanne sanatorium ("Give . . . Sympathize . . . Control," words from an Upanishad quoted in *The Waste Land*), Ginsberg found in Buddhist mantras and meditative practice.

Ginsberg's Buddhism seems to me to have had roughly the same effect on his lyrics that Eliot's Anglo-Catholicism had on his: a tension goes out of the poetry, and didacticism replaces it. In taming the uncontrollable, in regulating the nerves, the flinching person is made able to live; one cannot dispute the wisdom, in life, of staying out of the asylum. Yet the analysis of unregulated and baffling pain is a deep source of powerful lyric expression. The discipline that is taken up to regulate such pain is, of course, in itself a source of a different kind of deep pain—the pain of self-mutilation. Though the Eliot of "Four Quartets" recognizes this, Ginsberg is not very much interested in it. He finds consolation, rather than pain, in the atheist emptiness of his Buddhism.

The Ginsberg *Selected* is not entirely satisfactory. Many wonderful poems— from "American Change" to "Chances R," from "Ecologue" to "Black Shroud"—were omitted so that some sixty pages of Ginsberg's songs (none of which appeared in the 1984 *Collected Poems*) could be included. The songs may be convincing in performance, but they don't survive cold print, and Ginsberg's association with Bob Dylan is recalled rather too buoyantly: "I'm pleased with this intergenerational exchange of influence which confirms old traditions of artistic & spiritual transmission." Hardly an accurate interpretation: what of Ginsberg will enter the matrix of tradition is least likely to be the song lyrics imitating Dylan. But a truer statement follows: "The original task was to 'widen the area of consciousness,' make pragmatic examination of the texture of consciousness, even somewhat transform consciousness." That seems a fair summary of what Ginsberg's work has, in fact, done. Of course, his public appearances and his political activities in their own way helped to "widen the area of consciousness," just as have Czesław Miłosz's and Adrienne Rich's essays. But poetry has its own means, and they are not the same as marching in parades or writing persuasive prose.

Ginsberg's poetry gains much of its power from a cinematically detailed immersion in present-tense immediacy. You are there (as in any Ginsberg poem) when, in "Manhattan May Day Midnight," Ginsberg goes out at night to buy the newspapers and sees workmen tracking down a gas leak. He notices the bullet-shaped skull of the man in the manhole, he remarks the conjunction of asphalt and granite, he registers the presence of an idling truck:

At the Corner of 11th under dim Street-light in a hole in the ground
a man wrapped in work-Cloth and wool Cap pulled down his bullet skull
stood & bent with a rod & flashlight turning round in his pit halfway sunk
    in earth
Peering down at his feet, up to his chest in the asphalt by a granite Curb
. . . . .
Yes the body stink of City bowels, rotting tubes six feet under
Could explode any minute sparked by Con Ed's breathing Puttering truck
I noticed parked[.]
(703)

What is agreeable here is that there's no agenda. We are not asked to sympathize with the proletariat or to feel ecologically alarmed by the gas leak. Ginsberg's invincible interest in the real liberates us into a participatory disinterestedness. And his mind roams widely, in unpredictable ways. In another poem, the gas scene might have led to Ginsberg's own gas stove, or to comparable workers he had seen in India, or to the lure of night walking. In this case, his mind turns unexpectedly to Ancient Rome and Ur:

I passed by hurriedly Thinking Ancient Rome, Ur
Were they like this, the same shadowy surveyors & passers-by
scribing records of decaying pipes & Garbage piles on Marble, Cuneiform,
ordinary midnight citizen out on the street looking for Empire News[.]
(703)

One can't widen consciousness in poetry by having it follow a programmed path (as most ideologically committed poetry does). However noble its intentions, a programmed path *narrows* consciousness. Ginsberg, at his best, is alert, unprogrammed, free.

To examine "the texture of consciousness" means to find the million places existing in the interstices between our coarse terms for the activities of consciousness: "planning," "remembering," "memorizing," "grieving," "hoping." The texture of consciousness has had such marvelous explorers in our century (Joyce and Woolf in the novel, Eliot and Stevens in poetry) that it might seem that the task has already been accomplished. But Ginsberg has added something new. This has generally been thought to be the unspeakable (his mother's vomiting and defecating in the bathroom in "Kaddish," his own sexual grovelling in "Please Master," his embarrassment at the effects of Bell's palsy in "What You Up To?"). But, though Ginsberg has tracked shame and humiliation with great thoroughness, he has equally been the "Curator of funny emotions to the mob"—to borrow the title he bestowed on Frank O'Hara.

The comedy of consciousness was not the stock-in-trade of Eliot or Stevens, but it occurs with brio in Ginsberg, whose satiric eye is always ready to pick up a new contemporary genre—the "Personals" ad, for instance—and use it in "Personals Ad" for a CAT scan of his own psyche:

> Poet professor in autumn years
> seeks helpmate companion protector friend
> . . . . .
> to share bed meditation apartment Lower East Side,
> help inspire mankind conquer world anger & guilt,
> empowered by Whitman Blake Rimbaud Ma Rainey & Vivaldi
> . . . . .
> Find me here in New York alone with the Alone
> (970)

Which of us, Ginsberg's poem suggests, has not read the "Personals" ads and mentally composed one? Which of us has not recognized the intrinsic absurdity of self-description? The very levels of consciousness that exist to be explored are mocked by their jockeying for place in Ginsberg's ad: the tabloid self-epithet, "poet professor"; the helpless stock of cliché, "autumn years"; the archaic reversion, "seeks"; the casting about for names for homosexual partnership, "helpmate companion protector friend." (The writer's mental state alters slightly with each of these: from the Biblical "helpmate" to the euphemistic "companion" and on to the feudal "protector" and the longed-for "friend.") The impossibility of enumerating all the levels of consciousness shows up in the forced coexistence on a single line of Rimbaud and Ma Rainey, and Ginsberg's self-silhouetting—the last line echoes Lionel Johnson, who wrote, grandly, *"Lonely, unto the Lone I go; / Divine, to the Divinity"*—shows his determination not to forsake the (parodic) sublime.

In lyric poetry one transforms the consciousness of others solely by transforming one's own. Ginsberg's self-transformations (rather like Whitman's) license his readers to go and do likewise. "Sunflower Sutra" is one of the famous rhapsodic self-transformations ("You were never no locomotive, Sunflower, you were a sunflower!"), but there are also satiric ones, of which the most outrageously cheerful is the famous "Pull My Daisy":

> Pull my daisy
> tip my cup
> all my doors are open
> Cut my thoughts
> for coconuts
> all my eggs are broken
> (32)

It's hardly possible to say this without losing a lot of pompousness (if one happens to be harboring any). To become Ginsberg as one reads his poems is to undergo a powerful, if transient, alteration of consciousness. Under his spell, one is both more excited and more noticing, more tender and more mocking. As humor bests aggression, and curiosity bests xenophobia, the world improves.

Finally, Ginsberg's ever-reliable means of consciousness-raising is his rhythmic momentum, expressed by his long lines rolling in like breakers. Its urgency—at times strained, when Ginsberg is forcing the issue, but often genuine—means that some portion of life is demanding its place in the museum of history. If Ginsberg had not been mugged in New York, we would not have had the unstable rhythms of "Mugging":

I went down shouting Om Ah Hūm to gangs of lovers on the stoop
    watching
slowly appreciating, why this is a raid, these strangers mean strange business

with what—my pockets, bald head, broken-healed-bone leg, my softshoes,
    my heart—
Have they knives? Om Ah Hūm—Have they sharp metal wood to shove
    in eye ear ass? Om Ah Hūm
& slowly reclined on the pavement, struggling to keep my woolen bag
    of poetry address calendar & Leary-lawyer notes hung from my
    shoulder

(633)

Ginsberg's nonresistant chanting drives the muggers crazy—"Shut up or
we'll murder you"—and the poet concludes that it's easier to transform your
own consciousness than that of the man in the street. Yet, though the poem descends from its idealist hopes, and closes ruefully in the realm of the real, it
does not dismiss the premise that nonviolence as a response to violence is the
only alternative to an endless chain of aggression. In such poems Ginsberg's
"force field of language" still exerts a powerful imaginative pressure.

6

The Waste Land

Fragments and Montage

The Waste Land: in the medieval mythology of the Holy Grail, the land laid waste by sin or evil; the land where the king lies wounded and impotent; the land incapable of fertility; the land where April is the cruelest month because the shoots that appear are starved, frail, and doomed to wither. T. S. Eliot (1888–1965) adopted this myth (embodied in the nineteenth century by Wagner in *Parsifal*) as the governing metaphor for his daring 1921 sequence, a poem so disturbing to its first readers—in its darting among many languages, many centuries, and many religious systems—that some were prepared to believe it a hoax. But it was not a hoax: to its first admirers it seemed the replication on the page of postwar modernity itself. It was cosmopolitan, painfully self-aware, burdened by legacies of the past, overcome by the chaos of the present, and skeptical about the future.

Eliot, its young American author, although born in Saint Louis, came from an old New England family. He had had a brilliant career at Harvard, both as an undergraduate in literature and as a graduate student in philosophy; he then moved to France and Germany for postdoctoral study, leaving Europe for London in 1914 when war broke out. (Although Eliot himself did not serve in World War I, he knew its devastation acutely; his closest French friend was killed at Gallipoli.) Eliot would have been offered a post at Harvard had he returned from England for the oral defense of his PhD dissertation, but he declined to do so, and chose poetry. In 1915, Eliot had married an Englishwoman, Vivienne Haigh-Wood (to the disapproval of his parents), and was earning his living by working in the foreign department of Lloyd's Bank. When Eliot assembled the separately written poems that form *The Waste Land*, he was already the author of *Prufrock and Other Observations* (1917), and his name was becoming

known in the United States as well as in England. Yet his personal life was profoundly unhappy: his wife suffered from both physical and mental illness, and his
work at the bank prevented him from writing in any continuous way. His own
health broke down in 1921, and he had to ask for a medical leave from the bank.

Eliot's encyclopedic poem of 1921 is composed in many voices in part because Eliot found himself, after his breakdown, in a psychiatric hospital in
Lausanne that served patients from many countries ("At least," he wrote to his
brother Henry, "there are people of many nationalities, which I always like").
He had gone to Lausanne after a solitary rest at Margate (a seaside resort on the
Thames estuary) had proved insufficient to cure his depression, "nerves," and
persistent inability to work. The doctor in charge of the asylum in Lausanne
was Roger Vittoz (recommended to Eliot by his acquaintances Ottoline Morrell
and Julian Huxley); and although no medical records of Eliot's stay have been
found, Dr. Vittoz was known for what we might today call cognitive therapy,
convincing his patients that they could be in calm control of their minds and
emotions. Diagnosing his own breakdown, Eliot ascribed it "not to over-
work but to an aboulie and emotional derangement which has been a lifelong
affliction." (The French word "aboulie" is defined as "mental disease resulting
in loss of willpower.") Eliot retuned from Margate and Lausanne with, as Ezra
Pound remarked, "a damn good poem (19 pages) in his suitcase," a poem Pound
decisively edited into its present form, earning him Eliot's Dantean dedication:
"For Ezra Pound, il miglior fabbro"—the better maker. Although *The Waste
Land* incorporates pieces of poetry that Eliot had been writing since 1915, the
geographical extent of the (chiefly European) locales of the poem makes it, at
its core, not an American poem but a poem of Western Europe. (That is how
Pound saw it; he deleted the two American episodes Eliot had originally included.) For Eliot, even the European circumference was too small; he attempted
to make *The Waste Land,* by its close, a world-poem as well, embracing the
moral teachings of the Hindu Upanishads.

Eliot presents *The Waste Land* as a sequence grouped under five headings:
The Burial of the Dead (establishing it as an elegy), *A Game of Chess* (on sex as
a strategy of two antagonists), *The Fire Sermon* (on asceticism), *Death by Water*
(an elegy once more, but this time a personal one), and *What the Thunder Said*
(setting Hindu ethics against psychological collapse). The poem is prefaced by
a suicidal epigraph—"I want to die"—said by the Cumaean Sybil, imprisoned
in a bottle, and doomed by Apollo to immortality without youth.

We hear, just after the poem opens in its desolate April, the multilingual ca-
cophony of Eliot's fellow patients in Lausanne:

Summer surprised us, coming over the Starnbergersee

. . . .

Bin gar keine Russin, stamm' aus Litauen, echt deutsch.
And when we were children, staying at the archduke's,
My cousin's, he took me out on a sled,

. . . . .

In the mountains, there you feel free.
I read, much of the night, and go south in the winter.

Into this mélange, there breaks the despairing protagonist's dialogue with himself, carried on in a landscape of aridity, brokenness, and exposure to a pitiless sun. He addresses himself with the words God used to address Ezekiel in the valley of dry bones: "Son of man, can these bones live?"

What are the roots that clutch, what branches grow
Out of this stony rubbish? Son of man,
You cannot say, or guess, for you know only
A heap of broken images, where the sun beats,
And the dead tree gives no shelter, the cricket no relief,
And the dry stone no sound of water.

Eliot has begun his poem in the most theatrical way possible, with a suicidal epigraph, a paradoxical epigram ("April is the cruellest month"), a gabble of foreign voices, and then, with the dramatic rise of a curtain, a full view of his protagonist stranded in a desert under a pitiless sun, beset by thirst, his poetic ideals in a shattered heap, and the cricket's monotone his only music.

Both the protagonist and his landscape mutate in protean ways, but the bitter suffering underlying the central voice remains the same. Eliot's wealthy father had died in 1919, signifying his disapproval of his fugitive youngest son by leaving money only in trust to the impoverished Eliot (his siblings received their legacies outright). In one of its mutations, the Waste Land becomes a repellent London in which the prince-protagonist muses on two kings—his dead father and a "brother" lost by shipwreck (perhaps Eliot's friend Jean Verdenal, a medical officer killed in the Dardanelles, to whom, posthumously, Eliot dedicated his first book):

A rat crept softly through the vegetation
Dragging its slimy belly on the bank

> While I was fishing in the dull canal
> On a winter evening round behind the gashouse,
> Musing upon the king my brother's wreck
> And on the king my father's death before him.

The Waste Land's protagonist mutates later into the old prophet Tiresias, who had uniquely experienced sexual pleasure both as a man and as a woman. Eliot's note informs the reader that "Tiresias, although a mere spectator and not indeed a 'character,' is yet the most important personage in the poem, uniting all the rest." (The characters of the poem, in Eliot's metaphor, "melt" into each other until all the men are one man, "all the women are one woman, and the two sexes meet in Tiresias.") Tiresias begins his monologue with a reminiscence of Sappho's lyric hymn to the evening star—but like every other idyllic passage in *The Waste Land*, this one turns viciously anticlimactic as Eliot embarks on the squalid tale of the intercourse between a typist and her "young man carbuncular":

> I Tiresias, though blind, throbbing between two lives,
> Old man with wrinkled female breasts, can see
> At the violet hour, the evening hour that strives
> Homeward, and brings the sailor home from sea,
> The typist home at teatime . . .

As we watch Eliot's film evolve, episode by episode, montage by montage, anecdote by anecdote, all interspersed by the laments of the protagonist, the "melting" and reconstituting of the dramatis personae become elements of a surreal portraiture. The poem becomes an elegy for self and others, a ritual for the burial of the dead. At the center of *The Waste Land*, in *Death by Water*, there lies a drowned youth, Phlebas the Phoenician, commemorated in the hypnotic rhythms of ocean waves:

> A current under sea
> Picked his bones in whispers. As he rose and fell
> He passed the stages of his age and youth
> Entering the whirlpool.

The fear of bodily dissolution, that "fear in a handful of dust" encountered in the bleak desert, melts here into a fear of universal death by water:

> Gentile or Jew
> O you who turn the wheel and look to windward,
> Consider Phlebas, who was once handsome and tall as you.

Deaths multiply throughout the poem. "Fear death by water," says the fortune-teller Madame Sosostris. The protagonist sees a current of specters "flowing over" London Bridge: "I had not thought death had undone so many," He even meets a ghost he knows, one who has planted a corpse in his garden. Although the protagonist distrusts promises of the resurrection of the body, he expects a nightmarish resurrection of remorse:

> "That corpse you planted last year in your garden,
> Has it begun to sprout? Will it bloom this year?"

The silent husband in *A Game of Chess*, asked by his neurotic wife, "What are you thinking of?" answers from his own death-obsessed mind, "I think we are in rats' alley / Where the dead men lost their bones." His mind veers to his dead father, and remembering Ariel's "Full fathom five thy father lies," he quotes the mutation of the organic body into the inorganic: "Those are pearls that were his eyes." The deaths continue with the abortion carried out by Lil ("It's them pills I took, to bring it off, she said"), and with the archetypal images of Gethsemane and Calvary:

> After the torchlight red on sweaty faces
> After the frosty silence in the gardens
> After the agony in stony places
> . . . . .
> He who was living is now dead
> We who were living are now dying . . .

In this postwar poem, the mothers of the world are weeping, lamenting the death of their children:

> What is that sound high in the air
> Murmur of maternal lamentation . . .

And finally, the elegy that had mourned human death spreads to the deaths of great cities:

> Falling towers
> Jerusalem Athens Alexandria
> Vienna London
>
> . . . . .
>
> London Bridge is falling down falling down falling down.

The Waste Land, insofar as it is an elegy, begins with the title of the Anglican ritual of burial, continues with Eliot's mourning for Jean Verdenal, his musing on his father's death, and his own (and the Sibyl's) suicidal yearning, and—over all this—the deaths of young men, the destruction of Europe by the Great War, and the ruin of whole civilizations—Jerusalem, Athens, Alexandria.

W. B. Yeats once said that the only things to interest a serious mind are sex and the dead. If Eliot's mind is dwelling on the dead all through *The Waste Land*, it is also dwelling on sex, on both the human and the literary scale. There is an antiphony of sex and death throughout the poem, with the theme of sex culminating in two heartbreaking lines at the close. The first is a quotation from the *Pervigilium Veneris*, "The Vigil of Venus," in which the speaker, who has no mate, asks when he will gain a mate and be enabled to sing: *"Quando fiam uti chelidon"*—"When shall I be like the swallow?" The second is a quotation from Gérard de Nerval's sonnet "El Desdichado" ("The Disinherited One"), which recalls not only the princely protagonist's ruined tower, and his exclusion from his inheritance, but also the death of his beloved: he is darkened in spirit, a widower, inconsolable, his only star now dead, his lute emblazoned with the black star of melancholy:

> Je suis le ténébreux, le veuf, l'inconsolé,
> Le Prince d'Aquitaine à la tour abolie;
> Ma seule étoile est morte, et mon luth constellé
> Porte le soleil noir de la mélancholie.

These closing "fragments" are drawn from high art, but Eliot's startling originality in this poem is to bring low diction into the same frame as high. As an urban poet, he cannot live in fastidious withdrawal from the London crowds nor from their appetites and behaviors (in all of which he sees a tortured mirror of his own). Against the neurotic mutual cruelty of the cultivated couple who open *A Game of Chess* he sets, in the following pub scene, the disintegrating marriage of "Lil," the woman with decaying teeth who aborted her sixth child ("She's had five already and nearly died of young George"). Her "friend" warns Lil that she had better please her husband, demobilized from the War:

Now Albert's coming back, make yourself a bit smart.
He'll want to know what you done with that money he gave you
To get yourself some teeth. He did, I was there.
You have them all out, Lil, and get a nice set,
He said, I swear, I can't bear to look at you.
And no more can't I, I said, and think of poor Albert,
He's been in the army four years, he wants a good time,
And if you don't give it him, there's other will, I said.

The rhythms of Lil's traitorous "friend" are as cunningly chosen as anything else in *The Waste Land*. And they, in turn, dissolve first into the pubkeeper's loud "HURRY UP PLEASE IT'S TIME" and then into the fading rhythms of Ophelia's mad scene before she drowns herself: "Good night, ladies, good night, sweet ladies, good night, good night." The fluid antiphony of the beautiful and the sordid continues, as a refrain from Spenser's aristocratic wedding-poem ("Sweet Thames, run softly, till I end my song") is defaced by the detritus left by modern riverbank sex: "The river bears no empty bottles, sandwich papers, / Silk handkerchiefs, cardboard boxes, cigarette ends / Or other testimony of summer nights. The nymphs are departed." Down and up, Lil and Ophelia, up and down, the Spenserian nymphs and the littered condoms. We might consider this a rather stilted technique—a little high scenery, a little low scenery, a little irony joining them both—were it not for the complete absence of irony in the poem viewed as a whole. Irony may be the cartilage of this articulated body, but its heart is vulnerable flesh, at a pitch of perplexity and hurt that cannot but express itself.

The Waste Land belongs among that group of poems that poets write when they decide to risk all in disclosing the idiosyncratic, complicated, and chaotic contents of their own minds—which they then "set in order." The fragments that Eliot shores against his ruins are not those that we might choose if we were in his straits—but the experience of recalling literary phrases embodying our own suffering is not alien to the rest of us. Eliot's creating mind was set not on being "accessible" but on being true to his own sensibility. If others responded, that would be a later matter; but in Margate and Lausanne, when Eliot was assembling the segments of his personal and social observations that later became (with Pound's help) sections of *The Waste Land,* he was aiming more at authenticity than at "communication." Of course any formed expression in musical language is implicitly an attempt at aesthetic communication, and Eliot's extraordinary composition is no exception to that rule; but it is directed less to a possible audience than to the Muse, imploring from her a style adequate to the poet's depth and breadth of subject.

It is when we reach *The Fire Sermon* (Part III of *The Waste Land*) that we begin to grasp the extent of Eliot's ambition. The title baffles until Eliot reveals in a note that it refers to a sermon by the Buddha, urging asceticism. We also encounter in this section excerpts from St. Augustine's *Confessions:* "To Carthage then I came, where a cauldron of unholy loves sang all about mine ear. . . . I entangle my steps with these outward beauties, but Thou pluckest me out, O Lord, Thou pluckest me out." Eliot's note instructs us that "the collocation of these two representatives of eastern and western asceticism, as the culmination of this part of the poem, is not an accident." By this collocation, by this insistent note, Eliot suggests that although we may look to the past for literary embodiments of asceticism, it is up to us, by the collocation of such texts, to aid ourselves in personal spiritual choice. Yet Eliot cannot inform us of his own such decision: the most he can do is cite passages (from the Buddha, from Augustine) against his own distress, as he had done before by quoting Ophelia, quoting Ariel, quoting Spenser, quoting the Psalmist in exile ("By the rivers of Babylon, there we sat down, yea, we wept, when we remembered Zion": "By the water of Leman I sat down and wept," says Eliot by Lake Leman).

How efficacious can such quoting be? How reliable are such fragments in shoring up a collapsing self? Eliot's intertextual links—the veins through which the lifeblood of the poem flows—leave him arrested in situations like his own, while a recurrent self-denigration (here, in the decline from Marvell's "Coy Mistress" to an obscene Australian ballad) raises its mocking counterpoint:

> But at my back from time to time I hear
> The sound of horns and motors, which shall bring
> Sweeney to Mrs. Porter in the spring.
> O the moon shone bright on Mrs. Porter
> And on her daughter
> They wash their feet in soda water . . .

Revolted by Sweeney (Eliot's *homme moyen sensuel*) and his liaison with Mrs. Porter, Eliot leaps (via the closing line of Verlaine's sonnet "Parsifal") to the choir of sexless children singing at the heterodox religious close of Wagner's *Parsifal*—"Et O ces voix d'enfants, chantant dans la coupole!"—as if *Parsifal* (and Verlaine) could cancel out the "low" ballad (as of course they cannot).

The Waste Land remains, to most readers, Eliot's greatest poem, because it refuses any easy reconciling of its revulsion against the appetites of the sexual body and its aspirations toward the idealizing spirit. Eliot will not claim an achievement he has not reached. (Later, in *Four Quartets*, he will express a more settled spirituality by moving out of society and out of time to "the still point of the turning world.") Although *The Waste Land* has been a poem of the West (from Tiresias the seer to "dear Mrs. Equitone" the fortune-teller), it finds, in *What the Thunder Said,* that it has to move from the bankrupt West to the Ganges and the Himalayas, taking as its starting point (as Eliot's note reveals) a Hindu sacred text, the Brihadaranyaka-Upanishad, which explains the message of the sound of the Thunder. It is the voice of the Creator God, as he instructs the gods, human beings, and demons to surpass the ordinary limit of their natures: the minor gods should control their unruly selves, men should give alms despite their innate miserliness, and the demons should forsake their natural cruelty and sympathize. As the Upanishad says, "That very thing is repeated even today by the heavenly voice, in the form of thunder as 'Da,' 'Da,' 'Da.' . . . Therefore one should practice these three things: self-control, giving, and mercy."

What the Thunder says sounds remarkably like the reported advice of Dr. Vittoz—advice that is ethical rather than religious, universally applicable rather than sectarian. Eliot's study of the Upanishads at Harvard almost made him a Buddhist, but in the end his inherited culture was too strong for him, and he knelt at Little Gidding rather than at the Ganges. But here, the granted mercy ("a damp gust / Bringing rain") comes from Asia, from the thunderclouds over the Himalayas. Eliot's strikingly candid elaborations of the Thunder's three *Da* words—*Datta, Dayadhvam, Damyata*—restore, for a consoling moment, the possibility of a generous view of human relations:

> What have we given?
> . . . . .
> The awful daring of a moment's surrender
> Which an age of prudence can never retract
> By this, and this only, we have existed
> . . . . .
>
> I have heard the key
> Turn in the door once and turn once only
> We think of the key, each in his prison
> . . . . .
>
> The boat responded
> Gaily, to the hand expert with sail and oar
> The sea was calm, your heart would have responded
> Gaily, when invited, beating obedient
> To controlling hands . . .

These visions of giving, of sympathizing, and of happiness—even of gaiety—are impermanent not only because they are visionary but also because they are drawn from a Hindu tradition distant from the culture of the protagonist. Their offered expansion of selfhood shrinks, and the ruined Western psyche reasserts its ownership of the poem, shoring, against its *tour abolie*, its disintegrating European fragments—of London Bridge falling down, of a suffering poet sinking back into purgatorial fire, of a mind envying the singing swallow his mate, of a disinherited prince, of the mad and violent author Hieronymo. It is true that Eliot allows into his closing lines a faint reminiscence of the Thunder by repeating its three words, now "normalized" into English by the absence of their former italics. And yet he cannot remain in a normalized and translated version of the wisdom of the East: he ends his poem with the alien and untranslated self-echoing word "Shantih shantih shantih." The Thunder-words have been acceptably paraphrased within the poem, but "shantih" remains stubbornly unintelligible to a Western reader, promising only an unattainable ritual end recommended by a Sanskrit text. (Eliot added a note translating the import of "shantih," but within the poem it remains unexplained.)

The Waste Land surveys a domain of lost hopes, charlatan advisors (Madame Sosostris), destroyed cities, affectless sexuality, hordes of refugees, religious uncertainty, social hatred, lost ideals, and, above all, helpless loneliness and suffering in an arid desert. "Why not say what happened?" Robert Lowell was to ask defiantly, much later, in his final poem, "Epilogue." In 1921, Eliot was the first modern poet writing in English to say, in a very broad way, "what happened" to himself and to Europe during and after the Great War. Accusing his society of covering up its despair, he borrowed words from Baudelaire's "Au Lecteur" to double the force of his anger at social hypocrisy: "You! Hypocrite lecteur!—mon semblable,—mon frère!" But we must recall that in spite of the cultural and personal wounds uncovered and probed by *The Waste Land*, its literary fame arose not only from its investigations of death and sex but also from the memorable voices (not least the voice of its anguished protagonist) through which those obsessive themes arrived on the page.

Eliot had thought of calling the poem "He do the Police in different voices"— a quotation from Chapter XVI of Dickens's *Our Mutual Friend*, in which old Betty Higden says of her adopted foundling, Sloppy, "I do love a newspaper. You mightn't think it, but Sloppy is a beautiful reader of a newspaper. He do the Police in different voices." She means that Sloppy reads out the transcripts of court trials in full dramatic fashion, taking on a different voice for each of the participants: Eliot, too, does the social world in different voices, each with its own diction, each with its own rhythm. We have already heard the unstoppable pub monologue of Lil's companion; just as distinctive in *A Game of Chess* is the staccato discontented rhythm of the frustrated upper-class wife:

> "My nerves are bad to-night. Yes, bad. Stay with me.
> Speak to me. Why do you never speak. Speak.
>   What are you thinking of? What thinking? What?
> I never know what you are thinking. Think."

She is speaking aloud, as her quotation marks show; her morose husband does not answer aloud but responds in unquoted despairing thought:

> I think we are in rats' alley
> Where the dead men lost their bones.

Other voices intercut that of the protagonist: one with a snatch of song ("Frisch weht der Wind"); another with a reproach ("You gave me hyacinths first a year ago"). Or a different voice altogether will begin to speak in an elaborately Shakespearean pastiche:

> The Chair she sat in, like a burnished throne,
> Glowed on the marble, where the glass
> Held up by standards wrought with fruited vines
> From which a golden Cupidon peeped out . . .

A ragtime voice breaks in upon the neurotic woman, but she quickly resumes control of the page:

> "O O O O that Shakespeherian Rag—
> It's so elegant
> So intelligent
> "What shall I do now? What shall I do?"

Among his voices, Eliot makes room for a crowing cock—"Co co rico co co rico"—and a Whitmanian hermit-thrush—"Drip drop drip drop drop drop drop." Such interruptions and counterclaims of sound, such generic leaps—from stylized imitation to music-hall blare, from birdsong to Ariel's dirge—electrify Eliot's score for *The Waste Land*.

Several of Eliot's voices were edited out by Pound, notably the vulgar voice of a drinker who stops off at a bar, a music hall, and lastly a brothel. His lines originally opened the poem, serving as a prelude to "April is the cruellest month":

> First we had a couple of feelers down at Tom's place,
> There was old Tom, boiled to the eyes, blind. . . .
> . . . . .
> "I turned up an hour later down at Myrtle's place. . . .
> . . . . .
> Get me a woman, I said; you're too drunk, she said,
> But she gave me a bed and a bath and ham and eggs."

By cutting this American prelude and a later passage spoken by an American sailor, Pound made *The Waste Land* a consistently non-American poem. He also cut a prelude that opened *The Fire Sermon*, a coarse Swiftian pastiche in which an upper-class woman named Fresca is shown going through the motions of her morning: first, drinking hot chocolate (or tea) brought by her maid, then going to the toilet ("the needful stool"), then reading and answering letters, then bathing:

> This ended, to the steaming bath she moves,
> Her tresses fanned by little flutt'ring Loves;
> Odours, confected by the cunning French,
> Disguise the good old hearty female stench.

(Pound revised "cunning," with its obscene pun, to "artful," one of his many alterations, always for the better.) If it is true that Pound's deletions and pungent comments, visible in the margins of the 1971 facsimile of the *Waste Land* manuscript, shaped Eliot's several sections into their present form, it must be remembered that it was Eliot himself who wrote the marvelous lines of the poem, with their nervous rhythms, their musical counterpointing of voices, their religious yearnings and their satiric abysses, their imperious forays into other languages, their montage of social scenes, and their departures into eerie sexual surrealism:

> A woman drew her long black hair out tight
> And fiddled whisper music on those strings
> And bats with baby faces in the violet light

Whistled, and beat their wings
And crawled head downward down a blackened wall . . .

In such lines, the Renaissance *canzone* turns modern. And *The Waste Land* is an anthology of such lyric genres—the elegy, the prophecy, the lament, the homily, the vision, the pastoral, the satiric lyric, the love lyric, the lyric of remorse. While its every turn is literary and allusive, its anecdotes display the contemporary. Its dissonance of dramatis personae is countered by the exquisitely managed succession of its lyrical modes. Eliot may have said that the poem was "only the relief of a personal and wholly insignificant grouse against life; it is just a piece of rhythmical grumbling," but what else could he say—"My marriage is in ruins, my father has disinherited me, I have lost my faith, the social world disgusts me"? Hardly. Nor would such a confessional summary properly represent the extraordinary assemblage that we know as *The Waste Land*—a poem that reached so far beyond its origins in both life and literature that it revolutionized modern verse.

7

The Snow Poems and *Garbage*

Episodes in A. R. Ammons's Poetics

Ammons's *Garbage* (1993), that great *memento mori*, demands a return to *The Snow Poems* (1977). Imperfectly though I understood *The Snow Poems* on first reading that volume, I knew that I liked what I saw. That extraordinary document in the history of American poetry gave a foretaste of *Garbage*.[1]

The Ammons of *The Snow Poems* has literary antecedents, yes—in Williams's experiments in disjunction, in Stein's experiments with childish aspects of language, in Thoreau's wood watching, in Whitman's broad democratic vistas, in Frost's shapeliness of form, even in the Beats. Yet none of these poets, except occasionally Whitman, rises and falls from the geophysical sublime to the ignobly ridiculous in Ammons's daring way. Williams—most notably in *Paterson*—arranges his poem so that it rises, repeatedly, from the basso ostinato of the communal to the flute of solo lyric: he usually distinguishes melodic personal lyric from the *continuo* of the social. Ammons, however, insists in both *The Snow Poems* and *Garbage* that there is a *continuo* of the personal—the "noise" of the everyday mind—from which the lyric rises and into which it subsides. (Ashbery later suggested something cognate in *Flow Chart*.) This contextualizing of the lyric moment within its nonlyric "surround" is the fundamental device of the modern lyric long poem, from *The Waste Land* on; we distinguish among poets using this genre by their description of that surround as well as by the nature of their embodied lyrics. Ammons's context is an extraordinarily broad one, in one respect (he does not shrink from showing himself on the toilet, or telling dirty jokes, or experiencing severe, if sometimes comic, anxiety); yet in another respect, the surround of the Ammons lyric moment is narrow. Though amply extended into the natural world, and occasionally into the domestic one, it is rarely political, social, or commercial in the ordinary meanings of those words. It is even rarely literary in an overt sense (though covert literary allusions occur profusely as a form of in-joke). In short, Ammons's definition of the human person is different both internally and con- textually from the one we meet in the long poems of his fellow poets. And since that definition is made through poetic language, the language also defines what it is, for Ammons, to be human in this moment, in this country.

I want first to take inventory of many items in *The Snow Poems* that suggest principles in a poetics, and draw from each (hoping not to misrepresent the au- thor) a poetic "commandment" that it is obeying. I then want to suggest how many of these principles have survived in the later poem *Garbage,* but also to point out what has been modified in that work. *Garbage* is a masterpiece of a different sort from *The Snow Poems*—less whimsical (though by no means en- tirely grave), less linguistically arrogant (though not linguistically humble), less taunting (though not without mockery), less disjunctive (though not without its own leaps and gaps). Yet *Garbage* is recognizably a descendant of *The Snow Poems,* and I want to show what Ammons kept as well as what he discarded. I should begin by saying that all of Ammons's poems, long and short, descend from his first book, *Ommateum, with Doxology,* and from its initial manifesto, which reads, in part:

> These poems are, for the most part, dramatic presentations of thought and emotion, as in themes of the fear of the loss of identity, the appreciation of transient natural beauty, the conflict between the individual and the group, the chaotic particle in the classical field, the creation of false gods to serve real human needs. While maintaining a perspective from the hub, the poet ventures out in each poem to explore one of the numberless radii of experience. The poems suggest a many-sided view of reality; an adop- tion of tentative, provisional attitudes, replacing the partial, unified, prej- udicial, and rigid.[2]

The modern long poem, as has been frequently remarked, is the lyric poet's cast for epic breadth. In the nineteenth century, the novel so dominated utter- ance that Browning competed with it by writing his lyrically perspectival long poem, *The Ring and the Book.* Other lyric poets (from Wordsworth to Eliot to Frost) turned to the drama as a possible arena for breadth, but experienced a notable lack of success. The lyric temperament, with its commitment to inward- reflective form, is in most cases the enemy of the social temperament, which is committed to forms and themes that permit interactions among agents (agon, dialogue, marriage, social mobility, war). It is not that lyric dialogue-poems do not exist, but they enact the inner dialogue of the mind with itself, as Arnold (to his own wincing disapproval) saw. The tensions in *The Waste Land* (no matter what social metaphors they may borrow) project upon a screen not so much the social interactions of the twentieth century as the patterns of the ravaged Eliotic nerves.

By what strategy, then, can the long lyric poem, confined to the inwardly reflective as its material, achieve both breadth and depth? Each original poet answers the challenge differently. Eliot chose a far-ranging mental discontinuity—of scenes, of voices, of cultures, and of epochs; Williams chose to identify a man and a city as his version of the one and the many; Stevens (in *Notes toward a Supreme Fiction*) invented a series of allegorical personae (Nanzia Nunzio, Canon Aspirin) projecting different aspects of his own personality; Crane flung a single continental symbol (the Bridge) of his own Shelleyan aspiration over American times and places; Lowell dissected (in *Life Studies*) the typology of his own declining class of Boston Brahmins by means of sketches of his family *mis à nu*, or (in *History*) wrote a chronicle of his personal "takes" on famous people from Adam to Stalin; Berryman sang the Freudian self in Dream Songs that extended from his own Henry-Id to his whole generation of *poètes maudits*.

But these are thematic choices, and do not cover another, more exigent, requirement of the long lyric poem: that it represent contemporary language, both in depth and in breadth. Eliot's idea of depth in language was a class-stratified one (from the demotic to classical Greek, from the music hall to Wagner) and his idea of breadth in language was historical citation (from Jerusalem to London via Athens and Alexandria). To mention only one very different instance, Stevens's idea of depth (or height) in language was a philosophical one (from instantiation to abstraction); his idea of breadth in linguistic reference was a geographic one (Europe to the United States, North to South, Rome to "the more merciful Rome beyond").

And even theme and language range do not exhaust lyric strategy. A field of resemblance (metaphor, simile, analogy, allegory) tends to characterize any original poet, and can serve (as, for a lyric writer, narrative or agon cannot) as an organizing matrix on which the long poem can be plotted. I have mentioned how Williams "plots" the man Paterson on the matrix of the city: this is Williams's fundamental micro-macro field of resemblance, and, as he hovers over it, he makes the cataract of language equal the falls, the realm of innocent pleasure equal the park, the site of individual guilty violence the slums, and so on. Eliot's matrix of resemblance is the Dantesque one of Heaven, Purgatory, and

Hell, and almost any incident in *The Waste Land* can be plotted against those three allegorical places. Stevens replots reality as resemblance: "Things seen are things as seen" *(Adagia)*. Resemblance itself therefore becomes the originating ground of being, while "reality" (in all of Stevens's long poems) becomes a secondary derivation from an initiating resemblance perceived (or posited) by the poet.

And—to conclude this brief set of conditions of creation—the fourth consideration of strategy must be external form: What does the long poem look like on the page? The distracted forms summoned by the ruined mind in *The Waste Land* extend from the song to the heroic couplet, from free verse to metered verse, and from the continuous (the episode of the typist) to the discontinuous (scraps of language blown past the hearer). Nothing could be further from *The Waste Land*, in this respect, than Stevens's imperturbable blank-verse tercets—the emblem of his long-breathed speculative mind—unrolling down the page. And these do not resemble Lowell's phalanxes of sonnets—which by their form assert, for a considerable period, that the Procrustean bed of verse can control the mess of reality.

When we turn to *The Snow Poems*, what do we find to be Ammons's choice of unifying theme, linguistic depth and breadth, matrix of resemblance, and external forms? The volume, which covers a period from fall to spring, is thematically unified on the "outside" by its series of weather reports on "snow" (the word includes all hideous and beautiful Ithacan varieties of frozen water—icy rain, hail, sleet, slush, icicles, crystal, flake). Ammons's emphasis on his region of the United States explains the dedication of the volume: "for my country." The book is thematically unified on the "inside" by the author's turning fifty and by his father's death. For linguistic depth we are given a "social" scale from the rustic to the philosophic, a literary scale from the obscene to the sublime, and an emotional scale from terror to joy. For linguistic breadth we find a scientific scale extending from electrons through bacteria to galaxies (from quantum physics through biochemistry to astronomy), and a natural scale that runs from chipmunks to mountains. For a field of resemblance, we have the (mostly) visual scenes in the vicinity of Ammons's house, landscapes (from earth to sky) that are drawn on for metaphors of physical and mental dynamisms. And for external form, we have a free-verse ground (comprising 119 short-lined lyric poems, entitled by their own incipits) on which various entertainments are superimposed: small inserted lyrics, bearing their own titles; word lists linked by sound; little doodles on the typewriter while the writer waits for his compositional impetus to cohere; double and even triple columns; words running vertically instead of horizontally; and idiosyncratic punctuation (no periods, just colons and exclamation points, with the odd asterisk thrown in). *The Snow Poems* immediately says to the reader "variability," "oddity," "competing impulses," while yet showing these corralled into 119 distinct units. Ammons intended—as he remarked in 1963—a prosody in which "the movement is not across the page but actually, centrally down the page" (SM, 7). Ammons said, as late as 1994, that *The Snow Poems* remained his favorite among his long poems:

> It seems to me in that poem I had a more ready availability to the names of things and to images of them than in any of the other long poems. The other long poems were more nearly juggling by some program. (SM, 101)

Before I turn to *The Snow Poems* in more detail, I want to sketch a thematic and stylistic inventory for *Garbage*. Its unifying "outside" theme (what Ammons would call its "program") is named in its title: everything in the universe eventually loses function and is discarded as trash. The "inside" theme of the poem is the meaning (or meaninglessness) to the poet himself of his life and his art, given the certainty of personal death and the equal certainty of the eventual unintelligibility of all cultural production. The linguistic range of *Garbage* is narrower than that of *The Snow Poems:* there is less obscenity and less sublimity, and a less high-pitched (though no less moving) emotional expression: exclamation points are very rare. (In *Garbage,* as in most of Ammons's long poems, the usual terminal punctuation is the colon, the symbol of his commitment to provisionality of thought.) To the panorama of the natural world—Ammons's perennial matrix of resemblance—*Garbage* adds the terrifying vision of the landfill to which everything is eventually consigned for burning. Stevens's version of this was "the trashcan at the end of the world" ("Owl's Clover"), manifested also as a dump ("The Man on the Dump"); but those were cool approachable places on which one can even perch. Ammons's landfill is an unapproachable Florida pit where the silhouetted bulldozer, manned by its new Charon, heaves everything over the edge into a fire. In the fire, everything is cremated into smoke that rises and disperses in the air. Gulls wheel and scream over the site. In terms of external form, *Garbage* (a 121-page poem) is composed of eighteen "cantos": though these are of irregular length, they are all written (except for an occasional tercet or single line) in loose-pentameter blank-verse couplets, which are separated by stanza breaks that aerate the page. The impression given by the page is one of neatness, but the line breaks are sufficiently unexpected to keep the couplets from seeming conclusive. Though a steady ongoingness (rather than *The Snow Poems*' lyric fits and starts) is felt in *Garbage,* Ammons escapes, by his waywardness of development, a Lucretian finality.

The aim of any long piece in lyric form (as of any extensive art piece—drama, novel, opera, a painting sequence like that of the Sistine Chapel) is to equal the world, to be a "take" on the whole world. To this end, a long poem should be (in Ammons's thinking) as unmanageable as the world. His long poems are all strictly incomprehensible (though entirely understandable): one cannot get one's (mental) arms to encompass them. Yeats wanted to pull "the balloon of the mind" into the "narrow shed" of organized metrical form: Ammons wants the balloon to stay a balloon, to remain buoyant, to hover and float and rise, alluring and evading sight. Thus the uncontainable form of the long poem represents the poet's putting out tentative feelers toward understanding a world not yet delineated:

> The work of art is undertaken by the practitioner as a means of finding out and defining (if just tonally) something he doesn't already know. The elaboration of known or imaginable positions in morality, epistemology, politics, feminism needs no forms not already available to rationality and produces no surprise. In art, the form enables a self-becoming that brings up in its arising materials not previously touched on or, possibly, suspected. This confers the edge of advancement we call creativity. (SM, 28)

Readers have succeeded in memorizing Shakespeare's *Sonnets* and even *Paradise Lost,* but only a person with an eidetic memory could learn one of Ammons's long poems by heart; even then, the digressive form of the poem would militate against his comprehending it as a unity. Ammons's way of having his poems "resist the intelligence almost successfully" (Stevens) is to have them become all-inclusive, defeating not only the mind's will-to-consequence (its dependence on cause and effect, priority, hierarchy, and so on), and the eye's will-to-mapping (its dependence on a consistency of scene and focus), but also the heart's will-to-resolution (its dependence on a stable organization of feeling on which it can repose). In this respect, he makes his long poems emblems of a world that has become so full of information that it is no longer fully graspable (unlike, say, Milton's world as Milton portrays it, mastered by himself and by God).

To come to the particulars of *The Snow Poems:* the first thing to be said is how shocking a book it was in diction and tone and self-presentation (at least to this habitual reader of lyric) when it appeared. It was not that I was unacquainted with surrealism or futurism or the Poundian experiment of the *Cantos,* but those versions of shock were predominantly high-tech and high-culture (Pound's occasional Uncle Ez passages being the exception proving the rule).

And I had read Ginsberg's *Howl*, which permitted an urban vulgarity (and even obscenity) in serious writing. But Ammons consistently offered something quite different—a rural poetry in which the delicate lay cheek by jowl with the vulgar, the commercial next to the lyric, the momentarily unclear next to the clear:

Dawn clear
by sunrise
hazes riffles   you want to be
furrows and floats   bullfucked when
of fluff   mine is no longer
appear   than a penguin
so the sun
has too much   quilt raffle
to come through   antiques
to come through   handcrafted gifts
                       live country music
make verbal   whimsies, furbelows, and
things tangles   sundries
(SP, 71)

If I hadn't lived in Ithaca between 1960 and 1963, I might not have so joyously recognized the components of *The Snow Poems*, but the volume so completely transferred not only the weather and the scenery but the "handcrafted gifts" of that (then rural) town to the page that I was a hypnotized reader, ready to forgive (and at first I felt the need to forgive) any disturbances to my sense of the aesthetic from a poet so marvelously gifted at summoning up a known environment.

The language of *The Snow Poems* represents a new amalgam in American poetry. Ammons has a tendency to both the allusive and the parodic, so that some anterior form of expression is often playing hide-and-seek throughout his poems. Rustic diction, in his hands, is perhaps more shapely than it would be on the farm: but the "poetic" use of dialect (which has a long history in our poetry) has rarely descended to Ammons's glee in the "said song" of the vernacular:

I declare the crows have
come right in to hanging

around in the maple tree
and I jest bet you five
dollars since it's over
thirty today they got the
scent of that suet and
they jest a waitin' that's
what they doin' they jest
a waitin' sooner or later
they gonna plunk right
there on the porch and
start a grabbin' and a
tearin'

(SP, 136)

This laconic rustic repetition being one of Ammons's mother tongues (from his childhood in North Carolina), he insists on its occasional presence in his writing, but he reorders it into a slightly parodic form of itself.

The coarse, extending to the obscene, is another of Ammons's mother tongues (as it is of all men, and now increasingly of women). Ammons knows, I think, that it sits uneasily in the margins of his lexicon, but he will not fence it out entirely. It is often disturbing. In the poem I want to use as representative of the procedures of *The Snow Poems*, a piece called "Poetry Is the Smallest," coarseness (in a double-columned marital form representing a married couple) closes the lyric: at the end, by punning on the word "relief" to mean "urination" and "bas-relief," Ammons turns a man huddled in a urinal into a Parthenon metope:

poet friend of mine's
dick's so short   still his fat wife's
he can't pull it long enough   radiant every morning
to pee straight with: he humps well, probably,
not to pee on   stringing her out far and
anybody by surprise   loose on the frail hook:
sideways, he hunkers   and, too, I notice she
into the urinal so far   follows his words
he looks like, to achieve,   closely like one who
relief: knows what a tongue can do

(SP, 82)

The burden of this poem, as its title "Poetry Is the Smallest" implies, and as its earlier metaphors convey, is the apparent paltriness of lyric breath compared to the grand motions of the universal wind, the poet's insignificance in the landscape when he is placed against a mountain. The analogy of the surprising power of frail poetry to the surprising sexual success of the fellow poet's insignificant penis (aided by his tongue) makes the closing coarseness another manner of asserting what has been said twice before in the poem, first by didactic statement, second by allegorical dialogue. A twenty-line didactic statement had begun the poem, saying three times, "poetry is":

Poetry is the smallest	
trickle trinket	
bauble burst	
the lightest	f
windseed leaftip	r
snowdown	e
poetry is the breaks	e
the least loop	d
from	o
the general curvature	m
into delight	
poetry is	
the slightest	f
hue, hint, hurt	r
its dance too light	e
not to be the wind's:	e
yet nothing	d
becomes itself	o
without the overspill	m
of this small abundance	

(SP, 81)

This opening portion of "Poetry Is the Smallest" is a conventionally shapely four-stanza free-verse lyric (with the stanza breaks suppressed into invisibility); yet it is "disturbed" by the presence on the page of the word "freedom" twice inscribed vertically next to it. Still, we recognize the poem's kinship with earlier lyrics through its Dickinsonian definition-mode, its use of conventional praise-hyperbole, its alliteration, its "refrains" ("poetry is" and "freedom"), and its occasional rhymes ("lightest" and "slightest"; the Herber-

tian "light" and "delight"; "dance" and its portmanteau appearance in "abun-
dance"). As our eye strays to the right, we notice that the first vertical "freedom"
begins at the line "the lightest," while the second begins at the matching line,
"the slightest." The hosanna implicit in "freedom freedom" suggests the nature
of our delight when we arrive at a personal characterization of reality—an
idiosyncratic delight as available to those whom Wordsworth called "silent
poets" as to the speaking poets, whose perceptions are given permanence in
language.

If I could, as an early reader of *The Snow Poems,* assent to this exquisite hymn
to the lightness and yet consequentiality of the lyric breeze, I could equally well
assent to the allegorical Herbertian dialogue that follows it in "Poetry Is the
Smallest." This faux-naïf dialogue takes place between the poet, on his way to
an apparently minor height, and the mountain on whose terrain the poet asks
permission to intrude:

> you don't mind, do you, I
> said to the mountain, if
> I use this ledge or, like,
> inspiration pavilion to say
>
> a few things out over the
> various woods, streams, and
> so on: by all means, said
> the mountain: I was a little

concerned, I said, because	
the speech is, like, about	only
the individual vs. the major	where
structures and, like, I	we
	are
was thinking of siding with	to
the individual: but, of	lose
course, said the mountain:	all
well, but, I said, it	are
	we
doesn't make any difference	to
what I say if it doesn't	have
make any difference: please,	here
said the mountain, be my guest	and

(SP, 81–82)

Though the dialogue is self-contained in its five shy and apologetic quatrains (incorporating into poetry, in one of Ammons's characteristic forays into the colloquial, the now-universal adolescent marker "like"), it is not allowed to achieve equanimity because a new poem—consisting of one-word, mostly monosyllabic, lines—has "started up" within reach of our right eye.

The bicameral mind, earlier introduced into the poem by the single-word obbligato "freedom freedom" running alongside the initial praise-lyric, has now started up a second vertical effort, this time as a rival to the mountain-lyric. This second vertical poem, thirty lines long, reads (if conventionally punctuated and written out horizontally) as follows:

> [Only where we are to lose all, are we to have, here and there, a trifle; only where we are to lose all, are we to be here beholding everything.] (SP, 81–82)

We are forced, by the way Ammons runs this aphoristic mini poem down the right column, word by unpunctuated word, to read it as quasi nonsense, as it reiterates its weak, almost meaningless, phrases: "we are to" and "all are we to" and "lose all are we." Though a second reading parses it into sense, our first impression is that of bits and pieces of language offered as a flotsam-and-jetsam do-it-yourself-kit of verse. Its tentatively accreting vertical form stands, we can say, for the poet's gradual admission of the truth that its horizontally written version too summarily and too neatly announces.

Before the right-brain aphorism has concluded—in fact more or less at its halfway point down the right-hand margin—the left brain, having taken a three-line rest after its dialogue with the mountain, starts up its next lyric, a narrative on the transiency of any reality effect in nature, and on the consequent brevity of its lyric representation—a narrative, in short, that enacts the truth of the already-in-process right-brain aphorism accompanying it in the vertical column:

	there
	a
	trifle
a slice of clearing	only
widened over the ridge at	where
sundown and the sun	we
stood in it a minute,	are
full glow flapping up against	to

the garage and trees   lose
and through the windows against   all
the walls and it was very nice   are
say around four twenty,   we
gold effluvia gone   to
by four twentyseven   be
                                                     here
                                                     beholding
                                                     everything

(SP, 82)

Ammons's commitment to intensely patterned speech can be seen in the descending aphorism, at the same time that his commitment to inert quotidian expression ("and it was very nice / say around four twenty") can be seen in the landscape lyric—which pointedly throws in the word "effluvia" just so that we know the "very nice / say" is as deliberate as any other portion of the author's diction.

It is only at this stage—after we have seen the four-part quasi-Elizabethan fanciful praise-lyric "poetry is" (and its vertical "freedom" refrain); the five-stanza plain-style Herbertian allegorical mountain-dialogue; and the brief sunset-lyric (with its shared vertical aphorism on losing and beholding)—that we come to the already-cited poet friend's questionable dick (and *its* right-hand counterpart, his fat wife's apparent sexual satisfaction). Much could be said about this affronting closure of "Poetry Is the Smallest" as an index of Ammons's poetics in *The Snow Poems*, but since I am instancing this closure as an example of the coarse in Ammons's diction, let me say that in addition to paralleling the bicameral nature of the mind (lyric and philosophical) through the double columns of the marital verse, Ammons affirms (through his descent from the sublimity of language belonging to the mountain's inspiration pavilion—"gold effluvia"—to the comic relish of the urinary and the sexual) that the mind is stratified horizontally, too, and that lyric omits at its peril the material that is usually repressed in "polite" discourse. Ammons's poetry wishes to be both tragic and comic, high and low, concentrated and dispersive, and in *The Snow Poems* he resorts to scores of strategies (of which only a few are present in any one poem) to insist on the breadth of lyric as he conceives it. Yet Ammons's language for the sexual is not uniformly coarse: the cunnilingus hinted at in the ending of "Poetry Is the Smallest" turns up again, for example, in "You Can't Get It Right," in a diction mixing the romantic with the clinical:

the tongue, powerful,
moving organ, will in the
dark find bliss's button,
describe its contours,
buffet gently and swirl it,
and then swarm warmth (and
grease) into other areas
equally touchy and astonishing
suffusingly

(SP, 132)

I find the diction in this passage not entirely satisfactory, but I admire Ammons's attempt to describe a common sexual act that has been (as we say these days) "underrepresented" in poetry.

I want to give an example of a lyric in *The Snow Poems* where Ammons's experimentation seems unsuccessful—a short poem called "Teeth Out." It rages against the deformities of age—lost teeth and ingrown toenails and whatever else makes one feel ugly and odd and old (reading down on each right column yields "old guy ugly"):

Teeth Out

Teeth out	og	u
toenails in	lu	gl
	dy	y
when you're		
up you're		
out of this	le mismo	
world and when	difference	
you're down	chickweedo	
you're out	gone	
	to	
	goodness	

poetry is the life of criticism

(SP, 128)

We can see Ammons insisting here, as always in *The Snow Poems*, on aspects of writing:

a) the writer's workshop, which contains rearrangeable bits and pieces of language (here, the letters of three words—spelling "old" and "guy" and "ugly"—plus the stray word from Spanish);

b) the witty rearrangement of colloquial idiom (here "down and out") into lyric aphorism;

c) reference to anterior literary tradition (here, Arnold's dictum that poetry is a criticism of life);

d) the ethics of compensation (here, in the chickweed gone to goodness, just as the loss of teeth helps the necessary perpetual conversion, through decay, of matter into energy); and

e) the bicameral and tristratified (sublime, colloquial, coarse) mind.

The allusion to Arnold is not fully enough worked out in reference to the earlier parts of the poem to provide a coherent closure, nor is it clear why the Spanish is done wrong ("le mismo" instead of "el mismo"), nor why the chickweed is Hispanified into "chickweedo." But the occasional failure in *The Snow Poems* is part of its grand and outrageous raid on language and form.

It would be impossible to characterize every kind of experiment in the volume. Let me cite just one more, which occurs in a poem written on the first of March. Ammons is experimenting with the difference between a monocameral version of a lyric and its bicameral version. Here is lyric 1:

> march one and
> in the clear
> thicket highchoired
> grackles grate squeak,
> dissonant as
> a music school
> (SP, 189)

So far so good: the human analog (a music school, where in one room someone is playing the piano, in another someone is singing) will do for the conjoined dissonance of grackles, who have landed on high perches in the as-yet-unleafed thicket of early March. (The covert literary allusions are, of course, to Shakespeare's "choirs" of birds in Sonnet 73 and to Stevens's grackles in both "Snow and Stars"—"The grackles sing avant the spring"—and "Autumn Refrain"—"The skreak and skritter of evening gone / And grackles gone . . . / Some . . . residuum . . . grates.")

Now here is another version of the same poem, in which Ammons rewrote the monocameral lyric 1 into a split lyric, which I will call lyric 2. Nothing has changed, except that a curving—not straight—vertical gutter has been established within the poem, slowing it down:

march	one and
in the	clear
thicket	highchoired
grackles	grate squeak,
dissonant	as
a music	school

(SP, 189)

Though this looks "bicameral," it isn't, since the right-hand column does not have a justified left margin. But the new format emphasizes the activity of the mind, since it shows the hesitations implicit in composition. Shall I begin the poem with the month? Saying "march"? Well, why not be more precise and begin it "march one"? Shall I say "in the thicket"? Well, but that sounds like a leafy place, and the trees are still bare. Shall I say "bare thicket"? No, too Shakespearean, since I'm planning to say "highchoired" about the grackles. Let's make it visual and say "clear thicket." Grackles do what? Ah, Stevens tells me, "grate squeak," and they are dissonant as—as what? A music school.

Well, that's interesting, to reveal that the poem that in lyric 1 seemed a single burst of observation, was also—now that we have seen it via lyric 2 in its workshop form, fraught with the hesitations of the mind as it considers word choice. The poet is considering both of these potential printings of the lyric; to let us inhabit this fact, Ammons establishes on the page the vertical gutter of true bicameral opposition, showing us the two alternative lyrics, 1 and 2, competing formally for his attention. This arrangement I will call lyric 3, and this is what actually appears on the page as one portion of the poem called "It's Half an Hour Later Before":

march one and	march	one and
in the clear	in the	clear
thicket highchoired	thicket	highchoired
grackles grate squeak,	grackles	grate squeak,
dissonant as	dissonant	as
a music school	a music	school

(SP, 189)

If the poet presented the tight lyric 1 and the hesitant "revisionary" lyric 2 sequentially, one following the other, we would still see his considering mind, but we would not perceive it as split in two while he ponders his apparently imminent print choice between the two versions. The normal result of being split in two is that the poet acts to preserve one alternative by suppressing the other; it is a mark of the "reveal all" workshop poetics of *The Snow Poems* that the mind says, "I am divided *and* I choose both, so here they are, both kept in print, exhibiting a right-left standoff."

Of course, all these techniques—separating words into letters and phonemes, spelling words vertically, inscribing one-word-per-line poems vertically down the unpunctuated page, paralleling one version of a poem with its alternative version and letting both stand—are (like Ammons's many other tricks of allusion, punning, sound-string lists, and rewritten clichés) devices that prevent us from reading the poems as transparent "statements." At all costs, the Ammons of *The Snow Poems* wants us to know that the appearance of "spontaneity" in poetry arises from innumerable tinkerings and decisions that take place in the presence of historically anterior literary and colloquial expression. The tinkerings are one way of showing the reader that the poem, as Ammons always insists, is not merely a tissue of statements but a congeries of actions:

> Verbal actions imitate human actions or the actions of wind or river or rain. Poems are actions, of which one action is the making of statements. . . . Value is represented in poems. Poems exemplify ways to behave. . . . The poem can be accessible or distraught, harsh or melodic, abstract or graphic, and from these traits we can form our own models and traits. . . . Poetry's actions are like other actions. They are at once actions themselves and symbolic actions, representative models of behavior. (SM, 32–33)

All the ostentatious workshoppery of *The Snow Poems,* all its grasshopper-jumping among levels of diction, all its sly literariness, all its determination on the coarse and the colloquial mixed with the intellectual and the sublime, do not interfere with Ammons's commitment to a sustained, if abstract and stylized, revelation of human emotional life, both its highs and its lows. Nor do the tricks prevent the appearance of beautiful and shapely inner lyrics within the welter of language forms. I want to close my look at *The Snow Poems* by citing one of its classic lyrics, a Keatsian elegy written in couplets that anticipate the form of *Garbage:*

One Must Recall as One Mourns the Dead

One must recall as one mourns the dead
to mourn the dead and so not mourn too much

thinking how deprived away the dead lie
from the gold and red of our rapt wishes

and not mourn the dead too much who having
broken at the lip the nonesuch

bubble oblivion, the cold grape of ease at
last in whose range no further

ravages afflict the bones, no more
fires flash through the flarings of dreams

do not mourn the dead too much who bear no
knowledge, have no need or fear of pain,

and who never again must see death
come upon what does not wish to die.

(SP, 3)

Ammons remains a strong poet because he is always torn between his desire for shapeliness and his awareness of the ragged dispersions that are repressed in the tracing of any contour. Thought, emotion, and composition are congruent in Ammons, in that each must respect the world's Heraclitean strife: thought must acknowledge both creation and entropy; emotion must be torn between joy at love and rage at deprivation; poetic composition must respect both the truth of dynamic coherence into (temporary) form and the truth of chaotic dispersal into meaninglessness and death. In *Garbage,* the latter terms are no longer represented by the sprinkling of linguistic detritus over the page or by competing poem-forms as they were in *The Snow Poems*. Ammons's creation is no longer intent on revealing its doodling workshop methods. In that sense, *Garbage* appears to be a more conventional poem than *The Snow Poems*. Yet it too offers great resistance to the mind seeking an assimilable form of the long lyric.

To begin with the first difficulty in writing about *Garbage:* it is almost impossible to quote briefly from it, since its mind-loops are long, pensive arcs. Like *The Snow Poems* (and Ammons's other long pieces), *Garbage* can't be kept in the memory all at once, even if (like *The Bridge*) *Garbage* is unified by a powerful central symbol to which it consistently returns. Since the very subject of the poem is destruction, Ammons does not dedicate it to a single entity (such as "my country" in the case of *The Snow Poems*). *Garbage* is dedicated to multiple Shelleyan destroyers and preservers: "to the bacteria, tumblebugs, scavengers, wordsmiths—the transfigurers, restorers." Because Ammons—somewhat pragmatically—decided for optimism (though conscious of all the reasons for pessimism), the dedication concludes with the creative side of the law of the conservation of energy. Yet readers of *Garbage* may conclude that in this late poem Ammons's imagination is more actively committed to destruction than to transfiguration and restoration. In any case, its internal dynamic of perpetual change means that its cantos do not proceed in any easily foreseeable (and therefore graspable) form.

The poem begins, however, with a meditation that is Shelleyan in effect, if not in language. "Be through my lips to unawakened earth / The trumpet of a prophecy!" Shelley cried to the West Wind, asserting the social use of poetry in establishing new loci of value when the old values are in ruins. Ammons's version crosses Williams with Shelley in a self-mocking contemporary version of the Muse's summoning the poet to his vocation:

> Creepy little creepers are insinuatingly
> curling up my spine (bringing the message)
>
> saying, Boy!, are you writing that great poem
> the world's waiting for: don't you know you
>
> have an unaccomplished mission unaccomplished;
> someone somewhere may be at this very moment
>
> dying for the lack of what W. C. Williams says
> you could (or somebody could) be giving: yeah?
>
> so, these little messengers say, what do you
> mean teaching school (teaching *poetry* and
>
> *poetry writing* and wasting your time painting
> sober little organic, meaningful pictures)
>
> when values thought lost (but only scrambled into
> disengagement) lie around demolished
>
> and centerless because you (that's me, boy)
> haven't elaborated everything in everybody's

face, yet: on the other hand (I say to myself,
receiving the messengers and cutting them down)

who has done anything or am I likely to do
anything the world won't twirl without:[3]

To such a pass has the poet come that he questions not only his own authority
but that of the Muse, debasing her messengers into "creepy little creepers."
Yet this self-excoriation is followed by a long meditation on "elegance and simplicity," the qualities (one aesthetic, one primarily ethical) that Ammons names
as central to the poetics of his poem, a poetics that eschews both organized
religion (from Sinai or Zeus's thunderbolts) and the history of philosophy:

> . . . elegance and simplicity: I wonder
> if we need those celestial guidance systems
>
> striking mountaintops or if we need fuzzy
> philosophy's abstruse failed reasonings: isn't
>
> it simple and elegant enough to believe in
> qualities, simplicity and elegance . . .
> (G, 15)

Such a poetics of simplicity and elegance must rule out the fancy footwork
of *The Snow Poems*. The couplets of *Garbage* stand for its simplicity, while its
generic complexity and its manifold resources of diction and syntax stand for
its elegance.

"My hope," said Ammons of *Garbage*, "was to see the resemblances between
the high and low of the secular and the sacred":

> The garbage heap of used-up language is thrown at the feet of poets, and
> it is their job to make or revamp a language that will fly again. We are
> brought low through sin and death and hope that religion can make us
> new. I used garbage as the material submitted to such possible transfor-
> mations, and I wanted to play out the interrelationships of the high and
> the low. (SM, 102)

Both high and low participate in Ammons's characteristic turns of mind. In almost any canto of *Garbage,* no matter what the specific subject, the following
generic ingredients appear, sometimes in overlapping form:

a) An emotional meditation in the first person, either singular or plural;

b) A narrative;

c) A scene;

d) One or more aphorisms;

e) Something ugly or frightening (destruction, death);

f) Something beautiful or reassuring (an aspect of nature, love); and

g) Remarks about poetry.

This is all so cunningly managed that only someone studying the poem closely would see its recursive forms. A first-time (or even second-time) reader merely has the impression of a storytelling, meditating, far-seeing, celebratory, grieving voice unspooling its seductive language. Here are brief samples of the poem's seven recurrent genres:

First-person emotional meditation. Here, a reflection on the disappearance of Ammons's past, both in its remote North Carolina form and in its proximate Cornell form:

> I can't believe
> I'm merely an old person: whose mother is dead,
>
> whose father is gone and many of whose
> friends and associates have wended away to the
>
> ground, which is only heavy wind, or to ashes,
> a lighter breeze: but it was all quite frankly
>
> to be expected and not looked forward to: even
> old trees, I remember some of them, where they
>
> used to stand: pictures taken by some of them:
> and old dogs, specially one imperial black one,
>
> quad dogs with their hier*archies* (another *archie*)
> one succeeding another, the barking and romping
>
> sliding away like slides from a projector: what
> were they then that are what they are now:
>
> (G, 22–23)

Narrative. Here, a short anecdote from Ammons's life as a teacher in the Cornell English Department (housed in Goldwin Smith Hall):

I

was coming out of Goldwin Smith Hall after mail

call on a nova-bright late May day, the blues
and greens outdoing each other, when a dear friend

said, come and see, it's Ralph, he's in the car, and
thinking, I've never been asked to come see

Ralph before, I said, is anything the
matter, and she said, terminal cancer of the brain,

and I said, terminal cancer of the brain, and
she said, I found out a week ago, but don't say

anything to him: so, in the glaring light, his
window rolled down, I was talking with an old friend

as if the past twenty-five years of all three of us
as colleagues had shifted out of reach:

(G, 41)

Scene. Here, one from Ammons's return to his birthplace, the town of Whiteville in North Carolina:

I saw in Carolina morning flies

midair like floating stones: the dew, heavy;
the sun, blood red: a road dipping round a

pine grove down a hill to a pond, the spillway
clogged with cattails bent with breezes and with

redwings awilding day: a crippled old farmer
up early with his dog, noon likely to melt tar,

a benchlong of old blacks at the crossroads
gas station, dogfennel high on the woods' edge,

some scraggly roastnear corn used up, tomato
plants sprawled out, become vines: morning,

gentlemen, how you all doing: these bitty
events, near pangs commonplace on this planet

so strangely turned out, we mustn't take on so. . . .

(G, 95)

Aphorism. Here, one addressed to the reader, describing a Levinas-like relation with the ethically constituting other:

> In your end is my beginning, I repeat; also,
> my end; my end is, in fact, your end, in a way:
>
> are we not bound together by our ends: and when,
> end to end, our ends meet, then we begin to
>
> see the end of disturbing endlessness:
> (G, 63)

The ugly or frightening. Here, old people's knowledge of oncoming death:

> sometimes old people snap back into life for a
> streak and start making plans, ridiculous, you know,
>
> when they will suddenly think of death again
> and they will see their coffins plunge upward
>
> like whales out of the refused depths of their
> minds and the change will feel so shockingly
>
> different—from the warm movement of a possibility
> to a cold acknowledgment—they will seem not
>
> to understand for a minute: at other times
> with the expiration of plans and friends and
>
> dreams and with the assaults on all sides of
> relapses and pains, they will feel a
>
> smallish ambition to creep into their boxes
> at last and lid the light out and be gone,
>
> nevermore, nevermore to see again, let alone
> see trouble come on anyone again: oh yes, there
>
> are these moods and transitions, these bolt
> recollections and these foolish temptations. . . .
> (G, 53)

The beautiful. Here, the adaptive beauty of a web-worm, introduced, because of its motion, with an allusion to Gertrude's lament on the death of Ophelia

("There is a willow grows aslant a brook") and dismissed with an allusive nod to Whitman's dung-beetle:

> there is a web-worm falls
> sometimes aslant the honeysuckle hedge in spring
>
> breeze or other dislocation and finds itself
> asquirm dangerously dangled in the open air (I've
>
> seen hornets trim those babies right out of the
> air): this one I paused to view was wrestling
>
> up the single thread of web, nipping and tucking,
> reaching up for a hold on the tight and bringing
>
> itself up till the bit length could be added
> to the tiny cotton ball gathered at its
>
> head: but this is mere mechanics: down its
> back was a purplish streak exactly the color
>
> of honeysucklebushlimbstems, the top part (buds)
> of the stems: his feet, his laterals, were
>
> exactly the color of the lateralhoneysucklebush
> limbstems: while this waits explanation, I
>
> hold it a sufficient miracle. . . .
>
> (G, 71–72)

Poetry. Here, as a defense after looking into the pit of death: "I / looked into the pit of death and it was there, // the pit was, and the death" (G, 81), but with consequent guilt as to the time spent on poetry instead of on primary sensation:

> so I derived the nature
> of each thing from itself and made each derivation
>
> speak, the mountains quietly resounding and very
> authoritative, their exalted air perfect grain
>
> of the spiritual, the sense of looking down so
> scary half-love for height held: I made tongues

for adder's-tongue, periwinkle, and jimminycricket;
they wagged, and these tongues rang in my head

as in a chanson delicate of essence and point:
an assemblage, a concourse of intercourse, a

recourse: what is it, that you would turn down
a prairie for it, the prairie said as I went

on, my eyes set longsighted, and the turtle
eased needlepoint airholes up from swampwater,

his eyes quizzical in a downturn, and said,
where else does the shadow of the logknots fall

more sharply dark on the water, but I didn't
have time to take time: I spent every coin I

had into the good business of my own burning:

(G, 81–82)

While each of these excerpts is perfectly clear in itself, Ammons's interweaving of his generic set pieces makes any canto seem a farrago of crosscuts and jump starts, especially since the genre pieces can themselves be voiced in any one of Ammons's manners—the rustic, the scientific, the faux-naïf, the philosophical, the descriptive, the religious. Since the whole of *Garbage* is a hymn to the necessary principle of extinction (as life is "consumed with that which it was nourished by," the enlivening and extinguishing flame of the *calor vitae*), it is of the essence that the poem be engaged in constant change of both genre and diction. Ammons risks a great deal, since he asks from his reader more alertness than many readers can provide. Accustomed as we are to a narrative thread, or a temporal progression, or a hierarchical scheme, or a philosophical proposal ("It Must Be Abstract") as the clue to a long poem's labyrinth, we are surprised to find no such auxiliary pointers in Ammons. Indeed, we find ourselves in the refuse heap of language and literature, comparable to the Florida pit with its life detritus:

a priestly plume rises, a signal, smoke

like flies intermediating between orange peel
and buzzing blur: is a poem about garbage garbage

> or will this abstract, hollow junk seem beautiful
> and necessary as just another offering to the
>
> high assimilations (that means up on top where
> the smoke is; the incinerations of sin,
>
> corruption, misconstruction pass through the
> purification of flame:) old deck chairs,
>
> crippled aluminum lawn chairs, lemon crates
> with busted slats or hinges, strollers with
>
> whacking or spinningly idle wheels: stub ends
> of hotdogs:
>
> (G, 30–31)

The point of all Ammons's unsettling changes (thematic, generic, lexical) is to mimic a universe constituted of continual creations and destructions, to ratify a metaphysics acceding to the necessity of change, and to announce an ethics of protest, urgent (if helplessly so) against the human waste entailed by the universal principles of destruction—genetic, metabolic, political, catastrophic:

> how about the
> one who finds alcohol at eleven, drugs at seventeen
>
> death at thirty-two: how about the little
> boy on the street who with puffy-smooth face and
>
> slit eyes reaches up to you for a handshake:
> supposing politics swings back like a breeze and
>
> sails tanks through a young crowd: what about the
> hopes withered up in screams like crops in
>
> sandy winds: how about the letting out of streams
> of blood where rain might have sprinkled into
>
> roadpools:
>
> (G, 90)

Ammons may have in mind a particular dead youth, an individual Down's syndrome child, the events in Tiananmen Square, his own mother's tears at the death of his little brother, massacres in Europe, but he abstracts from the particular in his catalog of horror so as to make his indictment of human waste broadly applicable. He will not take refuge with the fortunate "who can in safety call evil essential to the / differentiations of good" (G, 90), but neither can he explain (or hope to eliminate) evil. He can merely ask, "After the balances are toted up, is there // a streak of light defining the cutting edge as celebration[?]" (G, 91). But he cannot hold firmly even to this hope. At the threshold of death we may, he speculates, decide that life, through the treasuring force of love, has had value; but it is equally probable that we end by admitting that the troubles caused by love have merely exhausted us:

> but, then, for the trouble of love, we may be
>
> so tired that indifference will join ours to the
> hills' indifference and the broad currents of
>
> the deep and the high windings of the sky, and
> we may indeed see the ease beyond our
>
> understanding because, till now, always beyond
> (G, 96)

It is Ammons's willingness to suspect, and say, and show, in *Garbage,* that at our end we are subsumed into the vast indifferent dynamics of the universe, that makes him a poet for our nonanthropocentric consciousness. The attempt to protect what is beloved, knowing the certainty of its destruction, is beneath all of Ammons's poetry. He said, "the most powerful image of my emotional life is something I had repressed and one of my sisters lately reminded me of":

> It was when my little brother, who was two and a half years younger than I, died at eighteen months. My mother some days later found his footprint in the yard and tried to build something over it to keep the wind from blowing it away. That's the most powerful image I've ever known. (SM, 71)

And yet Ammons does not adopt the "inhuman" perspective of Robinson Jeffers: he is acutely conscious of the place and worth of human attachment, human investment in others, human grief at the loss of love. It is his consciousness of damage and grief (suffered first in his own life, and subsequently known in historical and external ways) that makes for the tenderness that suffuses his poetry. It is a tenderness held in check—as indeed, all his passions are held in check— by an aesthetic responsibility to the law of form. Among Ammons's harshest passages in *Garbage* is a long excoriation of "hackers," those contemporary writers who, wishing to proclaim themselves *engagés,* exaggerate their rhetoric for audience effect:

> the hackers, having none,
> hack away at intensity: they want to move,
>
> disturb, shock: they show the idleness of
> pretended feeling: feeling moves by moving
>
> into considerations of moving away: real
> feeling assigns its weight gently to others,
>
> helps them meet, deal with the harsh, brutal,
> the ineluctable, eases the burdens of unclouded
>
> facts: the strident hackers miss no chance to
> dramatize, hurt, fairly or unfairly, for they
>
> fear their emptiness: the gentlest, the most
> refined language, so little engaged it is hardly
>
> engaging, deserves to tell the deepest wishes,
> roundabout fears: loud boys, the declaimers,
>
> the deaf listen to them: to the whisperers,
> even the silent, their moody abundance: the
>
> poem that goes dumb holds tears: the line,
> the fire line, where passion and control waver
>
> for the field, that is a line so difficult to
> keep in the right degree, one side not raiding
>
> the other:

(G, 120–121)

This is Ammons's most didactic expression of his poetic of "elegance and simplicity." As we read the late Ammons of *Garbage,* we can see that he kept, from *The Snow Poems,* the technique of a broad musing flow which gathers into an eddy of lyric; the rapid changes of lexicon; the turn to abstraction; the aphoristic summation; the rewriting of clichéd idiom; the preferred matrix of resemblance offered by the natural world; even the metaphysics of compensation of material loss by gain in energy. But in *Garbage* he restrained both his coarseness and his fancifulness; he was less concerned to toy with the concept of a bicameral mind; he added more narrative and a greater proportion of personal anecdote; and he adopted a regular ongoing scheme of long numbered cantos rather than *The Snow Poems'* more volatile scheme of individually titled short lyrics.

As the successive weather reports (emblematic of the ongoing and changing life of nature) connected the parts of *The Snow Poems,* so the symbol of the Florida funeral pyre (emblematic of the conversion of matter into energy) unifies *Garbage. Garbage* is a sadder poem than *The Snow Poems,* and a less showy one: if the exuberance of creation lies behind the earlier sequence, the certainty of destruction lies behind the later one. *Garbage* belongs, in the history of literature, to the category of restrained later works: among the monuments of poetry in English, *Paradise Regained, Four Quartets,* and *The Rock* have been customarily thought of in this way. In poems such as these, authors of great early display-poems decide that their subsequent sense of the world requires a less ostentatious style. Not everyone prefers the later moment; I continue to vary between my old attachment to the nervy, splashy, spontaneous, willing-to-be-silly *Snow Poems* and my current admiration for the grave canto-summations of *Garbage.* What is really remarkable is that the same poet should have written both these compelling poems.

8

All Her Nomads

Collected Poems, *by Amy Clampitt*

Amy Clampitt died in 1994, at the age of seventy-four; Knopf had published her first book of poems, *The Kingfisher,* in 1983. It was followed by *What the Light Was Like* (1985), *Archaic Figure* (1987), *Westward* (1990), and *A Silence Opens* (1994)—five books in eleven years.

   The *Collected* is preceded by an affectionate foreword by the poet Mary Jo Salter, a close friend of Clampitt's during the 1980s and 1990s; the biographical information below is drawn from this helpful introduction to both the person and the writing. Amy Clampitt was born on June 15, 1920, the first of five children, in New Providence, Iowa, on a three-hundred-acre farm belonging to her paternal grandfather; she lived on the farm until she was ten, when her parents, to Clampitt's lasting regret, moved to a new house. Her life was outwardly uneventful. After twelve years in the local public schools, where she felt out of place, she moved on to Grinnell College; then—after entering graduate school at Columbia—she dropped out and became a secretary at Oxford University Press. "She wrote advertising copy and won a company-sponsored essay contest, whose prize was a trip to England," Salter tells us, and adds, "It, and a follow-up journey around Europe a few years later, when she quit the Oxford job, changed her life."[1] There was an unhappy romance, and then a job as reference librarian for the Audubon Society. In the 1950s, Clampitt wrote three novels, which remain unpublished. She kept an apartment in Greenwich Village, but for the last twenty-five years of her life she also shared an apartment on the Upper East Side with Harold Korn, a professor at Columbia University Law School; they married shortly before Clampitt's death in 1994 of ovarian cancer. In the summers, they spent weeks in Maine, the location of many of Clampitt's poems of fog, sea, and sundews. Salter, in recounting her first meeting with Clampitt in 1979, gives a physical description that is very accurate:

> Tall, seemingly weighing nothing at all in her ballet slippers, she had a lightness of foot and manner that put one in mind, immediately, of a child. Her dark brown hair, greying only a little then, was put up behind with a hippie's leather barrette, though she had also trained two wide chin-length locks to fall over her rather comically large ears. She was less able (though she tried, with long, elegant fingers that were always flying upward) to hide a beautiful gap-toothed smile. (F, xvi)

Salter also fills in, for Clampitt's new readers, the moral background to the poems. It was Quakers who had settled New Providence, but a more amalgamated Protestantism was what Clampitt had been raised in. She was drawn in the 1960s into political action, and had joined the 1971 demonstrations outside the White House protesting the bombing of North Vietnam. When Salter asked Clampitt if she had ever wanted children, she replied: "Oh no, when we dropped the bomb on Hiroshima I knew that this wasn't a world I wanted to bring children into" (F, xvii). Salter, rightly, suspects that there were other reasons: it is clear from the poems that Clampitt was repelled by her mother's life, drained of personal energy by childbearing and household duties. Clampitt, Salter later learned, "left the Episcopal Church (after years of commitment so fervent she had considered becoming a nun) because she felt its leaders had not been sufficiently outspoken against the war" (F, xvii). But Clampitt also rebelled against being incorporated into any movement. She said in a 1993 interview in the journal *Verse* the year before she died:

> At least since the 1960s, I've had an urge to refer in some way to public issues—which is not the same as speaking for any identifiable group or point of view. There's a lot of fractious poetry being written; I've written some of it myself. What I'm really concerned with . . . [is] maintaining what I have to call a subversive attitude, the opposite of going along with anybody's program whatever. It amounts to wariness about being co-opted. Since part of being co-opted means having to accept somebody else's language, I see this wariness as a particular function of poets.[2]

Because of Clampitt's intense delight in nature—and her unlimited vocabulary for describing it (as befitted, and was natural to, a reference librarian)—the moral passion of her poems was slighted by some reviewers, who thought her a pedantic elaborator on natural scenery. By a few critics—whose vocabulary may have been less extensive than her own—she was resentfully branded an elitist poet, one whose poetry was not "accessible" to the ordinary reader. Clampitt was aware of this criticism but put it gracefully by: "There are enough readers who get turned on by the same kind of things that I do, so I don't terribly mind having people say, as they sometimes do: 'Where do you get all those words from?'" (V, 7). On the other hand, Clampitt's work was also greeted with high praise by readers who found her books "poetry for grown-ups"— J. D. McClatchy's phrase.

It is true that Clampitt's is an allusive and literary body of work, and that it asks for a literary reader. The novelist in her was attracted to the lives of the poets and she even wrote, toward the end of her life, a play *(Mad with Joy)* about the cohabitation of William Wordsworth, Dorothy Wordsworth, and Coleridge in Dove Cottage (her sympathies were with Dorothy). She also, more successfully, wrote a sequence on the life of Keats ("Voyages") and poems resuming the life of Dorothy Wordsworth ("Grasmere," "Coleorton," "Rydal Mount"), George Eliot ("George Eliot Country," "Medusa at Broadstairs," "High-Gate Cemetery"), Margaret Fuller ("Margaret Fuller, 1847"), and Pocahontas ("Matoaka"). Oddly, there was nothing similar on Hopkins ("the first poet she loved," according to Salter). These biographical poems, though they all have moving moments, do not equal in passion or art the pieces about Clampitt's own youth and the elegies for her parents; and they may, it is true, seem a little remote to readers who have no notion of the events in the writers' lives. For example, the first of the Keats poems, "Margate," begins:

> Reading his own lines over, he'd been
> (he wrote) in the diminished state of one
> "that gathers Samphire dreadful trade."
> Disabled Gloucester, so newly eyeless
> all his scathed perceptions bled together,
> and Odysseus, dredged up shipwrecked
> through fathoms of Homeric sightlessness—
>
> "the sea had soaked his heart through"—
> were the guides his terror clutched at.[3]

Yet even in her most allusive writing, Clampitt usually gives the reader enough human and lyric interest to propel him through the poem. "Margate," for instance, continues with Clampitt's ambivalent indictment of writing, an activity symbolized by the perilous trade of the seaweed-gatherer but also by the Whitmanian desolate collecting of "sea drift" and the Stevensian exposure to the "ice and fire" of the Northern Lights:

> How clannish
> the whole hand-to-hand, cliffhanging trade,
>
> the gradual letdown, the hempen slither,
> precarious basketloads of sea drift
> gathered at Margate or at Barnegat . . .
> .   The chaff, the scum
> of the impalpable confined in stanzas,
>
> a shut-in's hunger for the bodiless
> enkindlings of the aurora—all that
> traffic in the perilous.
> (CP, 143)

The biographical becomes a launching pad for the autobiographical and thence to the general: the articulation of the impalpable, Clampitt implies, presents difficulties to everyone throughout daily life.

But Clampitt will be remembered, I think, not so much for the imaginative gesturing toward past lives as for the registering of her own. In "Meridian," we are given the child's perspective on her mother's day:

> apathy at the meridian, the noon
> of absolute boredom: flies
> crooning black lullabies in the kitchen,
> milk-soured crocks, cream separator
> still unwashed: what is there to life
> but chores, and more chores, dishwater,
> fatigue, unwanted children: nothing
> to stir the longueur of afternoon
>
> except possibly thunderheads:
> climbing, livid, turreted . . .
> (CP, 18)

The rush of enumeration—nouns and noun phrases for the endless repetitiveness of housework—is the way Clampitt chooses to sketch an environment: "During my early years in New York," she said, "I . . . felt more at home with

painters than with most literary people. . . . Not being able to draw, I found myself exploring what words could do as an equivalent to drawing and brush-
work" (V, 7). When description turns to the mixture of indignation and regret
with which Clampitt elegizes her mother in the pained poem "A Procession at
Candlemas," it is past participles that bear the burden of the parental life,
generalized:

> the squalor of the day
> resumed, the orphaned litter taken up again
>
> unloved, the spawn of botched intentions,
> grief a mere hardening of the gut,
> a set piece of what can't be avoided:
>
> parents by the tens of thousands living
> unthanked, unpaid but in the sour coin
> of resentment.
> (CP, 24)

Finally, in the wake of the heaped-up inventories, comes the indictment of the
anonymous biological life women have been destined to; and here at last
Clampitt's syntax ignites into a whole sentence, as she asks how women relin-
quished the notion that they had a right to a soul, a "thread of fire," a personal
identity:

> Where is it? Where, in the shucked-off
> bundle, the hampered obscurity that has been
> for centuries the mumbling lot of women,
>
> did the thread of fire, too frail
> ever to discover what it meant, to risk
> even the taking of a shape, relinquish
>
> the seed of possibility?
> (CP, 24–25)

Clampitt is not a poet of conclusive stanzaic form; her breaking of a poem into
groups of seven lines ("Margate") or three ("A Procession at Candlemas") or
irregular verse-paragraphs of seven to eighteen lines ("Imago") seems not to
matter much in the structure of the whole. The tercet breaks are there to slow

down the cascading syntax of a single multiline sentence; the stanza breaks often represent the end of a sentence. At most, they alert the reader to a pause in thought rather than to a change of voice or a new symbolic system. To that degree, she is a poet more of thought and metaphor than of architectonics or symbol creation.

She is also more a poet of reflection and sorrow than of erotic drive, as might be predicted of an older poet writing from a settled life; the mad drive to locate one's sexual nature and one's place in the world (Keats's "love and fame") is the property of the young. She may be a poet best appreciated by those—young or old—who have reached the stage of life embodied in the poetry, or by those who are as intensely aware of natural beauty (and natural savagery) as she is. Her first memory was of an orchard field of violets under a canopy of maple trees: in "The Woodlot," she speaks of sliding under barbed wire

> to an enclosure
> whose ceiling's silver-maple tops
> stir overhead, uneasy, in the interminably
> murmuring air[.] Deep in it, under
> appletrees like figures in a ritual, violets
> are thick, a blue cellarhole
> of pure astonishment.
>   It is
> the earliest memory. Before it,
> I/you, whatever that conundrum may yet
> prove to be, amounts to nothing.
> (CP, 58)

Immersion in landscape seemed to return Clampitt to that presubjective moment of joy before self and object become two things. Consequently, nothing made her happier as a writer than the challenge to make the physical world appear to others as it seemed to her. The tornados of her childhood, for instance:

> Against
> the involuted tantrums of spring and summer—
> sackfuls of ire, the frightful udder
> of the dropped mammocumulus
> become all mouth, a lamprey

swigging up whole farmsteads, suction
dislodging treetrunks like a rotten tooth—
luck and a cellarhold were all
a prairie dweller had to count on.
(CP, 57)

Clampitt dwelt all her life on the nomadism that made her ancestors move westward, and that equally compelled her to move eastward. ("I'm too much of a nomad to be rooted anywhere," she said in the *Verse* interview published in 1993.) The Iowa prairie of her childhood is the fixed point from which all moves are measured, and the journeys represented in her poems range from the return to her mother's deathbed ("A Procession at Candlemas") to the terrifying displacement, endlessly repeated, of all nomads and immigrants, represented in her late poem "Sed de Correr." The poem is named from a phrase of Cesar Vallejo, meaning literally "a thirst for running away," but translated by Clampitt into

escape, the urge to disjoin, the hunger
to have gone, to be going: *sed de correr:*
Vallejo in Paris writing *(me alejo todo)*
of fleeing, of running away from what made one,
from everything.
(CP, 420)

The New York to which Clampitt once fled from the Great Plains now houses Puerto Ricans; and in coming to recognize that the journey is no escape, Clampitt is writing retrospectively about herself as much as about the new immigrants she sees on the elevated train or the subway:

escape that is no escape . . .
                                elevated
or submerged, the serial unseeing faces
within, the windows traveling, a delirium of them,
of arrivals, escapes that are no escape:
                     . . . these refugees
from the canefields' corridored, murderous green,
caught up in the wingborne roar, the breaking
wave of displacement . . .

> translated here, to
> the crass miracle of whatever it is that put up
> the South Bronx, street number after street number,
> the mailbox pried open, recipient unknown,
> moved on, shot down—and has made of it
> this byword, this burnt-out, roofless, windowless
> testimonial to systems gone rotten.
>
> (CP, 422)

Yet even as she attempts to write the poem of contemporary New York, Clampitt knows that she can see the new immigrants only en masse, cannot possibly speak from within their experience:

> The leaves of dispersal,
> the runaway pages, surround us. Who
> will hear? Who will gather
> them in? Who will read them?
>
> (CP, 423)

Her wrath at "systems gone rotten" extends far and wide. In a single poem, "The Prairie" (in part a history of her family), her topics range from the homeless in New York ("the houseless squinny at us, mumbling") to the expulsion (or corralling) of the Plains Indians and the imposition of mechanized large-scale agriculture on the Midwest:

> Demagoguery. Boundaries. Forced marches.
>
> Monoculture on the heels of slash and burn.
> Land reform. Drought. Insects. Drainage.
> Long-term notes. Collectives. Tractor lugs.
>
> (CP, 344)

The undertow of all such passages is a despair known perhaps only to those who have, like Clampitt, participated buoyantly and hopefully in social protest ("that freshet of anarchy") and have seen its ultimate powerlessness against the larger evils of the world. Years after the Vietnam War, she is still aghast at the slaughter. She writes an eighteen-line poem which is—of the many poems facing that mirror-black granite Plutonian cleft in the earth, the Vietnam War

Memorial—the most embattled against the historical gods of carnage. I quote
it in full:

The War Memorial

The rain-god Tlaloc, hungering for blood,
the war-god, hummingbird-gartered
Huitzilopochtli, the drugged booty

of a huger, cleverer hunger, stir
in a museum hall of nightmare, where
Asshur the bellicose and Marduk, who

rode forth to set the world in order,
are neighbors, where the drifts and dunes
of long-immobilized cuneiform begin

to move again, a bas-relief of dread
like the long scar, the black cicatrice
of memory not yet embalmed but raw,

those drifts of origami at its foot:
to trace whose length is to reopen
what George Fox, compelled at Lichfield

to take off his shoes, walked barefoot
in—the channel of the blood of those
who fell. For what? Can someone tell us?

(CP, 407)

The Vietnam War Memorial occasioned protest because it lacked the heroic
postures of most war memorials: designed by the young Maya Lin, it is, as
Clampitt says, a scar in the earth, commemorating name by name the 58,000
war dead, ghostly throngs that surround the tourist passing deeper and deeper
into the wall of countless names. (Clampitt alludes to the incident when George
Fox, thinking of his ancestors burned at Lichfield during the reign of Mary
Tudor, felt commanded by God to walk barefoot through the streets of the town,
which seemed to him channels of blood. After astounding the citizens by
shouting, "Woe unto the bloody city of Lichfield," he bathed his feet, put on
his shoes, and resumed ordinary equanimity.)

It is a Quaker anger against war that Clampitt here expresses, but it is also tinged with her feminism, which indicts male violence without averting its eyes from its female counterpart, the masochism of hysteria and mourning. In a remarkable poem called "Good Friday," she writes scornfully of female complicity in "the evolving ordonnance of murder." The celebration of the Passion of Jesus offers, she says, to its women devotees

> an ampoule of gore, a mithridatic
> ounce of horror—sops for the maudlin
> tendency of women toward extremes
> of stance, from virgin blank to harlot
> to sanctimonious official mourner—
> myrrh and smelling salts, baroque
> placebos, erotic tableaux vivants
> dedicated to the household martyr,
> underwriting with her own ex votos
> the evolving ordonnance of murder.
> (CP, 69)

To read Clampitt is to enter into the mind of a woman too intelligent not to see both sides of the gender question, too indignant not to want to change a hardhearted social system, too capable of exaltation to refrain from announcing joy. Feelings swarmed in her heart, words swam to her pen, and the flood of poems that she produced late in life delineate a self—silent for fifty-three years—that suddenly found a public voice. If she had died at fifty, we should never have known about her.

9

Seamus Heaney and the *Oresteia*

"Mycenae Lookout" and the Usefulness of Tradition

I want to examine, as a contemporary case history of the usefulness of tradition, the unsettling and surprising transformation, by Seamus Heaney, of the *Oresteia* of Aeschylus (especially the *Agamemnon*).[1] Never during the quarter century of hostilities in Northern Ireland had Heaney written openly inflammatory or recriminatory verse: even the "bog poems"—some of which concerned medieval sacrificial victims—refrained from matching the violence of much Irish political sentiment with violence of poetic language. His own intelligence and distrust of propagandistic rhetoric kept Heaney scrupulously away from language expressing the mad exuberance—felt by many, and a temptation to all writers—of those seeking vengeance by violent means.

With the final quelling (as it seemed) of the actual hostilities in the 1994 cease-fire, Heaney felt free at last to write violently of the war as it had been, to show what it had revealed of human nature, not least his own nature. In a totally unexpected move, Heaney published in *The Spirit Level* a five-poem sequence of unprecedented linguistic violence called "Mycenae Lookout." In an interview with Henri Cole in the *Paris Review,* Heaney described the origins of the sequence in several different traditions: Greek drama, Christian liturgy, Renaissance masque, and seventeenth-century lyric:

> Instead of being able just to bask in the turn of [cease-fire] events, I found myself getting angrier and angrier at the waste of lives and friendships and possibilities in the years that had preceded it. . . . And I kept thinking that a version of the *Oresteia* would be one way of getting all of that out of the system, and at the same time, a way of initiating a late-twentieth-century equivalent of the "Te Deum." . . .

I began to read the Aeschylus, and as I did, I also began to lose heart
in the whole project. It began to seem too trite—art wanting to shake hands
with life. Ideally, what I needed was the kind of poem Andrew Marvell
wrote on Cromwell's return from Ireland and what I was setting up for was
a kind of Jonsonian masque. At least that's what I began to feel. And
then the figure of the Watchman in that first scene of the *Agamemnon* began
to keep coming back to me with his in-between situation and his responsibilities and inner conflicts, his silence and his knowledge, and all this
kept building until I very deliberately began a monologue for him using
a rhymed couplet like a pneumatic drill, just trying to bite and shudder in
toward whatever was there.[2]

Traditions jostle in these remarks: the dramas of Aeschylus; "Te Deum Lau-
damus" (the early Christian Latin hymn of thanks); the Renaissance masques
of Ben Jonson; Marvell's "An Horatian Ode: Upon Cromwell's Return from
Ireland," which imitates classical Latin elegiacs; the rhymed pentameter couplet as one might find it in the political poetry of Dryden. The mention of the
"Te Deum" suggests that a thanksgiving ought to occur, and that the thanksgiving should be embodied in a ritual native to Heaney (perhaps the Catholic
use of the "Te Deum" on occasions such as a declaration of peace). The allusion to Marvell's Cromwell shows Heaney reflecting on the grim masculinity
of war, and on the rewriting of history by the conquerors. And Marvell's allusion to Horace's Odes may have turned Heaney's mind to Latin legend, since
we find, in the fifth poem of "Mycenae Lookout," that Heaney has inserted the
fratricidal story of the twin sons of Mars, in which Romulus murders Remus
over the proposed border of Rome. Heaney has his visionary Watchman, the
"Mycenae lookout" of the title, predict the future murder, as he sees

> . . . far-off, in a hilly, ominous place,
>
> Small crowds of people watching as a man
> Jumped a fresh earth-wall and another ran
> Amorously, it seemed, to strike him down.[3]

In this moil of tradition, Heaney feels a poem stirring, a poem of hitherto
pent-up historical anger. Heaney's description of "the moment of poetry"
illuminates the writing of his sequence: "The moment of poetry is the moment when all those complications and contradictions of history, politics, culture, fidelity, hostility, inner division, challenge, and change get themselves

gathered in words and become available to writer and reader as a mode of self-knowledge."[4]

To mediate his anger—and indeed all the other emotional complications he listed—Heaney first turns, in "Mycenae Lookout," to Aeschylus, assuming that the reader will remember the central situation of the *Agamemnon,* in which Agamemnon's sacrifice of his own daughter Iphigenia and his abduction of Priam's daughter, Cassandra, from Troy, end with the murder of both Agamemnon and Cassandra by Clytemnestra and her lover Aegisthus. Yet with all these violent personages to choose from, Heaney's eye lights on two nonviolent Aeschylean speakers, the Watchman and Cassandra, to serve as his surrogates.

Aeschylus opens the *Agamemnon* with the Watchman—whose first response, as he sights the victory blazes announcing Agamemnon's return, is one of joy. But then he realizes that he cannot tell his master of the adultery he has observed between Clytemnestra and Aegisthus:

> The ox is on my tongue. . . .
> I speak to those who know; to those who don't
> my mind's a blank. I never say a word.[5]

Aeschylus's Watchman becomes Heaney's persona, and the epigraph for the sequence is the Watchman's single (probably proverbial) phrase, "The ox is on my tongue"—a phrase from the *Agamemnon* mirroring Heaney's own long-guarded discretion of utterance during the war years. The only other speaking part in Heaney's poem, as I've said, belongs to Cassandra. Heaney reduces Cassandra's many speeches in the *Agamemnon* to her final tragic words, uttered after she has torn off her regalia as Apollo's priestess and stands revealed as a helpless girl. In Aeschylus, Cassandra's closing speech reads, in Fagles's translation:

> Oh men, your destiny.
> When all is well a shadow can overturn it.
> When trouble comes a stroke of the wet sponge,
> And the picture's blotted out.[6]

In Heaney's version, her speech is rendered freely:

> "A wipe
> of the sponge,
> that's it.

The shadow-hinge
swings unpredic-
tably and the light's

blanked out."
(33)

The Watchman's troubled speechlessness and the prophetess's disbelieved speech represent the dilemma of the poet in a time of dishonesty, victimage, murder, infidelity, and rape. From these beginnings, Heaney constructed a sequence with five named parts:

1. The Watchman's War
2. Cassandra
3. The Nights
4. His Dawn Vision
5. His Reverie of Water

Heaney's Watchman despairs of translating the truth of history into available language, since language already is a mark of civilization, while war is pure bestiality:

No element that should have carried weight
Out of the grievous distance would translate.
Our war stalled in the pre-articulate.
(33)

It is tradition, in the form of the *Agamemnon,* that enables Heaney to give voice to his "pre-articulate" anger, but the form of the Watchman's accusatory articulacy is shocking, as we hear it in the "pneumatic drill" (Heaney's description) of the Watchman's opening and closing couplets of the first poem in the sequence, "The Watchman's War":

Some people wept, and not for sorrow—joy
That the king had armed and upped and sailed for Troy.
. . . . .
I balanced between destiny and dread
And saw it coming, clouds bloodshot with the red
Of victory fires.
. . . . .

Up on my elbows, head back, shutting out
The agony of Clytemnestra's love-shout
That rose through the palace like the yell of troops
Hurled by King Agamemnon from the ships.

(29–30)

The Watchman looks on aghast as war-frenzy grips not only the yelling troops but also the civilian population. He hears, shuddering, the "love-shout" of the adulterous queen as it shakes the house of Atreus. The contamination of slaughter reaches the Watchman's own tongue, which feels like "the dropped gangplank of a cattle truck, / Trampled and rattled, running piss and muck, / All swimmy-trembly as the lick of fire, / A victory beacon in an abattoir." Heaney's distorted diction, as it finally breaks out here, suggests how difficult it was, during the quarter-century of the undeclared war in the North, for the poet to bridle his tongue while his mind felt agitated, polluted, inflamed, and appalled.

By the selectivity of his two telling quotations—the Watchman's ox-laden tongue, Cassandra's disbelieving despair—Heaney points up Aeschylus's own emphasis on speechlessness and prophecy, together with the incapacity of either response to stop the momentum of tragic event. By allowing the Watchman's later dawn vision (not in Aeschylus) to see forward (in Dantesque tercets) to the fratricide polluting the foundation of Rome, Heaney enlarges the reach of tradition in the poem, generalizing epic history from Greece to Rome, thence to civil strife in Dante's Florence and any later place. And finally, by bringing the sequence, at the close, home to contemporary Ireland (in the poem called "His Reverie of Water"), Heaney connects the Aeschlylean dream of moral ablution (dramatized at the end of the trilogy in the *Eumenides*) and the historical military struggle over possession of the well below the Acropolis of Athens to his contemporary hope for peace.

Under all allusion to a traditional text lies the fear that the primal cultural text is in danger of being forgotten, and that the poet, in consequence, has a responsibility to bear it out of the ever-threatening fire of oblivion. Resuscitating the Aeschylean myth for Irish purposes, Heaney must make it freshly seeable, transposing the House of Atreus into Irish circumstance. Merely to borrow the Greek plot and reimagine its actors will not suffice; the myth must also be given contemporary language. The rest of this essay will inquire into the strong measures Heaney took once the cease-fire allowed him, for the first time, a full-voiced anger against the prolonged carnage that took away from him, as from others in Northern Ireland, the possibility of a normal life. Measured eloquence and steady reflective meditation on life had been the staples of Heaney's poems written before the cease-fire, but these tones are discarded during most of "Mycenae Lookout," as if only outraged language could suit outrageous acts. By filtering his own anger through the parallels afforded by tradition, Heaney makes his own writing conscious and premeditated, rather than uncontrolled and self-pitying.

How is language made outrageous in "Mycenae Lookout"? In part by taking seriously the violence of Aeschylus's own language, in which words of sexual violation and words of bloodshed interchange so rapidly that the two categories are shaken into a single dark emulsion. So, too, Heaney's sequence begins and continues in a demotic coarseness relieved only in the closing poem of his sequence. At the opening, as Heaney's Watchman lies on the roof at night, he registers the erotic charge of killing, both in Argos and in Troy. Hearing night after night the wild lovemaking of Clytemnestra and Aegisthus, he, the confidant of each of them, speaks about their sexual confidences ("it was sexual overload / every time they did it") with the scorn of a soldier contemplating a decadent aristocracy. And the Watchman extrapolates the actions of his earthly rulers to the very heavens, likening himself to Atlas, patron of watchmen, who has to overhear a comparable sort of sexual grossness from the gods ("those thuds / and moans through the cloud cover"). The Watchman's tabloid terms ("every time they did it"; "[they] made out endlessly") turn bestial when he shows the erotic excitement of war inflaming even the Argives crouched in the Trojan Horse:

> When the captains in the horse
> felt Helen's hand caress
> its wooden boards and belly
> they nearly rode each other.
> (35)

But instead of indulging their frenzy homosexually, Agamemnon's soldiers take it out in rape: "In the end Troy's mothers / bore their brunt in alley, / bloodied cot and bed."

In his violent, self-loathing summary, the Watchman includes himself (the "roof-posted" one) among those whom the war drove mad, joining himself to the bull-like horned Agamemnon and the horsed soldiers, the boasting Argives and the bested Trojans:

> The war put all men mad,
> horned, horsed or roof-posted,
> the boasting and the bested.
> (36)

This adjectival list—*horned, horsed, posted, boasting, bested*—is a scrawled cartoon version of the epic personae of the Trojan War. Because of the Watchman's "low" language and his unrelenting rhythms (taking their cue from the heavy trochees of the name "Agamemnon"), no Heaneyesque softness, whether of exculpation or of human commiseration, can penetrate the language of "The Nights." Heaney refuses epic majesty to the Irish slaughter; instead, he brings down Aeschylus to language appropriate to vulgar brawling and war-lust.

But it is not in writing of Agamemnon's battle-frenzy, or Aegisthus's and Clytemnestra's adultery, or the cavorting gods, or the Argive rapes, that Heaney's invention of a "low tragic" language for epic material reaches its brutal peak. It is in the second poem of the sequence, "Cassandra," that tradition is most actively torn from its beginnings and made expressive of the present day. Though a reader of the *Agamemnon* (and of the *Iliad*) knows that Cassandra has been raped not only in Troy by Ajax but repeatedly by Agamemnon, and that she is Agamemnon's personal slave, other items of her Aeschylean presentation— that she appears in the ceremonial robes and wreath of a priestess, that she is King Priam's daughter, that she is a prophetess, that she rides in Agamemnon's chariot—suggest that she appears regal, elevated, and exalted, in spite of her status as slave. In a brilliant set of several poetic inventions, Heaney borrows Cassandra from tradition but reimagines her as she might appear in Northern Ireland, as one of the sullen young people caught up in sordid events, blurting out truth to bystanders in the midst of civic hatred and hypocrisy.

Cassandra's poem—spoken by the Watchman—is thin, even scrawny, like the raped adolescent's own body. Heaney gives Cassandra soiled punk clothing, an undernourished frame, the shaved head of a girl caught consorting with the enemy, a not-quite-innocent gaze:

> No such thing
> as innocent
> bystanding.
>
> Her soiled vest,
> her little breasts,
> her clipped, devast-

ated, scabbed
punk head,
the char-eyed

famine gawk—
she looked
camp-fucked

and simple.
(30–31)

The ostentatiously rhymed but sliced-up dimeter tercets of Cassandra are themselves a violated form of normal poetry. Heaney here presses the Watchman's
language into an obscenity quickened by his hatred of the "innocent" bystanders
who watch, erotically aroused, Cassandra's exposure. On the other hand,
Heaney gives Cassandra her own theatricality; she is not entirely innocent.
The bystanders know she tells the truth, because they recognize it within
themselves as she says it; yet, paradoxically, the Watchman sees something
slightly stagey about Cassandra's bewilderment. As a prophetess in Apollo's
temple, she is used to public appearances; or perhaps, as a victim, she has
learned to play the game of victimage:

People
could feel

a missed
trueness in them
focus,

a homecoming
in her dropped-wing,
half-calculating

bewilderment.
No such thing
as innocent.
(31)

In Heaney's hands, the fate of Cassandra becomes a perennial parable. The poet
has his Watchman describe Agamemnon—the slayer of Iphigenia, the rapist
of Cassandra—with jeering nicknames reducing him to type. Cassandra, too,

becomes typecast, as the parabolic lamb readied for slaughter, speaking not her native Trojan but prophetic Greek, resuming her role as the oracle of a vengeful Apollo:

> Old King Cock-
> of-the-Walk
> was back,
>
> King Kill-
> the-Child-
> and-Take-
>
> What-Comes,
> King Agamem-
> non's drum-
>
> balled, old buck's
> stride was back.
> And then her Greek
>
> words came,
> a lamb
> at lambing time,
>
> bleat of clair-
> voyant dread,
> the gene-hammer
>
> and tread
> of the roused god.
> (31–32)

Finally, Heaney gathers together all these themes—of raped virginity, erotically excited "innocent bystanders," clairvoyant prophecy, sovereign murder, adultery, vengeance, Fate, and historical oblivion—at the obscene climax, binding them together at the end through the quotation of Cassandra's last Aeschylean words:

> And a result-
>
> ant shock desire
> in bystanders
> to do it to her

there and then.
Little rent
cunt of their guilt:

in she went
to the knife,
to the killer wife,

to the net over
her and her slaver,
the Troy reaver,

saying, "A wipe
of the sponge,
that's it.

The shadow-hinge
swings unpredict-
ably and the light's

blanked out."

(32–33)

Here, Heaney has his Watchman revert to a different tradition, to the rhythm and manner of folk-ballads. From "in she went" to "the Troy reaver" we hear not only the simple singsong of nursery rhyme but also the abstractions of the twice-told tale—"the knife," "the wife," "the net," "the reaver." And the poet's final conspicuous action is to abort—in a Yeatsian move—his final tercet, making its two missing lines enact Cassandra's death.

How much is left of tradition after such violence has been done to it? After all, Heaney has in Cassandra's poem reduced Aeschylean high tragedy to amputated tercets in contemporary dress, tercets voiced in the lowest of styles, with interpolated vulgarity and obscenity. One answer to the question is that everything is left, that to understand Aeschylus today we need to read Heaney. The "spoiling" of form and language—in a sequence so antithetical to the ceremonious forms of Heaney's earliest writing—reflects accurately the "spoiling" of life brought about by war. The tragic loftiness that might have served to represent battle and betrayal at their epic origin falters after the political repetitions, in Ireland, of the twenty-five years of conflict, making epic decline into sardonic balladry, cynically singing the old scandals.

Heaney was unwilling to stop at the devastating amputations of "Cassandra," the depressed vision of eternal fratricide in the Watchman's dawn vision of the murder of Remus by Romulus, or the cynical view of peace in "The Nights," where "peace" is defined merely as the exhausted aftermath of the murderous "rope-net and . . . blood-bath." Yet he could not endorse a peace that would remain one of sectarian segregation. When he searches tradition for some equivalent to the restoration of moral equilibrium in the *Eumenides* he finds it in two recollections, one literary, one autobiographical: in the story of the military battle over the well at the Acropolis (described in the *Penguin Guide to Greece*) and in the memory of a well-digging at his birthplace.

The closing poem-of-wells of "Mycenae Lookout," called "His Reverie of Water," is, formally speaking, a brilliant set of three successive linked codas to the Mycenean-Irish war. The first four-tercet coda, literary and tragic, closes the Aeschylean borrowings proper with Greek tragic justice. This coda guarantees the literary relevance of the traditional genres of epic and tragedy: there will always be an innocent bath of fresh water, not yet bloodstained; and then the "far cries of the butchered on the plain" will die into it, ensuring that the war hero, in the violence begotten by violence, will be murdered, reddening the bath. Though such classical "justice" closes the *Agamemnon*, it is not what Heaney wants for Ireland, and so he proceeds to a second coda, one derived from historical, not dramatic, Greek tradition.

This second coda (in five tercets) uses the conquest and reconquest of the water supply below the Athenian Acropolis to take a long historical view. In this view, all cultural activity of the human species, including the making of war, is repetitive, will recur, and, since biologically determined, is innocent. Though the defenders of the Acropolis thought that only they knew of the secret staircase to the well, the besiegers discovered it:

> secret staircase the defenders knew
> and the invaders found, where what was to be
> Greek met Greek,
>
> the ladder of the future
> and the past, besieger and besieged,
> the treadmill of assault
>
> turned waterwheel, the rungs of stealth
> and habit all the one
> bare foot extended, searching.

(37)

The struggle for *lebensraum* is undifferentiated; land is always and everywhere struggled over, and the strugglers are, in evolutionary terms, "all the one / bare foot extended, searching." It is this very repetitiveness of human action, this stoic coda suggests, that guarantees the historical relevance of literary tradition, as a later period can always see itself in an earlier one.

This, however, is to take a view from an Archimedean anthropological distance; and although Heaney recognizes the inarguable truth of the long view, he, like Czesław Miłosz, also recognizes the necessity of balancing it with a perspective drawn to human scale. In the final, shortest, coda, a personal and hopeful one in three tercets, Heaney considers the fact—and moral solace—of ablution. Yes, he admits the poetic justice of the reddened water in the bath of the first coda; yes, he recognizes the historical treadmill of evolutionary biology in the perpetual territorial struggle of the second coda; but he also wants to assert the simple fact that the coming of peace can perform, on a human scale, the Keatsian "priestlike task / Of pure ablution round earth's human shores." Though the idea derives from tradition, in the *Eumenides*'s ritual cleansing of Athens from blood-guilt, Heaney does not summon up the Aeschylean "Kindly Ones," lest he find himself writing "a Jonsonian masque" with allegorical personae. (Besides, Eliot had preempted the Furies for *The Family Reunion*.) Instead, for the first time in the sequence, Heaney speaks as himself and stands on Irish home ground:

> And then this ladder of our own that ran
> deep into a well-shaft being sunk
> in broad daylight, men puddling at the source
>
> through tawny mud, then coming back up
> deeper in themselves for having been there,
> like discharged soldiers testing the safe ground,
>
> finders, keepers, seers of fresh water
> in the bountiful round mouths of iron pumps
> and gushing taps.
>
> (37)

As Heaney brings back the normalcy of his parents' prewar world and its bountiful water, he uses family memory to "wash clean" many of the polluted words and images that previously appeared in the poem. The Watchman's anguished nights are exchanged for "broad daylight": Agamemnon's yelling troops become relieved discharged soldiers; Cassandra the tragic seer gives way to "seers of fresh water"; the sinister nursery rhyme of the Troy reaver and his slave is re-placed by the innocent rhyme of "finders, keepers" (its sadder twin, "losers, weepers" suppressed here); and the blood-reddened water of the archaic murder becomes native water "in the bountiful round mouths of iron pumps / and gushing taps."

The closing rural scene of "Mycenae Lookout" is a retraction, to some de-gree, of the powerful reactive anger that generated the first four poems of the sequence. And yet, by putting his optimistic coda of ablution within the very same lyric as his other two codas—the tragic one of retributive justice, the stoic one of historical repetitiveness—Heaney at the end is (to borrow words from Wallace Stevens) "of three minds / Like a tree / In which there are three black-birds."[7] Heaney sought for ways in which to be true to the tangled complexity of his historical situation; to make three philosophically distinct but "co-equal" codas occupy his closing lyric is his means of being true to Aeschylus, to his-tory and evolutionary biology, and to his own incorrigible hope.

Literary tradition in the person of Aeschylus has been supplemented in "Mycenae Lookout" by several other factors: first, by political history, as Heaney views the military contention over access to the Acropolis water supply with Marvellian realpolitik crossed with anthropological evenness; second, by the poet's secular gratitude for the Anahorish well (replacing his initial impulse toward a religious "Te Deum"); third, by a vivid sense of the contemporary Irish scene in the figure of Cassandra and her postmodern amputated dimeters. Finally, literary tradition is supplemented by the one necessary thing in all lyric—a sense of the author's own internal predicament. There are many places in "Mycenae Lookout" where the Aeschylean persona becomes transparent, and we hear Heaney's own voice under that of the Watchman. Czesław Miłosz, whose life was shattered by World War II, writes, in "The Poor Poet," of any young poet's initial wish to celebrate the normal and beautiful:

> The first movement is singing,
> A free voice, filling mountains and valleys.
> The first movement is joy,
> But it is taken away.[8]

Heaney's original joy in nature, which, in another time, might have continued unperturbed, is now contaminated by historical circumstance. In a Dantesque moment, he reveals in "His Dawn Vision" the seepage of that contamination into the most innocent moments of life:

The little violets' heads bowed on their stems,
The pre-dawn gossamers, all dew and scrim
And star-lace, it was more through them

I felt the beating of the huge time-wound
We lived inside. My soul wept in my hand
When I would touch them.

(34)

If Heaney's voice was born to joy, the undeclared war in the North forced him—once the cease-fire gave him permission to unleash his long-suppressed anger and disgust—to take up the "pneumatic drill" of "Mycenae Lookout." When Henri Cole asked Heaney about "Cassandra," Heaney answered, " 'Cassandra' was written very quickly. It came out like a molten rill from a spot I hit when I drilled down into the *Oresteia* bedrock that's under 'Mycenae Outlook.' "[9] If we accept Heaney's metaphor of "bedrock" as shorthand for tradition, we can say, with Stevens in "The Rock," that poets cover the rock with the fresh leaves of the imagination. But if we look to the other half of Heaney's metaphor—to the rill to be found still under the fixed forms of the past—we can see that tradition also means, for the poet, access to a pent-up spring of emotion hidden in those apparently monolithic ancestral forms. If Heaney was the most subtle, apt, and exacting interpreter of events in the North of Ireland, it is not least because he could bring, to the characterizing of those turbulent events, a set of powerful traditional resources—classical, Christian, Celtic, and secular. All of these contexts critiqued each other in Heaney's mind; "Mycenae Lookout" is one striking product of that continual critique.

10

Melville

The Lyric of History

To literary history, Herman Melville (1819–1891) is above all the author of *Moby-Dick* and other novels. His arresting and wholly original poetry, written between 1850 and 1890, is visibly a product of the same mind that produced the greatest American novel, but it remains unknown to most readers. The chief monuments of that poetry are the volumes *Battle-Pieces and Aspects of the War* (1866) and *Clarel* (privately published in 1876, but begun much earlier, after Melville's 1856 tour of the Holy Land). The central event behind both books is the American Civil War.

To understand what the carnage of the Civil War meant to Melville—a definitive break with the ethical promise of the United States—one must know something of his life preceding it. He was born into a New York State family that had long been connected to American history: his ancestors had been in America since the seventeenth century, and both his grandfathers fought in the Revolution. His grandfather on his mother's side, General Peter Gansevoort, defended Fort Stanwix in the Revolutionary War, and was tendered official thanks by Congress for his actions. Many of Melville's relatives were involved in the Civil War, some as civilians, some as politicians, some as soldiers: his cousin Henry Gansevoort, whom he knew well, served as a militiaman, as a regular army officer, and as a volunteer in Virginia. For the United States to become disunited, for brother to kill brother, for the Constitution to be impugned—this was to Melville a destruction of all that his family had fought to accomplish.

Melville's formal education ended at fifteen, when his father declared bankruptcy. That the learned, philosophical, and considered poetry of Melville's maturity was produced by a writer with no university education is astonishing. The poet made up for his lack of formal training by two means: his wide and deep reading in his father's library, and his travels as a seaman ("The whaling ship," he later said, "was my Yale College and my Harvard"). Melville went to sea at seventeen and became a cabin boy on the *Highlander,* which took him to Liverpool. Though he then returned to New York, he shipped out again in 1841 on the whaler *Acushnet,* and the subsequent year-and-a-half voyage to the South Seas (before he jumped ship) gave Melville the foundation for *Moby-Dick.* He lived in the Marquesas and Tahiti before returning as an ordinary seaman to the United States in 1844. The years between 1837 and 1844 yielded fodder for several novels, of which the first two (the adventure stories *Typee* in 1846 and *Omoo* in 1847) made him famous as "the man who had lived among the cannibals." Melville, who had taken on family responsibilities by his 1847 marriage to Elizabeth Shaw, could have had a successful career as a novelist of exotic travel, but he had deeper motives governing his work, among them an adventurous and strenuous sense of the formal possibilities of the novel.

Disappointed by the uncomprehending reception of *Moby-Dick* (1851) and the total failure of *Pierre; or, The Ambiguities* (1852), Melville stopped writing and fell into a depression so severe that his family feared for his sanity. They persuaded him to go abroad, to the Holy Land. He consented, and the journal he kept on that 1856 journey formed the basis for his long-sustained writing of *Clarel,* a poem twice as long as *Paradise Lost.* (A few copies were printed privately, for family consumption, in 1876.)

When the Civil War broke out in 1861, Melville was a man in his early forties who had seen his genius unrecognized and misunderstood, and his ability to make money severely compromised. The shamefulness of his breakdown, and of his financial dependence on his own family and that of his wife, brought on a melancholy he could never wholly shake off. He was also disheartened by the inexplicable failure of his friendship with Nathaniel Hawthorne, which had reached such a high point during the composition of *Moby-Dick* that Melville dedicated the novel to him. Though in 1866 Melville was to receive an appointment as a customs inspector, during the war he was still applying, without success, for a government consulship like Hawthorne's (he was even introduced to Lincoln in Washington, but nothing came of it).

The Civil War arrived, then, as the external equivalent of Melville's inner crisis. Just as the America that his family had served had no use for him as its epic recorder, it had debased its own ideals in permitting the practice of slavery. Even before the Civil War, in the 1850s, Melville had written his own dark parable of a slave uprising in the story "Benito Cereno." The country had now fallen into a "conflict of convictions" (as one title in *Battle-Pieces* puts it) that could not be resolved except in the outburst of war. This fact confirmed all that

Melville had suspected concerning the irrationality of human nature and the chaos at the center of all political systems. Had *Moby-Dick* and *Pierre* not been such commercial and critical failures, Melville might have written a great novel of the War between the States. Instead, he turned to poetry, condensing whole episodes of the conflict into the lyrics of *Battle-Pieces and Aspects of the War*. These lyrics were for the most part composed after the hostilities ceased. They were not favorably received: even his family criticized them. His cousin Henry said that his writing in these pieces "never will really touch the common heart," and his sister Kate remarked, "I must say I cannot get interested in his style— of Poetry. It is too deep for my comprehension." Many public reviews were no kinder: "His poetry runs into the epileptic. His rhymes are fearful," said one critic, and William Dean Howells found the poems filled with "phantasms" rather than real events, showing "tortured humanity shedding, not words and blood, but words alone."

Two late volumes of Melville's verse were privately published for friends during his lifetime: *John Marr and Other Sailors* (1888) and *Timoleon* (1891). Neither of these has the sustained passion of *Battle-Pieces* or the philosophical depth of *Clarel*, but each contains unforgettable poems. Though Melville did return to prose, writing *Billy Budd* in the last year of his life, he never ceased to compose poetry. In his final years, he avoided society and passed into obscurity; when he died, his works were almost forgotten. It was not until the Melville revival in the twentieth century that *Billy Budd* and *Clarel* were published. Now, of course, Melville's canonical status as a novelist is secure, but as a poet he is still relatively ignored.

What sort of a poet is Melville? Why has he not achieved a popularity comparable to that of Whitman or Dickinson? These are both questions with complicated answers, but—to address the latter one first—it is enough to point out how profoundly Melville's grim view of history, war, politics, and religion differs from the Emersonian optimism that American readers have tended to prefer. Melville's gaze is not upward, like Dickinson's, nor directed in a democratic horizontal, like Whitman's; it is pitched downward, to the drowned under the sea, or to the fiery hell at the core of the earth. In "Pebbles," the unappeasable sea speaks: "Implacable I, the old implacable Sea: / Implacable most when most I smile serene—/ Pleased, not appeased, by myriad wrecks in me." Or the poet, walking on the placid grass of the New World but aware of imminent civil volcanoes, concludes in "The Apparition: A Retrospect":

> So, then, Solidity's a crust—
> The core of fire below;

> All may go well for many a year,
> But who can think without a fear
>   Of horrors that happen so?[1]

Like Keats in the epistle "To Reynolds," Melville had "seen too far into the core / Of an eternal fierce destruction." It made him the messenger of bad news, not only metaphysical or cosmic, but also personal and political:

> Found a family, build a state,
> The pledged event is still the same:
> Matter in end will never abate
> His ancient brutal claim.

Worse yet, even good actions tend to increase the sum of evil in the universe:

> Indolence is heaven's ally here,
> And energy the child of hell:
> The Good Man pouring from his pitcher clear,
> But brims the poisoned well.
>
> (234)

And there is nothing to be hoped from new political arrangements, not even from the U.S. Constitution, as the epigram "A Reasonable Constitution" asserts:

> What though Reason forged your scheme?
> 'Twas Reason dreamed the Utopia's dream:
> 'Tis dream to think that Reason can
> Govern the reasoning creature, man.
>
> (411)

Melville refuses to praise a Utopian America over a degenerate Europe: he sees original corruption everywhere. And though this belief is not incompatible with Calvinism, nineteenth-century America tended to forget the darker side of its own Protestantism. In its triumphant mercantile and industrial success, it lacked the long historical perspective that informs Melville's work. His poetry, even at its most political and social, is written from a conviction of the loneliness of thought in human life, and his consequent rhetorical aloofness estranges many readers.

Quite aside from Melville's philosophic gloom, his political attitudes did not render him popular with his contemporaries. He wrote with clear sympathy for the Indians, for instance, saying that they had been "all but exterminated in their recent and final war with regular white troops, a war waged by the Red Men for their native soil and natural rights." In 1860—a time when by no means all northerners were abolitionists—he called slavery "man's foulest crime" and saw with foreboding that it had been linked to democracy, "the world's fairest hope." In "Lee in the Capitol," he imagines Robert E. Lee, after the war, as having the long foresight gained by one who has studied the history of Empire, and knowing what Reconstruction will mean to the South:

> Forth he went
> Through vaulted walks in lengthened line
> Like porches erst upon the Palatine:
>   Historic reveries their lesson lent,
>   The Past her shadow through the Future sent.

(152)

In his poetry, Melville makes the divisive shadow of the Civil War reach through to the nation's future. The closing poem in *Battle-Pieces* is true to his conviction that the American conscience was profoundly violated by a governmentally "sanctioned" war pitting brother against brother. To Melville, all one could feel in the presence of such evil was "horror and anguish for the civil strife." His views were not shared by his fellow northerners, who were eager to blame the South. In "A Meditation" he writes, quoting and then answering them: "*'The South's the sinner!'* Well, so let it be; / But shall the North sin worse, and stand the Pharisee?*" (155).

Precisely because of his exposure of the moral ambiguities in American history, the poet Melville has not been incorporated into American culture in the way that Whitman and Dickinson have. Whitman is more conventionally patriotic, more anecdotal, more colloquial, more genial, and more personal; Dickinson is briefer, less forbidding, less historical. Both are in their outer reaches as heretical as Melville, but the schoolbooks and anthologies for the general reader never look to their outer reaches. Almost anything by Melville, on the other hand, is subversive enough to raise hackles. Melville's broad analysis of the war is, for instance, a mixed one, ascribing evil to both sides: it emphasizes (along with heroism in both armies) needless death, mistaken strategy, the atrocities during the draft riots (in the poem "The House-Top"), huge battle losses, stiff-neckedness in the winner, nobility in the loser. And if Melville's tragic sense of history is repugnant to American optimism, his religious nihilism, also present in *Battle-Pieces,* is even more so. It is certain that our literary history has not yet fully absorbed Melville's lyrics into its picture of nineteenth-century culture.

As we look at Melville's poetic works, admitting their documentary and historical relevance, we are bound to ask about his poetry's claims to greatness. The most evident claim is the depth of reflective thought in them; in some 1862 notes, he listed "the greatest number of the greatest ideas" as desirable for an artist. If one wishes to be sure of grasping Melville's ironies, the most gnarled and compressed of the "Battle-Pieces" demand rereading. An unusual structural principle, too, makes his historical poetry difficult. It is typical of Melville to reverse the usual manner in which lyric poems unfold. While the normative lyric presents at its beginning a first-person narrative with its accompanying feelings (and only secondarily, when plot and emotion have been exposed and clarified, turns to philosophical generalization), Melville tends, by contrast, to offer first an impersonal philosophical conclusion, next the narrative that has produced it, and last the lyric feelings accompanying it. This is the most original method Melville discovered by which he could fold the epic matter of history into lyric, and it is this and other strategies in his Civil War lyrics that I want to examine in some detail.

Melville's most famous poem, "The March into Virginia" (10–11), is composed in the back-to-front fashion I have just mentioned. The poem was occasioned by the disastrous Union losses in the first and second battles of Bull Run (1861), fought on the plain of Manassas. The newly recruited federal troops marching toward First Manassas had no idea of the slaughter they were to encounter in battle. Were the poem to begin not with line 1 but with line 16, offering Melville's narrative of the uninitiated troops soon to be sacrificed to the god Moloch, the reader would have a story to grasp, one about blithe young soldiers:

> The banners play, the bugles call,
> The air is blue and prodigal.
>   No berrying party, pleasure-wooed,
> No picnic party in the May,
> Ever went less loth than they
>   Into that leafy neighborhood.
> In Bacchic glee they file toward Fate,
> Moloch's uninitiate;
> Expectancy, and glad surmise
> Of battle's unknown mysteries.

Melville's spectatorial observation—"Moloch's uninitiate"—full of historical and prophetic irony, reveals to the reader the boys' eventual fate.

But Melville refuses to begin his poem with this straightforward narrative. The passage just quoted is preceded by fifteen lines of grim brooding on youth's wish *not* to know what lies ahead (which would foreclose all surprise) and by the poet's sardonic appreciation that all wars need the ardors of ignorant youth as "preparatives of fate." This philosophic overture would make perfect sense if one had already read the narrative of the naive boys off to battle, but as the first statement offered to the reader, it perplexes. One opens *Battle-Pieces* and reads:

> Did all the lets and bars appear
>   To every just or larger end,
> Whence should come the trust and cheer?
>   Youth must its ignorant impulse lend—
> Age finds place in the rear.
>   All wars are boyish, and are fought by boys,
> The champions and enthusiasts of the state:
>   Turbid ardors and vain joys
>   Not barrenly abate—
> Stimulants to the power mature,
>   Preparatives of fate.

The reader accustomed to a lyric "I" will wonder where the speaker of these opening generalizations is hiding. The speaker is Melville as omniscient narrator—a personage not often found in nonballad lyric, though regularly present in epic. The storyteller of a ballad, however, does not philosophize like Melville. And instead of retelling his own emotions, as the usual lyric speaker does, Melville's narrator focuses on the feelings of the young soldiers—first, as they go into battle ("a rapture sharp, though transitory"); second, as some of them die in battle ("enlightened by the vollied glare"); and third, as some of them survive First Manassas and, as the shamed and defeated successors of their decimated companions, fight the second battle of Manassas:

> But some who this blithe mood present,
>   As on in lightsome files they fare,
> Shall die experienced ere three days be spent—
>   Perish, enlightened by the vollied glare;

> Or shame survive, and, like to adamant,
>> The throe of Second Manassas share.[2]

The theoretical phrase in the poem, revealing its implicit poetics, is "like to adamant." The response of the experienced survivors to their humiliating defeat and their traumatic knowledge is to harden themselves to adamant, to take on the stony posture of one who knows all—historically, metaphysically, and ethically—that it is possible to know about life's evil. This is Melville's posture, too, in his poetry: he knows the volcano below the crust, the storm that wrecks the ship, the estrangement that ends the friendship. He will, at all cost, write the poetry of the enlightened, not of the naïve. Therefore what takes first priority in "The March into Virginia" is the philosophic and political knowledge that a historical experience has produced. After the announcement of philosophical conclusions, and only then, will he offer the primal narrative. And only after that can he allow the lyric feelings of the soldiers—first rapture, then enlightenment, then shame—to take their place in the poem. It is this reversal of the usual order of lyric—the way he goes "backwards" from generalization to originating feelings—that makes Melville's best poetry both so oblique and so formally exciting.

Even the most topical of Melville's history poems tend to begin somewhere other than their actual locale. "The Battle for the Mississippi" (April, 1862) starts, for instance, not at the Mississippi but at Migdol, with the Israelites of Exodus 14, as Melville invokes typological precedent:

> When Israel camped by Migdol hoar,
>> Down at her feet her shawm she threw,
> But Moses sung and timbrels rung
>> For Pharaoh's stranded crew.
> So God appears in apt events—
>> The Lord is a man of war!

Yet if the reader persists through the indirect and intriguing opening, a Melville poem often hurls itself into thrilling realist description, as this one does:

> The shock of ships, the jar of walls,
>> The rush through thick and thin—
> The flaring fire-rafts, glare and gloom—
>> Eddies, and shells that spin—

The boom-chain burst, the hulks dislodged,
    The jam of gun-boats driven,
Or fired, or sunk—made up a war
    Like Michael's waged with leven.
  (42)

Many balladeers on the winning side might have written such a stanza; but they would neither have begun typologically nor have proceeded to Melville's mournful conclusion, which focuses on the slain: "The living shall unmoor and sail, / But Death's dark anchor secret deeps detain." Melville risks incoherence by letting triumph end in elegy, and at least one critic has found a comparable poem, "The Battle for the Bay," a failure on that account. The latter poem, about Farragut's victory at the Bay of Mobile, first pays philosophical homage to the knowledge of the sea that comes from long experience:

O mystery of noble hearts,
    To whom mysterious seas have been
In midnight watches, lonely calm and storm,
        A stern, sad discipline.
  (72)

The poem continues with the narrative of the sea fight at Mobile, cast as a battle between Good and Evil. On the Union side,

No sprightly fife as in the field,
    The decks were hushed like fanes in prayer;
Behind each man a holy angel stood—
        He stood, though none was 'ware.
  (73)

And "The Battle for the Bay" concludes with an elegy for the Union vessel *Tecumseh,* the leader of the fleet, sunk when it hit a Confederate mine. The poem, in short, follows the same plan as "The March into Virginia"—philosophical reflection, brisk narrative, and closing grief. But according to Stanton Garner, the most serious commentator on Melville's Civil War pieces, "The Battle for the Bay" is "a long, disunified, ultimately incomprehensible poem":

The three sections . . . are essentially immiscible. . . . On what note, then, could the poem close, a reaffirmation of the educative powers of the sea

or a crescendo of God-on-the-side-of-the-Union hokum? Both are abandoned when, unaccountably, the poem shifts its focus to the stricken
[*Tecumseh*]. . . . Precisely why a ship that—on the periphery of the poem—
had the misfortune to detonate a mine should be thought of as having
earned a glory that will thrill the timbers and the cannon of navies
throughout eternity is left to the reader's perplexed imagination.

The poem is more about a poet in creative difficulty than it is about a
battle. Confused about the point of the action, perhaps, in attempting to
write one poem, Herman wrote fragments of three—one about moral maturity, one about moral and divine values in conflict, and one about the
men of the *Tecumseh,* who . . . have been carried down to the bottom of
war's waters. Had he focused on any one of the three, the poem might
have succeeded.[3]

But Melville can never focus on one aspect, is never content to be single-minded:
for the poet, the cost borne by the brave men drowned in the *Tecumseh* must
haunt the close of the victory narrative, just as the college colonel, in the brilliant poem of that name, cannot forget, as he leads his exhausted but victorious
regiment home, the unspeakable truth that came to him in battle. And just as
"The March into Virginia" began not with epic narrative but with reflection,
and closed not with narrative but with the tragic knowledge gained both by
those who perished and those who lived to fight another day, so "The Battle
for the Bay" begins in wisdom, continues with narrative, and ends in the tragedy
that must qualify every deeply felt battle-song, even one of victory.

Melville has attempted to invent a lyric structure adequate to the complex
feelings generated by the epic event of battle. Besides showing formal innova-
tion in his battle poetry—as he makes a hybrid of the paean, the narrative, and
the elegy—Melville displays in his poetry, as in his novels, an instinctive recourse to many forms of symbolic expression. These include, in *Battle-Pieces,*
various staples of lyric writing: typology, analogy, personification, myth, allegory, refrain, allusion, proper name, synecdoche, and so on. Some of these
devices, however familiar in theory, are striking in Melville's practice, such as
his frequent allusive analogies of American events to civil wars in Rome and
England: "Not Rome o'ercome by Roman arms we sing, / As on Pharsalia's
day," he remarks in "The Surrender at Appomattox"; and he claims, through
an English spokesperson in "Battle of Stone River, Tennessee," that "In North
and South still beats the vein / Of Yorkist and Lancastrian." By such large historical reference, the American conflict is swept into Melville's panoptic view
of the perennial eruption of human aggression: "War yet shall be, and to the

end" ("A Utilitarian View"). On the other hand, Melville was vividly aware of historical difference: though the substance of war might be forever the same, its means had changed from spears and chain mail to ironclad ships; and though the epic impulse to record might be a recurrent one, the function of the bard was now being fulfilled by the newspaper reporter. These technological changes were ones he reflected on, and found formal equivalents for. The armored ships require, he sees, a new sort of language and rhyme. In "A Utilitarian View of the Monitor's Fight," he advocates a plain style devoid of "fans / Of banners" and "the gaud / Of glory," and offers rhyme in only two lines out of six:

> Plain be the phrase, yet apt the verse,
>   More ponderous than nimble;
> For since grimed War here laid aside
> His Orient pomp, 'twould ill befit
>   Overmuch to ply
>   The rhyme's barbaric cymbal.
>
> (39)

And the poet aligns himself, not with the past feudal celebrant singing his lord's victory, but rather with the contemporary journalist sending daily dispatches that are scanned by worried civilians. Melville retells the story of the Union siege of Fort Donelson in Tennessee through the reporter's fluctuating and not always reliable messages, posted on a bulletin board:

> About the bulletin-board a band
> Of eager, anxious people met,
> And every wakeful heart was set
> On latest news from West or South.
> "No seeing here," cries one—"don't crowd"—
> "You tall man, pray you, read aloud."
>
> (17)

After this genre scene, resembling so many nineteenth-century paintings, comes the first tacked-up bulletin:

> IMPORTANT.
>
> *We learn that General Grant,*
> *Marching from Henry overland,*
> *And joined by a force up the Cumberland sent*

> *(Some thirty thousand the command),*
> *On Wednesday a good position won—*
> *Began the siege of Donelson.*
> (18)

Melville imitates even the time headings of the bulletins ("1 P.M."; "3 P.M."), and lets them break into headlines—but Melville's headlines repeatedly (if inconspicuously) rhyme:

> GLORIOUS VICTORY OF THE FLEET!
>
> FRIDAY'S GREAT EVENT!
>
> THE ENEMY'S WATER-BATTERIES BEAT!
>
> WE SILENCED EVERY GUN!
>
> THE OLD COMMODORE'S COMPLIMENTS SENT
> PLUMP INTO DONELSON! (24)

Such experiments in the plain style and in new lyric genres fitted to the new technologies of war show Melville's unwillingness to settle (as did many Civil War poets) for a rousing, thoughtless ballad or a victory narrative in the old style. The fallibility and interruptedness of the daily newspaper bulletin becomes, in Melville's hands, a symbol of the unknowability of war; modern battles are always too complex to be fully grasped. The successive headlines become a symbol of modern epic discontinuity.

Melville was acutely conscious of the broad sweep of troop movements, and of the difficulty of getting that epic panorama into the lyric. He frequently places his observer at a vantage point from which the whole course of an event can be followed, as he does General Grant in "Chattanooga":

> Grant stood on cliffs whence all was plain
>
> . . . . .
>
>   He, from the brink,
>   Looks far along the breadth of slope,
> And sees two miles of dark dots creep.
> (59)

The many poems of far focus serve as nerve centers for *Battle-Pieces:* they gather large social disturbances into the X-ray vision of the watcher, who analyzes the intricate vectors of a many-faceted action. One such episode was the New York draft riots of 1863, which erupted after the Enrollment Act for conscription became law. Since the well-off could hire a substitute or pay a commutation fee to avoid being drafted, the law was in effect discriminatory; riots broke out in July, and before they were put down by the police and the army, more than a hundred people had been killed. Melville's speaker looks out from a housetop; he is scornful of the actions of the mob as he hears "the Atheist roar of riot" and sees "red Arson—there—and there": "The Town is taken by its rats—ship-rats / And rats of the wharves." Yet the speaker is equally disillusioned by the actions of the government, which orders out cannon to disperse the mob:

> Wise Draco comes, deep in the midnight roll
> Of black artillery. . . .
> . . . . .
> He comes, nor parlies; and the Town, redeemed,
> Gives thanks devout; nor, being thankful, heeds
> The grimy slur on the Republic's faith implied,
> Which holds that Man is naturally good,
> And—more—is Nature's Roman, never to be scourged.
>
> (57)

Because Melville's speaker can see—from his high circumspection—all sides of a question, he is ironic toward all: toward the republic's faith in man, which has been disturbed by the sudden violence of the riots; toward the Draconian actions of the state, which have betrayed the faith on which the republic is founded; and toward the persistence in America, under republican pieties, of the pessimistic aristocratic "code corroborating Calvin's creed / And cynic tyrannies of honest kings." (As a nod to the epic nature of his subject, Melville closes "The House-Top" with a Virgilian hexameter alluding to the rights of Roman citizens.) All through *Battle-Pieces*, far-focus viewing is one of Melville's ways of inserting, into short lyrics, factional complexity of grand proportions. Yet he mistrusted any vantage that claimed to explain the whole: he said of the battles in the Virginia Wilderness,

> None can narrate that strife in the pines,
>   A seal is on it—Sabaean lore!
> Obscure as the wood, the entangled rhyme
>   But hints at the maze of war—

> Vivid glimpses or livid through peopled gloom,
>> And fires which creep and char—
> A riddle of death, of which the slain
>> Sole solvers are.
>
> (69)

These doubts about anyone's ability to convey the persisting enigma and riddle of war suggest why, to Melville, the single grim detail, seen up close, can be as explanatory as the high vantage point and far focus of the roof-perch. If the distanced view gives the map of events, the detail relates their pang:

> A path down the mountain winds to the glade
>> Where the dead of the Moonlight Fight lie low;
> A hand reaches out of the thin-laid mould
>> As begging help which none can bestow.
>
> (64)

The detail is often, as here, severed from the whole that it explains. Out of the earth extends an upraised hand—but whose?

Though the poems of far focus represent Melville's most significant attempt to encompass epic breadth in lyric form, poems of the single detail represent the aspect of his genius that yearned to condense reality into epigram, or—carried to the utmost reach—into a single word. Melville hopes that by emphasizing proper names in his lyrics—names of battles, of generals, of ships—he can finally enclose within a single word an entire "aspect" of the war. "The Cumberland," concerning a sunken Union sailing ship, begins,

> Some names there are of telling sound,
>> Whose voweled syllables free
> Are pledge that they shall ever live renowned;
>> Such seems to be
> A Frigate's name (by present glory spanned)—
>> The Cumberland.
>
> (34)

Each stanza closes with a rhyme on "Cumberland," and separating the stanzas is a three-line refrain, four times repeated (with slight variations): "Sounding name as ere was sung, / Long they'll roll it on the tongue—/ Cumberland! Cumberland!"

The aura that names can carry in legend is of course a part of popular lyric transmission, and here Melville is imitating refrain poetry, such as the hymn that repeats "Maryland, my Maryland." Many other poems in *Battle-Pieces*, among them "The Stone Fleet" and "Donelson," exhibit a comparable faith in the single word or name as a powerful repository of epic memory. But condensation into a name is, I think, less successful as a technique of detail (perhaps because it is essentially a choral response) than Melville's use of the lone upraised hand or, in "A Utilitarian View," a single attribute of the warrior's dress. In commenting that technology has replaced earlier forms of warfare, Melville gestures toward those vanished forms with two antithetical details, severed from the bodies of their wearers—the lace of the feudal coat, the feather of the Indian brave—and adds a supplementary word, "singe," to represent their imminent destruction:

> War shall yet be, and to the end;
>   But war-paint shows the streaks of weather;
> War yet shall be, but warriors
> Are now but operatives; War's made
>   Less grand than Peace,
>   And a singe runs through lace and feather.
>
> (40)

Arresting as the use of lace and feather may be, the true Melvillian detail—the one with the pang in it—comes in the words "a singe runs through": lace and feather are scorched not by battle but by what Frost would call "the slow smokeless burning of decay," an effacement by technological advance. As yet, lace and feather are neither entirely destroyed nor even uniformly discolored. Their end is forecast in their aesthetic unloveliness as the detail isolates it for our attention; the marring singe shows both lace and feather to be streaked, as was the earlier war paint, by the "weather" of obliteration.

I have emphasized the qualities in Melville's battle poetry that have made it unassimilable to his own epoch and to ours—his stoic irony, his steely view of warfare, his insistence on the ambivalence felt by any spectator, his refusal to pronounce easily on the whole, his invention of a species of epic lyric comprehensive enough to include metaphysics, narrative, panoramic tragedy, and individual pang. But I would not want to end without glimpses of the other, more tender, Melville. In "Time's Long Ago," the poet's memory of a tragic period of his past is now solace in a bleak present that can imagine no future. In the serenity of a backward look, even

> . . . Fates and Furies change their mien.
> Though strewn with wreckage be the shore
> The halcyon haunts it; all is green
> And wins the heart that hope can lure no more.
> (388)

Beautiful though this is, suffused with nature's green and taking as its presiding genius the bird who appears in calm weather, it is not so beautiful as Melville's late lyric absolving the hurt inflicted on him by life's four winds and bitter seas. Untypically, this seraphic poem begins with direct feeling:

> Healed of my hurt, I laud the inhuman Sea—
> Yea, bless the Angels Four that there convene;
> For healed I am even by their pitiless breath
> Distilled in wholesome dew named rosmarine.
> (206)

The Stoic and Christian doctrine of the compensatory moral value of suffering is rephrased in a set of images that could have been invented only by Melville. The four winds shown at the corners of old maps (here transmuted to angels) replace the Holy Spirit as the breath of inspiration. The "wholesome dew" of seaspray—Ovid's *ros maris*—replaces the baptismal water that obliterates sin. Though the ministers of experiential conflict are themselves inhuman and pitiless, the human mind can distill their assaults on the body into salutary healings of the soul. What it cost Melville to write this epigram, after all he had seen of personal tragedy and civil war, makes us pause, reading it. With *Clarel* and its companion poems—especially the epic-lyric *Battle-Pieces*—it is enough to win the poet Melville, in this century at least, what he prophetically named "the belated funeral flower of fame."

11

Lowell's Persistence

The Forms Depression Makes

Lowell's moral and aesthetic persistence in writing poetry concerning, and enacting, crushing depression was an act of courage. Poems about depression are nothing new: we can all recall Herbert's "Affliction," or Coleridge's "Dejection," or Hopkins's "terrible sonnets." Each of these earlier poets found characteristic ways of representing depression in verse: Herbert's weary iterations ("I read, and sigh, and wish I were a tree"); Coleridge's exaggeration of nature into an unnatural and premonitory peculiar tint of yellow-green as he muses that "not to think of what I needs must feel, / But to be still and patient, all I can"; and Hopkins's flat notations ("I wake and feel the fell of dark, not day"). These utterances have in common their stylistic reduction (with the exception of Coleridge's word "patient") to monosyllables. It seems to me that to find an adequate style for true depression is curiously difficult, because the abjection of self—the hallmark of depression—requires also an abnegation, at least an apparent one, of flourishes of personal eloquence.

Existence seen under the sign of depression is not only flat, stagnant, stale, and blank, it is also incoherent: in Lowell's words, "All's misalliance." The depressed poet is wary of too remarkable a style, too neat a form; both are inimical to the sheer tiredness and baffled searching of the depressed spirit. Yet poems, even depressed ones, need a style and need a form—and to see what Lowell makes of this conundrum of construction and diction is my purpose here. I will draw all but one of my examples from *For the Union Dead* (published in 1964, after the exhaustion of yearly attacks of mania and depression, before Lowell gained a new lease on life from lithium).[1] My last example, however, the poem "Notice," is taken from his 1977 volume *Day by Day*. "Notice" was composed by Lowell out of a different sort of depression: his third marriage was ending, and he feared death from the congestive heart disease that indeed killed him shortly after the publication of *Day by Day*.

The themes of most of the poems in *For the Union Dead* are depressed ones: among them are madness, the death of friends, the desiccation of old relationships with Elizabeth Bishop and Jean Stafford, flawed vision, drinking to excess, personal cruelty, and the threat of nuclear war. I leave out of consideration here poems printed in *For the Union Dead* but written earlier—such as the title poem, composed in 1960, and "Beyond the Alps," previously published in the 1960 *Life Studies*. I dwell instead on the poems exhibiting the laconic style most characteristic of the volume. Lowell himself said about *For the Union Dead:*

> Depression's no gift from the Muse. At worst, I do nothing. But often I've written [during depression], and wrote one whole book—*For the Union Dead*—about witheredness. It wasn't acute depression, and I felt quite able to work for hours, write and rewrite. Most of the best poems, the most personal, are gathered crumbs from the lost cake. I had better moods, but the book is lemony, soured, and dry, the drought I had touched with my own hands. That, too, may be poetry—on sufferance.[2]

The style of *For the Union Dead* is, at first glance, both obstructive and repetitive. The first poem of the volume, "Water" (321–322), throws down a challenge to the reader expecting the florid volatility of Lowell's early style, which he himself called "mechanical, gristly, alliterative." The first, and chief, tic of style in "Water" is its repetition of the word "rock," together with a compulsion to circle back to the word's concluding sound, a "hard c." This sound, occurring in initial, medial, or especially final, position in the words composing the poem, yields a sound-chain of fourteen such words in thirty-two short lines: "quarries," "bleak," "stuck," "rock," "stick," "rock," "color," "rock," "rock," "flake," "flake," "barnacles," "rock," "cold"—with eight of them serving as line-ending words or rhyme words. The cruel foregrounding of the word "rock"—used to end a line in four of the eight stanzas—weighs against the hopeful title, "Water," and foreshadows the rock-bound close: "In the end, / the water was too cold for us." It is clear that the obstructiveness in the repetitive style of "Water" comes not only from the pervasive images of stasis and trappedness, but also from its refusal to let lines run free. Again and again the lines come up against the wall of the hard c and stop short: we see "dozens of bleak / white frame houses stuck / like oyster shells / on a hill of rock." Line breaks with the c-sound become especially obstructive when they violate the natural joining of adjective to adjective or adjective to noun in "bleak / white frame houses" and "match-stick / mazes"; but even when the c-sound doesn't phonetically stop a sentence in its tracks, the line breaks purposefully violate naturalness. The peculiar subject-synecdoche "boatloads of hands" waits in mid-air before being completed by its verb "pushed off," just as the verb "lapped" has to hang over two line endings before finding its direct object, "maze"; and the noun "the color" has to pause at the linebreak before finding its phrasal complement, "of iris."

On the page, this peculiarity of short-line stoppage at odd syntactic places, widely present in the poems of *For the Union Dead*, may look like a practice derived from William Carlos Williams. But it could not in fact be further from Williams's poetic. Williams's line breaks usually generate a dynamic imaginative movement between one line and the next—such as the descent from the metaphysical to the physical in "So much depends upon / a red wheel barrow," or the slide from substance to accident in "a red wheel barrow / glazed with rain water," or the hop from one piece of visual stationing to another in a different location, as in "glazed with rain water / beside the white chickens." In *For the Union Dead*, Lowell's stoppages reflect a mind moving sluggishly to organize its materials, as though it were an effort to find a piece of wit to join subject to object ("boatloads of hands / pushed off"), or to progress from a perfectly ordinary adjective to its inseparably linked noun ("granite / quarries"), or to relate a color to its name ("the color / of iris"). A "normal" person speaking would say "granite quarries" or "the color of iris" with absolutely no pause: if we heard someone say that workers were headed for "granite"—and then a pause—and then "quarries," the pause would be inexplicable, since no word other than "quarries" could conceivably follow "granite" in this context.

So much for the repetitiveness and obstructiveness of style as a symbol of depression: we have seen thoughts circling round the same sound-place obsessively, unable to move on; and we have seen the degree of effort required to push ordinary articulation from one word to the next, even when the next is an intimately related one. We can notice as well another characteristic of the depressed style: it can imagine no possible future. It stays in the present while making occasional forays into a conceivably better past. Yet the nostalgic flashbacks to better moments are themselves corrupted by being recollected in a climate of present depression. In "Water," the flashback to a moment when Lowell and Bishop sat together on a rock long ago ought to convey the warm incipience of the moment when they might have become lovers. But the seepage of compositorial depression corrupts the colors of the past, both by finding the simile of rot for the remembered hue of the rocks, and by aggressing against that false visual appearance of purple by insisting on the true and banal substratum of gray:

> Remember? We sat on a slab of rock.
> From this distance in time,
> it seems the color
> of iris, rotting and turning purpler,
>
> but it was only
> the usual gray rock
> turning the usual green
> when drenched by the sea.
> (321)

If the corrupted flashback in "Water" is in any way characteristic of what I have called "the depressed style," we should—and do—find comparable flashbacks in other poems of *For the Union Dead*. There are, for instance, attractive phrases in the nostalgic flashback of "The Old Flame" (323–324), in which we see the snowbound lovers reading in bed, with the wife speaking in her "voice of flaming insight." Yet, just as in "Water," even that recollection of past companionship is soured by Lowell's comment that since new people have entered the house "Everything had been swept bare, / furnished, garnished and aired." The allusion here is to Jesus's parable of the man possessed by an unclean spirit in Matthew 12:43–45:

> When the unclean spirit is gone out of a man, he walketh through dry places, seeking rest, and findeth none.
> Then he saith, I will return into my house from whence I came out; and when he is come, he findeth it empty, swept, and garnished.
> Then goeth he, and taketh with himself seven other spirits more wicked than himself, and they enter in and dwell there: and the last state of that man is worse than the first.

Since madness was thought to be possession by the devil, Lowell suggests not only that there was an unclean spirit in him during the recollected flashback when he first lived in the house, but also that the swept and garnished house remains defenseless against the advent of worser spirits. In another instance of a corrupted flashback, even Lowell's nostalgia for his beloved Florence—"The apple was more human there than here" (330)—is malignly spoiled by events blighting the poet's time in the city; these include the monthly fever Lowell suffered there, the fate of the strangled horseshoe crabs, and the defeat of the ungainly but pitiable monsters.

In addition to spoiling recollection, depression kills off continuity of memory and, with it, all sense of the unfolding leisure of recalled experience. In *Life Studies*, Lowell could roam for extended periods in the past, but any moment of benign memory in *For the Union Dead* is immediately foreclosed. "Those Before Us" allows merely a glimpse of lounging ancestors taking their ease before the maelstrom-whirl of the hourglass makes "sands drop from the hourglass waist and swallow tail." And "Those Before Us" ends with Lowell's acknowledgment of his inability to maintain his nostalgic memory of those ancestors: "We have stopped watching them. They have stopped watching" (333). The asymmetry of the two sentences—did our ancestors ever watch, or watch over, us?—gives a depressive blur to the stasis of these empty mirroring sentences.

In his glimpses of recollected but curtailed time in *For the Union Dead*, Lowell resorts several times to the word "flash": I take this as a sign of the immediate evanescence of past experience when it is considered in a state of depression. Lying in bed with a cut cornea, the poet in "Eye and Tooth" learns to flinch "at the flash" (334) of the match light. As a boy, he tells us, he watched when women's bodies "flashed" in the bathroom. The poem "The Law" says that as he fished in monotonous nature, he once saw, "in a flash," fresh ground, "a manmade landscape," unique rather than repetitively organic (340). In "The Public Garden," "The fountain's failing waters flash around / the garden. Nothing catches fire" (341). Of Hawthorne, the poet says that "even this shy distrustful ego" once "felt those flashes / that char the discharged cells of the brain" (357). Looking at marital gravestones in a cemetery provokes the poet's remark to his wife, "In a flash, / I see us whiten into skeletons" ("The Flaw," 373). I could mention analogous moments that use some synonym for "flash": in "Night Sweat" the poet says, "I see my flesh and bedding washed with light / my child exploding into dynamite" (375). Such extreme evanescence destroys any hope of a Proustian duration, any guarantee of continuous steady light, the coherence of the ego over time. The poems of depression in *For the Union Dead* portray life as disjunctive, undependable, and static or unprogressive. At best, as in "Going To and Fro," one can go only "to and fro" and "up and down," counting one's steps. The steps get nowhere but "to the noose" (343–344).

The experience of nonprogression or stasis finds its stylistic equivalent in a structure that resists narrative plot. Any new experience has to be stationed, at best, next to the old one, not beyond it. This law—that in depression no experience, not even aesthetic experience, can escape monotony—is articulated most clearly in the poem called "Law" (340). Its weary first-stanza overture declares that it scarcely matters whether one lives under the law of nature or the law of God, one is in any case dead on the battlefield of life—unsleeping though appearing to sleep, because one is sleeping the eternal sleep of death:

> Under one law,
> or two,
> to lie unsleeping,
> still sleeping on the battlefield . . .

It is true that the poem then launches itself into the old *Life Studies* mode of narrative. The beginning of "Law" recalls the inviting opening of "Dunbarton," the poem of Lowell's habitual excursions with his grandfather—"On our yearly autumn getaways from Boston. . . ." "Law" (340) seems to begin its narrative of the poet-as-outlaw in the same genially habitual mode:

> On Sunday mornings,
> I used to foray
> bass-plugging out of season on
> the posted reservoirs.
>
> Outside the law.

But whereas "Dunbarton" is full of narrative incident between grandfather and grandson, advancing the plot—"He took the wheel . . . / We stopped . . . for brownies . . . / Grandfather and I / raked leaves . . . / I borrowed Grandfather's cane . . . / I lanced it in the fauve ooze for newts"—"Law" cannot muster a continued narrative. Instead, it runs into the characteristic depressive perception of all moments as one of dead sameness, a perception here projected onto nature:

> At every bend I saw
> only the looping shore
> of nature's monotonous backlash.
>
> The same. The same.

Once again the poem attempts narrative, passing from the imperfect of "used to" and "saw" via the characteristic verbal token of a "flash," as the bored poet is glad to come upon mowed lawns, a man-made canal, and little stone bridges—works of art that are, like himself, outside the law. It looks as though a little narrative plot has at last been achieved: "First I saw nature, then I saw art." We move, consequently, into the active preterites of "shot" and "arched," and into an adjectival vivacity:

> Then once, in a flash,
> fresh ground, though trodden,
> a man-made landscape.
>
> A Norman canal
> shot through razored green lawns;
> black reflecting water arched
> little sky-hung bridges of unhewn stone—
> outside the law.

However, the poem does not, and cannot end with the man who is "outside the law" successfully finding, and remaining in, a congenial place "outside the law." The hopeful reprise of lawlessness—conveyed by freedom of action and adjectival energy—is followed by another static scene. Granted, the closing scene still contains "each unique set stone" of the man-made bridges, but these artifacts are resumed into the unadorned colors and elements of a verbless monotonous nature, in which the "stone" of gray rock is echoed by the "stone" of art:

> black, gray, green and blue,
> water, stone, grass and sky,
> and each unique set stone!

"Law," in short, as its title implies, foils its own narrative plot by which the outlaw would find joyful activity in an outlaw-home, freed from "nature's monotonous backlash." The depressed mind, even if capable of momentary relief, knows the immobile backdrop is always there unchangingly waiting: "water, stone, grass and sky."

A comparable immobility—but this time one of pain—is repeated, via the word "same" (so emphasized in "Law") at the end of a similar poem, "The Lesson":

The barberry berry sticks on the small hedge,
cold slits the same crease in the finger,
the same thorn hurts. The leaf repeats the lesson.

(332)

An equally motionless non-plot conspicuously organizes the poem "Eye and Tooth" (334–335). Its stasis is generated by the absence of remedy for pain— an absence that ensures the persistence of depression. "Eye and Tooth" repeats, throughout its second half, its obstructive negatives:

Nothing can dislodge
the house with my first tooth
noosed in a knot to the doorknob

Nothing can dislodge
the triangular blotch
of rot. . . .

No ease from the eye
of the sharp-shinned hawk in the birdbook there. . . .

No ease for the boy
at the keyhole. . . .

Nothing! No oil
for the eye, *nothing* to pour
on those waters or flames.

The prolonged obstruction by negatives foils any narrative advance. How, then, can such a static style, incapable of any resort to meaningful plot, be made interesting and, even more, beautiful?

Because it is the aim of style to create intelligible formal structure, human focus, emotional movement, and aesthetic shimmer, we must come to the question of the kind of beauty the depressive style can aim at and create. Decorum, as Milton taught us, is the great masterpiece to observe. I have been mentioning how the depressive style observes negative decorum: its rhythm and sound must be obstructive, repetitive, paralyzed; it must appear to come from an ego that lacks continuity, duration, and coherence; it must, if it allows itself remembrance at all, find that the flash of remembrance vanishes as fast as it appears, extinguished by its proximity to the soul's grimness. The depressive style cannot be seen to get anywhere; if it goes to, it must go fro; if up, down. It represents "all those settings out / that never left the ground," as Lowell says in celebrating his "Tenth Muse, . . . Sloth" ("Tenth Muse," 357). These negative aspects of the depressive style are all, we could say, characteristics of one beauty of writing, which is (as Stevens observed) an accuracy with respect to the structure of reality.

But there is another beauty besides the beauty of accuracy. It is the beauty of vividness, of the arresting image. What would arresting images of depression look like? Lowell was a powerful creator of images and, as we know, he began by depending on the thunderous metaphors of a Puritan apocalypse, in which the soul is given grandeur by the magnitude of its spiritual importance. Depression can offer no such transcendent images, nor can the poet any longer implore, using images borrowed from the Counter-Reformation and Hopkins, the Virgin Mary's "scorched, blue thunderbreasts of love to pour / Buckets of blessings on my burning head" ("In Memory of Arthur Winslow," IV, 862–864). What images, we ask, can be both arresting enough to vivify a paralyzed page and true enough to represent the dulled and static ego of depression?

Of the many such images in *For the Union Dead*, the most memorable—or at least the most quoted—is the image, in the poem "Florence" (330–331), of the disarmed, powerless, dead monsters, vanquished by the cool Davids and Judiths of the dispassionate swords. These conquering heroes and heroines, "Greek demi-gods of the Cross, / rise sword in hand" above the male monsters Goliath and Holofernes—

> above the unshaven,
> formless decapitation
> of the monsters, tubs of guts,
> mortifying chunks for the pack.

Under the sword of Perseus, the Gorgon, Lowell's parallel example of a female monster falls equally undone: her "helpless, big bosomed body / lay like slop." These images of literal depression—as the monsters are ground underfoot by their vanquishers—are an unnerving mixture of the human (the monsters are respectively unshaven and big-bosomed) and the dehumanized (the monsters are formless, decapitated, sloppy "chunks"). The literal snapshots of the depressed Lowell that we see elsewhere in *For the Union Dead* show him (in "The Drinker" [349–350], for instance) to be not unlike the monsters, as he lies in bed with cigarettes and Alka-Seltzer, unable to rise:

No help from his body, the whale's
warm-hearted blubber, foundering down
leagues of ocean, gasping whiteness.
The barbed hooks fester. The lines snap tight.

The Judith to the poet's Holofernes is his wife, whose engagements seem to him
indictments of his inertia, whose personal address book seems "a quiver full of
arrows." The juridical phallic woman, with her arrows and barbed hooks, her
calendar and address book and indictments, represents one source of the poet's
fellow-feeling for the monsters:

Ah, to have known, to have loved
too many Davids and Judiths!
My heart bleeds black blood for the monster.

Just as the monsters are wonderfully found images for the formless, nonthinking,
"decapitated," foundering, and festering state of the depressed body, so the
phrase "my heart bleeds black blood," with its spondaic and alliterative monosyllables and its gradually thickening vowels—from the scream of "ee" to the
flatness of "a" to the subvocalic clotting of "uh"—offers a feeling image (in
appropriate language) for the festering, oozing decline of the depressed soul.

Yet attractive as the monsters may be to us as examples of Lowell's figural
inventiveness, they are rather too baroque and materially substantial to represent the more bled-out states of depression. The monsters represent depression
felt in the body—corporeal heaped-ness, mental vacuity, sexual failure. If we
look through *For the Union Dead* for an arresting image of spiritual bleakness,
we are more likely to turn to such a poem as "The Mouth of the Hudson" (328).
In thinking about poetry, it is often useful to scan down a poem for its chief
words or phrases, ignoring for the moment what is being "asserted" in favor
of what is being displayed. Here are the images constituting "The Mouth of
the Hudson," every one of which is a figure, I think, for Lowell himself in the
state of spiritual depression:

A single man
a discarded gray . . . cable drum
chains of condemned freight-trains
        [that] jolt and jar and junk
wild ice ticking seaward like a clock

the blank sides of a jig-saw puzzle
A Negro
a punctured barrel
chemical air
smells of coffee
suburban factories [that] tan
the sulphur-yellow sun
the unforgivable landscape.

These phrases might all be interpreted more subtly, of course, if replaced in the sentences they came from, but for the moment I merely want to translate these splendid images into the literal first person, creating the flat, imageless sentence that they could be said to stand in for. If he were speaking literally, the poet would say, "I am a social outcast, graying, discarded, once a bearer of messages with a destination, now alienated and disequilebrated, condemned by time, moving toward my death, wild and medicated at once, unable to give any meaning to the aspects of my life, my ego punctured, living on chemicals and coffee, segregated, my atmosphere poisonous, my mental functions obscured, my crimes unforgivable." By finding an image for each noun or adjective in this literal sentence of antecedent feeling—by splitting the incoherent self of spiritual depression into Negro and cable drum, chains of condemned trains and ticking ice, chemical air and punctured barrel, "tanning" factories, acid sun, and unforgivable landscape—Lowell fills his Hudson River School painting with a sizable population of people and objects. Yet this poem offers—except for the "sulphur-yellow sun"—a monochrome landscape which resembles its "pepper and salt" snow. The man's "eyes drop," the poem tells us: they cannot see the polychrome world. "He has trouble with his balance," too: unable to walk the world, he can only stand and scuffle the snow. The speaker is a parody of stout Cortez on the peak in Darien; he "cannot discover America by counting / the chains of condemned freight-trains / from thirty states." Like the trains on the siding, the man is on the sidelines. There is nothing to drink at all in the drought of this poem, and nothing to eat but the few wheat-seeds toasted over coke fumes by a vagrant Negro. There is nothing to breathe but the chemical air, with its undrinkable coffee smell.

Lowell's poetic handling of his weirdly disparate self-images—pepper and salt snow, a cable drum, freight trains, wild ice, the Hudson, a jigsaw puzzle, a clock, a Negro, wheat-seeds, coke fumes, a punctured barrel, chemical air, coffee, suburban factories, sulphur-yellow sun—succeeds in assembling them all into a relatively plausible visual scene. But if one can imagine the poet's original aesthetic puzzle—"Take a handful of images that seem to you reflective of your inner state and contrive a short static film-in-words into which they will all fit"—one can conceive of Lowell's poem as an ingenious set of imaginative radii around a single depressed center. Creative writing teachers—in order to liberate the imagination of their students—sometimes give an exercise beginning with the command "Write a poem in which these words (or images) are contained," followed by a list of implausibly disparate things—"orchestra," "grave," "elbow," "squirrel," "turbine," "brush." It is hoped that through such an exercise the student will learn that a poem with linked surprises in it is more interesting than a poem containing either squirrels alone or orchestras alone. Because the vice of poems about depression is to become as featureless as the state they endeavor to describe, Lowell counteracts one set of distinctive qualities of the depressive style—such as repetitiveness and obstructiveness—by his almost unnaturally wide-ranging and disparate images.

However, it should be remembered that even in a poem so multifigured as "The Mouth of the Hudson," many stylistic features of the depressive style remain. Monosyllables and repetition, for instance, are oppressively present: "the chains . . . of trains" that "jolt and jar / and junk"; "the wild ice ticking seaward . . . The ice ticks seaward"; "A single man stands . . . and scuffles . . . / He cannot discover . . . / He has trouble . . . / His eyes drop . . . / he drifts." And we note in the second stanza of "The Mouth of the Hudson," the reappearance of the blocking sounds we noted in "Water," sounds picked up here from the entropic ticking ice: "ticks," "clock," "coke," "punctured," "chemical," "coffee." The extinction of the ego, too, is punishingly enacted: in the single most startling depressive strategy of the poem, the man—so insisted on in the string of sentences making up the first half of the poem, of which only one ("They jolt and jar") does not have him as subject—disappears entirely in the second, impersonal half, where he is at first replaced as the focal human figure in the landscape by the homeless Negro. For the poet to make his surrogate "man" disappear entirely, in the half-lives of diminishing stanzas (thirteen lines, seven lines, four lines) is perhaps the most devastating means by which he can represent his own sense of extinguished ego.

In the closing stanza of "The Mouth of the Hudson," even the Negro—the last human surrogate—is made to disappear. Though this has been a gray-and-white winter landscape, it has at least included human inhabitants. Now, suddenly, it is vacant of human beings and is lit by an apocalyptic sulphur-yellow sun—harsh, glaring, judgmental, unforgiving. The static industrial landscape of New Jersey, tanning slowly in the sun, now replaces—in the geographical focus of the film-poem—the motion of the river, the ice, and even the jolting trains. The gradual extinction of the human figure (even in the third person, even in surrogate form), and the gradual accompanying subsidence of motion into stasis, are aspects of the depressive style that exist in coordination with the appropriate but surprising and unsettling variations in image as the poem unfolds. The counterpoint between the repetitive and the diminishing (in syntax, in sound, in proportion, in population), on the one hand, and the unusual and new (in the images and final palette) is what makes the depressive style, as we see it in Lowell, beautiful. This counterpoint declares, in equal proportion, both "I am depressed," and "I am inventive in finding equivalents for depression." The moral accuracy (enacted in blockage, repetitiveness, and extinction) and the inventive resources of the poet's aesthetic (conveyed by the procession of images) visibly contend, and display themselves equally. I hardly need say that Lowell's will to write of depression, when emerging from depression sufficiently to be able to write, is an example of both moral and aesthetic persistence that is handsomely rewarded in the best depression-poems of *For the Union Dead*.

My final example of the depressive style, as I promised, will come from *Day by Day*. Some remarks Lowell made about other poets' work can be helpful here. He said of "Little Gidding" that it was "written in a revolutionary and lax language" (CP, 211); he praised Elizabeth Bishop's "exploring quality" (CP, 245); and he mentioned the presence, in Laforgue, of the "whimsical, minute, tender, small emotions that most people don't feel," adding that Laforgue "has fragility along the edges and a main artery of power going through the center" (CP, 245–246). These remarks are all useful in approaching *Day by Day*, and Lowell's emphases in them reveal why some critics—nostalgic for the old Lowell of density and drama—were not prepared for the compression, restraint, fragility, pathos, and "laxity" of the last volume.

In 1957, closing his asylum-prose called "Near the Unbalanced Aquarium," Lowell expressed the hope that composing his autobiography would supply him "with swaddling clothes, with a sort of immense bandage of grace and ambergris for my hurt nerves" (CP, 362). In this complex remark, the poet is at once a newborn child needing swaddling clothes, a multiply wounded victim needing bandages, a sinner needing grace, and a maker of soothing perfume from the "morbid secretion from the intestines of the sperm whale" (to use the *OED* definition of "ambergris"). By the time of *Day by Day*, twenty years later, Lowell might have used a more "lax" language than this for the hoped-for results of writing, but the mixture in the poet's self of naïveté (in the child), hurt (in the victim), aspiration (in the sinner praying for grace), and sensual relish (in the presence of perfume) can still be seen in *Day by Day*.

Though "Notice" (828) is not an especially remarkable poem, it offers Lowell's last word on depression and poetry. Poetry here is conceptualized as the result of merely "noticing." This humble verb—"to notice"—partakes of neither inspiration nor craft. It has to do with paying attention to the appearances of the world. Only after noticing will one be able to name. The poet utters three questions in the course of the poem, of which the last, almost absurd, one, is "Is this what you would call a blossom?" (Lowell's myopia motivates this self-caricature; he once asked at Harvard, as he emerged squinting into the Dunster House courtyard—which was almost entirely occupied by a huge blossoming apple tree—"Is that an apple tree?" and was reassured to be told it was.) In the question, "Is this what you would call a blossom?" the "Is this" represents the pointed direction of the eye, the noticing; the "what you would call" represents the urge to name in a common language; and "blossom" represents the tentative stab at naming. The poetics of noticing is decidedly unflashy; it is one reduced by depression to its most basic dimension.

"Notice" has two stanzas. The first is a short one that takes place in an English asylum, and it shows us the poet as a recovering patient able to participate in a rational colloquy with his doctor. The second stanza ("I am free") is a longer one tracing the rush-hour train journey by the restabilized and discharged poet as he returns home to London. The first stanza emphasizes the solitude and helplessness of the marginalized and confined person; the second emphasizes the hopeful reintegration of the poet into the human crowd. In the first stanza, the doctor, understandably nonplussed by his famous patient, invokes a high idea of art, and apologizes for not being "deep in ideas, imagination, or enthusiasm." Those words are ones we associate with a Romantic aesthetic of poetic composition: sublime ideas, creative imagination, inspired enthusiasm. His patient replies, asking for help:

> "These days of only poems and depression—
> what can I do with them?
> Will they help me to notice
> what I cannot bear to look at?"

These childlike questions—"What can I do?" "Will they help me?"—are, we could say (recalling the prose sentence of Lowell's quoted earlier), the "swaddling clothes" of this poem. The terrible paradox of needing to look at, yet being unable to bear to look at, one's hurt state—a state precisely defined as "what I cannot bear to look at"—is, then, the wound needing the "bandage" of the poem. The poet has yet to be rewarded with ambergris: that balm will arrive in the second stanza, when the doctor is forgotten and the patient is free.

In the second stanza, the poet is connected to other human beings in several ways. He is at last returning home; he jokes about forgetting the maiden name of the wife of one of his friends; he rides "elbow to elbow" with other people on the train; he is carrying a letter, using the back of it to compose a poem. The new poem itself—we see only its unfinished beginning—is about the mutual embrace and warmth of trees after their winter separateness:

> "When the trees close branches and redden,
>   their winter skeletons are hard to find."

This fragmentary poem-within-a-poem admits that even under reddening new growth, the "winter skeleton" of depression persists, but wants to notice the new intertwining and reddening growth more than the underlying skeleton. Each of the patient's minor but accretive approaches to freedom in the second stanza—being able to forget his doctor's name, riding the train, beginning a poem, noticing dryly "that the much-heralded spring is here" and mentioning it to someone else, then heading for home on a walk so familiar he could walk it blindfolded—is carefully added to the score. The poem does not allow itself any real exhilaration: there is no youthful spring to its step except in the single line "I am free," which generates a series of infinitives of action—to ride, to copy, to know, and to say—before the final step, "Then home." The hidden ambergris of the poem lies, we could say, first in the quiet but cumulatively successful exercises in sanity practiced in the second stanza, second in the continuity of memory and growth implied in the poem of the newly reddening and embracing branches, and third in the final command of aesthetic will: "But we must notice." And why must we notice? Because "we are designed for the moment."

This odd conclusion stems from the poet's own perception of his returning sanity as he returns home. Sanity is realized moment by moment, step by step: "Yes: I can forget all about the doctor; I can make a joke; I can introspect; I can bear to be with other people; I can want to write; I can notice the spring; I can talk to someone else; I can find my way home by myself." None of these trivial achievements would be noted by an untroubled person. The poet's serial noticing of them reveals by contrast his "skeletal" previous state, in which the

doctor was the most important person in the world to him. Then, he was isolated from others, he was indifferent to the seasons, he couldn't write, he was
distracted and unsociable, he needed the hospital, he couldn't be let out on his
own. In becoming conscious of his recovery by becoming aware, literally moment by moment, of his new capacities for the most ordinary actions of life,
the poet sees that "we are designed for the moment"—that our consciousness
chiefly functions moment by moment, action by action, realization by realization. Biologically, "we are designed for the moment" of noticing. This revelation is to the poet peculiarly consoling: in a sane state, he comes to understand,
he is already in gear for creation, of which the first, primal step is noticing. The
sense of completion and understood causality that resides in the last two lines
of "Notice" replaces the baffled "swaddled" helplessness of the hospital and the
tentative, even "bandaged," serial exploration of normal life. The ambergris—
the healing intellectual and emotional resolution of the pilgrimage—is reached
in the blessed notion that normal biological consciousness and creative noticing
are "designed" on one and the same template.

The gratitude for a return to health that we find in the poem "Thanks-
Offering for Recovery" uses the same words as "Notice": "I am . . . free"
(828). "Notice" itself puts in counterpoint two different motions. The first of
these—the narrative pilgrimage from hospitalization to freedom—is emphat-
ically not a depressive structure, but a progressive one; but the bare repetitive
infinitives in which the narrative is framed—"I am free to ride, to copy, to know,
to say"—is "left over" from the time of depression. The poet has departed from
the helpless questioning of the original depressive state, but he has not yet
reached—except in the progressive verb "redden"—any lexical exhilaration
corresponding to progressive imaginative freedom. The primitive question of
nomenclature—"Is this what you would call a blossom?"—and the resort to
ironic cliché—"the much-heralded spring"—suggest the blank slate of the still-
depressive mind, which must once again relearn original expressive language.
So, although the plot structure of "Notice" is indeed one of progressive libera-
tion from nakedness (or, in the poem-within-a-poem, skeletal branches) to
bandages to ambergris, the language of the poem continues to linger—in its
primer-like evolution—in the depressive shadow. Only in the energetic assertion of health against illness—"But we *must* notice—/ we are *designed* for the
moment"—do we feel the poet coming into genuine moral and intellectual
strength.

Lowell inventively counterpoints a "depressive" style of monosyllabic, hes-
itating, repetitive, and "primitive" words and structure against the contrasting

qualities which give these poems their originality and vivacity on the page—qualities of surprising image, fluctuation of tonal energy, or striking "flash" of memory. He becomes a notable conveyor of depressive states via their linguistic and narrative equivalents, while remaining a poet who insists on the capacity of art to turn even the bleakest material into a striking set of lines. "What I cannot bear to look at" moves in his hands to "What I must notice," and thence to the naming work of poetry: "Is this what you call it?" If we as readers can answer, "Yes, this is what we call it," then the poem has done its aesthetic work. Art can sometimes thrive on such stinted raw material; Lowell's perception that something could be done with his stationary, parched, and sad moments—something so far from the ringing Miltonic pentameter prophecies of *Lord Weary's Castle*, the rich, prolonged, familial reminiscence of *Life Studies*, and the brisk Marvellian tetrameter swing of *Near the Ocean*—suggests his power as an artist of the inner life, not flinching before its deserts of drought and paralysis. His persistence won through the "witheredness" he spoke of into a poetry of strange aesthetic ambergris.

12

Wallace Stevens

Hypotheses and Contradictions, Dedicated to Paul Alpers

The torment of fastidious thought grew slack,
Another, still more bellicose, came on.
—*The Comedian as the Letter C*[1]

"The Concept of the Arrière-Penseur"
"Reason's Constant Ruin"
—(Two of Stevens's titles for poems never written)[2]

There is no reality; there is the human consciousness ceaselessly forming, reforming, earning, suffering, spiritually stamping worlds from its creative property. . . . In this capacity . . . the uppermost [step] says: there is only the idea, the great, objective idea. It is eternity; it is the world order; it lives by abstraction; it is the formula of art.
—Gottfried Benn, "The Way of an Intellectualist"[3]

Your art has deserted the temples and the sacrificial vessels, it has ceased to have anything to do with the painting of pillars, and the painting of chapels is no longer anything for you either. You are using your own skin for wallpaper, and nothing can save you.
—Gottfried Benn, "Artists and Old Age"[4]

At Harvard Graduate School Paul Alpers and I were fellow students, fellow teaching assistants, and members of the small group of people who were interested in poetry—a group including Stephen Orgel, David Kalstone, Dan Seltzer, John Carroll, Neil Hertz, Grace Billings, Martin Wine, Mary Ann Miller, Bill Youngren, and Bill Pritchard. We sought out teachers whose main interest was poetry: Douglas Bush, Rosemond Tuve, Reuben Brower, John Kelleher. We soon realized that poetry—in some cases, Renaissance poetry in dramatic form—was where our hearts lay. (Some of us were capable of writing on fiction, too, but most of us had no such desire.) Paul seemed to me terribly learned: he was working on Edmund Spenser, had read widely in classical literature as well as in the Renaissance, and he spoke with seriousness when he spoke of literature. I looked up to him, and to the original way he had found to think through Spenser's figurative language (which to me was, and still is, the most difficult in English poetry).

Our generation was thought of as "New Critics" or "Formalists"—terms that have come in for a fair amount of abuse. We were said to practice something called "close reading"—a rather absurd term, since what, if anything, would "far reading" be? It was popularly thought that "New Critics" believed that one needed nothing but "the words on the page" in order to construct a description or an interpretation of a passage of literature. Of course, the original "New Critics"—and any followers worthy of them—were very learned men: Allen Tate and John Crowe Ransom in the United States, and, in England, I. A. Richards and his pupil William Empson. They brought, to any text they touched, all their knowledge of classical and modern languages, ancient and modern history and philosophy and religion, other art forms, and so on. They had learned, in short, whatever they thought they needed to know in order to approach the passage in question. Their fundamental choice, as critics, was a choice of attention: they chose to give more time to the intrinsic qualities of the work than to its contextual penumbra. They were far from declaring learning (historical, social, psychological) unnecessary to interpretation. They simply assumed that any thorough critic would not begin to write unless the necessary elements of learning had been gathered. They preferred to memorize the poem before teaching it or writing on it; Douglas Bush was famous for having memorized *Paradise Lost*, and Richards's memory was legendary.

Almost the first thing I knew of Paul after he began teaching at Berkeley was that he had won an American Council of Learned Societies Fellowship to take a study leave to learn Latin better. His subsequent work on pastoral had its roots in that study leave, and though Paul's approach to pastoral is primarily that of a genre-critic (one version, I suppose, of the "formalist" undertaking), no reader could deny the profound learning underpinning Paul's formal observations on variation in pastoral, both classical and modern. Paul changed the way we see both Spenserian epic and Renaissance and modern pastoral lyrics. By offering in Paul's honor this essay in Stevensian stylistics, I want both to recall my admiration of his mind when we first became friends and to hail his enlarging of a field that needed his shaping hand.

Though my title names hypotheses and contradictions as two aspects of the work of the poet Wallace Stevens, I think of these practices as his *if*s and *or*s and *but*s.

These three words, representing speculation on the one hand, and obstruction of speculation on the other, play a visibly large role in Stevens's poetry. To remark on Stevens's need for these forms of thought, and yet his late resistance to them, is one way to track his evolution—and his idiosyncrasy—as a poet. I hope to show that by using, questioning, and eventually forsaking these rhetorical means, Stevens over time seeks out truth in different ways. First, by dialectical means, he looks for "the" truth; then, adopting a Nietzschean multiplicity, he argues for "truths"; but in his late work he aims to approach, by a series of asymptotic figures, "a" truth plausible to his exacting mind.

Stevens's poems were written during the fifty years between his matriculation at Harvard and his death at seventy-five. His long life was relatively without incident: He was born in 1879 in Pennsylvania, of Pennsylvania Dutch—that is to say German—extraction; his father, Garrett Stevens, was a lawyer who wanted his sons to be lawyers, and all three of them eventually obeyed him. Garrett Stevens was willing to send his brilliant son Wallace to Harvard, but would support him there for only three years, since one could enter law school after three years at the university. On his departure without a degree from Harvard, Stevens, disregarding his father's wishes, did not immediately enter law school, but became a newspaper reporter in New York. Discouraged by both the work and the salary, Stevens capitulated and went to New York University Law School, after which he had various disappointing short-term positions as a lawyer in New York. In 1916, at thirty-seven, he found a job as a surety lawyer with the Hartford Accident and Indemnity Insurance Company of Connecticut, where he remained till he died in 1955.

In the first years of Stevens's employment at the Hartford his work was arduous, requiring frequent train travel across the United States to investigate insurance claims, and in those years Stevens wrote little poetry. Eventually, as he rose in the company, his life became less harried, and when he was forty-four he published his first book, *Harmonium*, with Knopf. Other volumes followed steadily, and in 1954, some months before his death from cancer, his *Collected Poems* won the Pulitzer Prize and the National Book Award. Since his death, his fame has grown steadily, but he remains, in the eyes of us all, a difficult poet, the one who wrote, both in "Man Carrying Thing" and in a collection of *pensées* to which he gave the Erasmian title *Adagia,* that a poem "must resist the intelligence almost successfully."

Although Stevens's life had many ecstatic moments, it was not in the usual sense a happy one. His marriage became increasingly difficult, as his beautiful but uneducated wife, Elsie (once the model for the American Liberty dime), retreated into homesickness, estrangement, and suspicion: no friends or acquaintances could be invited to the house, not even by their daughter, Holly. Each night, after dinner, Stevens retreated to his small separate study and bedroom upstairs, where he read, listened to music, wrote letters, and composed poetry. It was an intensely lonely life, relieved by occasional trips to New York museums, and by his eventual good relations with his daughter and her son.

At Harvard, Stevens had abandoned the Protestantism of his parents for the skeptical Lucretian naturalism of his acquaintance George Santayana. This philosophic materialism was buttressed by Stevens's intimate knowledge of the natural world: he was a great walker in his youth, often covering thirty miles in a single day. Spring warmed him into life; winter chilled him into despair. He became the most exquisite poet of seasonal change since John Keats, by whom he was permanently influenced. Many of Stevens's early poems became intelligible to readers through their relation to Romantic verse: "Sunday Morning," for instance, ends in homage to Keats's "To Autumn." Instead of Keats's agricultural and domestic landscape, populated by lambs, robins, and swallows, Stevens's American scene offers mountains and an uncultivated wilderness, populated by deer, quail, and pigeons. Keats's goddess of the season has vanished, and human beings exist in isolation:

> Deer walk upon our mountains, and the quail
> Whistle about us their spontaneous cries;
> Sweet berries ripen in the wilderness;
> And, in the isolation of the sky,
> At evening, casual flocks of pigeons make
> Ambiguous undulations as they sink
> Downward to darkness, on extended wings.
>
> (56)

As a young reader, I could move easily into such a poem; it was only a step from Keats to the Keatsian elements in Stevens. I had far more trouble understanding why Stevens would write certain other poems, among them the one that opened *Harmonium* (and which is still the first piece one sees in the *Collected Poems*). I realized that this strategically placed poem, "Earthy Anecdote," must be some sort of manifesto, but of what was it the proclamation? Like most conceptual art, this 1918 poem[5] offers no elaboration of its stubbornly repeated plot—that of a daily contest between deer (fiercely charging straight ahead) and a mountain lion (named by its folk appellation, "firecat") that obtrudes itself in the path of the bucks:

Earthy Anecdote

Every time the bucks went clattering
Over Oklahoma
A firecat bristled in the way.

Wherever they went,
They went clattering,
Until they swerved
In a swift, circular line
To the right,
Because of the firecat.

Or until they swerved
In a swift, circular line
To the left,
Because of the firecat.

The bucks clattered.
The firecat went leaping,
To the right, to the left,
And
Bristled in the way.

Later, the firecat closed his bright eyes
And slept.

(3)

The firecat's only purpose in his waking hours is to make the bucks swerve. The game goes on all day, conceived and prolonged by the bright eyes of the firecat, and it comes to an end only when the firecat sleeps. Had the firecat not "bristled in the way," the bucks would have unswervingly clattered over the plain of Oklahoma in an unimpeded straight line.

At least one way of reading this little parable is to see it as an enacting of the response of the mind's original inertia when it encounters new hypotheses and then contradictions of these very hypotheses. Once our thoughts are set on an inertial straight path, they will not become inventive unless blocked, and one can see the bucks as a form of uncreative life forced into creativity by the bright-eyed obstacle of intelligence. In Stevens, the obstacle that forces the swerve is dialectically self-created: and *ors* and *buts*, with their bright-eyed queries, force the mind into alternative paths. I believe that this apparently trivial little poem revealed to Stevens, as he wrote it, how much his art depended on obstructions and the consequent swerves provoked by them, and that he therefore gave "Earthy Anecdote" pride of place both in his first volume and in the final collection of his poems.

When in 1922 Stevens comes to organize his long Browningesque autobiography in verse, *The Comedian as the Letter C*, he does so by means of successive geographic hypotheses, each contradicting the former. Should the poet remain in Bordeaux, within the European tradition? Or translate himself to the Yucatan, where the new world is the savage landscape discovered by Columbus and the conquistadors? Or move to North America's placid and warm English-settled southern states? Stevens eventually decides for the last of these, and his hero Crispin, treated with comic irony, settles down in the Carolinas, in "a nice shady home" with a "prismy blonde" for a wife, and four "daughters with curls" (32, 34, 35). Mistakenly, Stevens stops while Crispin is still dwelling in the South: "Crispin knew / It was a flourishing tropic he required / For his refreshment" (28). Later, in 1936, affected by the failure of his marriage and the shock of the Depression, Stevens will write the elegiac "Farewell to Florida," declaring that he must now seek his fate in the North: "My North is leafless and lies in a wintry slime" (98). Because Stevens's speculations in *The Comedian* on the poet's proper geographic home and the contradiction of Crispin's Romantic aspiration by domestic curtailment are ensconced within a plot, they are, for this reason, both more visible (because narrated of a protagonist) and less visible (because overgrown by picaresque picturesqueness) than they will be when they appear in more metaphysical form, in those brief parables and anecdotes that Stevens came to prefer, because of their abstraction, to quasi-mimetic, even if allegorical, narrative.

If we turn away from Crispin's narrative to Stevensian lyric, we can see how hypothesis becomes for Stevens a firecat-stimulus to a creative swerve. In a 1923 manifesto, "The Idea of Order at Key West," Stevens examines, by means of successive hypotheses and contradictions, the relation between lyric language and the element of nature it purports to translate. The speaker, walking with a companion, hears a girl singing on the shore, and asks the relation of her song to the sea:

Whose spirit is this? we said, because we knew
It was the spirit that we sought and knew
That we should ask this often as she sang.

The question, "Whose spirit is this?" prompts a set of hypotheses followed, as we might expect, by a contradiction:

If it was only the   *dark*   voice
                                                                                                  of the *sea*

    that rose
        or even
[if]   *colored* by many *waves;*
If it was only the   *outer*   voice
                                                                                                  of *sky* and *cloud,*
                                                                                                  of the sunken *coral* water-walled,
                                                                                                                                        however clear,

    it would have been   deep *air,*
        the heaving   speech
                                                                                                  of *air,*
                                          a summer   sound
                                                                                                  repeated in a summer without end
                                              and   sound alone.
But it was more than that,
        more even than   her   voice
                                                                                                  and ours,

    among the meaningless plungings
                                                                                              of *water* and the *wind,*

        theatrical   distances
        bronze   shadows heaped on high horizons
        mountainous   atmospheres
                                                                                              of *sky* and *sea.*

(105)

    This sort of elaboration becomes typical of Stevens's opulent middle style. Of what use to him, we ask, are such *if*s, such *but*s? The *if*s here represent temptations toward certain theoretical positions, especially those attributing human art to nothing grander than animal instinct, an evolutionary instinct that prompts us to reflect the various items of our environment, as, say, the mockingbird does. Perhaps we do nothing but transcribe blindly the example of the sea, and the darkness of our song reproduces its darkness; if our song takes on colors, they have been conferred by the colors of the sea's iridescent waves. Or perhaps if our song by the seashore takes on yet other colors, not of the sea, they are borrowed from the surrounding context—blue sky, white cloud, and red coral. Were blind imitation the case, the girl's song, Stevens argues, would have been sound alone, breath alone, as birdsong is. Her song would have been an imitative vocalise, as meaningless—in its exercise of the animal instinct for melodic expression—as the great physical displays of the natural sublime of sky and sea.

To elaborate, in this way, a possible biological theory of poetry, and to enclose in it a theatrical Wordsworthian mimetic hymn to the "mountainous atmospheres of sky and sea," sets in relief the alternate poetic Stevens is about to proffer, which is introduced by one of his useful contradictory *buts*—"But it was more than that." The new poetic is neither instinctual nor mimetic; it is an abstract one of intellectual artifice, of exact measurement, of geometric lines and demarcated spatial zones. At the end of the poem, when the poet and his companion turn away from the shore toward the town, they find that their surroundings have been charted and made intelligible by the words of the singer, in the same invisible way in which the globe has been charted by geographers who create invisible lines of latitude and longitude, marking out the North and South Poles and fixing zones above and below the equator. Because of the singer's song,

> The lights in the fishing boats at anchor there,
> As the night descended, tilting in the air,
> Mastered the night and portioned out the sea,
> Fixing emblazoned zones and fiery poles,
> Arranging, deepening, enchanting night.
> (106)

Stevens's final interpretation of the maker's *furor poeticus*, the "blessed rage for order," is secure only because it has been arrived at after he has given a full display, by means of his *ifs* and *buts*, of both Darwinian determinism and the submissive mimetic sublime of William Wordsworth's *Elegiac Stanzas*, "that rueful sky, that pageantry of fear," a phrase akin to "mountainous atmospheres / Of sky and sea." Stevens's inching progressions—"If . . . or . . . If . . . But . . . more . . . more"—track a mind at work investigating its first thoughts and rejecting them for a more accurate one, one that announces the spirit's mastery, by the geometrical abstraction afforded by lyric language, of the sublime landscape of the night sky.

How far can the poet carry speculative hypotheses and fertile contradictions? In deciding to write, in 1937, "The Man with the Blue Guitar," a theoretically interminable sequence in a new populist style, Stevens proposes that one can entertain multiple hypotheses and successive contradictions if they are juxtaposed to one another in a cubist multiperspectival space:

> Is this picture of Picasso's, this "hoard
> Of destructions," a picture of ourselves,
> Now, an image of our society?
>
> (141)

In this Nietzschean realm, every description destroys another description, every mouth proclaims a different point of view. We find ourselves in a Mallarméan world in which the supreme ruler is the plural poetic word (of which the "amorist Adjective aflame" of the sky's unlimited "blue" is the paradigm). Here, the demands of logical consistency are repudiated as unwelcome "pale intrusions into blue":

> The pale intrusions into blue
> Are corrupting pallors . . . ay di mi,
>
> Blue buds or pitchy blooms. Be content—
> Expansions, diffusions—content to be
>
> The unspotted imbecile revery,
> The heraldic center of the world
>
> Of blue, blue sleek with a hundred chins,
> The amorist Adjective aflame . . .
>
> (140–141)

Although we find, in "The Man with the Blue Guitar," many hypotheses and contradictions, Stevens in this sequence experiments with deleting, in various instances, the expected prefacing signals, *if* and *but*. This tactic produces, as in Canto XXVII, obdurate sets of implied hypotheses in which parallel statements either mutually contradict one another or else stand in logically oblique relations to each other. Here we find the sea again, but it is far less intelligible than it was when it stood simply for physical nature in "The Idea of Order at Key West." Many speculative hypotheses about the sea, in no clear relation one to the other, are entertained, but no *ifs*, *or*s, or *but*s are allowed to appear. The mind's conjecturings, obstructions, and swervings give rise to a series of independent statements, with all logical junctures suppressed as they might be in a succession of objective *prises,* or seizings, of a natural phenomenon:

> It is the sea that whitens the roof.
> The sea drifts through the winter air.
>
> It is the sea that the north wind makes.
> The sea is in the falling snow.
>
> This gloom is the darkness of the sea.
> Geographers and philosophers,
>
> Regard. But for that salty cup,
> But for the icicles on the eaves—
>
> The sea is a form of ridicule.
> The iceberg settings satirize
>
> The demon that cannot be himself,
> That tours to shift the shifting scene.
>
> (147)

To shift the shifting scene is now the perplexing task of the poet's "daimon" that cannot be himself, cannot possess a fixed identity or enunciate a fixed truth. Stevens does not want to remain in a masked world of unfixed phenomena, since he still yearns for truth and a stable poetic. Yet, "There is no place, / Here, for the lark fixed in the mind, / In the museum of the sky" (149–150). Where will stability, then, be found? Nowhere, in much of "The Man with the Blue Guitar."

Stevens's contradictions reappear in a slightly later poem, one despairing of any future stability, the 1942 "Cuisine Bourgeoise," a piece composed almost entirely of hypotheses, denials, and questions. It begins with a grim scene: "These days of disinheritance, we feast / On human heads" (209). After a dismissal of the moribund past ("But that's all done. It is what used to be"), "Cuisine Bourgeoise" launches itself into a frustrating present of betweenness. It does this by means of a series of arid definitions, hypothetical similes, mini-hypotheses in the form of words in apposition, and—in a final alienation in which the governing pronoun changes from "we" to "they"—hopeless questions:

> It is like the season when, after summer,
> It is summer and it is not, it is autumn
> And it is not, it is day and it is not,
> As if last night's lamps continued to burn,
> As if yesterday's people continued to watch
> The sky, half porcelain, preferring that
> To shaking out heavy bodies in the glares
> Of this present, this science, this unrecognized,
>
> This outpost, this douce, this dumb, this dead, in which
> We feast on human heads . . .
> . . . . .
> This bitter meat
> Sustains us . . . Who, then, are they, seated here?
> Is the table a mirror in which they sit and look?
> Are they men eating reflections of themselves?
> (209)

In Stevens's work, a series of words in apposition almost always represents a set of compressed hypotheses. In order to show the rapidity with which Stevens, in his later period, adopts and discards speculative proposals, I stop a moment here on his serial nouns describing the present in "Cuisine Bourgeoise." This series is remarkable because in it there appears the one distinctly *nonhopeless* word of the poem, the French adjective *douce*, here transformed into a noun. "This present" is interestingly first hypothesized to be "this science"—since science is the dominant modern frame demanding from the poet a fresh description of the universe. This characterization of the present is dismissed by declaring that we find more unsettling than the knowledge purveyed by science the vast quantity of ignorance ("this unrecognized") it reveals. No longer the Ptolemaic center of the universe, we have become "this outpost," a planet knowing nothing of the center from which it originated. In the middle of such a bleak portrayal of the present we are surprised to find a new, wholly alternative Stevensian hypothesis in the unexpected phrase, "this douce." Admitting the melting sweetness of physical experience even in an unintelligible world, Stevens at last has something to write about—but how can he do so in "this dumb," a hypothesis that recognizes a failure of speech intensifying the failure of cognition expressed in "this unrecognized"?

Why does Stevens present some of his appositive hypotheses here as nouns, and some as adjectives-turned-nouns? We can see that the hypotheses about the present embodied in true nouns are focused on *external* reality—this *present* (the twentieth century), this *science* (the new frame), this *outpost* (the marginalized planet). By contrast, the hypotheses that are phrased in nouns derived from adjectives have to do with the poet's *inner* world—what it recognizes, what it finds sweet, what it wants to utter in language. This grammatical division of labor makes the hypothesis articulated in the final adjectival noun, the climax of the series, so cutting: "this *dead*" is, by its adjectival grammar, seen to be an internal quality. Although earlier in the poem death was imagined externally as a quality belonging to the ingested "human heads" of the past, it now migrates into the subjective world of the poet himself. It is no coincidence that "head" rhymes with "dead."

Stevens attempts to contest his nihilist deadness even as he voices it, and we can see his first efforts toward a recovery of confidence in certain minor poems, such as "Forces, the Will & the Weather" (210) and "On an Old Horn" (210–211). In the second of these, the Darwinian doubts seen in "The Idea of Order" return in force ("The bird kept saying that birds had once been men, / Or were to be, animals with men's eyes, / Men fat as feathers"), and the poet finds solace only in a precarious set of wavering self-contradictory assertions:

> In the little of his voice, or the like,
> Or less, he found a man, or more, against
> Calamity, proclaimed himself, was proclaimed.
> (211)

Yet in spite of such transitory consolations, the deadness of "Cuisine Bourgeoise" persists. In *Transport to Summer* (1947), a Darwinian bestiality returns in force as the once-joyous man with the guitar reappears in the poem "Jouga," its title deformed from the Spanish *jugar*, "to play." Both the physical world of "The Idea of Order at Key West" and the human world of "Cuisine Bourgeoise" are now meaningless. The name of the guitar player, "Jaime" (Spanish for "James"), is distorted into a series of the meaningless phonemes of its pronunciation, Ha-eé-me, just as his notes become unmelodic "noise," and his guitar is dehumanized to a beast:

Jouga

The physical world is meaningless tonight
And there is no other. There is Ha-eé-me, who sits
And plays his guitar. Ha-eé-me is a beast.

Or perhaps his guitar is a beast or perhaps they are
Two beasts. But of the same kind—two conjugal beasts.
Ha-eé-me is the male beast . . . an imbecile,

Who knocks out a noise. The guitar is another beast
Beneath his tip-tap-tap. It is she that responds.
Two beasts but two of a kind and then not beasts.

Yet two not quite of a kind. It is like that here.
(295)

The *but*s and *or*s and *perhaps*es and *not*s here reveal the bitterness and self-loathing of the poet confronting an apparently untransformable external world. When Stevens's last resort of joy, the physical world, becomes meaningless it renders the virtual world of language and music meaningless as well. The instability of the physical world had already reached, in the 1939 "Variations on a Summer Day," as far as Keats's North Star, elegiacally subjected by Stevens to a drifting delineation that thins down further and further:

Star over Monhegan, Atlantic star,
Lantern without a bearer, you drift,
You, too, are drifting, in spite of your course;
Unless in the darkness, brightly-crowned,
You are the will, if there is a will,
Or the portent of a will that was,
One of the portents of the will that was.
(213)

A poet cannot write indefinitely in this oscillating and self-repudiating vein, qualifying his every statement with *unless* and *if* and *or*. How will Stevens escape his uncertainty? Can he arrive at a point of more stable assertion? If steadfast truth does not reside in the North Star, where is it to be found?

Stevens escapes uncertainty at first—and perhaps even at last—by incorporating into his poetics the idea of necessity. This necessity may be moral or aesthetic or historical, or it may be referred to the physical laws of nature. It has already made its appearance, rather theatrically bearing its Greek name, in the 1936 *Owl's Clover:* "Fatal Ananke is the common god" (580). Its more common appearance in Stevens is by means of the repeated modal forms *has to* and *must*, visible in the 1940 manifesto "Of Modern Poetry": Here, philosophical truth is defined not as proposition but as process: the mind's "act of finding / What will suffice." And the new poetics of process is prompted by moral obligation; the mind of the modern poet is bound by social and historical duty:

> It has to be living, to learn the speech of the place.
> It has to face the men of the time and to meet
> The women of the time. It has to think about war
> And it has to find what will suffice. It has
> To construct a new stage. It has to be on that stage[.]
> . . . . .
>   It must
> Be the finding of a satisfaction. . . .
> (218–219)

There is much that could be said about this hinge of modal obligation and necessity, which mediates between middle and late Stevens, but I can only remark here the change it represents. There is not an *if* nor an *or* nor a *but* to be seen in this passage; not an *as* nor a *like*. (Later in the poem Stevens's signals of qualification—*like, not, but*—do appear briefly, but they are firmly put aside in favor of another *must*.) The Stevens who earlier luxuriated in dialectical speculation now prefers the blind assertions of a desperate necessity. To justify the necessity, Stevens leaves solitude behind and demands that his work "face the men of the time" and "meet the women of the time." "Of Modern Poetry" voices Stevens's temporary conversion to the colloquial and the social, and to the use of a public rhetoric.

This "conversion," prompted by the social convulsions of the Depression and World War II, was not one that Stevens could always maintain; but the poetics of process, of "finding," that it elicited did spring the poet free from the sterile consumptions and reflections of "Cuisine Bourgeoise," forcing him to think of a means for looking forward. He begins by analyzing his own rebellious disposition, which had always prompted him to contest the received truths of his culture. In the 1940 poem "Landscape with Boat," Stevens chastises himself for having been hitherto insufficiently fertile in "supposing," in spite of all the supposing he had done earlier with his *if*s and *or*s. He was mistaken, he tells us, in supposing that there existed a final propositional "truth beyond all truths," one that would forever put an end to conjecture. He advances, now, by an inching logic of contradiction and hypothesizing, to a final positive assertion. In saying "the world itself was the truth," Stevens accepts a materialist, rather than a propositional, notion of truth:

> It was his nature to suppose,
> To receive what others had supposed, without
> Accepting. He received what he denied.
> But as truth to be accepted, he supposed
> A truth beyond all truths.
>
>   He never supposed
> That he might be truth, himself, or part of it,
> That the things that he rejected might be part[.]
> . . . . .
>
>   . . . He never supposed divine
> Things might not look divine, nor that if nothing
> Was divine then all things were, the world itself,
> And that if nothing was the truth, then all
> Things were the truth, the world itself was the truth.
>
> (220–221)

This dismissal of "*the* truth" as an intellectual figment—"Where was it one first heard of the truth? The the," as Stevens says in the 1940 poem "The Man on the Dump" (186)—and the substitution for it of the laws (and beauties) of the material universe, each of which, in Emersonian fashion, has *a* symbolic truth to tell, liberated Stevens from the constant undermining of speculation by contradiction, while leaving him open, at least from time to time, to using hypotheses and objections more casually.

In working toward a poetics that is one of process, but also one that can make positive assertions that can resist subversion or contradiction, Stevens reaches increasingly often—as in the 1943 poem "Somnambulisma"—for formulations that will not deny poetry's origin in the animal evolution of language, but that will equally not deny poetry's role in the highest domain of knowledge. Even in that highest domain, the Stevensian poet is not Plato's philosopher king: in a democracy, he is surrounded not by regalia but (winningly) by personalia.

The origin of what the poet pours forth in language is in part animal, in part spiritual: but whether we choose to see the poet as evolutionary bird or Emersonian American scholar, he undeniably makes the material world pregnant with reflected human meaning. As "Somnambulisma" returns to the shore of "The Idea of Order at Key West," we can see how the necessary social relation of the poet to his fellows, declared in "Of Modern Poetry," rescues Stevens from materialist solipsism, and enables a triple hybrid figure of the poet as the vernacular ocean, an archetypal restless bird, and a solitary scholar:

Somnambulisma

On an old shore, the vulgar ocean rolls
Noiselessly, noiselessly, resembling a thin bird,
That thinks of settling, yet never settles, on a nest.

The wings keep spreading and yet are never wings.
The claws keep scratching on the shale, the shallow shale,
The sounding shallow, until by water washed away.

The generations of the bird are all
By water washed away. They follow after.
They follow, follow, follow, in water washed away.

Without this bird that never settles, without
Its generations that follow in their universe,
The ocean, falling and falling on the hollow shore,

Would be a geography of the dead: not of that land
To which they may have gone, but of the place in which
They lived, in which they lacked a pervasive being,

In which no scholar, separately dwelling,
Poured forth the fine fins, the gawky beaks, the personalia,
Which, as a man feeling everything, were his.

(269)

Without the poet, according to "Somnambulisma," those of his generation would be deprived of a living sense of their own emotional experience; and the world surrounding them, if uncommented-on by the poet, would be "a geography of the dead." The Stevensian compulsion to speculate and hypothesize is here imagined first as the restless rolling of the ocean and next as a bird's inability—represented by intensives of the present progressive tense—to settle on a nest. The "generations" of the poem are borrowed from Keats's odes to the nightingale and the Grecian urn—from "No hungry generations tread thee down" and "When old age shall this generation waste." The music of "Somnambulisma" comes from Tennyson's song, "The splendor falls on castle walls . . . Dying, dying, dying," and from "The Passing of Arthur"—"And hollow, hollow, hollow all delight." What is uniquely Stevensian, here, is the hybrid creation of the ocean-bird-scholar and the startlingly complex effusion of marine fins, aerial beaks, and human personalia that pour forth from the intensities of the solitary scholar's feeling. He feels, after all, "everything."

In admitting the function in the formation of poetry of both animal instinct (in the bird) and emotional intellect (in the scholar feeling everything), Stevens can lay to rest his Darwinian suspicion that poetry might not be a form of knowledge. What he has discovered is the indispensable contribution of the poet's "invisible geography" to the "visible geography" of the Earth, a "geography"—as he wrote in an essay—that would be intolerable except for the nongeography that exists there" ("The Figure of the Youth as Virile Poet," 684).

What becomes of Stevens's speculative *if*s and *or*s and *but*s in his late work? These words cease for the most part to represent obstacles and become—to put it briefly—accretive, elaborative, and asymptotic instead of alternative and exclusive. In 1949, the thirty-one-canto sequence *An Ordinary Evening in New Haven* begins by announcing its subject—"The eye's plain version . . . , / The vulgate of experience"—and adds, "Of this, / A few words, an and yet, and yet, and yet—/ As part of the never-ending meditation" (307). The *and yet*s are resistant yet additive, like the turning leaves of a book in this "endlessly elaborating poem." Elaboration, rather than contradiction, has now become a fundamental principle of composition. And although Stevens begins *An Ordinary Evening* with two rebuttals—saying that the poem is "Part of the res itself and not about it," and that the poet speaks the poem "as it is, / Not as it was," these merely clear the ground for positive assertion. The space where the poem takes place is increasingly an ever-mobile and yet—because it is fixed in words—immobile present:

> The poem is the cry of its occasion,
> Part of the res itself and not about it.
> The poet speaks the poem as it is,

Not as it was[.]

. . . . .

                       . . . There is no

Tomorrow for him. . . .

. . . . .

The mobile and the immobile flickering
In the area between is and was are leaves,
Leaves burnished in autumnal burnished trees

And leaves in whirlings in the gutters, whirlings
Around and away, resembling the presence of thought,
Resembling the presences of thoughts, as if,

In the end, in the whole psychology, the self,
The town, the weather, in a casual litter,
Together, said words of the world are the life of the world.

(404)

Multiple truths here coexist additively without strain. The flickering is both mobile and immobile; the leaves exist (in life) in burnished trees and (as pages) in whirlings in the gutters; the leaves (as a single poem-gestalt) resemble the presence of thought while (as an evolving sequence of processes) they resemble the presences of thoughts. Just as the life of the world is multiple, so are the words of the world.

But by the end of *An Ordinary Evening in New Haven*—a poem that tends to abandon a materialistic poetry for a virtual one—even the accreting leaves and thoughts seem insufficiently immaterial symbols for the mind's attempt to create a coalescence of outer and inner reality. In Canto XXXI, Stevens represents "the edgings and inchings of final form" as activities by which desire asymptotically approaches its goal:

The swarming activities of the formulae
Of statement, directly and indirectly getting at,

Like an evening evoking the spectrum of violet,
A philosopher practicing scales on his piano,
A woman writing a note and tearing it up.

(417)

Each of these instantiations of "getting at" complements the others: we see the evening investigating more and more tints as it tries to evoke the whole spectrum of violet; a philosopher hoping to progress from scales to, say, a Chopin étude; a woman resorting to destruction so as to approach more nearly to perfection. The successive attempts in all these activities lead Stevens to his finest discrimination as he concludes that reality itself need not be conceived of in material terms:

> It is not in the premise that reality
> Is a solid. It may be a shade that traverses
> A dust, a force that traverses a shade.
> (417)

The first of Stevens's two closing suppositions calls attention to itself because it is unidiomatic: we do not normally refer to "a" dust. This traversable dust resembles the biblical pillar of cloud: it is a shape that we must interpret as our physical self imagined as the sum of its mortal collective atoms. This "dust" is sufficiently permeable to be traversed by a shade—a tint, a hue. Or, in the second of the suppositions, reality may be not a shade but a force—like gravity, like electricity—that traverses the self, which is now not a permeable dust, but a ghostly shade. We scarcely have words for these elusive and delicate traversings, but at least Stevens's language makes us aware that—as the title of a late poem asserts—"Reality Is an Activity of the Most August Imagination":

> There was an insolid billowing of the solid.
> Night's moonlight lake was neither water nor air.
> (472)

"Central experiment is one of the constants of the spirit which is inherent in a true record of experience." This 1948 statement by Stevens (823) suggests that what we have been following, in tracking the poet's hypotheses, contradictions, accretions, and asymptotic figures, is his struggle to render first philosophical "truth," then cubist perspectival "truths," then "a truth," something more personal and intimate. When he is seeking philosophical "truth," conceiving of it as an absolute, he relies on a dialectical *either/or* characterized by hypotheses and contradictions. When he is seeking perspectival "truths," he relies, as in "The Man with the Blue Guitar," on endless elaboration. When he is seeking "a" truth, he approaches it asymptotically, suggesting various metaphors, each of which comes in some way close to the essence of that goal.

There are many beautiful late poems with which to close my topic, but I want to single out two, both composed in 1954, Stevens's last full year of life. The first of these poems was written in March, the second in November. The March poem, "Not Ideas About the Thing but the Thing Itself," is significant as the piece with which Stevens chose to conclude his *Collected Poems*—the pendant to "Earthy Anecdote," with which the collection, and this essay, began. "Not Ideas About the Thing but the Thing Itself"—a Kantian title claiming knowledge of the *Ding-an-sich*—harks back to many earlier poems: the desolate winter poem "The Snow Man"; the poem called "The Sun This March" ("The exceeding brightness of this early sun / Makes me conceive how dark I have become"); the many bird poems; and the assertion in "An Ordinary Evening in New Haven" that the poem is the "cry" of its occasion. In "Not Ideas About the Thing but the Thing Itself," Stevens's voice is the (lowercase) "c" that preceded the choir; the lowercase exemplifies the humility of the old, by contrast with Stevens's earlier self-naming in uppercase "C" in "The Comedian as the Letter C." "Not Ideas" exhibits the familiar counters *but, not, or,* and *like,* but uses them without the uncertainty that used to attend their presence in Stevens's poems.

The plot of "Not Ideas" is a simple one: an aged speaker who has doubted that he would live to see another spring wakes up uncertain whether the bird-cry he has heard is real or part of a dream. The poem traces his growing conviction that it is real: yes, the sound must be coming from outside because the advancing season is confirmed by the earlier rising of a rejuvenated sun; and though the pale sun and the scrawny cry are merely premonitory heralds of the "colossal sun" and the "choir" yet to come, the eventual grandeur of the much desired spring is already implicit in its inception. The leap of the heart as the speaker realizes that the axis of the seasons has turned, that spring is miraculously his once again, is like "a new knowledge of reality." We can watch, here, how all the early torturing words of uncertainty—*but, not, seem, like, or, part*—are now recruited to play felicitous parts in a drama of the renewal of life:

Not Ideas About the Thing but the Thing Itself

At the earliest ending of winter,
In March, a scrawny cry from outside
Seemed like a sound in his mind.

He knew that he heard it,
A bird's cry, at daylight or before,
In the early March wind.

The sun was rising at six,
No longer a battered panache above snow . . .
It would have been outside.

It was not from the vast ventriloquism
Of sleep's faded papier-mâché . . .
The sun was coming from outside.

That scrawny cry—it was
A chorister whose c preceded the choir.
It was part of the colossal sun,

Surrounded by its choral rings,
Still far away. It was like
A new knowledge of reality.

(451)

Stevens could not sustain this spring joy. "The Region November," written five months before he was diagnosed with advanced stomach cancer, reveals that every sign of the mind's lively responses—conjectures, hypotheses, qualifications, comparisons, contradictions—can be abolished by the inertia of age and illness. In "The Region November," the title suggests that the month has become the space to which living has been reduced. As the poet hears the north wind, he watches it compel the monotonous swaying of the treetops. The trees say only the same thing, over and over, without fluctuation, modulation, correction, apposition, or speculation. They display the melancholy of the contentless, even if effortful, agglutinative inertial repetitions of age, void of any substance, divine, material, or human. The rich American wilderness of "Sunday Morning" has become a waste land of spiritual entropy:

The Region November

It is hard to hear the north wind again,
And to watch the treetops, as they sway.

They sway, deeply and loudly, in an effort,
So much less than feeling, so much less than speech,

Saying and saying, the way things say
On the level of that which is not yet knowledge:

A revelation not yet intended.
It is like a critic of God, the world,

And human nature, pensively seated
On the waste throne of his own wilderness.

Deeplier, deeplier, loudlier, loudlier,
The trees are swaying, swaying, swaying.

(472)

It is like Stevens to counter the benign and inclusive elaboration of his late phase, visible in the prophesied springtime expansion of "Not Ideas," with its desolate reverse, the agglutinative elaboration of the meaningless into a repetitive swaying and a predicateless saying. Even Ha-eé-me had his conjugal beast and its meaningful, if minute, sonic oscillation—tip-tap-tap. But here tautology rules: deep is deep and loud is loud and *deeplier, deeplier, loudlier, loudlier* repeat a single monotonous sound that leads to no crescendo of promised being such as the colossal sun and its surrounding choir. In "The Region November," the mind is in abeyance, and with it, all its wonderful speculative instruments.

Recalling earlier poems, we can say that here the bucks have no firecat, the landscape no measuring singer, the world no cornucopia of parts, the guitar player no instrument, the world no responsive audience of men and women, the earth no scholar-bird effusing personalia. It is here, feeling the lack of the exhilarating Stevensian mimesis of the mind's fluctuations, that we realize that even in thematic bleakness, Stevens was above all a poet of fertility of verbal invention. His swerves, hypotheses, contradictions, hybridities, cubist multiplicities, accretive elaborations, and asymptotic progressions establish in his poetry a mental landscape anything but bleak, one that matches the distributed richness of the material world with its own unfailing wealth of emotional, intellectual, and linguistic forms.

13

Ardor and Artifice

Merrill's Mozartian Touch

The poet James Merrill (1926–1995) was wealthy (by a trust from his father, Charles Merrill, of Merrill Lynch), finely educated (first by a governess who spoke French and German, then by St. Bernard's, Lawrenceville, and Amherst), and homosexual. His poetry reflects all of these facts, but in no plain manner. Merrill was unafraid of swathing in a sinuous syntax all the words and languages that he knew, not to speak of practicing most of the lyric forms invented by the Western tradition. He became unafraid, as time went on, of being explicitly homosexual in his chronicling of the affections. His poetics was not one to please an anti-intellectual and homophobic public; in fact, the *Times,* in an editorial, stung by the award of Yale's Bollingen Prize to Merrill's "Braving the Elements," objected to it on January 16, 1973. Supposedly, the critique was aimed not at Merrill himself ("a poet of solid accomplishment and sure craftsmanship") but, rather, at the taste of the administrators of the prize, for believing that "poetry is a hermetic cultivation of one's sensibility and a fastidious manipulation of received forms." Setting up Whitman as a counterexample, the *Times* thundered, "There is a whole world west of New Haven." I mention this only to show what Merrill was up against in persisting on his path.

Merrill's work falls into two parts: a late seventeen-thousand-line "epic visionary poem" (his editors' description) issued in parts between 1976 and 1980, and published in its entirety in 1982 under the title "The Changing Light at Sandover"; and an exquisite body of lyrics assembled in *James Merrill: Collected Poems,* edited by Merrill's fellow poets and appreciative critics J. D. McClatchy and Stephen Yenser. "Sandover"—because of its Ouija-board origins, its massiveness, and its difficulty—got the lion's share of critical attention during the poet's later years. Now the balance may be righted to emphasize what many of us think of as Merrill's best work—his lyric poems.

Proust and James were the godfathers of Merrill's syntax; Auden of his experiments in form; and Constantine Cavafy (1863–1933)—the Greek lyric poet of homosexual encounters—the patron of his sexual explicitness. Merrill was unashamed of his allusiveness; his relation to literary tradition was convivial rather than oppositional. The rebellious Anglophobic strain of American literary primitivism was not to his taste, any more than it was to Eliot's; both Eliot and Merrill thought of the European literary tradition as fully theirs, and fully America's. How could it be otherwise if one's mind had been formed by Dante and Valéry and Rilke?

Merrill was not admired by those American writers and reviewers who tended to repudiate European literature as the fruit of what they considered an exclusive and exclusionary tradition. He nonetheless proceeded intrepidly through their accusations of snobbery, affectation, preciousness, artifice, perversity, and élitism. He once said in his own defense, speaking of his use of formal meters and stanza forms:

> The attention they require at once frees and channels the unconscious, as Auden kept reminding us. Even if your poem turns out badly, you've learned something about proportion and concision and selflessness. And at best the form "received" by the next poet to use it will have taken on a new aspect because of what you learned there.[1]

Although he never had a job (aside from short stints at teaching), Merrill worked intensely at poetry as a daily occupation, writing for fifty years about lovers, friends, opera, travel, landscape, and his various homes: an apartment in New York that had belonged to his grandmother and beloved houses in Stonington, Athens, and (later) Key West.

Merrill's chief subject, emotionally speaking, is the pain occasioned through relations with parents and lovers; yet he is a comic writer, not a tragic one, and persists in making the pain yield gracefully either to solace or to insight ("Think of music. . . . You don't *end* pieces with a dissonance"; CP, 118). What he is drawn to, as he says in "Nine Lives," is the complex blend of joy and poignancy in Mozartian comedy:

> There is a moment comedies beget
> When escapade and hubbub die away,

Vows are renewed, masks dropped, La Folle Journée
Arriving star by star at a septet.
It's then the connoisseur of your bouquet
(Who sits dry-eyed through *Oedipus* or *Lear*)
Will shed, O Happiness, a furtive tear.[2]

A Mozartian treatment of love became, for much of his life, Merrill's occupation. After the appearance of love-as-rapture in the early poetry, the inevitable frayings in intimate relations began to demand their say, and an elegiac tone, present in "The Summer People," tinged the poetry as Tenderness met Time:

These two are the past masters
Of rime, tone, overtone.
They write upon our faces
Until the pen strikes bone.

Time passes softly, scarcely
Felt by me or you.
And then, at an odd moment,
Tenderness passes, too.

(281)

"To preserve the lyric impulse during the middle years," Merrill once wrote, "is no easy matter."

The last poems, as Merrill anticipated his own death from AIDS, made gallantry their final form of comic resolution. In "164 East 72nd Street," a friend ventures a question:

"Do you ever wonder where you'll—" Oh my dear,
Asleep somewhere, or at the wheel. Not here. . . .
                              The point's to live in style,
Not to drop dead in it.

(661)

In fact, Merrill died just as he was discharged from a brief hospital stay in Tucson, still up and about, still traveling. A few months before his death, emaciated and frail, he had attended a gathering in his honor at Washington

University in Saint Louis, courteously giving every appearance of interest and pleasure.

Merrill lived in style, in both senses of the phrase. It is true that his earliest poems were often driven more by style than by feeling, becoming a "melodic, empty-headed *fin de siècle* sort of thing," as he once said. The last poems in his first book, though, were ones in which he felt "humanly more involved. . . . 'Real' experience had grazed them, somehow." As the inseparability of manner and matter grew, style and subject began to converge rather than to run on parallel planes. The poet's need for arbitrarily complex stanza forms receded: "I'm no less formal now," he said in a 1968 interview, "but I no longer dote on elaborate stanzas." (That wasn't entirely true, but in the later work elaborate stanzas were less the motive for the work than its obbligato accompaniment.)

The poems of Merrill's first book, *The Black Swan*, in spite of their obliquity, reveal the young poet's sense of himself as a misfit. His first self-image in the title poem is that of a solitary black swan, which, unlike the harmonious white swans, "draws / A private chaos warbling in its wake." Its neck is like a question mark; its swan song is silence; but it succeeds in transforming "time's damage" by finding "sorrow's lost secret center," which exhibits, of all things, a maypole that prefigures Merrill's determined lifelong creation of bliss in the face of blight:

> Enchanter: the black swan has learned to enter
> > Sorrow's lost secret center
> Where like a maypole separate tragedies
> Are wound about a tower of ribbons.
> (3)

The child-Merrill ends the poem crying "aloud / In anguish: I love the black swan." A tenacity in sticking by his socially "wrong" choices was to persist both in Merrill's life (as, defying his parents' wish that he be "All Boy," he established a household with his friend, the writer and artist David Jackson) and in his work (as he refused the demotic plainness of expression that might have pleased the *Times*).

In another prescient early poem, "Variations: The Air Is Sweetest That a Thistle Guards," Merrill announces love as his chief subject, placing it under the sign of Stendhal, "for whom love was / So frankly the highest good":

> Love merely as the best
> There is, and one would make the best of that

By saying how it grows and in what climates, . . .
To say at the end, however we find it, good,
Bad, or indifferent, it helps us, and the air
Is sweetest there. The air is very sweet.
(22)

There are many problems (encountered by Western poets from Petrarch on) in electing "love" as a subject, and almost all appear in Merrill: the felt contrast between an altruistic concept of morals and the narcissism and opportunism of erotic experience; the self-incrimination that follows on mistaken choice; the repetition-compulsion that convicts one, eventually, of apparently irremediable stupidity in love matters; the tendency of sexual intensity to fade; the incongruity of erotic feeling in an aging body; infidelity to a life partner. One of the compelling and page-turning attractions of the poems is viewing the author's unsparing self-analysis (conducted on the best Stendhalian principles) as the years and volumes pass before the reader's eye.

In love, Merrill is ever "pulled two ways at once by the distant star / Called Plenitude and the bald planet Ebb" (29), recognizing, even in the first book, his own complicity in the ending of any love affair: "It appears we seek whatever we do seek only / That we may cry Enough!" (46). The lasting hope is that art may transmute the disappointments of life into something more radiant and stable; the lasting bitterness is that although art may guide "what pangs there be / Into a bearable choreography" (49), it does not repair the original life-rift.

As he recognized the irrational recurrence of erotic compulsion, Merrill came sometimes to think of himself—of all of us—as puppets of the god Eros (later enlarged in "Sandover" to "God B," the "B" standing for "biology"). As a young man, the poet was shocked by his possession by Eros, a reaction manifest in the 1959 poem "The Dunes." The dunes are relieved at their escape from the jaws of the ocean: "at last a way / Out of its insane frothing, those white jaws / In which they were nothing." Yet there remains a subterranean desire to repeat the experience—"a certain creeper yearning seaward / Over a dry admonitory drift"—and soon enough there appear in the poem "a burning couple far away":

Absolute innocence, fiery, mild. And yet
Soon even they were lost behind the dunes.
(82)

Since no one can pretend for very long to the "absolute innocence" of those lovers, Merrill takes on, in the same volume, the foreseeably successive nature of his present and future love affairs. His surrogate becomes the phoenix, forever dying in its bed of flame and then resurrecting itself from the ashes:

> So that a sumptuous monotony
> Sets in, a pendulum of amethysts
> In the shape of a bird, keyed up for ever fiercer
> Flights between ardor and ashes. . . .
>   And in the end, despite
> Its pyrotechnic curiosity, the process
> Palls.
>
> (110)

Up to this point, Merrill has represented himself as helpless under the onslaught of desire. Nonetheless, his future reminiscences—comic, poignant—never entirely absolve him from responsibility, and he begins to see, in his thirties, his poetic duty: to admit the darker and more repellent side of life, love, and his own promiscuity. After a new experiment in love, he swears an oath to a new poetics:

> Upon that book I swear
> To abide by what it teaches:
> Gospels of ugliness and waste,
> Of towering voids, of soiled gusts,
> Of a shrieking to be faced
> Full into, eyes astream with cold—
>
> With cold?
> All right then. With self-knowledge.
>
> (128)

The problem with this vocabulary of ugliness, waste, and soiled gusts is that it doesn't lend itself to a poetics of comedy. The intricate task Merrill took on, during the rest of his writing life, was to enfold love's worser moments—ranging from the minor irritants of quarrels and disappointments to the major scars of betrayal and death—in a light and gauzy texture, to lift them by sheer style to the essentially comic realm of the seen and seen-through. The meta-

phors of tragedy—abysses, cyclones, shrieks—were replaced by the metaphors of comedy: theatre, prisms, magicians. The tone of doom was lightened
by the diction of the everyday: seeing in Istanbul the emptiness of Hagia So-
phia (which has passed from cathedral to mosque to "flame- / less void"), and
feeling an interior resemblance between his own mind and the cathedral's
"transcendental skull," he remarks dryly to himself that he had cooperated in
his own decline:

> You'd let go
> Learning and faith as well, you too had wrecked
> Your precious sensibility. What else did you expect?
> (177)

The last stage in this lightening of the tragic by the texture of the comic is
reached in "Family Week at Oracle Ranch," a wonderfully funny and sad sequence (twelve poems composed in *abca* quatrains). We are in Merrill's last
volume, *A Scattering of Salts,* and the poet's lover is spending a month at a
therapeutic center. The poet does not feel much hope that Oracle Ranch will
help their strained relationship, and his flippant scorn trails off in wistfulness:

> As if a month at what it invites us to think
> Is little more than a fat farm for Anorexics,
> Substance Abusers, Love & Relationship Addicts
> Could help *you,* light of my life, when even your shrink . . .
> (654)

The poet, as he visits and participates in some of the doings for "Family
Week," is first appalled by the crudity of the psychology of the place and its
clichés: one is allowed only seven words ("AFRAID, / HURT, LONELY, etc.") with
which to express oneself.

> The connoisseur of feeling throws up his hands:
> Used to depicting personal anguish
>
> With a full palette—hues, oils, glazes, thinner—
> He stares into these withered wells and feels,
> Well . . . SAD and ANGRY?
> (655)

Astonishingly, the old words work, in all their worn familiarity, better than his fancy ones. He watches satirically the transparent theatrical strategies of the "counsellors"—Gestalt therapy with a teddy bear (oneself as a child), finding a "safe place" in the room when the group therapy becomes acrimonious, visualizing one's childhood home, enumerating and regrieving past griefs, and listening to therapeutic mantras ("You are a brave and special person"). Yet, for all Merrill's resistance, the tricks succeed: at the visualization of "home," "Tears have begun to flow / Unhindered down my face. Why? / Because nobody's there" (657).

It's evident that Merrill's response to the psychic magic is not uncorroded by doubt as to the long-term efficacy of the seven therapeutic words. Yet the plunge into primal expression ("SAD") and schematic remembrance ("home") has occasioned not only satire directed at Oracle Ranch and its language but also a rueful acknowledgment of the elementary nature of feeling, no matter how elaborate its eventual transmutation into art.

By the end of Merrill's life, a broad democracy of suffering replaces both the youthful isolation of the earliest work and the somewhat larger, but still restricted, social compass of the middle poems. As "Family Week at Oracle Ranch" amply shows, Merrill has become far more interested in American culture, low as well as high, and has redefined the "love lyric" not necessarily as the secretive record of phoenix ecstasy (or even phoenix monotony) but as a part of a contemporary social canvas. The poet can admit that his emotional life doesn't differ very much from that of other people. As "Ken" the counsellor says:

> We hope that we have shown you just how much
> You have in common with everybody else.
> Not to be "terminally unique"
>
> Will be the consolation you take home.
>
> (659–660)

Merrill, who had begun by thinking of himself as a "terminally unique" black swan, discovers an odd relief in this.

Since, as Merrill once said, "the Muse matures with her poet," his second large subject, art—standing in for the larger subject of consciousness itself—changes, like love, over time. How do we receive, sift, symbolize, and stylize our experience? It wasn't always clear to Merrill, rhetorically speaking, whether his patron was to be the divine Apollo or Apollo's mortal rival, Marsyas (flayed to death for his ambition). In a wonderful 1959 sonnet, Marsyas sets up the opposition between his own demotic verses and his rival Apollo's lofty forms:

> I used to write in the café sometimes:
> Poems on menus, read all over town
> Or talked out before ever written down.
> One day a girl brought in his latest book.
> I opened it—stiff rhythms, gorgeous rhymes—
> And made a face.

But Marsyas, flayed and hanged, loses out to Apollo:

> They found me dangling where his golden wind
> Inflicted so much music on the lyre
> That no one could have told you what he sang.
> (96)

Apollo's is a Paterian poetry that overwhelms sheerly by its music, a poetry in which the matter is subordinate to the manner. Merrill tried, in his youth, under the influence of "the impenetrable quatrains of Mallarmé," to "create a surface of such impenetrability and, at the same time, such beauty that it wouldn't yield up a meaning easily, if at all. Maybe eventually one gets tired of that kind of thing, though in my weak moments I still find myself drawn to it" (CP, 21). By the time of this sonnet, however, the poet is already visibly tempted by the colloquial voice of Marsyas, which gets along without the "stiff rhythms, gorgeous rhymes" of Apollo.

The rivalry between Apollo and Marsyas for Merrill's soul never faded. "Oracle Ranch" is largely written in the everyday tone of Marsyas (who became a more dominant figure as Merrill increasingly allowed himself a relaxed and conversational style). But even in the last poems, Merrill is still obsessed, as an artist, with understanding the secret life of language. Language begins with the letter, progresses to the word, advances to the rhyme, and ends in the stanza. In a 1995 poem called "b o d y," the individual letters interest Merrill in their shape, their symbolism, and their sound. As Merrill, mortally ill, thinks of his body, so soon to disappear, the letters of the alphabet begin to glow with their own significance. The "o" seems to him like a little black-outlined moon; "b" and "d" not only incorporate "o" in their graphic shapes but also can become shorthand for "birth" and "death"; and "y," sounded out, says "Why." Reflections of this sort bring "b o d y" into being:

> Look closely at the letters. Can you see,
> entering (stage right), then floating full,
> then heading off—so soon—
> how like a little kohl-rimmed moon
> *o* plots her course from *b* to *d*
>
> —as *y*, unanswered, knocks at the stage door?
> (646)

The pang in "so soon—" gives pathos to the little journey of the deathwards "o."

Not all poets are so minutely interested in the tiniest elements of language: each poet has, so to speak, a chief plane of linguistic interest—sonic, etymological, lexical. Merrill is unusual in that almost every plane of the linguistic, including the pun (a taste he shared with Keats), appeals to him. He possessed an enormous facility in rhyme, but he also enjoyed its simplest games, such as finding words that enclosed within themselves a more or less exact rhyme word: "dread" and "read," "heart" and "art," "stairs" and "stars," "shame" and "same." Struck by the vowel change from "a" to "oo" in the phrase "the man in the moon," he assembles (in another game) words or parts of words that resemble each other except for the middle vowel, and makes a song out of them. This is the first half of the poem, set as he somewhat unwillingly flies (emotionally and literally) from Byzantium:

> Up spoke the man in the moon:
> "What does that moan mean?
> The plane was part of the plan.
> Why gnaw the bone of a boon?"
>
> I said with spleen, "Explain
> These nights that tie me in knots,
> All drama and no dream,
> While you lampoon my pain."
>
> He then: "Lusters are least
> Dimmed among the damned.

The point's to live, love,
Not shake your fist at the feast."
(252)

For many readers—and even many critics—writing this way is merely doing tatting around the edges of art. And although this dialogue certainly doesn't represent the height of Merrill's accomplishment, the curiosity about sounds that it displays lies behind the surprise of many of his beautiful and unusual rhymes. Merrill enjoys the wit of finding "bath to" as a rhyme for "Matthew," or "décor" as a rhyme for "war," but his real genius, in terms of form, is to write rhyming narrative stanzas that ripple effortlessly down the page. (Less skillful hands tend to distort something—sense, rhythm, syntax—to force rhymes into place.) Here is a short incident (rhyming *abba*) from the close of a 1972 poem, "Up and Down." Merrill's mother has taken him down to the bank vault where the jewels his father had given her are stored. She wants to give her son one of her rings, an emerald, so that he can give it to his future bride (keeping up the pretense that someday there will *be* a bride):

> She next picks out a ring. "He gave
> Me this when you were born. Here, take it for—
>
> For when you marry. For your bride. It's yours."
> A den of greenest light, it grows, shrinks, glows,
> Hermetic stanza bedded in the prose
> Of the last thirty semiprecious years.
>
> I do not tell her, it would sound theatrical,
> *Indeed this green room's mine, my very life.*
> *We are each other's; there will be no wife;*
> *The little feet that patter here are metrical.*
>
> But onto her worn knuckle slip the ring.
> Wear it for me, I silently entreat,
> Until—until the time comes. Our eyes meet.
> The world beneath the world is brightening.
> (342)

Later poems adopt stanza forms freer than this. An ironic and touching self-elegy called "Self-Portrait in Tyvek (TM) Windbreaker," in the last book, amuses itself rhyming "crystals" with "whistles," "puffins" with "coffins," using an eight-line stanza for which the only fixed rule is that the first line must rhyme with the last, and at least two rhymed lines must be found within. In his self-portrait, Merrill—once again the culture critic—is describing the New Age shop where he bought his world-map-imprinted white Tyvek Windbreaker:

> I found it in one of those vaguely imbecile
> Emporia catering to the collective unconscious
> Of our time and place. This one featured crystals,
> Cassettes of whalesong and rain-forest whistles,
> Barometers, herbal cosmetics, pillows like puffins,
> Recycled notebooks, mechanized lucite coffins
> For sapphire waves that crest, break, and recede,
> As they presumably do in nature still.
>
> (669)

By the end of his life, Merrill can sketch in this easy and deft way anything that passes under his alert eye, and find for his description a flowing line and a chiming rhyme.

If you like poetry composed (in Hopkins's words) in "the current language heightened," Merrill will please you. If you like a wry refraction of contemporary institutions, from "imbecile emporia" to therapeutic ranches; if you have despaired of finding words subtle enough for all that goes on between lovers over time; if you are delighted by poetic invention, Merrill will please you. If you are eager for a window into the pangs and pleasures of gay existence, or if you want to know what a person of ever-attentive receptivity might have seen between 1926 and 1995, Merrill will please you.

Above all, if you value lightness of touch, Merrill will please you. He tells, in a Class Day talk he gave at Amherst College, of a speech by the former president of the college introducing a reading by Robert Frost: " 'The winkles,' said Dr. Cole, 'the winkles that you see on Mr. Fwost's bwow do not come from old age or wowwy, but the weight of the wreath' " (CP, 351). The weight of the wreath is heavy on all poets, but Merrill rarely allowed the weight to be felt, or the wrinkles to show.

14

The Titles

A. R. Ammons, 1926–2001

> I hope my philosophy will turn
> out all right and turn out to be a philosophy so as
> to free people (any who are trapped, as I have been)
>
> from seeking any image in the absolute or seeking
> any absolute whatsoever except nothingness:
> —"Hibernaculum"

Poets invite us into their volumes by the titles they choose; and at the end of a poet's life, the work often becomes symbolically represented by the successive volume-titles: we can think of Robert Frost's *North of Boston* and *New Hampshire;* or Eliot's *The Waste Land* and *Four Quartets*, or Lowell's *Life Studies* and *History;* or Bishop's *North and South* and *Geography III*. Now that, to our grief, the canon of A. R. Ammons's work has closed, what will we find of him symbolically present in his volume-titles? There are twenty of them—not counting such titles as *Selected Longer Poems*—and they are:[1]

> *Ommateum, with Doxology* (1955)
> *Expressions of Sea Level* (1964)
> *Corsons Inlet* (1965)
> *Tape for the Turn of the Year* (1965)
> *Northfield Poems* (1966)
> *Uplands* (1970)
> *Briefings: Poems Small and Easy* (1971)
> *Sphere: The Form of a Motion* (1974)
> *Diversifications* (1975)
> *The Snow Poems* (1977)

Highgate Road (1977)

A Coast of Trees (1981)

Worldly Hopes (1982)

Lake Effect Country (1983)

Sumerian Vistas (1987)

Garbage (1993)

The North Carolina Poems (1994)

Brink Road (1996)

Glare (1997)

Bosh and Flapdoodle (2005)[2]

We begin with the 1955 *Ommateum, with Doxology,* the title of that slim vanity-press volume that brought in, as royalties for its first year (as Ammons once told me) four four-cent stamps, and that is now, as a rare book, valued almost beyond price. Alexander Pope, in *The Essay on Man*, had asked, ironically, "Why has not man a microscopic eye? / For this plain reason, man is not a fly." Ammons's title, refuting Pope, tells us that he aspires to the fly's compound eye—its ommateum—that sees its surroundings from every angle, not merely from one. This god's-eye—or fly's-eye—view commands an instantaneous and spatial omniscience. In his foreword to that first volume, Ammons announced his lifelong themes: "fear of the loss of identity, the appreciation of transient natural beauty, the conflict between the individual and the group, the chaotic particle in the classical field, the creation of false gods to serve real needs." And he defined his poetic form: "While maintaining a perspective from the hub, the poet ventures out in each poem to explore one of the numberless radii of experience. The poems suggest a many-sided view of reality; an adoption of tentative, provisional attitudes, replacing the partial, unified, prejudicial, and rigid."[3] The word *Ommateum* reminds us of Ammons's training as a scientist; he is the first American poet to use scientific language with manifest ease and accuracy, as part of his natural vocabulary—and this is one of his great contributions to the language of modern poetry. But an even greater contribution is his exposition of a philosophical view of humanity built on the constructs of modern science: we are matter that came from energy and that will dissolve back into a slush of energy. Ammons did not find this view of life incompatible with the deepest human affections and gratitude for them, as the second half of his title tells us; nor was it incompatible with his conviction of the importance of the invisible realm, from the perfect spheres of geometrical abstraction to the physical laws governing the immense motions of the universe to the creative human spirit itself. *Ommateum, with Doxology,* a title combining science and thanksgiving, bravely began Ammons's heterodox form of poetry.

The titles of the two following volumes, *Expressions of Sea Level* (1963), and *Corsons Inlet* (1965) reflect Ammons's experience of the Atlantic shore. Though he was born inland, Ammons grew to know the sea well in his wartime Navy watches in the Pacific. In New Jersey, walking by the sea, he came into intimate relation with the coastal landscape. The poem that made him famous is the title poem of his third volume, *Corsons Inlet,* which is less an ars poetica—though it is that—than a poem declaring itself for freedom and variability and a consciously expanding mental universe. Though psychic terror is still present in the poet, it arises now from nature and not from the pulpit threatening divine wrath. Order, as Ammons sees it, is not an imposed and static system, but rather something that springs from an accumulation of small physical events, "orders as summaries," and with this view, the poet finds, "there is serenity":

> no arranged terror: no forcing of image, plan,
> or thought:
> no propaganda, no humbling of reality to precept:
>
> terror pervades but is not arranged, all possibilities
> of escape open:[4]

"Corsons Inlet" symbolizes experience as a walk—a different walk each day, with no permanent stopping-place—a conviction insisted on by Ammons's lifelong use of the colon in preference to the period. Like *Ommateum,* with its compound eye, *Corsons Inlet* aspires to a form of omniscience, but Ammons now locates omniscience in a temporal unfolding, as he embraces it in a walk, rather than in the instantaneous glance of a compound eye. The poems of the two New Jersey volumes testify not only to Ammons's lifelong capacity for attachment to a specific place—first, his North Carolina farm country, and, after New Jersey, Ithaca, but also to his love of persons—especially Nelly Myers, a household member in his childhood—and of animals—Sparkle, his hog, and Silver, his mule.

Ammons's intense response to the unscrolling of time, which he first acted out fully in the walk around Corsons Inlet, was repeated in the quixotic enterprise of composing a long poem in short lines on a roll of adding-machine tape, resulting in the 1965 volume *Tape for the Turn of the Year.* In that poem-volume,

Ammons charts not only the absolute length of a fragment of time but also the changes, even the most minuscule ones, taking place within it. The wintry "turn of the year" often found the poet depressed; in both *Tape for the Turn of the Year* and the 1977 *Snow Poems* there is a time of complete cessation of poetry, weeks of cold and darkness in which no poem stirs in the mind. Ammons's strong responses to the deaths and resurrections of the natural world mirrored his own oscillation between extreme emotional poles—from panic to joy, or from miserable anxiety to hope. His great poem, "Easter Morning," to which I'll return, finds a redemption from such torturing extremes of feeling in the simultaneous eddyings and order of the natural universe, symbolized—when the desolate beginning of the poem comes to a conclusion—in the varying but stable routes of great migratory birds, one of the many signs of the turn of the year always observed by the poet.

Ammons continued his habit of drawing titles from place-names and landscape in the 1966 *Northfield Poems* (from Northfield, New Jersey, where his wife, Phyllis, came from and where they lived after their marriage), the 1977 privately printed *Highgate Road* (named after a road in Ithaca), and the 1970 *Uplands*, as well as in the 1994 *North Carolina Poems*. Despite their titles grounded in the earth, the first three of these often rose sharply to philosophical abstraction. In them Ammons formulated his shapely poetical helices, poems inhabiting the upper regions of his worldview. But in the 1971 title *Briefings*, Ammons departed from his place-titles to call attention to form itself rather than to content: the very short poems of *Briefings* offered, like the items in Thoreau's notebooks, briefings on and briefings to the world expressed with epigrammatic concision.

Although Ammons brought the short abstract lyric to a quintessential perfection in *Northfield Poems*, *Uplands*, and *Briefings*, he also wanted to write the sort of poetry that, in Beckett's words, "includes the mess" of life. Writing long poems is a way to include the mess, and the oscillation between very short poems and very long poems is one that has attracted many of our poets British and American: we can see it in Blake and Wordsworth, Merrill and Ashbery, as well as in Ammons. Long poems are not congenial, perhaps, to the "purest" lyric poets, those without any sustained wish to expound a "philosophy" or to burden their poems with novelistic detail: George Herbert, Robert Herrick, Emily Dickinson, and Elizabeth Bishop come to mind as such poets. But Ammons, like Wordsworth, had a life-project: it was to formulate the consciousness of the poet as it must operate in a secular, scientific, and, above all, information-laden environment. "The Growth of a Poet's Mind"—the subtitle given on publication to *The Prelude*—would equally well describe Ammons's long poems. They delineate the intellectual and imaginative scope of the poetic mind in the twentieth century.

Sphere, Ammons's 1974 volume, adopts a title belonging to solid geometry and chooses a subtitle—*The Form of a Motion*—apparently more proper to calculus and the physics of dynamic systems than to poetry. About the volume and its title, Ammons once said:

> *Sphere* had the image of the whole earth, then for the first time seen on television, at its center. I guess it was about 1972. There was the orb. And it seemed to me the perfect image to put at the center of a reconciliation of One-Many forces. . . . The earth seemed to be the actual body around which these forces could best be represented.[5]

Such a title draws our attention to the Platonic side of Ammons's mind—the side that wanted to draw in a lyric a perfect two-dimensional arc and then from it create, via a long poem, a perfect three-dimensional sphere and set it in motion. The extreme idealism of Ammons's yearning for achieved perfection struggled with his refusal to accept an inhuman perfection that could not include lowly things ever engaged in an evolutionary dynamic.

Sphere, we are not surprised to find, was followed by a countertruth of dispersal in the 1975 volume of short poems called *Diversifications*. Diversification of species is a formal drive of Darwinian selection, as natural to poets as to flora and fauna; and with this title Ammons is again, as he was in the earlier title *Briefings*, creating an aesthetic pun: versification, when multiplied, yields diversifications—in this case a multitude of short, pungent lyrics closing with the long lyric "Pray without Ceasing," in which the poet, usually apolitical in verse, mentions, and judges, the war in Vietnam.

Ammons's 1977 title, *The Snow Poems*, offers us a return to the natural world after the abstract titles *Briefings*, *Sphere*, and *Diversifications*. *The Snow Poems* suggests that the weather, as the most complex of visible dynamic systems, is the best symbol for human moods. For Ammons, the weather plays the role that color plays in painting (and we might recall that Ammons was a painter in his spare time). Just as each collocation of colors has for both painter and spectator its own emotional weight, and each collocation of words, for both writer and reader, has its own atmosphere, so the weather—down to its minutest aspects—determines the "feel" on our skin and our senses of any given day. Ammons (resembling in this Hopkins and Frost) was an expert weather watcher; he could sense the humidity, the temperature, the wind direction, the cloud movements, the weight of snow on a branch, the strength of ice-retaining twigs, the force of water as it splits rock. His assemblages of weather facts are in truth assemblages of soul facts; but his role as reporter on the soul did not prevent the *Snow Poems* from being also a theatre of the absurd: its Sternian pages allow typewriter doodles, concrete poetry, verbal games, collapses into bathos, jokes (including dirty jokes), and almost anything personally embarrassing to the writer. Ammons fought a long battle with lyric decorum, determined as he was to represent fully even the unpleasant aspects of daily life, even if such a reso- lution meant—as in a late poem published in the *New Yorker*—reporting on lugging large jugs of urine to the doctor's office for tests. Characteristically, Ammons discovers, during the early depressing errand, the beauty of dawn snow, untouched but for his footprints.

A Coast of Trees, the volume published in 1981, has a title that does not give us much information; we see in it a landscape of earth, water, and trees. This is Ammons's way of giving us the generality from which the poet must deduce his minute particulars, as the title poem, "Coast of Trees," affirms: "with nothing, we turn to the cleared particular, not more / nor less than itself." A coast of trees is a landscape distinctly different from Ammons's perennial mountains, Biblical desert, or backyard or farm or creek. A coast is a humanly friendly, but larger-than-human, vista; because it has trees it must have water and shade and birds and grass, and is therefore a place conceived of as beau- tiful; but it is also uninhabited. The title gives us nature as habitable but as yet uncivilized, the rural but not the agricultural or the domesticated. It is not sublime, and therefore not Wordsworthian or Shelleyan; it is not yet accultur- ated to man, therefore not Frostian; it has no fauna, therefore not Mooresque; it is not urban, therefore not Williamsesque. *A Coast of Trees* is a painter's title. *Lake Effect Country* (1983), which follows *Worldly Hopes*, is another reminder of Ammons's domestication in Ithaca, where the most salient geographical fact is the presence of Lake Cayuga, which modifies the weather it undergoes, just as the idiosyncratic spirit of the poet modifies the successive weathers of the soul inflicted on him.

Worldly Hopes (1982), on the other hand, is a title drawn from Ammons's Protestant upbringing. We all know what worldly hopes come to, in religious systems; but if we are not religious, what can we have but worldly hopes? Am- mons's secularism operates always in a dialectic with religious language, to which he often resorts as the best formulation we yet have of certain longings and certain dilemmas. But he always uses religious terms in a secular, and some- times ironic, context, as he does in this title. The volume allows itself bursts of anger, as in the poem called "The Role of Society in the Artist": after initially repudiating the artist, society grovels to him once he becomes famous, and the artist, although he pretends gratitude, "every night went out / into the forest to spew fire / that blazoned tree trunks and set / stumps afire." Such occasional bitterness puts into relief the self-conquest that generates Ammons's mildness and humor.

The 1987 title *Sumerian Vistas* came to Ammons's younger readers as something of a surprise. How did we get from Ithaca to Sumer? Older readers would remember the Sumerian grave and its inhabitant described in "Requiem," a poem from *Expressions of Sea Level:*

> Returning silence unto silence,
> the Sumerian between the rivers lies. . . .
> The incantations, sheep trades, and night-gatherings
>   with central leaping fires,
> roar and glare still in the crow's-foot
> walking of his stylus on clay.[6]

Sumer is the culture where writing began, in the cuneiform inscriptions made on clay tablets; and the poet's reversion, in the title *Sumerian Vistas,* to the ancient world reminds us of another of Ammons's invocations of ancientness. His first symbolic name for himself, voiced in 1955 when he was in his late twenties, was the Biblical and prophetic name Ezra, borne by a school friend and adopted in order to give himself—an acutely shy and unrecognized person—authority to speak. He eventually placed this self-naming as the first item in his 1971 *Collected Poems:*

> So I said I am Ezra
> and the wind whipped my throat
> gaming for the sounds of my voice . . .
> Turning to the sea I said
>   I am Ezra
> but there were no echoes from the waves . . .[7]

Every poet must somehow insert himself into the ancient as well as the modern: Ezra and the Sumerian scribe embodied Ammons's claim to be part of a prophetic and inscriptive genealogy stretching back, in its vistas, as far as the historical eye can see.

Ammons's 1993 title, *Garbage,* was surprising in a different way. It seemed parodic. Can a book of poems be called *Garbage?* Can one go lower in a title-search? *Garbage* turned out to be, of course, a great book-length poem about death. If you look at bodies from a materialist position, you know that all organic materials become garbage: they are destined to be buried and to rot, or to be incinerated and turned to smoke—"unity's angelic spire / rot lit in rising fire" ("Lofty," from *Highgate Road*). With equanimity, humor, curiosity, and vivid particular interest, Ammons sees a huge mound of garbage heaped up beside the Florida interstate—his first inspiration for the poem. Later, he visits the Ithaca garbage dump, where the debris of human culture, pushed by the front loader into an almost bottomless pit, is incinerated to the screams of hungry gulls haunting the perimeter for food. Mortality is seen steadily and whole as the poem rises and falls; and, as matter is piled up uselessly to molder, or fed to the fire to burn, *Garbage* gathers itself into interior smaller lyrics, disperses itself into bits and pieces, and becomes a sustained tragic and comic meditation on the Heraclitean conversion of matter into energy.

The 1996 title *Brink Road,* on the other hand, speaks (literally) of human inroads on the virgin landscape. There is a road called Brink Road (carefully defined by Ammons in the Acknowledgments as lying "off NY 96 between Candor and Catatonk"); it has been built because human beings have come to live in upper New York State; it has been named by its originators; it has a location and direction and destination; it makes a human demarcation of the natural world; and, symbolically, as the poem "Gung Ho" tells us, recalls to us by its name the brink of death on which Ammons now stands:

> Arriving takes
> destination
>
> out
> of destination:
>
> the grave's
> brink,
>
> to late
> years,
>
> dismantles remnant
> forwardness.[8]

The title *Brink Road* reminds us that Ammons is not only a poet of nature: he is also a poet of the constructed. In his work we see—besides roads—houses, garages, hospitals, automobiles, nursing homes, and garbage dumps, those places and things that human beings have had to build or dig or invent in order to make life livable. Ammons regards these cultural artifacts with the same dispassionate interest he bestows on nature and its phenomena. This dispassionateness, combined with Ammons's equal and balancing sense of human pathos, gives his poetry its special tone of objectivity. One can't imagine associating Ammons with any sort of special pleading—not even for the geographic and temperamental categories into which he himself might be said to fall: the Southerner, the misfit, the genius, the neurotic. He contemplates himself with ironic inquiry, just as he observes his neighbors and everything else. I can't forbear to quote the poem "Boon," from *Brink Road,* in which Ammons resuscitates an old genre, the dialogue between the soul and some divine principle. "Boon" speaks of three qualities of Ammons's verse: its universality, its constant drive toward inception and fresh being, and its tragic awareness:

> I put my head
> down low
> finally and said
>
> where then do I
> belong: your
> belonging
>
> is to belong nowhere:
> what am I
> to be:
>
> your being is to be
> about to be:
> what am I to
>
> do: show
> what doing comes to:
> thank
>
> you
> for this office,
> this use.[9]

The virtue of brevity is combined, in Ammons, with the virtue of loquacity, which we see at work in the book-length poems such as *The Snow Poems, Sphere,* or *Garbage*. The title *Sphere* speaks of wholeness, summation; *The Snow Poems* speaks of that number of months in which Ithaca sees some sort of snow, from sleet to ice storms to blizzards; *Garbage* speaks of the endless recycling, in the universe, of matter from its macro version in human life through mortal decay or incineration to its resurrection in atomic and molecular form. These large subjects require, for Ammons, entire volumes, in each of which poetic process dominates over lyric product. Or rather, as in each of these volumes the expanding discourse coalesces over and over into incorporated lyrics, we see poetic products in their own self-creation and self-extinguishing, rather than in a realized stasis. Although these books owe something, in their large-limbed motion, to Wallace Stevens's long meditative poems, Stevens's poems are divided into cantos that are orderly, measured, isometric, while Ammons's long meditative poems give themselves over, recklessly, to a stream of consciousness that can pass from a pang of grief to the reckoning of the repair bill at the garage, from a surging love of wife and son to the chilly movement of galaxies. The sheer arbitrariness of consciousness is one of Ammons's great formal challenges, one he rises to by an appearance of randomness. I say "appearance," because in Ammons's poems the musical unfolding of a stream of consciousness has its own selectivity of pace, tone, and syntax. The volatility of the speaker's language keeps the reader turning the pages for fresh samples of the enchanting and lonely mind performing its concerto of American English.

Ammons's last book-length poem, *Glare* (1998), derives its title from a few lines obscurely buried halfway through the volume. But those lines are among the most searching, and the most devastating, of Ammons's autobiographical revelations. We had been told, by the 1981 poem "Easter Morning," that Ammons's eighteen-month-old baby brother had died, and that the death had left the adults in the family undone, so much so that they could not afford to be aware of the blow the death had inflicted on their stricken but exceptionally intuitive four-year-old son, who never recovered from that irreversible loss. But we had not known, until *Glare* was published, the event that preceded the death. The poem's thirty-fourth segment shows us the parents, accompanied by a neighbor and their small son, taking the sick child, at night, to the woods. There they halve a sapling at its middle, and pass the child through the split in the tree trunk, which is then bound together to heal. The parents resort in desperation to this uncanny act of folk medicine in the hope of saving the sick baby by sympathetic magic. But the observance of the superstition did not prevent death; and a truth—the rock-bottom glare of extinction—was revealed to the poet-to-be that he has never since been able to suppress in memory:

> I see the eye-level silver shine of
> the axe blade the big neighbor carried
>
> at our house at dawn, and I see the
> child carried off in arms to the woods,
>
> see the sapling split and the child
> passed through and the tree bound
>
> back: as the tree knits, the young
> rupture heals: so, great mother of
>
> the muses, let me forget the sharp
> edge of the lit blade and childish
>
> unknowing, the trees seeming from
> our motion loose in motion, the deep
>
> mysteries playing through the ritual:
> let me forget that and so much: let
>
> me who knows so little know less:
> alas, though: feeling that is so
>
> fleeting is carved in stone across
> the gut: I can't float or heave it
>
> out: it has become a foundation:
> whatever is now passes like early
>
> snow on a warm boulder: but the
> boulder over and over is revealed,
>
> its grainy size and weight a glare.[10]

The dynamism propelling such a passage is visible in everything Ammons wrote, short or long. To him, a poem is an action, bodily and mental; as it passes from its beginning to its end, it describes a curve comparable to a geometrical curve—a parabola, an ellipse, a circle. Every poem starts, for Ammons, with a gesture that goes on to complete itself, ending in a spot other than the place where it had begun. That is why so many of his best-known poems (such as "The Eternal City," "Transaction," and "Easter Morning") have to do with reconstruction following destruction, life following death, motion resumed after a catastrophe. Because Ammons believes in inclusiveness as an aesthetic prin- ciple, the body of the poem has to be open to anything the real body can con- tain or sustain, from wounds to excreta. Because Ammons is a symbolist, his poems can be read as moral, quasi-Biblical parables of the emotional life; he himself says as much in the foreword to *Ommateum:* "The imagery is generally functional beyond pictoral evocation of mood, as *plateau,* for example, may suggest a flat, human existence, devoid of the drama of rising and falling." There was, Ammons has said, no book in the house when he was growing up except a rarely opened Bible; and the psalms and the parables heard at Sunday school and in sermons meant more to him, I think, than the historical parts of the Old and New Testaments (which are rarely mentioned in his poetry). The psalms, as lyrics chiefly of suffering and praise, spoke to the deepest motives of his own later poems; and the parables, as abstractions of life, may have been for Ammons models for his own tendency toward symbolic incident. He has often spoken in interviews, too, of the effect on him of the hymns sung in church, where it is always true that "the imagery is functional beyond pictoral evoca- tion of mood."

As we evoke his titles, Ammons's character becomes present to us, as it walks over uplands and by Corsons Inlet, through lake-effect country and on Brink Road; as it looks back to Sumer while taping the turn of the current year; as it scrutinizes—with and without irony—worldly hopes; as it makes small brief- ings and large gestural spherings; as it notes with its ommateum the infinite forms of snow through an Ithaca winter; and as, in the last two of its book-length diversifications, it describes the glare of the harshest reality, the endless recy- cling of human bodies into elemental fire and ash.

We never know, with respect to a contemporary poet, which poems will seem most valuable to posterity. But it seems to me certain that "Easter Morning"— which I first saw with amazement and gratitude in the pages of *Poetry*—will last.[11] It is Ammons's elegy in a country churchyard, and is conscious, I am sure, of its lineage from Gray's elegy. "Easter Morning" belongs to Ammons's beginnings in Whiteville, North Carolina, where "there were 40 aunts and uncles" *(Glare),* but it knows the migratory distance he has traveled since his beginnings. It is the saddest of poems as it opens: "I have a life that did not become," and yet it becomes sadder as it tells why that stunted life could not progress beyond the tragedy of his little brother's death. It becomes even sadder as it sees this event as typical of all human life rather than singular to his own; and it bursts out in its most violent statement:

> now
> we all buy the bitter
> incompletions, pick up the knots of
> horror, silently raving, and go on
> crashing into empty ends not
> completions

Not stopping at the tragedy of death alone, the poet's Easter morning in the family churchyard progresses even to extinction of meaning and intelligibility in the "flash high-burn / momentary structure of ash." Yet the poem ends with what Ammons calls "a sight of bountiful / majesty and integrity"—an ending of the sort Thomas Gray, with his wistful quiet classicism, could not have written, but which marks this poem as distinctively American in its turn to wildness and the width of sky. "Easter Morning" rewrites the most sacred of Christian myths in ordinary American speech.

In 2005, four years after Ammons's death, there appeared—to everyone's astonishment—another book, one composed in 1996, for which Ammons had chosen the arrangement of the poems and the title. He gave the volume an off-putting and self-satiric title: *Bosh and Flapdoodle*. (I think the expression must have been a phrase used in the South, perhaps by Ammons's family.) This last volume begins with a serious poem, reciting the motto, one could say, of the book, and of Ammons himself, a praise of motion:

> motion,
> the closest cousin to spirit and spirit the
>
> closest neighbor to the other world, haunted
> with possibility, hope, anguish, and alarm.[12]

Bosh and Flapdoodle has familiar passages of weather, social observation, and humor, but it specializes in superb social satire linked to grandiloquent titles. The poet, after a coronary bypass, has been sent, we gather, to a nutritionist, and being told to diet, thinks of all America dieting. This is how the grandly named "America" begins:

> Eat anything: but hardly any: calories are
> calories: . . . .
>
> eat as much of nothing as you please, believe
> me: iceberg lettuce, celery stalks, sugarless
>
> bran
> (27)

Yet next to this peerless absurdity there will be a revelation of the Ammons of anguish:

> did I take my bristled nest of humiliations
> to heart: what kind of dunce keeps a fire
>
> going like this: what do people mean coming
> to hell to warm themselves:
> (39)

Up and down the keyboard from hilarity to misery, from anger to vulgarity, goes Ammons's voice: reminiscence, dirty jokes, ridiculous play with capital letters (DRAB POT, which reverses to TOP BARD), the speedup of time as address books become palimpsests, as cards for holidays "drop clean away into sympathies" (30), as narratives turn into elegies. Ammons is more a storyteller here than ever before; the high abstractions appear rarely, and then only to revert from their loneliness to the familial and the familiar. The poet professes to be writing "prosetry" (141) though dropping in a "poem" now and then. He responds to critics of his digressive lines:

> Don't you think poetry should be succinct:
> not now: I think it should be discinct:
> (157)

Ammons plays on the etymology: "succinct" poetry is "cinctured": "discinct" poetry is unbelted, unbuttoned, the "bosh and flapdoodle" of the human lexicon.

Ammons unveils—in a sad and tender recollection of the Christmas he was
four—the presence of joy as the most precious index of time remembered:

I

remember an ancient Christmas morning with my
tin toy mule and milk wagon on the quilt:

I was four and that little thing tied a world
together: it was a miracle: but that is a

story too old to save. . . .
(138)

With that, the voice fades into ellipses, but the story has been saved. Had *Bosh
and Flapdoodle* never been written, we would never have known Ammons
entire.

15

Poetry and the Mediation of Value

Whitman on Lincoln

In raising the question of how the art of poetry conveys value, I take as my texts Walt Whitman's four poems on the death of Abraham Lincoln.[1] Lincoln was shot by John Wilkes Booth, in conspiracy with others, on April 14, 1865, while the Civil War was still ongoing. In the twenty days between the assassination and Lincoln's May 4 burial in Springfield, Illinois, many events occurred. There was first the shocked five-day interim following the assassination; then the thronged April 19 state funeral for Lincoln in Washington; then the seventeen-hundred-mile ceremonial journey of the funeral train bearing Lincoln's coffin through Baltimore, Harrisburg, Philadelphia, New York City, Albany, Buffalo, Cleveland, Columbus, Indianapolis, Michigan City, and Chicago. On April 26 Booth had been apprehended and shot, and by April 27 eight conspirators were in jail (awaiting the trial that would end in the hanging of four of them on July 7). All of these events were available to Whitman as he wrote his four poems, as was the fact that the body of Lincoln's son Willie (who had died three years earlier) was exhumed from its grave in Washington and reburied in the Lincoln tomb at Springfield.

Whitman's poems on Lincoln were composed in the following order: the short occasional poem "Hush'd Be the Camps Today" (dated April 19, 1865, the day of Lincoln's funeral service in Washington, and printed in the May 1865 edition of *Drum-Taps*); the formally rhymed poem "O Captain, My Captain" and the free-verse elegy "When Lilacs Last in the Dooryard Bloom'd" (both added to the second edition of *Drum-Taps*, September 1865); and the later epitaph "This Dust Was Once the Man" (1871). The assassination of Lincoln of course provoked a flood of writing—journalistic, biographical, poetic. Of the many poems then written, Whitman's memorials have lasted the best; and in considering what values they select, enact, and perpetuate, I want to ask by what aesthetic means they make those values last beyond the momentary topical excitement of Lincoln's death.

Poetry mediates values differently from prose. In prose, values are usually directly stated, illustrated, clarified, and repeated. One has only to think of the classical form of the oration—and its descendants the sermon, the stump speech, and the university lecture—to see the importance placed, in an oral form, on reduplication of matter. Whitman's poetry retains many vestiges of the oration, and we can see such vestiges in "Lilacs."[2] But most lyric poetry, being short, cannot avail itself of the ample terrain of oratory; it has consequently had to find extremely compressed ways by which to convey value. Readers of poetry not only become adept in unfolding the implications of a poetic language; they also learn to see—by exercising historical knowledge—what is being left out that might well have been present. In respect to the conveying of value, what is left out is always as important as what is put in. Let me give one quick example: Lincoln was assassinated on Good Friday, and commentary on his death quickly attached to him—probably for that reason—the word "martyr" with its overtones of Christ's sacrifice. Whitman offers no word placing Lincoln in the context of Christ's passion, Good Friday, or Easter Sunday. He does not put Lincoln in a Judeo-Christian frame at all—even though contemporary commentators such as Bishop Matthew Simpson at the Washington funeral compared Lincoln to Moses.

I will come back to what is left out by Whitman, but I want to return now to the main question: how we can examine poetry's mediation of value. To relate what is left out to what is put in is a task relatively easier with respect to narration than with respect to lyric. One can see that a novelist (say, Herman Melville in *Moby-Dick*) has included no female characters and suggest what effects and values are enabled by, and also prohibited by, this stratagem. But in lyric, there is no such obvious norm. A symphony score employing no violins would be visibly anomalous; but nobody noticed at first when Georges Perec wrote a novel *(The Void)* without the letter *e* because letters—and words—are less visible than women or violins.

It is imagination, then, that is our first recourse in thinking about poetry and value—the imagination of what is left out. This imagination operates not simply on the grosser level of images (such as the Jewish and Christian ones of Moses or Christ that I have mentioned) but also on the level of syntax—in what other manner could this sentence have been framed?—and of diction— what words might have occurred by contrast to the ones we have? The critical imagination must operate even in the realm of sound, especially at crucial poetic moments, asking what alternative phonetic effects might have been used instead of the given ones.

It is generally agreed that images and the semantic content of words mediate value, but syntax and sound are rarely conceded that potential. In prose, syntax and sound are generally less powerful than in poetry; in poetry they provide a crucial expressive ground to the assertions of value carried by images and words. And, since a short poem is in fact a single complex word in which all individual components are bound together in an inalterable relational syntax, there is, strictly speaking, nothing that does not become a carrier of value in poetry (even such harmless-looking particles as the indefinite and the definite article).

Every lyric belongs to one or more theoretical paradigms of genre. The paradigm may be a formal verse-whole, such as the sonnet, which brings with it certain values—those of courtly life—and general expectations (that it might concern, for instance, love or politics). Or the paradigm may be a formal stanza, such as *terza rima*, which brings with it overtones of Dante, the afterlife, and the value of spiritual self-scrutiny. Or the paradigm may be that of a genre that has no formal shape: the English elegy, for instance, can take any verse shape, but must reflect the death of one or more persons and must meditate on the value of a given sort of human life. Or the paradigm may be that of a genre which, while having no prescribed shape, does have a prescribed length and tone: an epitaph, for instance, must be short and impersonally phrased, and it must assert a final judgment. Or the anterior paradigm may prescribe only one part of the stanza: the presence of a refrain at the end of each stanza, for instance, suggests the value of folk-motifs and of incremental intensification of emotion. A poem can ally itself with the first-person singular paradigm (which is the most common lyric self-presentation, valuing individual experience), or it may depart from that norm by choosing a first-person plural paradigm, in order to claim collective utterance and, with it, collective value.

A poem is expected not only to inscribe itself within the subject matter and values implied by its paradigms but also to extend, reverse, or otherwise be original in respect to those very paradigms. It is in the use and critique of its own antecedent paradigms that a poem most fully reveals its own value system. It is this that I hope to show in reflecting on Whitman's poems concerning Lincoln. The value system of an original poet—and therefore of his or her poems—will be in part consonant with, in part in dispute with, the contemporary values of the society from which he, and they, issue. Were the poetry not intelligible with respect to those social values, it could not be read; were it not at a distance from them in some way, it would not be original. The most disturbing lyrics are those, such as Whitman's, in which one finds so many shared social values that one is surprised when interior divergence manifests itself. Whitman's memorials of Lincoln are patriotic ones, devoted to the image of Lincoln, voiced in solidarity with the Union army, participating in the nation's grief at Lincoln's death and at the carnage of the Civil War, and (in "Lilacs") proud of the much-celebrated beauty of the American landscape. What is it, then, that makes them original? And what values does that originality consecrate? And why is "Lilacs"—the longest of Whitman's poems about Lincoln—also the best? What does it allow that the others do not?

"To have great poems, there must be great audiences, too," Whitman once wrote.[3] His poetics depended on a close connection, even an erotic one, with his imagined listeners: he not only wished to be their spokesman, he wanted *them* to call out to *him* to *be* their spokesman, thereby legitimating his writing. It is not surprising, then, that Whitman's first literary response to Lincoln's death—after the wordless silence that followed the ghastly news of the assassination—was to speak in the collective voice of the Union army, as soldiers call on the poet to "sing . . . in our name . . . one verse" (285). They ask that the subject matter of this verse should be "the love we bore him." What the soldiers want is not a eulogy of Lincoln's personal life and actions, of the sort pronounced from the pulpit in Washington, but rather an articulation of their mourning. It is the soldiers themselves, as the poem opens, who devise the liturgy appropriate to the death of their commander in chief: "Let the camps be hushed, let the weapons be draped, and let us each retire"—to do what? To mourn, to muse, yes, but above all to "celebrate"—in the liturgical, not the festive sense—"our dear commander's death." Any human being can perform these personal acts of silence, weapon draping, and musing, just as any human being can voice the consolation of the second stanza, as the soldiers say that Lincoln has escaped "time's dark events, / Charging like ceaseless clouds across the sky."

Only after they have invented a collective ritual, and offered a collective consolation, do the soldiers feel the absence of something necessary to their ceremony—an elevated, that is, sung, form of utterance offered in their name. It is significant to them that it should be sung by one who, because he has been a "dweller in camps," knows the particular heaviness of soldiers' hearts. This short poem values collectivity—in the voice it adopts, in the rituals it devises. It not only values—more than all pomp-filled state memorials—the love borne by the common soldiers, but it also views poetry as merely one ingredient in an indigenous ritual, devised by the people for the people. Why, then, do the soldiers need a verse at all? The poem answers by showing the omnimobility of words. The soldiers remain bound in their camps, but their poet's invisible verse, as the syntax shows, can insert itself into the very circumstance and moment of far-off burial: "As they invault the coffin there, / Sing—as they close the doors of earth upon him—one verse." Lincoln is valued in this collectively voiced poem less as the president of a country than as the beloved commander of a brave army, themselves accustomed to "time's dark events, / Charging" at them. Yet the view of Lincoln is still a hierarchical one—not in a feudal, but in a military, sense. He is not hailed as king or president, but rather as the commander. It is not surprising that the democratic Whitman will eventually turn to valuing Lincoln outside a military hierarchy.

Now that he has written the collective call beckoning him to sing, Whitman can compose the verse that will show, from the inside, the army's love and their heavy hearts. "O Captain, My Captain" (284) is sung in the voice of a Union naval recruit. He is a young boy; he has sailed on the ship of state with his captain, whom he calls, Oedipally, "dear father"; the tide of war has now turned and victory is in sight, as cheering crowds welcome the captain's ship. At this very moment the captain is shot, and dies. The moving turn of the elegy comes two-thirds of the way through the poem. In the first two stanzas the boy addresses the captain in the second person as someone still living, a "you" who, cradled in the boy's arm, can hear the words directed to him. But in the third stanza the young sailor unwillingly resorts to third-person reference, marking his captain as dead: "My Captain does not answer, his lips are pale and still." The hierarchical rank of commander—remote from his troops—has been lowered to the rank of captain—sharing a ship with his men—and then lessened further to the familial hierarchy of father and son, as Lincoln's relation to others becomes ever more democratic, even intimate.

Two stylistic features—its meter and its use of refrain—mark "O Captain" as a designedly democratic and populist poem. In each stanza, four seven-beat lines (each the equivalent of two standard ballad lines of tetrameter and trimeter) are followed by a slightly changing ballad refrain. The refrain—after two trimeters—returns to the tetrameter/trimeter ballad beat. The poem, by its form, implies that soldiers and sailors have a right to have verse written for them in the sort of regularly rhyming stanzas that they like best. And because Whitman has chosen to speak now as a sailor-boy, the diction of the poem offers the clichés of victory that such a boy might use: "Our fearful trip is done, / The ship has weather'd every rack, the prize we sought is won, / The port is near." Everything on shore adheres to the boy's expected conventions of popular celebration—"For you the flag is flung—for you the bugle trills, / For you bouquets and ribbon'd wreaths." Even "the bleeding drops of red," the "mournful tread" of the sailor, and the captain "fallen cold and dead" come from the clichés of war journalism.

Whitman was not, I think, hypocritical in writing such a poem; he was answering his first poem with the second poem that he thought the first had called for. But in adopting the naïve voice of the young boy mourning his "father," Whitman had sacrificed his own voice entirely. Because he valued, and validated, the claim of his audience that he represent their heavy hearts, Whitman thought at first to do so by becoming one of them. Wanting to value democracy, he thought he had to exemplify it by submitting to the rhythms and rhymes and clichés of the popular verse prized by the soldiers, rather than inventing a democratic form of his own. Because he was bent on registering individual response as well as the collective wish expressed in "Hush'd Be the Camps," he took on the voice of a single representative sailor, silencing his own idiosyncratic voice. And wanting to show the sailor and his father-captain as participants in a national endeavor, he adopted the popular cliché of the Ship of State as the ruling metaphor of his poem.

Though we do not know, factually, that "O Captain" was composed before "Lilacs," it seems to me that the sailor-boy's dirge must have been the direct response to the call in "Hush'd Be the Camps." "Lilacs" is, by contrast, the outburst of individual voice following on Whitman's attempt to honor collectivity by writing in the voice of the heavyhearted soldiers and to defend representativeness in verse by writing in the voice of the mourning sailor. He was valuing Lincoln as commander in the one and captain-father in the other; he was valuing poetry as a contributor to collective ritual in the one and as a form of populist expression in the other. When we come to "Lilacs," all the values change.

"Lilacs" is written not collectively, and not representatively, but in Whitman's own original lyric voice. In it, Lincoln is not placed in a vertical social hierarchy as president, commander in chief, captain, or even father, but is rather placed horizontally, as a fellow man, even if one distinguished by superlative wisdom and sweetness. There is ritual in the poem—even received ritual, carried out by other mourners but even by the poet, as he lays conventional bouquets of lilies and roses on the coffins of the dead; but there are also strange new rituals, to which I will come, outnumbering the conventional ones. And— most striking of all—there is a suppression of the coincidence of the day of the assassination with Good Friday, as well as a refusal to echo the Christian rituals of services and sermons and hymns that pervaded the twenty days preceding Lincoln's burial.

In "Lilacs," the coffin train indeed makes its long and mournful journey—in a funereal ritual unprecedented in American history, and therefore attractive to Whitman as an original event—but aside from the mentions of the mourning ceremonies attending the train at each of its stops, nothing in the poem transmits historical fact. The poem never mentions the assassination, the assassin, or the jailed and executed conspirators; the Emancipation Proclamation and other acts of Lincoln's presidency are passed over in silence. Even the startling fact of the reburial of Lincoln's son is omitted. We are given, instead of facts, three symbols: the star of the evening sky, the lilac of this earth, and the hermit thrush of the dark swamp. By apportioning his poem among the classic three realms of upper-world, middle-world, and underworld, Whitman gives cosmic importance—rather than the political importance ascribed to it by historians—to Lincoln's death. The poem does not value facts: it does not value politics; it does not value Christianity; it does not value speaking in a voice other than one's own. It is written in free verse of the most original sort; it does not value debased popular taste in poetry. Has Whitman repudiated "Hush'd Be the Camps" and "O Captain"? Or does something of them linger in "Lilacs"?

What does "Lilacs" value? And how are its valuings enacted? And what aesthetic value do they exhibit? These questions have answers too complex to be fully enunciated here, but let me give some brief observations. "Lilacs" is a sequence constructed of sixteen cantos ranging in length from five to fifty-three lines. It builds up to its longest and most lyrical moment in Canto 14, achieves its moral climax in Canto 15, and ends with a coda of "retrievements out of the night" in Canto 16. The nonreligious "trinity" that opens the poem (perennial lilac, Lincoln-star, and the "thought of him I love") will become, by the end, the trinity of "lilac and star and bird": that is, the bird and its carol become the equivalent of the "thought" of the poet. It is unusual for Whitman to establish such a firm symbolic constellation; his secular trinity is set as a memorable elegiac emblem of the formality that is one of the poem's values. This is not an intimate elegy: Lincoln is named a "friend," but he is also the "powerful western fallen star" who is due formal honor as a symbol of the ideal. That honor is given character in the symbolic trinity dedicated to his memory.

The first act of the speaker—after he has initially lamented his helplessness in the grasp of the "harsh surrounding cloud that will not free my soul"—is to break off a sprig of lilac from the lilac bush growing in the dooryard (line 17). No explanation is given for this act; it is not until line 45 that we learn why he took the sprig. It is to have a flower to lay on Lincoln's coffin: "Here, coffin that slowly passes, / I give you my sprig of lilac." This is not the conventional sort of floral offering; it has passed through no florist's hands. The speaker knows the conventions of arranged "bouquets" made of the rarer-than-lilacs "roses and early lilies" and indeed later observes these conventions, as his mourning becomes generalized to "the coffins all of you." Still, he prefers his roughly torn and unarranged lilacs:

> All over bouquets of roses,
> O death, I cover you over with roses and early lilies,
> But mostly and now the lilac that blooms the first,
> Copious I break, I break the sprigs from the bushes,
> With loaded arms I come, pouring for you,
> For you and the coffins all of you O death.

The poem dismisses the idea of personal immortality; when the star sinks, it is gone forever:

> . . . I watch'd where you pass'd and was lost in the netherward black
>   of the night,
> As my soul in its trouble dissatisfied sank, as where you sad orb,
> Concluded, dropt in the night, and was gone.

What the poet can confirm, as a principle of hope, is the natural vegetative resurrection from which Jesus took the metaphor of the risen wheat: the funeral train, Whitman says, passes "the yellow-spear'd wheat, every grain from its shroud in the dark-brown fields uprisen." And in the old woods, "lately violets peep'd from the ground, spotting the gray debris."

The chief stylistic trait of this first part of the poem is the long-withheld subject of its "periodic" sentences. The run of sentences with postponed subjects and predicates begins in the one-sentence, six-lined Canto 3: "In the dooryard . . . / Stands the lilac-bush . . . / With many a pointed blossom . . . / With every leaf a miracle—and from this bush in the dooryard . . . / With delicate-color'd blossoms . . . / A sprig with its flower I break." In Canto 5, with its seven-line sentence, the continuo is carried by a series of adverbs and participial adjectives—"Over . . . / Amid . . . / Amid . . . / Passing . . . / Passing . . . / Carrying . . . / Night and day journeys a coffin." We can see that this drawn-out sentence form imitates the long passage of the train across the eastern third of the North American continent. It is important to Whitman to ally his single tributary sprig of lilac with all the preceding civil and religious ceremonies honoring the dead hero, and Canto 6 is the poem's chief concession to factual reporting; but this canto is staged so that the public observances lead up to the poet's anomalous, solitary, and unarranged lilac sprig:

> Coffin that passes through lanes and streets,
> Through day and night with the great cloud darkening the land,
> With the pomp of the inloop'd flags with the cities draped in black,
> With the show of the States themselves as of crape-veil'd women
> 　　standing,
> With processions long and winding and the flambeaus of the night,
> With the countless torches lit, with the silent sea of faces and the
> 　　unbared heads,
> With the waiting depot, the arriving coffin, and the sombre faces,
> With dirges through the night, with the thousand voices rising strong
> 　　and solemn,
> With all the mournful voices of the dirges pour'd around the coffin,
> The dim-lit churches and the shuddering organs—where amid these
> 　　you journey,
> With the tolling tolling bells' perpetual clang,
> Here, coffin that slowly passes,
> I give you my sprig of lilac.

The poem here gives what all the contemporary photographs of the journey cannot: movement, silence, sound, tonality, atmosphere. While other poems about Lincoln's death mostly contented themselves with abstractions of praise and grief, Whitman renders the very scenes of mourning in present-participial form, making them unroll before our eyes in what seems real time. The journey comes to a telling climax—after all the elaborate tributes of the cities—in the single lilac sprig. The poem, it is evident, values showing over telling, and the senses over abstraction; it emphasizes the contribution of each individual act to the tally of mourning gestures. It also values drama—not only in the changing chiaroscuro tableaus of homage presented here but also in the narrative syntactic drama of the sentence that presses toward the gift of the dooryard lilac.

One might think that the poem could end here. The poet has contributed his flower: is that not enough? We soon learn that it is not: he puts aside the summons of the bird heard in Canto 9 to ask the three questions of Canto 10: "How shall I warble? . . . / how shall I deck my song? . . . / what shall my perfume be for the grave?" The last problem is easily solved: the perfume will be the sea winds and the breath of the poet's chant. But the first two are less rapidly answered. In fact, the first—"How shall I warble?"—is not at this point replied to at all, while "How shall I deck my song?" mutates into the specific question, "What shall the pictures be that I hang on the walls, / To adorn the burial-house of him I love?" This question originates from Whitman's knowledge of Egyptian tombs, decorated on the interior with idyllic pictures of daily life. He will renew this convention in Canto 11, making resonant pictures of American landscapes and action: "Pictures of growing spring and farms and homes . . . / And all the scenes of life and the workshops, and the workmen homeward returning." He includes no religious iconography on the walls of the tomb; he employs only the iconography of the land, catalogued in terms breathing aesthetic bliss: "With floods of the yellow gold of the gorgeous, indolent, sinking sun, burning, expanding the air . . . / In the distance the flowing glaze, the breast of the river, with a wind-dapple here and there." The praise of the beauty of America and its "gentle soft-born measureless light" almost distracts the poet from the still-unanswered question "How shall I warble?"; and though he once again turns toward the chant of the bird, "limitless out of the dusk," and calls it, unexpectedly, a "loud human song, with voice of uttermost woe," he represents himself as still held back from "the swamps, the recesses" by the star above, and the lilac beside him.

He is really held back by his prolonged cataloguing of beauty, which spills over into the beginning of Canto 14, as the poet glosses "the large unconscious scenery of my land." Whitman valued highly, as a poetic structure, the accumulation of sentences of inventory. Beyond the formal triad of his symbols, beyond the conferring of cosmic significance on Lincoln's death by showing its consequence to upper and lower and middle worlds, beyond the drama of the periodic sentence pressing toward its climax, beyond the rendition of theatrically lit atmospheres, he valued the multiplicity and beauty of the world's objects, landscapes, and inhabitants, even in the moment of mourning. Inventories fill most of the poems of *Leaves of Grass* (and all parodies of Whitman begin with a swell of egotism followed by unbridled lists of categories).

But the beautiful categories of Canto 13, though they overflow into Canto 14, continue under a shadow. While the poet, ravished by the "heavenly aerial beauty . . . / and the summer approaching with richness," watches the ample scene, "—lo, then and there, / Falling upon them all and among them all, enveloping me with the rest, / Appear'd the cloud." The poet finds "the knowledge of death" walking on one side of him and "the thought of death" walking on the other side, "and I in the middle as with companions, and holding the hands of companions." He finally flees to the swamp, which is then revealed as an underworld of "shores of . . . water" and "solemn shadowy cedars and ghostly pines so still." This is not the Christian afterlife, but the underworld of shades and ghosts at the shores of Lethe and the Styx inherited from Greek myth. By annexing the afterworld of classical Greece to the preceding tomb decorations of Egypt, Whitman tells us that he prefers these ways of knowing and encountering death to those offered by the Christianity in which he had been raised. In 1891, the last year of his life, after he had suffered strokes and other disabling illnesses, he wrote: "The philosophy of Greece taught normality and the beauty of life. Christianity teaches how to endure illness and death. I have wonder'd whether a third philosophy fusing both, and doing full justice to both, might not be outlined" (PW, 708). But when he was writing "Lilacs," it was the "normality" of Egypt and Greece, rather than Christian patience, that Whitman valued.

We have reached, in the second half of Canto 14, the lyric center of "Lilacs," the song of the hermit thrush, where the supreme aesthetic value of the poem—the value of free musical language—resides. Though this is the poetic center of the elegy, it is not its moral climax, which will arrive in Canto 15, when the poet fully accedes to vision. However, we must for the moment suspend attention to that moral climax, and ask ourselves first about this lyric center. "And the charm of the carol rapt me," says the poet: what is that charm? The "carol" is a hymn to a goddess, Death, and is therefore allied to the earliest lyrics we have, the Orphic hymns to abstractions such as Death and the Homeric hymns to the gods and goddesses such as the maternal goddess Demeter, mother of the lost Persephone in Hades. The song of the thrush, beginning in invocation ("Come lovely and soothing death"), and becoming a song of praise ("praise! praise! praise! / For the sure-enwinding arms of cool-enfolding death"), invents a celebratory ritual ("Dances for thee I propose saluting thee, adornments and feastings for thee") to replace the mourning ritual of somber dirges and tolling bells and shuddering organs invented by Christianity. Yet the repudiation of Christian melancholy, forceful as it is, is less memorable than the seductive oceanic rhythms of lyric loosed to be itself. Whitman "overwrites," with this rhythm, the dragging journey of the train. As the train moved across the land, we heard it go "Over the breast of the spring, the land, amid cities": now we hear the carol float above the train, over the same landscape:

> Over the rising and sinking waves, over the myriad fields and the
>   prairies wide,
> Over the dense-pack'd cities all and the teeming wharves and ways,
> I float this carol with joy, with joy to thee O death.

As the song of blissful death "overwrites" the journey of melancholy death, lyric claims its right to the creative joy that resides in art, even in art of tragic import.

As the bird sings the acceptance of death, the poet, tallying the song in his soul, finds that as he lets go of his former fear and denial, his imprisoned vision awakes: "My sight that was bound in my eyes unclosed, / As to long panoramas of visions." The painful silent moral visions, gifts of memory, replace, with a wrench, the aesthetic sights of the earth seen earlier by the grateful eye of sense. Whitman first admits to a "screen vision" of mutilated battle-flags ("pierc'd with missiles / . . . and torn and bloody, . . . / And the staffs all splinter'd and broken"). As he persists in his resolve to remember all, the splintered flags of the obscuring "screen vision" dissolve into the greater mutilations of flesh they were hiding:

> I saw battle-corpses, myriads of them,
> And the white skeletons of young men, I saw them,
> I saw the debris and debris of all the slain soldiers of the war.

At this point, the elegy for Lincoln resumes in an explicit way its earlier guarded collective gesture ("For you and the coffins all of you O death") toward all those ordinary soldiers who have died in the war. This is the moment of highest moral value in the poem, as the poet allows himself to see all that the war has cost. At the same time, by resurrecting a word used earlier, apparently casually, in the mention of the violets that peeped from the ground, "spotting the gray debris," Whitman reminds us that debris is the compost of new growth. It was the Union that was to grow strong from the battle-corpses.

The drama of Canto 15 is enacted in the style of a chronicler of apocalypse:

> And I saw in the right hand of him that sat on the throne a book. . . . And I saw a strong angel proclaiming. . . . And I beheld, and lo. . . . And I saw when the Lamb opened one of the seals. . . . And I saw, and behold a white horse. (Revelation 5, 6)

> And I saw askant the armies,
> I saw as in noiseless dreams hundreds of battle-flags. . . .
> I saw battle-corpses, myriads of them,
> And the white skeletons of young men, I saw them,
> I saw the debris and debris of all the slain soldiers of the war.

This style claims boldly, if implicitly, that Whitman expects his vision to be granted the same credence as that granted the book of Revelation; the passage is his most blasphemous transvaluation of Christian value.

In the coda of Canto 16, the poet resumes his earlier themes, and finds his trinity complete—"Lilac and star and bird twined with the chant of my soul"—but unexpectedly is not permitted to leave, in memory, the underworld. Though in real life the lilac is "there in the door-yard, blooming, returning with spring," the poet finds "Lilac and star and bird twined with the chant of my soul, / There in the fragrant pines and the cedars dusk and dim." Because the underworld is "there," the poet is by implication "here" in the normal world—but the poem cannot enact the "here" in which he finds himself: rather, the lilac is also distant, "there" in the door-yard. The living part of his soul remains in the dusk and the dimness of Hades, twined with his trinity.

If we seek out the originality of "Lilacs"—beginning with its refusal to name Lincoln and its suppression of his civic and military roles—we can see that though it indeed obeys many paradigms of its genre, the English elegy, it wears its rue with a difference, subduing Christian symbols to those of Egypt and Greece, celebrating the natural beauty of life rather than the prospective beauties of heaven, finding its consolation in new joyous rituals of death, and asserting that its revelation of corpses and skeletons is as prophetically binding as Saint John's revelation of heaven. Its style asserts the value of showing rather than telling, the value of the idiosyncratic voice over the collective or representative voice, and—in its journeying sentences that climax in a definite halt—the value of acceptance, rather than denial, of the full stop of death. Its other striking sentences, phrased not in the progressive pressure to end, but rather in arias ebbing and flowing without resolution, assert the fluctuating harmonies and contrasts of the expansive but inconclusive rhythms of experience:

> Victorious song, death's outlet song, yet varying ever-altering song,
> As low and wailing, yet clear the notes, rising and falling, flooding the night,
> Sadly sinking and fainting, as warning and warning, and yet again bursting with joy,
> Covering the earth and filling the spread of the heaven.

After "Lilacs," Whitman composed another poem concerning Lincoln—the one as yet unwritten—Lincoln's epitaph (285). It was published in 1871, six years after Lincoln's death. Lincoln is no longer friend or wise and sweet soul; he is reduced to dust. The poet grasps the dust in his hand: "This dust," he says. He does not point to the grave, saying, "That dust." This is not a poem gesturing outward toward the "there" of the lilac or the "there" of the underworld.

This dust was once the man,
Gentle, plain, just and resolute, under whose cautious hand,
Against the foulest crime in history known in any land or age,
Was saved the union of these States.

The epitaph is massively imbalanced: the four words "This dust was once" make up the left half of the copula, while the right half requires thirty words. The proportion is therefore appropriate to the light dust versus the complex description of the consequential man. Lincoln, in becoming dust, becomes historical, "the man who guided the preservation of the Union." The initial adjectives characterizing Lincoln are themselves complex, as the personal "gentle" is played off against the final official "resolute," while in between we see the "plain" of Lincoln's upbringing set against the "just" character of his legal profession. I hear the line with the emphasis on "and": "Gentle, plain, just—*and*—[when the hour came] resolute." The next adjective, applied not to Lincoln but to his guiding hand, is "cautious"—this speaks to his wisdom. What is most surprising about the epitaph is that it, unlike most such honorific inscriptions, gives no active verb to its subject. Lincoln is not said to be "the man . . . Who saved the Union of these states." That would give him the power of a monarch. It was the thousands of soldiers, alive and dead, who saved the Union; the president, *primus inter pares*, was merely their supervising fellow participant. But the soldiers are left unmentioned as such: they exist only subsumed within the passive verb "was saved." Yet they are the saviors, and as such they are the ultimate repository of individual value, even in an epitaph praising their leader. The very peculiar syntax of this epitaph reserves the main subject and verb of the subsidiary adjective clause—"The Union of these States was saved"—to the very end and inverts the normal word order to "Was saved the Union of these States," thereby putting the Union in the final climactic syntactic position of national value, placed even above the actions taken to save it. Tucked in between the presiding cautious hand and its salvific agents is the averted horror: the continuation of slavery. Slavery is here named by euphemism, as though its actual name should never again be uttered in human hearing. It becomes, superlatively, "the foulest crime," and it is placed in a cosmic spatiotemporal field: it is "the foulest crime known in any land or age."

What makes this epitaph a poem? Above all, its tortured syntax, which tries to tuck into thirty words the personal, professional, ethical, and prudential qualities of a single historical personage; his relation to the Union Army; the soldiers' relation to the winning of the war; the chief result of that victory; and a description of the ancient, widespread, and evil crime against which both president and soldiers opposed their lives. Syntax, when tortured, becomes a sign of a complexity too great to be naturally contained within a single sentence and yet bent on being thus contained because all the elements of that given complexity are inextricable one from another and must therefore be named in the same breath. Whitman's last word on Lincoln emphasizes his historical greatness, based on greatness of character, while reserving to him merely a guiding role in the ultimate value, the salvation of the Union. This is a poem of Roman succinctness and taciturnity, betraying its depth of feeling chiefly in the implicit figure of the scales of justice—in which a handful of dust is equal in weight to the salvation of the Union, with the copula serving as the needle of equilibrium. In it the poet speaks not collectively, not representatively, and not idiosyncratically and lyrically; he speaks impersonally, as the recording angel. This poem places value on the voice of history in final judgment. Walt Whitman, the man, is sublimed away; this poem is—to use Elizabeth Bishop's words—one of those "admirable scriptures of stone on stone." One can see its words chased on a tablet: it is itself a tombstone. But did any tombstone ever carry such an epitaph?

There is more to say about the values imaged and implied by these four poems. In attempting the subject of Lincoln from four different perspectives, Whitman (who had often seen Lincoln and had described him in prose of a journalistic and mimetic nature) turns away from personal and historic mimesis of the man and president to symbolic mimesis, framed for the conveying of value. In each case the aesthetic vehicle—the collective voice of the soldiers in the camps, the single voice of the grieving novice-sailor, the idiosyncratic voice of the poet coming to know death, and the impersonal voice of historic judgment—offers a different possibility of expression. The shorter poems show us, by contrast, how and why "Lilacs" reaches its heights and its amplitudes. All of the poems reveal Whitman debating what stance the American poet should adopt when speaking of important national events. If each stance—collective, representative, idiosyncratic, impersonal—has something to be said for it, then we are shown that value can be mediated by poetry in any number of ways and that both the poet and his audience are modeled differently in each. We are warned, by the greater success of the most original of the four poems, of the dangers to the poet in attempting to speak collectively or within the bounds of popular taste—or even with the impersonal voice of historiography. It is chiefly when a public crisis evokes some crisis in the soul of the poet—here, Whitman's crisis in asking what could be truly said of human mortality—that a public poem takes on lasting aesthetic value.

16

"Long Pig"

The Interconnection of the Exotic, the Dead,
and the Fantastic in the Poetry of Elizabeth Bishop

When I first read "In the Waiting Room," I puzzled over Bishop's representation of a male corpse about to be eaten by cannibals. The poem is generally thought to center on the poet's discovery of her own identity as a female, since she emphasizes, in the course of the poem, her reluctantly made connection with her aunt, with the *National Geographic* tribal women and their horrible pendulous breasts, and with her female name, "Elizabeth." Yet, factually speaking, the most revolting photograph the young speaker sees in the magazine is certainly that of the human being about to be cooked, the meat reductively named "long pig" by the cannibals:

> A dead man slung on a pole
> —"long pig," the caption said.[1]

It is clear that the young Elizabeth is concentrating on the more exotic and sensational details visible in the magazine: she singles out volcanoes rather than rice paddies, naked black women rather than clothed white or Asian ones, a meal of "long pig" rather than one of wild boar. The link between these troubling visions and the poem's speaker is the relatively "normal" appearance of the white explorers Osa and Martin Johnson in the midst of the tropical scenes. Still, the insertion of "long pig" and, at the end of the poem, of "the War" (previously unmentioned) suggests that Bishop had to include, even in a poem principally about female sexuality and vulnerability, the ultimate facts of cultural cruelty—the tribal hunting and eating of men by men, and its contemporary equivalent, modern warfare.

Yet the picture of "long pig" is not merely an instance of cruelty and death: it is also, and perhaps more centrally, an instance of the fantastic—by which

I mean a metaphor that calls attention to itself by its own far-fetchedness. "Long Pig" inserts into the poem—as the late mention of war does not—Bishop's inveterate fascination with cultural difference. There are in the poems many neutral exhibitions of that fascination—for example, the handmade clogs, each with a different tune, in "Questions of Travel"—but here I want to point out how often the fantastic, in Bishop, is allied not only to the exotic but also to a diseased or dying thing. Another way of putting this is to say that the details that appear most gratuitous in her poems—such as "long pig"—are often inserted in the service of a compulsion by which the exotic, the fantastically imagined, and the dead or diseased or mutilated are joined in one complex object.

The most savage instance of this complex occurs in "Pink Dog," as the Brazilian hairless scabies-ridden female dog is imagined, fantastically, as decked out in a carnival costume and mask:

> You are not mad: you have a case of scabies. . . .
>
> Now look, the practical, the sensible
>
> solution is to wear a *fantasía*.
> Tonight you simply can't afford to be a-
> n eyesore. But no one will ever see a
>
> dog in *máscara* this time of year.
> (190–191)

Just as a human corpse is one degree removed from actuality by being seen metaphorically as "long pig," so the pink dog will be one degree removed from the threat of being murdered by disguising herself in a fantastic costume. In each case, the faraway exotic, the imaginatively fantastic, and the dead (or, in the case of the dog, one threatened with death) rise up at once together in a single image. "In the Waiting Room" buries that triply significant image ("long pig") in the middle of the poem, while "Pink Dog" places the image of the dog in *máscara*, in a climactic position, at the end.

I believe that Bishop is compelled, over and over, to invent or adopt such images: that the exotic alone, or the fantastic alone, or even the exotic and the fantastic combined, did not suffice to convey one complex of her sensibility. Somehow death—or its equivalent in the mutilated or the spectral—had to join the exotic and the fantastic to make the complex complete.

The earliest examples I have found in Bishop's work of this triadic convergence represent it as a tidal wave capable of destroying an idyllic scene. The 1929 poem of sexual temptation, "The Wave" (217), prevents, however, the convergence from occurring. It allows house-room to both the exotic and fantastic, but refuses the menace of erotic self-annihilation, "total immersion" in the threatening "wave" of sexual experience. As "The Wave" opens, the Baudelairean exotic-erotic sets the scene: "How still, how blinding is the light! / Spellbound and golden shines the foam." As the dangerous incoming wave hovers, it incarnates itself in a series of fantastic metaphors: its "helmet" rises, it is a "radiant bird," a "wonder." The slightest gesture of erotic acknowledgment from the speaker to the other half of the "we" of the poem would allow the wave to fall on the land:

> . . . the motion
> Of a hand,
> A tiny quickening
> Of the heart,
> And it will fall
> And nothing more
> Can keep the sea and land apart.

However, the gesture of assent is not made, and the wave recedes, doubling back on itself and subsiding dully into the sea. "We are too innocent and wise, / We laugh into each other's eyes."

A fantastic underwater drowning actually is allowed to occur in a 1933 poem, "The Flood" (220), but the ingredient of the exotic, as well as any treatment of death, is absent. The flood is rendered as a regional and known phenomenon, and the familiar New England town of its occurrence is rendered fantastic only by its lively subaqueous existence after the flood:

> And slowly down the fluid streets
>   the cars and trolleys, goggle-eyed,
> enamelled bright like gaping fish,
>   drift home on the suburban tide.

In short, in this poem Bishop tames the flood, permitting the fantastic, but not any actual annihilation.

It is in the tortured and baroque "Three Sonnets for the Eyes," also written in 1933, that the triadic complex of death, the exotic, and the fantastic is first allowed full development. At the opening, Bishop imagines the living eye sockets as basins in which illusions withdraw, as in an ebb tide, but then replenish themselves fully. This steady-state universe of ebb and flow is destroyed in the last of the three sonnets. The exotic location of the final sonnet is a cemetery; the eyes are truly dead; and the fantastic is represented by the surreal image of eyes as organic machines exploded from their bone-nests into malfunction and disappearance:

> Either above thee or thy gravestone's graven angel
> Eyes I'll stand and stare.
> . . . . .
>   I'll
> Look in lost upon those neatest nests of bone
> Where steel-coiled springs have lashed out, fly-wheels flown.
> (224)

Bishop will remember, and reuse, this closing on "flown" in "At the Fishhouses."

Although the complex of the exotic, the fantastic, and the dead naturally does not occur in all of Bishop's poems, it appears often enough to be notable. In "The End of March"—to cite a late instance—the exotic realm is the sky, inhabited by a fantastic lion sun who has descended to make majestic paw prints on the beach before returning to the sky. The "dead" thing in the poem is a tangle of floating white string, seen at the tide line by Bishop and her companions, but transformed by the poet into a fantastic ghost:

> a thick white snarl, man-size, awash,
> rising on every wave, a sodden ghost,
> falling back, sodden, giving up the ghost. . . .
> A kite string?—But no kite.
> (179)

It is not until the very close of "The End of March" that the fantastic dead mass of string is brought together with the exotic sun, a lion sun "who perhaps had batted a kite out of the sky to play with." The Hardyesque carelessness of celestial fate, amusing itself with a kite but then "killing" the kite and its string, brings the poem to ironic resolution.

The closeness, for Bishop, of these three realms—the exotic, the fantastic, and the deathly—seems to be accounted for in part by the uncanniness of death itself, the most exotic of all destinations. Since it is the undiscovered country from whose bourne no traveler returns, it generates the most intensely fantastic analogies for and around itself. In the early canonical poems, the complex shows itself in the imaginary and exotic iceberg of "cloudy rock" that "like jewelry from a grave" adorns only itself ("The Imaginary Iceberg," 4); the conjunction is also evident in Bishop's appropriation of Felicia Hemans's Casabianca on the Nile ("The boy stood on the burning deck, / Whence all but he had fled"). In Bishop's hands, the tableau "while the poor ship in flames went down" becomes a congeries of representations of love, death, and a fantastic melting-together of identities:

> Love's the obstinate boy, the ship,
> even the swimming sailors. . . .
>   And love's the burning boy.
>
> ("Casabianca," 5)

Just as the Nile renders the scene exotic, so Eros-multiplied renders it fantastic; and the burning boy, like Southwell's Burning Babe, fixes the scene iconically to death.

The complex can be seen, if in mitigated form, in the fantastic comparison— in "Wading at Wellfleet" (7)—of the waves of Cape Cod to the Assyrian chariot wheels that were armed with knives. However, the sea "hasn't put in action yet" its destructive potential aimed at the wader's shins, so the ingredient of actual death, although threatened, is evaded, as it had been in "The Wave." Similarly, in "The Gentleman of Shalott," the envisaged destruction of the fantastic half-man—"If the glass slips / he's in a fix—/ only one leg, etc." (9–10)—is kept at bay, and his exotic existence in the country of the mirror continues to be viable. The Man-Moth, too, living in his exotic subterranean realms, knows, but cannot bear to look at, a constant genetic yearning for suicide. In his dreams of rushing in a train through tunnels,

> He does not dare look out the window,
> for the third rail, the unbroken draught of poison,
> runs there beside him. He regards it as a disease
> he has inherited the susceptibility to. He has to keep
> his hands in his pockets, as others must wear mufflers.
>
> ("The Man-Moth," 15)

The fantastic comparison of the inorganic third rail to an organic inherited disease completes the triad of the exotic underground, the mortal threat, and the fantastic Man-Moth; but again, the worst is evaded. What would the Man-Moth do with his hands if he took them out of his pockets? He might commit not suicide but murder. The late poem "Crusoe in England" permits the hands their deadly work, in actuality and in dream. In actuality, Crusoe's hands fantastically "dye" a baby goat bright red, "just to see / something a little different. / And then his mother wouldn't recognize him" (165). "Dyeing" turns into "dying" for the unrecognized and consequently unnourished baby goat. In Crusoe's dream, the hands do worse: "I'd dream of things / like slitting a baby's throat, mistaking it / for a baby goat" (165).

In inserting these two fantastic death-dealing actions—the one of actuality, the other of dream, and neither present in Defoe's original—into the story of Robinson Crusoe on his exotic island, Bishop allows her three-part complex its full imaginative activity. We can see, in "Crusoe in England," how long it takes her to "creep up" on the fascinating but unsayable scene of dyeing and murder, and to say it. A similar delay, followed by a "screen version" of the complex, followed by the full complex, occurs in "Over 2,000 Illustrations and a Complete Concordance." In this poem, the exotica occur first ("The Seven Wonders of the World . . . / the squatting Arab") followed quickly by a gesture—unembroidered by the fantastic—toward mortality ("the Tomb, the Pit, the Sepulcher" [57]). I call these latter items realistic because they are still in the realm of the guidebook cliché: they have not yet been internalized within the poet's imagination.

As the poem moves to Mexico, we find a "screen version" of the complex, in which the word "dead," after being used of a man, is "neutralized" by being immediately predicated of volcanoes:

> In Mexico the dead man lay
> in a blue arcade; the dead volcanoes
> glistened like Easter lilies.
> (58)

The fantastic makes its appearance in the unlikely comparison of the volcanoes to Easter lilies, a resurrective image invoked to cancel out the disturbing corpse in the arcade. At last, after one more postponement via the divagation to the Marrakech lesbian brothels, the full complex of the exotic-fantastic-deathly appears, making real the previous offhand tourist references to "the Tomb, the Pit, the Sepulcher." The speaker sees "what frightened me most of all." This is a grave, a "holy" grave located, exotically, in the desert under a stone canopy.

But it is not unique—not *"the* Sepulcher"—it is one of many, and it does not look "particularly holy." The exotic and the (disappointingly) sepulchral now being present, it is time for the fantastic to appear, and it does, with the unforeseeable comparison of the grave, or its inscriptions, to—of all things—yellowed cattle-teeth. And the actual presence of the sepulchral (which we recall from one of its earliest appearances in "The Monument," where the monument may or may not contain "the bones of the artist-prince" [25]) is gone one better here by becoming the despoiled sepulchral: someone has presumably robbed the tomb of the body of the "poor prophet paynim who once lay there." Here at last is Bishop's compelled coarticulation of the exotic, the deathly, and the fantastic:

> An open, gritty, marble trough, carved solid
> with exhortation, yellowed
> as scattered cattle-teeth;
> half-filled with dust, not even the dust
> of the poor prophet paynim who once lay there.
> (58)

Why is this complex—an exotic location, a corpse, a leap into the fantastic— so frequent in Bishop's imaginative excursions? Another way of putting this question is to ask what would be the contrary of the compelled triadic complex, its antidote, its exorcism? It would be something not exotic, but familiar, combined with something not deathly, but life-filled, expressed in a metaphor not fantastic but natural. We see this antidote in the tableau with which "2000 Illustrations" comes to its yearning end:

> Why couldn't we have seen
> this old Nativity while we were at it?
> —the dark ajar, the rocks breaking with light,
> an undisturbed, unbreathing flame,
> colorless, sparkless, freely fed on straw,
> and, lulled within, a family with pets. . . .
> (58–59)

The empty "holy grave" is exorcised by the peopled holy cave; exotic Arabia is exorcised by the familiarly Christian little town of Bethlehem; and the death-fantasy of scattered cattle-teeth is exorcised by the comfortable presence of the ox and the ass as family pets. The exorcism of the demonic is enabled by a specialized form of inspiration, represented—in an old and natural metaphor—as light and flame. This miraculous flame—which is the substitute for an image of the divine infant lying on straw, or for Southwell's Burning Babe—breaks out from rocks, has no color or sparks, is nourished on straw, and is both undisturbed by the agitations of existence and independent of the animate energy of breath. Bishop's undisturbed, unbreathing flame may be a descendant of the purgative flame of Yeats's "Byzantium":

> At midnight on the Emperor's pavement flit
> Flames that no faggot feeds, nor steel has lit,
> Nor storm disturbs, flames begotten of flame,
> Where unbegotten spirits come
> And all complexities of fury leave,
> Dying into a trance
> An agony of dance,
> An agony of flame that cannot singe a sleeve.[2]

The "negative theology" of definition by subtraction, used by Yeats in the form of "no . . . nor . . . nor . . . un . . . cannot," reappears in Bishop in the form of "un . . . , un . . . less, . . . less. . . ." Both passages share the theme of that which is fed but cannot be disturbed, both ascribing that quality to flame.

The light-filled, positive, "normal," triad of the familiar, the life-giving, and the homely reveals contrastively, by the form it takes of the Christian Nativity imagined as "a family with pets," the origin of Bishop's dark compelled triad of the exotic, the deathly, and the fantastic. One can explain, at least in part, the tableau of life instead of death, and the familial instead of the exotic, as the reverse of Bishop's orphaned state and her displacement from Massachusetts to Nova Scotia and back again. But the fantastic is harder to account for. Of course, the fantastic is only the metaphorical raised to some level of exhibitionism. Yet such exhibitionism consorts oddly with Bishop's level tone and modesty of self-presentation. One might at first guess that the fantastic, for Bishop, is a symbol of the aesthetic realm. Yet she often represents art as a solacing encounter with the recognized (as in "The Map" or "Poem"), or as a form of life-giving or cherishing ("The Monument"), or as a "watery, dazzling dialectic" resolving contraries (as in "Santarém") rather than as a disquieting confrontation with the bizarre.

The fantastic must be, then, a special subgenre of the aesthetic. When art is represented as an excursion into the fantastic, it is because the poet has been evading the ruthless demands of art on the mind. When the poet is "sleeping on the ceiling," she is peaceful; but such peace can be felt only because she is avoiding a necessary encounter with the demons of the unconscious:

> We must go under the wallpaper
> to meet the insect-gladiator,
> to battle with a net and trident,
> and leave the fountain and the square.
> But oh, that we could sleep up there. . . .
>
> (29)

The poet's inner demons take on, when she doubts her strength to confront them, the grotesque form of an insect-gladiator waiting under the wallpaper when one doubts one's strength to confront it. "Pink Dog" exhibits the same dynamic: we find, inside the costume and mask, Bishop's demon as a scabied bitch who has abandoned her children; still elsewhere, ornamenting the desert tomb, the demons are exhortations yellowed like scattered cattle-teeth. Still elsewhere, in "Arrival at Santos," Bishop's anxieties produce the empty wasps' nest—judged "ugly" by another traveler—instead of the traditional filled honeycomb of the poet. In "The End of March," lengths of meaningless white string replace what should be a string buoyantly keeping a kite aloft; and in "Going to the Bakery," the poet's inner demons have so tainted the innocent items of confection that they appear mortally ill:

> the round cakes look about to faint—
> each turns up a glazed white eye.
> The gooey tarts are red and sore. . . .
>
>   the loaves of bread
> lie like yellow-fever victims
> laid out in a crowded ward.
>
> (151)

The anxiety behind the creation of such a fantastic fever-ward of cakes and tarts and loaves suggests that merely seeing something exotic—unfamiliar Brazilian pastries, in this case—was to Bishop a particularly powerful stimulus to her most primitive repressed terrors of abandonment, illness, and failure. In short, the more a poem evaded confrontation, the more it was likely to represent art as something grotesquely fantastic. Because of the depths stirred up unexpectedly in her by an unfamiliar sight, Bishop prized the exotic as an anteroom to self-discovery and writing; because of the primitive resistances and anxieties it provoked in her, the exotic moved her to fantastic conjunctions of death and bizarrerie.

Even when the triad of death, the exotic, and the fantastic is muted, it declares itself to the eye that has learned to recognize it. The grandmother's house in Nova Scotia is the first exotic location for the New England child that Bishop was: she was not brought up to believe that her destiny lay in remaining in Great Village; rather, she knew her destiny lay in Massachusetts (as her removal there, and her attendance at the Walnut Hill School, bear evidence). In "Sestina," the unnamed and ungendered child persistently draws the missing parental generation—not "a family with pets" but an unmated "man with buttons like tears" (the mother being suppressed entirely in an unacknowledged "death"). The fantastic almanac dropping its little moons into the child's flower bed, and the grandmother's surreal teacup full of dark brown tears add the element of the inscrutable, as the child Elizabeth—for who doubts that the anonymous child is she?—struggles with the demons of double parental absence (unexplained in the poem, but biographically linked to the death of the father and the madness of the mother). The exotic, the deathly, the fantastic: even in their mild forms in "Sestina" they unite like cells bearing tailor-made receptors for each other.

In their more violent forms, as in "Brazil, January 1, 1502," the exotic becomes the arena of conquistadors, the deathly becomes *"L'Homme Armé,"* and the fantastic becomes the erotic landscape-tapestry of Sin, represented as one aroused female lizard eyed by four male lizards:

> The lizards scarcely breathe: all eyes
> are on the smaller, female one, back-to,
> her wicked tail straight up and over,
> red as a red-hot wire.
>
> (92)

This demonic image, equating Sin with animal lust, prepares us for the final violence, when the "Christians, hard as nails" "ripped away into the hanging fabric." "Ripped" modulates into the unsaid "raped" as the Christians are each "out to catch an Indian for himself—/ those maddening little women who kept calling" (92). The exotic venue, the death-dealing armed men, and the fantastic emblem-image of Sin mobilize Bishop's harshest poem of cultural encounter and primitive erotic drives of cruelty.

Bishop needs to transmute even the familiar into the exotic in order to provoke the state of writing. Or perhaps it is truer to say that unless the familiar scene or object appears in an unfamiliar aspect it cannot engender verse. The Nova Scotian parlor of "First Death" becomes exotic because of the coincidence of the frozen red-eyed loon and Arthur's frosty coffin; even what should be an ordinary fish becomes fantastic because of his five lip-embedded hooks and lines; the familiar Atlantic shoreline in "At the Fishhouses" is rendered exotic as it is gradually painted a homogeneous silver; and the Atlantic itself becomes fantastic because it is conceived of as a burning and briny analogue to knowledge, in which total immersion means death to any mortal. The exotic engenders the fantastic, and the fantastic the deathly—or the exotic engenders the deathly, and the deathly the fantastic, until the triad is complete.

The involuntary magnetism of the three terms for each other is broken, in certain poems, not by the evasion of one of the three terms as in "The Wave" or "The Flood," but by the poet's courageous examination of an anxiety palpably present in the poem. The preeminent poem of this kind is "At the Fishhouses." It makes the familiar shoreside scene exotic, as I've said, by covering it over, stroke by stroke, in all-pervasive silver. And though the poem draws in passing a minor fantastic image of death—the rusting capstan is said to be stained "the color of dried blood"—its two major fantasies (emphasized by introductory ellipses) are those of the seal and the fir trees, both invoked as mental resting-places for anxiety, both serving to stave off the dangerous passage down the ramp into the ice-cold water. The seal, already immersed, does not fear the water; the stationary fir trees do not have the mobility to be endangered by it. Twice the Atlantic note is prematurely sounded—"Cold dark deep and absolutely clear"—but in each case the speaker skitters away from it, first into a meditation on the seal and next into a meditation on the fir trees. Finally, the Atlantic note is liberated into unhindered being: "dark, salt, clear, moving, utterly free." This is the note of death, since the water is an "element bearable to no mortal." But instead of moving away from the ocean, as she had done as the young speaker of "The Wave," or instead of pretending that an alternate form of life could go on underwater, as in "The Flood," Bishop nerves herself to encounter the sea, because she has come to know that she is "a believer in total immersion." She fully grants the ache and the burn and the indifference of the sea, and her terror before it. But as she finally represents the ocean, it gives not only an ultimate death but an interim nourishment "derived from the rocky breasts forever, flowing and drawn." The sea suckles us on the milk of necessity; and the acknowledging of necessity and reality—our voluntary "drawing" from those "rocky breasts"—is a form of life, not death. To be "utterly free" is to be at the opposite pole from death, even if our free knowledge is flowing, and eventually flown. In seeing flown-ness as part of flowing-ness, Bishop exorcised the fear of death, and the anxiety of her own demons, from this grand conjunction of the exotic silver shore and the fantastic burning tide. She could not do so until she realized the involuntary nature of earlier compelled conjunctions of the triad. Once she had disjoined its components, consciously and deliberately, from each other, she could conjoin them voluntarily and majestically in her clear portrait of elegiac anxiety faced and overcome in "At the Fishhouses."

There are other such "involuntary" conjunctions in Bishop, such as that of the domestic and the strange, or the knowable and the inscrutable. In every case, the best poems are those in which the psychologically "inevitable" magnetisms are recognized as such, separated, scrutinized, and then aesthetically rejoined. The deep contribution of the exotic to Bishop's poetry is one that has already been amply acknowledged, and I have only added, here, that it frequently presents itself as inseparable from two other strong components of her art— death and the fantastic. Her art needed the abrasion of the exotic and the permission of the fantastic to expose the worst of her terrors. In the posthumously published "Edgar Allan Poe and the Juke Box," we find Bishop praising Poe— that connoisseur of the exotic, the fantastic, and the deathly—for being "exact." Poe the artist is contrasted in the poem with the sexually mechanical modernity of the jukebox. Bishop must have sensed that if she was not to be the captive of her compulsions, she had to join Poe in being exact about them.

17

Stevens and Keats's "To Autumn"

Reworking the Past

Throughout his long life as a poet, Stevens returned again and again to Keats's ode "To Autumn." The history of those returns provides a classic example of how literary materials can be reworked by a modern artist. We are accustomed to this process in modern visual art, especially in painting and sculpture. Gombrich has pointed out how artists reproduce, not what they see, but some amalgam of that and an antecedent pictorial schema already in their minds. For Stevens, Keats's ode offered an irresistible antecedent model; Stevens hovered over the ode repeatedly in his musings. He became, to my way of thinking, the best reader of the ode, the most subtle interpreter of its rich meanings. Our understanding of latent significance in the older poem broadens when the ode is seen refracted through Stevens's lines. At the same time we may perceive, in Stevens's departures from the ode, implicit critiques of its stance.

A modern work of art may comment on an older one in several different ways. Stevens defined poetry in his *Adagia* as an art embracing two different "poetries"—the poetry of the idea and the poetry of the words.[1] My own writing on Stevens has hitherto been chiefly a commentary on the poetry of the words, but here I turn to the poetry of the idea. Stevens helpfully remarked that the idea of God was a poetic idea; it seems from "The Motive for Metaphor" that he considered the idea of a seasonal cycle a poetic idea as well, since it embodied the natural counterpart to the poetic "exhilarations of changes," the motive for metaphor:

> You like it under the trees in autumn,
> Because everything is half dead . . .

In the same way, you were happy in spring,
With half colors of quarter-things.

(257)

The seasonal idea, though immemorially present in lyric, seems to have been mediated to Stevens through Keats, no doubt through the sonnet on the human seasons as well as through the odes. In commenting on a received aesthetic form, an artist such as Stevens can take various paths, as Harold Bloom taught us in *The Anxiety of Influence*. The poet may make certain implicit "meanings" explicit; he may extrapolate certain possibilities to greater lengths; he may choose a detail, center on it, and turn it into an entire composition; he may alter the perspective from which the form is viewed; or he may view the phenomenon at a different moment in time. We are familiar with these strategies in painting, in the expansion and critique of classical forms practiced by all subsequent schools, but most noticeably for us, perhaps, in the dramatic and radical experimentation with classic forms in our own century. Stevens is modern as Cézanne is modern; he keeps the inherited shapes, is classic in his own disposition of materials, is rarely bizarre, and stays within the central tradition of Western art. Stevens's "copies" never forget their great originals; but we may see, in following Stevens's experiments with the materials of the autumn ode, how a modern originality gradually declares itself, while deliberately recalling the earlier master's prototype.

The presence of Keats's ode within a great many of Stevens's poems is self-evident. The single most derivative moment in Stevens is the end of "Sunday Morning";

We live in an old chaos of the sun,
Or old dependency of day and night,
Or island solitude, unsponsored, free,
Of that wide water, inescapable.
Deer walk upon our mountains, and the quail
Whistle about us their spontaneous cries;
Sweet berries ripen in the wilderness;
And, in the isolation of the sky,
At evening, casual flocks of pigeons make
Ambiguous undulations as they sink,
Downward to darkness, on extended wings.

(56)

In "Credences of Summer" and "The Auroras of Autumn" Stevens composed two "panels" to the autumn ode; and there are lesser appearances of fragments of the ode throughout Stevens's work. Anyone familiar with "To Autumn" will recognize in Stevens's verse the replication of Keats's fruits, autumnal female presence, cottage (transmuted to an American cabin), cornfields (changed to American hayfields), wind, muted or unmelodious birds, stubble plains (reduced to bare stalks or thin grass), clouds, and bees. Our recognition of such echoes is usually intermittent; but to read through Stevens's poetry with the ode "To Autumn" in mind is to be suffused by the lights that Stevens saw presiding over "the trash can at the end of the world," the urn of "Owls' Clover":

> . . . Above that urn two lights
> Commingle, not like the commingling of sun and moon
> At dawn, nor of summer-light and winter-light
> In an autumn afternoon, but two immense
> Reflections, whirling apart and wide away.
> (156)

The end of "Sunday Morning" is a rewritten version of the close of Keats's "To Autumn"; such obvious and unashamed risk taking in a young poet argues a deep engagement with the earlier poem. The resemblances have been often remarked. Both poets use successive clauses of animal presence (gnats, lambs, crickets, redbreast, and swallows in Keats; deer, quail, and pigeons in Stevens); both poems close with birds in the sky (gathering swallows in Keats, flocks of pigeons in Stevens) and with the sense of sound (including a whistling bird in each); Keats's soft-dying day becomes Stevens's evening. Stevens's stance, unlike that of Keats, is the homiletic and doctrinal one inherited from religious poetry and dear to American poets. However, Stevens, as a modern poet, offers no single doctrine but rather a choice among truths: we live either (1) in chaos, or (2) in a system of mutual dependency, or (3) in a condition of solitude, which may itself be seen as (3a) lonely ("unsponsored") or (3b) liberated ("free"), but which is in any case inescapable. The passage allowing doctrinal choices is followed by the passage on deer, quail, berries, and pigeons (those wilderness forms replacing Keats's domestic ones), in which the doctrinal options are alluded to but, in the end, left undecided. The quail utter "spontaneous" cries, and their adjective hearkens back to our "unsponsored" state; the pigeons fly in an "isolation" etymologically resembling our "island" solitude; the "chaos" of the sun recalls orthographically the "casual" flocks of pigeons. In the end, as Stevens's pigeons inscribe their transient motions in the air, their calligraphy is read (by the poet seeking significance) as elusively ambiguous, and doctrinal choice dissolves in mystery. But although metaphysical certainty remains unattainable, the truth of mortal existence is clear. The final motion, whether or not definable as one of chaos, dependency, solitude, freedom, or unsponsoredness, is "downward to darkness." In such an ending, *be* is finale of *seem*, and death is the only certainty uninvaded by metaphysical doubt. While Keats rests in the polyphony of the creatures in their autumnal choir, Stevens (although his adoption of Keats's principal trope, enumeration, shows him as not insensible to the plenitude around him in the scene) makes his landscape depend for its significance on what it can explicitly suggest about metaphysical truth.

With the example of Keats's beautiful implicit meanings before us, we may tend to recoil from what seems crudity in Stevens, as he speckles the visible scene with invisible queries: chaos? dependency? solitude? unsponsoredness? freedom? isolation? casualness? ambiguity? The coercion of cadence forces the innocent landscape to enact a Stevensian entropy:

> And,
> in the isolation of the sky,
> at evening,
> casual flocks of pigeons make
> Ambiguous undulations as they sink,
> Downward to darkness,
> on extended wings.

Stevens's final clause is, of course, imitated from Keats's passage on the gnats among the river sallows:

> aloft   lives
> borne   or   as the light wind   or
> sinking   dies.

Keats's imitation of randomness is changed by Stevens into an imitation of decline. But Keats, after writing about the gnats, went on to forbid himself such evident stylistic equivalences:

> And full-grown lambs loud bleat from hilly bourn;
> Hedge-crickets sing; and now with treble soft

> The red-breast whistles from a garden-croft;
> And gathering swallows twitter in the skies.

These clauses are the source for Stevens's earlier ones (such as "Deer walk upon our mountains"), but Stevens has reversed Keats's rhetorical order. Keats writes a long clause about the gnats, then follows it with shorter ones dwindling to "hedge-crickets sing," then broadens out to end his poem. Stevens writes short clauses followed by a final long one. The result is a gain in climactic force and explicit pathos, but a loss in stoicism and discretion of statement. Keats's pathos (at its most plangent in the small gnats who mourn in a wailful choir, helpless in the light wind; less insistent but still audible in the bleating lambs; but largely absent in the whistle and twitter of the closing lines) reaches us with steadily diminishing force, in inverse relation to Keats's recognition of the independent worth of autumnal music, without reference to any dying fall. Stevens's pathos, on the other hand, is at its most evident in the closing lines. In short, Stevens has adopted Keats's manner—the population of animals, the types of clause, the diction, even the sunset landscape—without embracing Keats's essential stylistic argument against nostalgia. Nor has he imitated Keats's reticent diction and chaste rhetoric; instead, he writes with an increasing opulence of rhetorical music, and imposes explicit metaphysical dimensions on the landscape.

The imitation, however inferior to its source, argues that Keats's ode had penetrated Stevens's consciousness and imagination and was already provoking him to see the world in its light, even if he found the world insufficient without attendant metaphysics. Keats's ode continued to provide Stevens with material to the very end of his life. In the *Adagia*, Stevens asks the question the ode, among other works, must have prompted: "How has the human spirit ever survived the terrific literature with which it has had to contend?" (907).

If, on the total evidence of Stevens's poetry, we ask how he read "To Autumn," we can isolate, for the moment neglecting the chronology of the *Collected Poems*, elements of his understanding of the ode. He thought, at first, that Keats was being evasive in the stasis of the first stanza, that he was avoiding the most repellent detail of natural process—death. (Stevens was, in taking this severe view, misinterpreting Keats, whose subject was not natural processes, but human intervention in natural process—harvest, rather than death.) In "Le Monocle de Mon Oncle" and "Sunday Morning," Stevens, insisting that everything "comes rotting back to ground" and that "this luscious and impeccable fruit of life /

Falls, it appears, of its own weight to earth," writes what seem taunts directed at the changeless ripeness of Keats's first stanza:

> Is there no change of death in paradise?
> Does ripe fruit never fall? Or do the boughs
> Hang always heavy in that perfect sky?
>
> (55)

Allowing the fruit to follow its natural trajectory, Stevens lets Autumn not only "swell the gourd" but doubles the gourd into a human couple. The gourds are strained beyond their normal ripeness until they become distorted in shape and their skin becomes streaked and rayed:

> It comes, it blooms, it bears its fruit and dies . . .
> Two golden gourds distended on our vines,
> Into the autumn weather, splashed with frost,
> Distorted by hale fatness, turned grotesque.
> We hang like warty squashes, streaked and rayed,
> The laughing sky will see the two of us
> Washed into rinds by rotting winter rains.
>
> (13)

In spite of this "realist" critique of Keats's benign autumn, Stevens's poetry here is still Keatsian: no new style of language has been invented to support the new harshness of position. And the unfairness of the modern poet's revisionary critique is of a piece with the "realist" position. Stevens comes much closer to the true Keatsian stance in a later poem, "On the Road Home," where plenitude is seen to stem not so much from any group of items in the landscape as from the refusal of doctrine in favor of perception, of measuring the world not by thought but by eye:

> It was when I said,
> "There is no such thing as the truth,"
> That the grapes seemed fatter . . .
>
> It was at that time, that the silence was largest
> And longest, the night was roundest,
> The fragrance of the autumn warmest,
> Closest and strongest.
>
> (186)

Whatever the objections that could be urged against the final formulation here, it is, in its near-tautology and solemn playfulness, recognizably Stevensian and not Keatsian in language. Even when metaphysically in agreement with Keats, the later Stevens speaks in his own twentieth-century voice.

When Stevens writes, in "The Rock," his final retraction of the "realist" view expressed in "Le Monocle," he alludes to his own dictum from the early poem ("It comes, it blooms, it bears its fruit and dies") but he quietly corrects himself by omitting the death. The leaves that cover the rock, standing for the poem as icon, "bud and bloom and bear their fruit without change." This is not written in agreement with Keats, who allowed his fruit to change, if not through death at least through harvest, winnowing, and cider making. But neither is it written to correct him. It is written to give credence to the plenty of the world as it is preserved not on the earth but in the mind, always Stevens's chosen territory. The leaves

> . . . bloom as a man loves, as he lives in love.
> They bear their fruit so that the year is known,
>
> As if its understanding was brown skin,
> And honey in its pulp, the final found,
> The plenty of the year and of the world.
> (446)

Here, precisely because he is speaking of internal, not external fruition, Stevens is able to leave the fruit on the tree, the honey in the hive, without irritably reaching out to force them to fall and rot, or to be harvested.

No other source in poetry was so rich for Stevens as Keats's second stanza. Keats's goddess of autumn, nearer to us than pagan goddesses of fertility because, unlike them, she labors in the fields and is herself threshed by the winnowing wind, varies in her manifestations from careless girl to burdened gleaner to patient watcher—erotic in her abandon to the fume of poppies, the intimate of light in her bosom friendship with the maturing sun, worn by her vigil over the last oozings. She reappears in innumerable guises in Stevens's work, but is more often than not maternal: "The mother's face, / The purpose of the poem, fills the room" ("The Auroras of Autumn," 356). It is probable that her maternal nature was suggested by Keats's ode (which itself borrows from Shakespeare's image of "the teeming autumn, big with rich increase, / Bearing the wanton burden of the prime, / Like widow'd wombs after their lord's decease"). Keats's season is an earth-goddess whose union with the sun makes her bear fruit; the sun, his part in procreation done, departs from the poem as the harvest begins, and the season gradually ages from the careless figure on the granary floor to the watcher over the last drops of the crushed apples. Finally, when she becomes herself the "soft-dying day," she is mourned by creatures deliberately infantine, as even full-grown sheep are represented as bleating lambs: these creatures arc filial forms, children grieving for the death of the mother. Stevens, I believe, recognized these implications and brought them into explicitness.

The most beautiful modern commentary on Keats's invention of a humanized goddess of the ripe fields occurs in Stevens's poem "The Woman in Sunshine":

> It is only that this warmth and movement are like
> The warmth and movement of a woman.
>
> It is not that there is any image in the air
> Nor the beginning nor end of a form:
>
> It is empty. But a woman in threadless gold
> Burns us with brushings of her dress
>
> And a dissociated abundance of being,
> More definite for what she is—
>
> Because she is disembodied,
> Bearing the odors of the summer fields,
>
> Confessing the taciturn and yet indifferent,
> Invisibly clear, the only love.
>
> (381)

The "poetry of the idea" here comes from Keats, the "poetry of the words" from Stevens. The iconic "image," surrounded by words like "empty," "dissociated," "disembodied," "taciturn," "indifferent," and "invisibly clear," is wholly Stevensian, as is the rhetoric of "it is only," "it is not," and "it is empty." Stevens has taken a detail from his source—Keats's form of an autumn goddess—and has enlarged it to fill a new and more modern space. This goddess assumes various forms in Stevens, most of them beneficent. When Stevens is depressed, "mother nature" (as she is named along with a matching invention, "father nature," in "Lulu Morose") turns either actively malevolent (curdling the kind cow's milk with lightning in "Lulu Morose") or, worse, devouring but indifferent (as in "Madame La Fleurie," where mother and father nature are conflated into one androgynous mother who feeds on her son, "a bearded queen, wicked in her dead light"). But such "corrections" of Keats's goddess are infrequent in Stevens. Rather, Stevens tends to expand Keats's figure until she becomes one of "the pure perfections of parental space, / . . . the beings of the mind / In the light-bound space of the mind" (374–375). Though he acknowledges fully the fictive nature of the goddess, Stevens can move insensibly into speaking of her as if she were real, as if she were in fact all there is of reality. In this, he learned from Keats's fully formed and fully imagined relation to the autumn goddess, whom Keats begins by celebrating in tones of worship and ends by consoling in the accents of intimacy: "Think not of them, thou hast thy music too."

Keats's third stanza gave Stevens his crickets, his bare spaces, and all his autumn refrains of thinning music. But, more centrally, it invited him to participate in its debate on the value of a diminished music, and in its speculation on the relation of that music to the ampler choirs of spring. Stevens recognized, I think, that Keats's ode is spoken by one whose poetic impetus arises from recoil at the stubble plains; the method of the ode is to adopt a reparatory fantasy whereby the barren plains are "repopulated" with fruit, flowers, wheat, and a providential goddess. But Keats subsides, at the end, into the barrenness that had first stimulated his compensatory imagination, and he leaves in the fields nothing but his poem—that autumnal thin music—where there had briefly been an imagined feast for sight and touch.

Nostalgia, so gently put aside by Keats when his goddess sighs for the songs of spring, is more vindictively suppressed by Stevens in one of the more astonishing poetic descendants of the ode. "Think not of them," says Keats to that part of himself which has looked longingly backward to the nightingales' spring songs. Stevens begins his corresponding late passage in "Puella Parvula" (390) by telling us that "every thread of summer is at last unwoven." It is the "season of memory, / When the leaves fall like things mournful of the past." But over the dissolving wind, "the mighty imagination triumphs," saying to inner nostalgia not Keats's kind words but rather,

> Keep quiet in the heart, O wild bitch. O mind
> Gone wild, be what he tells you to be: *Puella*.
> Write *pax* across the window pane. And then
>
> Be still. The *summarium in excelsis* begins.

The taming of mind to the season is common to Keats and Stevens, but Stevens's regret, the regret of the man who rarely had the satisfactions of summer, is more bitter. What is left from romance is "the rotted rose," and the later poet must squeeze "the reddest fragrance from the stump / Of summer" (255). The violence of the modern supervenes on the Romantic sunset.

These, as Stevens would say, are only instances. For Stevens's grandest meditation on "To Autumn" we must look to two of his long poems. "Credences of Summer" (322) centers on the moment when "the hay, / Baked through long days, is piled in mows," the moment before the stubble plains. "The Auroras of Autumn" (355) centers on the approach of "boreal night" after "the season changes." The light wind of Keats's soft-dying day modulates into a fiercer form: "A cold wind chills the beach." The stubble plains, at the end of "The Auroras," are metaphorically ignited to form the flares of the aurora borealis, "the lights / Like a blaze of summer straw, in winter's nick." In between "Credences" and "Auroras," radiating back to the one and forward to the other, stands Keats's ode.

The boldness of "Credences of Summer" lies in its suggestion that the perception of Keats's bees—that "warm days will never cease"—is no self-deception to be patronized, however wistfully, by the poet, but rather one of the authentic human states of being:

> . . . Fill the foliage with arrested peace,
> Joy of such permanence, right ignorance
> Of change still possible.
> . . . . .
>   The utmost must be good and is
> And is our fortune and honey hived in the trees.

And yet Stevens knows that the song of "summer in the common fields" is sung by singers not themselves partaking of that summer, just as Keats's ode of summer fruition and repose is sung by one gazing at the shorn stubble fields. Stevens's singers are "far in the woods":

> Far in the woods they sang their unreal songs,
> Secure. It was difficult to sing in face
> Of the object. The singers had to avert themselves
> Or else avert the object. Deep in the woods
> They sang of summer in the common fields.

> They sang desiring an object that was near,
> In face of which desire no longer moved,
> Nor made of itself that which it could not find.

In spite of this admission that singers sing out of desire rather than out of satisfaction, Stevens's poem begins, as Keats's does, with the benevolent fiction that the singers are in the midst of the landscape they celebrate:

> Young broods
> Are in the grass, the roses are heavy with a weight
> Of fragrance and the mind lays by its trouble.

This is the moment of the marriage of earth and sky, the time of conspiracy between the sky-god, the sun, and the earth-goddess, the queen, to produce the young broods: this is "green's apogee // And happiest folk-land, mostly marriage hymns."

Keats had begun his ode with the symbolic marriage of earth and air, but had sketched it with the lightest of suggestions: in Stevens the family constellation appears and reappears, as he draws Keats out to iconic completion:

> These fathers standing round,
> These mothers touching, speaking, being near,
> These lovers waiting in the soft dry grass.

The queen is "the charitable majesty of her whole kin," and "the bristling soldier" is "a filial form and one / Of the land's children, easily born." Like the earthly paradise where flowers and fruit coexist, this paradise contains harmoniously all stages of human existence—the young broods, lovers, fathers and mothers, and an old man—but its chief emblem is "the youth, the vital son, the heroic power," the filial form whom age cannot touch. Yet, after the admission that "a mind exists, aware of division," the heroic attempt to maintain the privileged moment falters, and Stevens's more grotesque version of stubble fields makes its appearance, with a presiding form resembling Keats's redbreast. There is even a recollection of Keats's river sallows:

> Fly low, cock bright, and stop on a bean pole. Let
> Your brown breast redden, while you wait for warmth.
> With one eye watch the willow, motionless.

> The gardener's cat is dead, the gardener gone
> And last year's garden grows salacious weeds.

Keats's twice-repeated "soft" appears in this canto: "Soft, civil bird," and "not /
So soft." For the agricultural laborer-goddess and her creatures Stevens substitutes the gardener and his cat, deriving the gardener perhaps from Keats's
"gardener Fancy" in the "Ode to Psyche." Stevens's way of solving the en-
croachments of decay on his scene of happiness is to attribute to his singers,
although they are only the creations of "an inhuman author," a will of their
own, as though the author is himself mastered by the rise of desire in the hearts
of his characters:

> . . . The characters speak because they want
> To speak, the fat, the roseate characters,
> Free, for a moment, from malice and sudden cry,
> Complete in a completed scene, speaking
> Their parts as in a youthful happiness.

These characters who speak of their own free will resemble Keats's creatures,
who, in spite of the season's sadness, sing their own music. It is clear from
Stevens's ending that "malice and sudden cry" are likely to be the ordinary states
of the characters of the inhuman author, and that the miraculous lifting for a
moment of their usual oppressive state enables, not youthful happiness, but a
state resembling it. Seen in this way, "Credences of Summer" becomes, like
"To Autumn," a backward-glancing poem, as its author, for a moment liberated from misery, looks for the perfect metaphor for the feeling he experiences
in that moment and decides that youthful happiness (after spring's infuriations
are over, after one's mortifying adolescent foolish selves are slaughtered) is the
vehicle he needs. It is only in retrospect that we see the hovering of a divided
mental state at the end of the second stanza:

> This is the last day of a certain year
> Beyond which there is nothing left of time.
> It comes to this and the imagination's life.

"This"—the perfect day—staves off for a while the full realization of the
other—the imagination's life. But by the end of the poem, in the meditation
on the observant mind, imagination is in the ascendant and the rich day has
decayed into the salacious garden. The war in the poem between the warmth

of Keatsian language and the chill of metaphysical analysis means that Stevens has not achieved a style that can embrace both the physical pine and the metaphysical pine. The presentation of summer cannot coexist, in tone or diction, with the anatomy of summer; and the anatomy, skirted and then suppressed in Keats in favor of self-forgetfulness, is allowed full play by Stevens. If the summer-prolonging bees are given credence, so is the undeceived questioning of the aloof, divided mind, and Stevens's poem, unable to maintain a Keatsian harmony, divides sharply in consequence of its "mind, aware of division."

If "Credences of Summer" goes both backward from Keats and further with his questioning (thereby losing the miraculous, if precarious, Keatsian balance), "The Auroras of Autumn" fastens on the question "Where are the songs of spring?" and makes a poetics of it. Keats stops in autumn to imagine spring and rebukes himself for his nostalgia, which implies a criticism of the season in which he finds himself. "Think not of them," he says of the spring songs. Stevens, in contrast, decides to think deliberately about them. What does it mean—for life, for poetry—that we cannot rest in the present, in any present? It means that the desire for change is more deep-rooted than the pleasure of any permanence, no matter how luxurious:

> Is there an imagination that sits enthroned
> As grim as it is benevolent, the just
> And the unjust, which in the midst of summer stops
>
> To imagine winter?

Every making of the mind moves to find "what must unmake it and, at last, what can." After being "fattened as on a decorous honeycomb," "we lay sticky with sleep," like Keats's bees. Stevens is Keatsian in accepting the fact of change; he is also Keatsian in his elegiac strain, substituting a Keatsian "farewell" for the even more Keatsian "adieu":

> Farewell to an idea . . . A cabin stands,
> Deserted, on a beach.

Stevens is Keatsian, too, in making the goddess who presides over the dissolution of the season a maternal figure who says not farewell or adieu but (as to children) goodnight, goodnight:

> Farewell to an idea . . . The mother's face,
> The purpose of the poem, fills the room.

She gives transparence. But she has grown old.
The necklace is a carving not a kiss.

Stevens offers a critique of Keats by leaping over Keats's set piece of sunset and twilight bird song and taking his poem beyond the death of the mother, after sunset, into boreal night. The birds, instead of going downward to darkness or gathering into a Keatsian flock, are set wildly flying:

The theatre is filled with flying birds,
Wild wedges, as of a volcano's smoke.

Across his sky Stevens displays his auroras, his earthly equivalent to the heavenly serpent-god sloughing skins at the opening of the poem, both symbols of change. The auroras are beautiful and intimidating at once; they leave us in the state of Keats's gnats and bleating lambs, "a shivering residue, chilled and foregone." The auroras change "idly, the way / A season changes color to no end, / Except the lavishing of itself in change." All natural changes are equal; there is no entropy in nature; all events are simply songs of "the innocent mother." The spectre of the spheres, like the inhuman author of "Credences of Summer," contrives a balance to contrive a whole. This new poetics wishes not only to relish everything equally (in itself a Keatsian ideal), but to relish everything at once, to imagine winter in summer and summer in winter, to meditate

The full of fortune and the full of fate,
As if he lived all lives, that he might know,

In hall harridan, not hushful paradise,
To a haggling of wind and weather, by these lights
Like a blaze of summer straw, in winter's nick.

This finale of "The Auroras" is an implicit boast of imaginative triumph. Everything, however, is intrinsically less expressible than something. The close of the poem is less beautiful than the vision of the aurora itself. In this respect Stevens is Keatsian, substituting one form of landscape, the later auroras, for another, the Romantic sunset.

An earlier poem of Stevens arises from the Keatsian injunction that prompted "The Auroras"—"Think not of them"—and is in fact an extended thinking-

and-not-thinking; "The Snow Man" might well be called "The Man Standing in the Stubble Plains." Snow, like harvest, eliminates vegetation; and Stevens, like Keats, faces the question of how to praise a world from which the summer growth has disappeared. Keats's "light wind" blowing over the bare fields is intensified, always, in Stevens into a "wind" of "winter" (and Stevens relishes the phonemic echo). Oddly enough, beheld with a mind of winter, the world does not appear bare: the boughs of the pine trees are crusted with snow, the junipers are shagged with ice, the spruces are rough in the distant glitter of the January sun. It is only with the introduction of the wind, and misery and the few remaining leaves on the deciduous trees that the world becomes "the same bare place" and the regarder and beholder—who saw such a rich world—becomes a listener who, nothing himself, "beholds / Nothing that is not there and the nothing that is." The turn from beholding to listening, borrowed from Keats's ode, coincides, as it does in Keats, with a pained turning from plenitude to absence. But Keats finds a new plenitude—of the ear—to substitute for the visual absence. Stevens, finding it impossible to acknowledge the plenitude perceivable by a mind of winter—that plenitude of encrustation, shagginess, and rough snow-glitter—reverses Keats and finds bareness in listening. He turns, therefore, from the Keatsian trope of plenitude—enumeration—which he had employed in his listing of pines, junipers, and spruce trees, and uses instead a trope of reductiveness, becoming a modernist of minimal art: he hears, in a deadly repetition of the same few words (italics mine),

> *the sound of the wind*
> *the sound of a* few leaves
> *the sound of the* land
>   full *of the same wind*
>   that is blowing *in the same* bare place
>   for the *listener* who *listens in the* snow
>   and, *nothing* himself, beholds
>   *nothing that is* not there
>   and the *nothing that is.*

Another fairly early attempt at "thinking with the season" occurs in "Anatomy of Monotony" (90) where Stevens, conceding the pathetic fallacy, urges us to have it on nature's terms, not our own. Since the Earth "bore us as a part of all the things / It breeds," it follows that "our nature is her nature":

> Hence it comes,
> Since by our nature we grow old, earth grows
> The same. We parallel the mother's death.

But the Earth has a wider vision than our narrow personal pathos:

> She walks an autumn ampler than the wind
> Cries up for us and colder than the frost
> Pricks in our spirits at the summer's end,
> And over the bare spaces of our skies
> She sees a barer sky that does not bend.

This widening of perspective is borrowed from Keats, too, though it applies Keats's technique of expansion (broadening from the cottage and its kitchen garden and orchard to the cornfields and outbuildings and finally extending to the horizon, the boundary hill and hedges, the river, and the sky) only to the bare spaces of Keats's final stanza. It seems, as we read Stevens, that each aspect of the autumn ode called out to him to be reinterpreted, reused, recreated into a poem.

Much later, in "World without Peculiarity" (388), Stevens "rewrites" "Anatomy of Monotony," achieving at last, however briefly, the power to think with the season. What is most human is now no longer (in Stevens's hard saying) sadness, pathos, nostalgia—that projection of ourselves into and onto other things which fail, die, or wane—but rather solitary existence as a natural object. Stevens may be remembering, in his extraordinary central stanza, Whitman's line about "the justified mother of men":

> What good is it that the earth is justified,
> That it is complete, that it is an end,
> That in itself it is enough?

> It is the earth itself that is humanity . . .
> He is the inhuman son and she,
> She is the fateful mother, whom he does not know.

> She is the day.

Though there are here no verbal echoes of Keats, this seems to me a poem that could not have been thought of except by someone who had incorporated into his imagination that sense of the independent life of nature voiced in the autumn ode.

Just as Stevens's "Woman in Sunshine" removes the mythological solidity from Keats's goddess in the fields and reminds us of what she is, a fictive construct, so "Less and Less Human, O Savage Spirit" (288) wishes for a god both silent and quiet, "saying things," if he must, as light and color and shape "say things," a god who "will not hear us when we speak." This god, unable to say "Where are the songs of spring," is at once more earthly and more disembodied than Keats's goddess, pressing further toward the fictive and the inanimate at once.

Always in Stevens there is a new precipitate from the Keatsian solution, because mind and sense cannot coexist in equilibrium. No writer, in Stevens's view, could avoid the asking of the fatal question about the songs of spring. Stevens writes, in "The Ultimate Poem is Abstract" (369), a second-order reflection on the inevitability of questions: Keats (or a poet like him) is treated ironically and called "the lecturer / On This Beautiful World of Ours," who "hems the planet rose and haws it ripe, / And red, and right." But his hemming and hawing into roses and rosehips and red haws cannot last:

> One goes on asking questions. That, then, is one
> Of the categories. So said, this placid space
>
> Is changed. It is not so blue as we thought. To be blue,
> There must be no questions.
>
>   . . . It would be enough
> If we were ever, just once, at the middle, fixed
> In This Beautiful World of Ours and not as now,
>
> Helplessly at the edge, enough to be
> Complete, because at the middle, if only in sense,
> And in that enormous sense, merely enjoy.

Such a poem is a rewriting, at a second-order level, of the Keats ode; it recounts in an abstract way Keats's attempt to remain "at the middle" of the beautiful world, praising its generosity to all the senses, its plenitude of being. The invasion of Keats's enjoyment by questioning, an *event* in the ode, becomes a *topic* for Stevens. And in other poems Stevens comments on each stage of the Keatsian process—how one sees first the earth "as inamorata," but then sees her "without distance . . . and naked or in rags, / Shrunk in the poverty of being close" (413). She has been a celestial presence among laborers, an angel surrounded by paysans, an "archaic form / . . . evoking an archaic space" (421).

But then her appurtenances fade (the moon is "a tricorn / waved in pale adieu") and "she is exhausted and a little old" ("Things of August," 422).

Stevens's late poetry of receptivity and inception, coming after the poetry of age and exhaustion, is nothing short of astonishing. Here Stevens follows Keats's "Human Seasons" beyond the winter of gross misfeature, finding "the cricket of summer forming itself out of ice," "not autumn's prodigal returned, / But an antipodal, far-fetched creature" ("A Discovery of Thought," 459). As he listens to winter sounds in "A Quiet Normal Life" (443), he hears "the crickets' chords, / Babbling each one, the uniqueness of its sound," and decides to do without the archaic forms:

> There was no fury in transcendent forms.
> But his actual candle blazed with artifice.

Stevens forgoes (in "Looking across the Fields and Watching the Birds Fly," 439) "the masculine myths we used to make" in favor of "a transparency through which the swallow weaves, / Without any form or any sense of form," and he decides that our thinking is nothing but our preestablished harmony with the grand motions of nature:

> We think, then, as the sun shines or does not.
> We think as wind skitters on a pond in a field[.]
>
> The spirit comes from the body of the world[.]
> . . . . .
> The mannerism of nature caught in a glass
> And there become a spirit's mannerism,
> A glass aswarm with things going as far as they can.

This sublime self-transformation into a modern version of an Aeolian harp immolates the mind. If we pose questions, it is because the earth poses them. There is no longer any need to say "Think not of them": everything is permitted, because everything is a natural motion.

Stevens's last tribute to the stubble plains is his transmutation of Keats's bareness into "The Plain Sense of Things" (428). This poem presses Keats's *donnée* to its ultimate point. There is no goddess, even a dying one; there is no memorial gleam cast through rosy clouds; there is no music; there are no touching filial forms; the surrogate animal for the human is not the laden honeybee, but the inquisitive pond rat:

After the leaves have fallen, we return
To a plain sense of things. It is as if
We had come to an end of the imagination,
Inanimate in an inert savoir.

. . . . .

Yet the absence of the imagination had
Itself to be imagined. The great pond,
The plain sense of it, without reflections, leaves,
Mud, water like dirty glass, expressing silence

Of a sort, silence of a rat come out to see,
The great pond and its waste of the lilies, all this
Had to be imagined as an inevitable knowledge,
Required, as a necessity requires.

"To Autumn" represented, for Keats, a retraction of the "Ode to Psyche."
In the earlier ode Keats had hoped that the imagination could be fully reparatory for an external absence; piece by piece, in "Psyche" he constructs his interior fane to compensate, warmly and luxuriously, for the earthly temple that
the goddess lacks. By the time he writes "To Autumn," he has lost, not the impulse toward plentitude (his impulse on seeing uninhabited stubble plains is to
go home and write a stanza loaded and blessed with fruit and to invent an in-
dwelling harvest goddess), but the ability to close with erotic anticipation
"a bright torch, and a casement ope at night; To let the warm Love in!" "The
absence of fantasia" in the bare fields might have tempted Stevens earlier to a
compensatory opulence of reconstruction (like his populating his cabin with
four daughters with curls in "The Comedian"), but now he finds a discipline
in poverty, in another detail borrowed from Keats and expanded into its own
poem: an unmusical bird cry. The "wailful choir" of the autumn sunset gives
way, in Stevens's poetry of old age, to an imagined choir of aubade, as Stevens
draws the ode forward from its twilight into the new sunrise of "Not Ideas About
the Thing But the Thing Itself" (451):

At the earliest ending of winter,
In March, a scrawny cry from outside
Seemed like a sound in his mind.

. . . . . .

That scrawny cry—it was
A chorister whose c preceded the choir.
It was part of the colossal sun,

Surrounded by its choral rings,
Still far away. It was like
A new knowledge of reality.

There is no "new reality": there is only a "new knowledge of reality." Crispin, the "marvelous sophomore," had boasted, "Here was the veritable ding an sich, at last" (23). But his boast was premature. Stevens did not find "the thing itself" until very late, and then in a scale Keatsian in its humility. "Not Ideas About the Thing But the Thing Itself" (451) is Stevens's most beautiful late reflection on his own beginnings (as the comedian as the letter "C" becomes the chorister whose "c" preceded the choir) and on Keats's ode and its minimal music. Nonetheless I close not with this last successful meditation but instead with a poem that in its own interlacing of lines shows Stevens's stubborn ambition, even at the expense of violent dislocation of form, to have plenitude and poverty at once, to possess Keats's central divine figure opulently whole and surrounded by her filial forms, while at the same time asserting the necessary obsolescence of her form and of the literature about her. She remains, he asserts, for all her inevitable vanishing, the inhabitant of "The Hermitage at the Centre" (430):

The leaves on the macadam make a noise—
    How soft the grass on which the desired
    Reclines in the temperature of heaven—

Like tales that were told the day before yesterday—
    Sleek in a natural nakedness,
    She attends the tintinnabula—

And the wind sways like a great thing tottering—
    Of birds called up by more than the sun,
    Birds of more wit, that substitute—

Which suddenly is all dissolved and gone—
    Their intelligible twittering
    For unintelligible thought.

And yet this end and this beginning are one,
   And one last look at the ducks is a look
   At lucent children round her in a ring.

Stevens's response to Keats's ode was so long-lived that the central problems of the ode—process, termination, interruption of ripeness, the human seasons, the beauty of the minimal, the function of nostalgia, the relation between sense and thought, and so on—became central to Stevens's poetry as well. His attempts to go "beyond" Keats in various ways—to take the human seasons further, into winter, into boreal apocalypse, into inception; to find new imagery of his own, while retaining Keats's crickets and bees and birds and sun and fields; to create his own archaic forms in the landscape, defining in their evolution Stevens's own emerging originality. Though he retains a classical structure to his verse, his diction and rhetoric become ever less visibly Romantic, as a plain sense of things and an absence of fantasia clear the air. Everywhere we hear Stevens meditating on Keats, whose fashion of beholding without comment must have seemed to Stevens prophetically modern. Stevens sensed that the poem of presentation was the poem of earth: just to behold, just to be beheld, what is there here but weather—these are the assumptions Stevens found and grasped for himself in the most untranscendental of the great Romantic odes.

18

"The Circulation of Small Largenesses"

Mark Ford and John Ashbery

Writers influenced by John Ashbery more often imitate his manner than grasp his import. They can scramble a metaphor, write a melting close, insert pop icons, make a comic allusion. But the essence of Ashbery does not lie in these tricks. When in 1992, I read, with instant joy, Mark Ford's *Landlocked*,[1] I found a poet who had internalized the inner, more than the outer, Ashbery. But, as I hope to show, Ford's poetry, even while benefiting from Ashbery's example, retains its own different quirkiness, both in that first volume and in his second collection, *Soft Sift* (2001).[2]

Ashbery's importance, to my mind, lies in his being the first notable American poet to free himself, stylistically and thematically, from nostalgia for religious, philosophical, and ideological systems. His modernist predecessors thought such systems necessary to human dignity, and they either remained Christian, like Marianne Moore; returned to Christianity, like T. S. Eliot and John Berryman; adopted an alternative political ideology (fascism in Ezra Pound, political conservatism in Robert Frost, a quasi-socialism in William Carlos Williams, feminism in Adrienne Rich); turned to Buddhism like Allen Ginsberg and Gary Snyder; or to science as a substitutive omni-system, as in the case of A. R. Ammons. Many poets who have tried to do without such systems— Wallace Stevens, Robert Lowell, Elizabeth Bishop, Sylvia Plath, and Charles Wright—nonetheless have expressed explicit imaginative regret for the loss of religious sublimity. One feels the pull, in all these poets, toward a system of belief or an organized form of collectivity, a wish for a way to give honor, dignity, and greater-than-personal significance to human life. Only within and by means of such systems, it seems to many writers, can the human subject be situated and understood.

Ashbery, by contrast, is wholly without a religious creed or a political ideology. And—more crucially—he gets along without the nostalgia for credences or, to be more precise, he includes systems and creeds in his general mild nostalgia for everything transient, from sunsets to Popeye. But in Ashbery's work a comedy of plenitude and inception, both in theme and language, is constantly—and effortlessly—canceling out the general wash of nostalgia. His little two-line poem says it all: "The Cathedral Is," says the title; "Slated for demolition," says the poem.[3] Sturdy architectural existence in the title; then a white space; then the one-line glee of the wrecking ball. The diction of cathedral destruction is neither tragic nor sublime, but pragmatic and demotic. What such a poem honors is the human capacity for change (a Stevensian value) and the equally human delight in demolition (which is *not* a Stevensian value; Stevens prefers, as we can see from the beautiful late poem, "St. Armorer's Church from the Outside," the coexistence of the emergent new with the declining old).

Even when "demolition" is in view, Ashbery usually avoids ringing closure (though lingering closure pervades his volumes). He is more likely to start up a new poem in the last several lines of the old than to let the old come to a complete halt. As he writes in "Grand Galop,"

> But we say, it cannot come to any such end
> As long as we are left around with no place to go.
> And yet it has ended, and the thing we have fulfilled we have become.
>
> Now it is the impulse of morning that makes
> My watch tick. As one who pokes his head
> Out from a under a pile of blankets, the good and bad together,
> So this tangle of impossible resolutions and irresolutions:
> The desire to have fun, to make noise, and so to
> Add to the already all-but-illegible scrub forest of graffiti on the
>   shithouse wall.[4]

Genial though this ending may sound, it is also savage in implication: the *monumentum aere perennius* is unmasked as a "shithouse wall," and the "formed trace," to use Ezra Pound's phrase,[5] has become a scribble of "graffiti" growing as lawlessly and stuntedly as a scrub forest. Yet, the impulse to write, however denigrated, is affirmed:

> And one is left sitting in the yard
> To try to write poetry

> Using what Wyatt and Surrey left around,
> Took up and put down again
> Like so much gorgeous raw material.
>
> (SP, 177)

If the "raw material" is "gorgeous" enough, it will remain so when embodied in our forms as it was in those of the sonneteers. The quest, for instance, is one piece of that perennial "gorgeous raw material," one of the inescapable modes in which life presents itself. In Ashbery then, Browning's Childe Roland will approach the dark tower yet once more, but this is how it happens in "Grand Galop":

> So it is that by limping carefully
> From one day to the next, one approaches a worn, round stone tower
> Crouching low in the hollow of a gully
> With no door or window but a lot of old license plates
> Tacked up over a slit too narrow for a wrist to pass through
> And a sign: "Van Camp's Pork and Beans."
>
> (SP, 178)

The characteristic postmodern pratfall of anticlimax is here, as Ashbery represents the lyric tradition by the "license plates" of former poets, and parodies the way we say "Spenser's *Faerie Queene*" by signing the location "Van Camp's Pork and Beans." But also visible is the ever-present, if often comically occluded, Ashbery pain: one "limps carefully" from one day of the quest to the next. And the sickening anti-aesthetic of a new order is always rising to view:

> . . . morning saw a new garnet-and-pea-green order propose
> Itself out of the endless bathos.
>
> (SP, 178)

Yet the implied task of the poet, bafflingly enough, has not changed: it is to find a way of raising human beings to a larger exponential power:

> Impossible not to be moved by the tiny number
> Those people wore, indicating they should be raised to this or that power.
> But now we are at Cape Fear . . .
>
> (SP, 179)

We can say, then, that in existence as we find it in Ashbery, nothing is to be taken seriously for long; everything is to be taken seriously in essence as "raw material"; and pain and bathos are forever setting the poet new aesthetic conundrums in "garnet" blood and "pea-green" bile.

What is it that Wyatt and Surrey left lying around? Love and pain, scenery, and an order of archetypes (such as the quest). Ashbery is a poet of all of these. As he holds the Petrarchan inheritance up to the light, Laura and Stella mutate into randomly named contemporary girls, just as inherited philosophical questions metamorphose into journalistic banalities:

> How to explain to these girls, if indeed that's what they are,
> These Ruths, Lindas, Pats and Sheilas
> About the vast change that's taken place
> In the fabric of our society, altering the texture
> Of all things in it?
>
> (SP, 182)

There is nothing for the poet to do but to drag the clichés into plain view and, like Wyatt and Surrey, before him, "babble about the sky and the weather and the forests of change," seeking a contemporary texture of words to match the altered texture of society. "Aloof, smiling and courteous," like life in "Haunted Landscape" (SP, 263), this poet who admires everything and wonders at nothing babbles on, naïveté and sophistication his changes of garments. There is in his poetry a persistent sense of plot aborted, of journeys on circular tracks, of aspiration engaged in and mocked, of synapses of allusion constantly making electrical sparks and then fizzling out. Human meaning is made and exploded, and no larger backdrop of sustained systematic thought or belief guarantees either its fittingness or its permanence. Yet the intelligence that understands itself and its own evolving forms raises human biological organisms to a higher power, even as they helplessly undergo the vicissitudes of their physical being in love, fear, and pain.

Is this what life feels like in Mark Ford's rendering? As I read Ford, I answer "Yes" and "No" and "Sometimes." Yes, there are, as in Ashbery, many parodic and inconsequential moments, and yes, there are, as in Ashbery, forms of suffering, usually understated, subtending the comic anticlimax. But let me take an example of "No." While Ashbery tends to write within explicitly human terms, Ford is more allegorical in his protean changes. He can be a "misguided angel" (the phrase is the title of a poem; SS, 17) or a "huge green amphibian," who in the cartoon-poem "Outing" follows the poet's girlfriend as she shops:

> If only it were truly impossible, and less like being a huge green
>   amphibian
> made to inch my home-sick coils between the different counters
> of your favourite store, taking all these fancy cautions
> to keep my head down, and out of other shoppers' way.
> Your ankles I can just make out . . .
> The dusty floor is cool, like a fountain,
> worn smooth and comfortable by so many feet. . . .
> Now as I glide towards the whirr of sliding doors, I half-hope
> its electric eye won't respond to my irregular approach. Another
> spanking clean threshold! "Open Sesame," it cries, "Hold tight!"
> (L, 51)

Ford's interjection of the clichéd cries, "Open Sesame" from *The Arabian Nights*, and "Hold tight" from *The Waste Land* exhibits the tag-ridden overload of the Ashberian literary synapse, but the comic film of the self as a homesick dragon about to confound the high-placed electronic sensor of the automatic doors has more fairy-tale jollity and more consistency of plot than is natural to Ashbery. Ford's lyrics frequently rest, then, as Ashbery's do not, on a story line—but of course an absurd and allegorical one. The inventiveness in a characteristic early Mark Ford poem—"A Swimming-Pool Full of Peanuts" (L, 36–38)—lies in its comic-strip sketches of the protagonist's successive Chaplinesque efforts to deal with a single unexpected situation—coming across a swimming pool full of peanuts. First the scene is set, in a paratactic style partly borrowed from another influence on early Ford, Frank O'Hara:

> I come across right in the open
> a whole swimming-pool full of peanuts I think
> I've gone mad so I shut my eyes and I count
> to five and look again and they're still resting there
> very quietly an inch or so I suppose below
> the high-water mark they're a light tan colour
> and the tiles around are a lovely cool aqua-blue
> only there's no water just these peanuts.

There follow the speaker's attempts to deal with the anomalous contents of the pool:

> Well this is a hoax . . . / unless they're painted . . . / so I kneel down / and with a loud snigger I dip in my finger / just to see it sinks into small grainy nuggets.

Queasiness sets in at the thought of what the peanuts might be hiding (piranhas, perhaps?), but he continues his exploration: when "fistful after fistful" of peanuts uncovers nothing underneath, he takes a nine-iron from his golf bag and after fruitlessly swinging away "reckless in that peanut bunker" he jumps in,

> but there's more and more always / so I say let sleeping dogs lie / and I crawl to the side and haul myself out and . . . / angrily I throw my nine-iron into the middle of the pool where it sinks / without trace and I storm back to my car and . . .

Ashbery often makes use of a comparable paratactic style but would not have pursued the anecdote so consistently. The deadpan detail includes the saltiness and greasiness of the peanuts, the masculine bravado in the brandishing of the golf club, the intimation of a dark conspiracy between the constructor and the filler of the pool, and so on. The poem is a perfect mimicry of the absurd medieval trial, the protagonist rising to a furious zeal; but the knight of the swimming pool, in lieu of finding victory, succumbs ingloriously to collapse.

Such a parabolic poem—applicable to any persistent, heroic, deranged, and deranging effort to make sense of the confounding world—aims to make us believe entirely in its frustration while disbelieving its farcical story. It asks us to remember the enormous and angry strivings of youth while judging them, from our later perspective, as absurd and demeaning. The means of Ford's poem are its dogged Disney animation, its lively successive verbs, and its despair of finding—even for a single incident—coherent similes, whether for self ("like a madman . . . like one possessed . . . like a good soldier") or for peanuts ("like sand-flies . . . like golf- / balls . . . like buff-coloured hail"). The Ashberian comic perplexity at the resistance of life to articulated description, and the equally Ashberian drive to describe it nonetheless, compete in Ford. And though the initial premise is absurd, nothing that follows is: Ford makes us believe in the quixotic heroism of our efforts to cope, even though our plight may extort ridiculous self-exposure. "A Swimming-Pool Full of Peanuts" could not have been written without the example of Ashbery and Frank O'Hara, but the young Ford had his own comic élan, more orderly than that of Ashbery, more aggressive and metaphysical than that of O'Hara.

One of Ashbery's most constant attitudes—underlying his display of intelligence and self-mockery that raises us to a higher power—is that of being of (at least) two minds. Dividedness drives almost every Ashbery poem, and is visibly manifest in the vertically split pages of his "Litany." A comparable doubleness—but in interestingly altered and much-condensed form—can be seen in Ford; my example is a three-stanza poem from *Landlocked* called "Then She Said She Had to Go," in which the two halves of each stanza of the poem, left and right, are separated by a columnar mid-gutter of white space. Here, to show the gutter, is the first of the three stanzas:

> The drawing-room was full.   The commuters half-turned
> At last the angry hostess   to wave good-bye to
> approached and   their friends. About their
> whispered   feet fell the
> black words
> into my   of their
> unsuspecting ear.   evening newspapers.

(L, 43)

On the left side of the gutter there appears a scene and there is a matching scene on the right, of precisely equal shape. The first left-hand scene, given above, is located in a "drawing room" where a party is taking place; in the second stanza, the left shows a pastoral field enclosing a wandering cow; in the third, the left gives us a seaside village being drenched by a large sea swell. In the right-hand scene of the first stanza, given above, "commuters" wave good-bye to their friends; in the second stanza, the protagonist eats lunch in a hall full of birds; in the third stanza, his girlfriend angrily stalks out of the relationship. We are instructed to read these scenes across as well as down because the scene on the left always holds its fifth line in common with its partner on the right. In each case, however, the shared line changes meaning, depending on whether we insert it into the left scene or the right.

In the first stanza, for instance, "black words" is the phrase shared by the two matched scenes: although in the left-hand narrative snippet the phrase "black words" has sinister psychological import, the identical phrase, read into the more routine right scenario, has only innocent visual significance. This is an Ashberian demonstration of the comic slipperiness inherent in language. Read separately in either scene, the phrase held in common is in no way ambiguous; but just as "black words" shifts its meaning like a chameleon as it moves from left to right, so does the shared phrase in each of the subsequent two matched sets of stanzas. In the second set, a cow swishes "away flies" on the left, while on the right, "away flies" a carrot in the beak of a bird. In the third set, after the ocean floods on the left, "salt water" is found far inland, while on the right, the lover tries to imagine the "salt water" of tears in his girlfriend's eyes.

Whereas the pieces of Ashbery's bicameral mind in the two columns of "Litany" never become pervious in this way to each other, Ford wants to insist on the way language leaks across from one mental compartment to another. The first of Ford's puns here is lexical (as "black" is first moral then visual); the second is grammatical (as "flies" is first noun and then verb); and the third zooms from the macro- to the microcosmic (as "salt water" is first oceanic then lachrymal). Such puns suggest how language shimmers in a poet's consciousness, where a word, as it enters into different combinations, behaves with quantum variability—a wave one minute, a particle the next. And it is characteristic of Ford's practice that this lyric is so firmly condensed: he has shown no disposition toward Ashbery's characteristic constantly digressive expansiveness. In fact, Ford has located his writing in the line of the sonnet, saying,

> Every form I try is a variation on a sonnet, or rather an attempt to disguise the fact the poem secretly wants to be a sonnet. . . . In the end they simply end up squashed or stretched sonnets, elastic sonnets, sonnets that have stayed on the train a couple of stops past their destination.[6]

Ford's more recent poetry is less indebted to the Ashberian comic, but continues to practice the silent Ashberian undermining of the ground one stands on. "I plunge," says Ford in a poem entitled "Penumbra," "Towards remote vanishing points, where one man's / Loss unravels and becomes another man's / Devastation" (SS, 34). We had expected that one man's loss would become another man's gain, but we were second-guessed—both men lose out. The passage from "loss" to "devastation," by the undertow of circumstance, unsettling our clichés in the process, is pure Ashbery. Here as in Ashbery's verse, the "Discordant Data"—to quote the title of a recent Ashbery poem dedicated to Ford[7]—will not add up. Even so, the frustrating wish to create order persists. As Ford puts it in "Living with Equations," "as I emerged from my hip-bath it suddenly dawned / The facts might be remarshalled and shown to rhyme," but the poem nevertheless comes to grief in a very Ashberian way: after a time of more reassuring equations,

> The remainder can only imperceptibly dwindle, retreating
> Backwards until their long lost premises turn inside out.
> (SS, 13)

The Möbius strip of the human, like a Yeatsian gyre, can only undo itself; but we are at least enabled, by our ability to take the long view, to track the dimensions of our own undoing. Ford's ending here, in its equal avoidance of the comic, the tragic, the sublime, and the just, places his poem in the human-scale aesthetic defined by Ashbery.

Yet one aspect of Ford's work especially differentiates him from Ashbery. Ford includes in his writing a physically sensuous documentation that is not present in the ever-theatrical, ever-virtual John Ashbery. One could say that Wordsworth and Gerard Manley Hopkins, with their sense of skin against wind, breath against earth, lie behind the moments of natural presence we come across in Ford. In the very poem, "Penumbra," where we found the Ashberian satiric bon mot that one man's loss is another man's devastation, we see that Ford brackets that piece of Ashberian dark comedy with bleak scenic passages:

> I lean into the wind that blows
> Off the lake, and scours the sodden fields; the sky's
> Reflections ripple between ruts and bumps[.]
> . . . . .
>   Crops,
> Sludge, restless drifts of leaves absorb
> The haggard light.
> (SS, 34)

The depressive moods of the body, one could say, frame in Ford the comic aphoristic verdict of the mind. And the poet's micro-noticing of "ravaged spores" and "downy nettles" manages to hover, in its adjectives, on the border between the real and surreal without losing a grasp on the actual scene. In this way Ford belongs to the line of British poets, from Shakespeare to Hardy and Hopkins, who are willing to describe unlovely moments in nature; but he differs from them in giving the introspective reflections arising from such depressed physical moments an Ashberian inconsequence and ironic comedy.

Mark Ford has praised in James Tate qualities that can be found in his own work: the "refusal to elide the illogic of experience," the "treacherous instability" of meditation, and the ways in which poems work by "collaging disparate materials into a seamless fluency."[8] And the kind of lyricism that Ford finds in Tate—one both "intimate and impersonal"—is the sort he delights in in Ashbery and desires, I think, for himself. Poetry must be "intimate," or it would scarcely be true to itself; yet it must be "impersonal," so that it can be true for others. Writing in the *New Republic* on Mina Loy, Ford praised a poem that, he said, "embodies a devastating critique of outdated rhetorical conventions and ossified belief-systems," one that "anticipates the decentering fluidities of postmodern poetics."[9] There is perhaps something a little too pat about the approval extended here to something called "post-modern poetics" as though the Shakespeare of *Hamlet* and the Shelley of "The Cloud" were not aware—as they surely were—of "decentering fluidities." Ford is on surer ground when he speaks of every major poet's war on "outdated conventions and ossified belief-systems." Ashbery's war on them has proved, especially in its comic attachment to those very "conventions" and "belief-systems," buoyantly liberating for many younger poets, in England for Ford especially.

I have said one of the aspects distinguishing Ford from Ashbery is the felt presence of the body in an actual landscape. Ford is also likely to set himself in a recognizable location or to narrate a stable incident. Where Ashbery is protean, an absent center through which all discourses move, Ford lets us see himself in a given posture and location, irritated (in a poem called "Plan Nine") by the "dreadful telephone again," facing every morning a supervisor whose "reign of terror / And mind like glue" are relentlessly present (SS, 8). Horrible twentieth-century prescriptions for good living are, in the same poem, imposed on a "case" resembling, we are sure, the poet's own, as a "caustic voice" says to "a clutch of bright-eyed interns," "No mohair, no alcohol, / Lots of plain yoghurt certainly, no foreign languages, no tête-à-têtes." One can see, from that parodic mockery of medical discourse, why Ashbery appeals to Ford; and yet such a passage is more firmly located in an actual event—here, a medical consultation—than Ashbery's work tends to be.

Ford, though impersonal, is also confessional in a way closer to Hart Crane than to Ashbery. There are recognizable lyrics of disquieting self-exposure, such as "Misguided Angel," which begins with a mock-Miltonic self-challenge:

> Where will you ride in this minute that stretches
> Its wings, and soars aloft, and turns into
> An unplanned, devilish interval?
> (SS, 17)

Upon this taunt, the "ossified belief-systems" and confusing bewilderment of
the flesh immediately put in their appearance:

> Serial
> Misadventures have shattered the grip
> Of barbed rubric and corporate logo; enigmas
> Swarm at the brink of the five senses.

Finally, the poet's initial hyperbolic self-challenge—"Where will you ride
in this minute?"—becomes a more actual one, almost a vow, in which the poet
admits the three inescapable unfreedoms of the creative mind: one cannot
censor one's thoughts, one cannot deny one's wounds, and one cannot escape
the "inflexible etiquette" of art. That "inflexible etiquette"—the phrase, in its
combination of the necessary and the decorative, could have come from Hart
Crane—demands that gesture be brought to coincide with memory:

> [T]here is no controlling
> One's renegade thoughts, nor striking
> The fetters from blistered limbs. Inflexible etiquette
> Demands every gesture be also a memory: you stare
> Into space where fractions and figures still pursue
> Their revenge[.]
> (SS, 17)

An unknown frontier lies ahead in which the misguided angel is to stake a
claim, but

> Whoever claims
> A stake out there must rise and speak in guttural tones
> Of all they mean—or meant—to do, and why, and where.
> (SS, 17)

We have moved entirely out of the pose of ultimate inconsequence and charming
dissolution that is Ashbery's own, and into a Stevensian and Crane-like seri-

ousness in which the poet's muttering will be judged by an exacting ethical standard, at once internal and social.

Hart Crane's verse, as Ford commented in a review of his *Selected Letters*,[10] was motivated by the poet's "need to embody the physical, the mundane, the fleeting." The "mundane" and the "fleeting" are amply present in Ashbery, but the "physical" less so. And it is the "physical," with its irruptions of sensuous transcendence, that appeals to Ford in Crane—what he, quoting Crane, calls the poet's "blanket-like absorption in experience." The quintessential Ford can be found in the grafting of a felt physical ambience on the Ashberian metaphysical one, as well as the grafting of a Fordian allegorical story line on the Ashberian aslant angle of incidence. A recent Ford poem, "Twenty Twenty Vision," remarking centrally that "my doom is never to forget / My lost bearings," opens in a mode of cartoon metaphysics learned from Ashbery:

> Unwinding in a cavernous bodega he suddenly
> Burst out: Barman, these tumblers empty themselves
> And yet I persist.
>
> (SS, 29)

Very shortly "Twenty Twenty Vision" turns into a wonderfully exact lyric autobiography, reminiscent by turns of Wordsworth, Eliot, and Crane, but dominated by no one influence.

The fact that we can read such an oblique poem with understanding is due to our training by Ford's precursors in modernism, including Ashbery. But the memorable lyric itself—its story line, its alternately understated and overstated emotional vicissitudes, its surreal scenic vividness—is all Ford's own. I want to quote its closing lines, prefacing them by saying that the Ford narrative departs from the usual Wordsworthian plot by ending, as well as beginning, in medias res by framing both beginning and ending in a setting sun; by symbolizing birth as a death-wound; and by representing the awakening to life as coterminous with the terrible thirst with which "Twenty Twenty Vision" will end:

> *In medias res* we begin
> And end: I was born, and then my body unfurled
> As if to illustrate a few tiny but effective words—
> *But—oh my oh my—avaunt.* I peered
> Forth, stupefied, from the bushes as the sun set
> Behind distant hills. A pair of hungry owls

Saluted the arrival of webby darkness; the dew
Descended upon the creeping ferns. At first
My sticky blood refused to flow, gathering instead
In wax-like drops and pools: mixed with water and a dram
Of colourless alcohol it thinned and reluctantly
Ebbed away. I lay emptied as a fallen
Leaf until startled awake by a blinding flash
Of dry lightning, and the onset of this terrible thirst.

(SS, 29)

Although the posture here is not heroic, one feels the poet's sheer joy at the discovery of language, even in its most primitive forms of childish response: "but" (the objecting mind); "oh my oh my" (dismay one day, wonder the next); "avaunt" (the first thrill of the literary). For the "terrible thirst" parching the poet's throat from the onset of his vocation, no words, of course, will ever be entirely adequate—but the mind has nevertheless begun to amass its lexicon.

Michael Hofmann once called Mark Ford's work "unmistakably mid-Atlantic," and yet Ford's verse is also "unmistakably"—to this transatlantic reader—English in its attachment to the line of English romantic and modern lyric.[11] In an interview with Graham Bradshaw, Ford repudiated the contemporary genre of the literally autobiographical poem:

> I can't bear poems about grandfathers, or fishing expeditions, or what it's like to move into a new house, unless they're very *very* good poems. . . .
> I start off prejudiced against them because I find the subject-matter so boring. . . . I guess basically I'm always looking for gaps, little fissures where "a thought might grow," to use Derek Mahon's phrase.[12]

I associate the literal lyric with the United States, where it has lately been thought that specification of gender, ethnicity, class, and family relations adds authenticity to a poem. The classic lyric, from which Ford derives, has in the past engaged in various sorts of despecification so as to make its voice assumable by many readers, and Ford assents to that despecification as he reinvents himself as alligator, angel, or body unfurling into language. In the lyric of the past, the generalized speaker was, however, expected—by an invisible convention—to pursue his thoughts along normal logical lines. Pound, Eliot, Moore, and Crane, by allowing more wayward associations, created a modernism that curved the rails of thought in lyric, while Ashbery, disciple of Rimbaud and Mallarmé, dared to create actual gaps along the length of the rails. Ford, too, makes such leaps in logic native to his poems.

But the enthralling thing about Ford's lyrics is that although he has adopted the newer techniques of curves and gaps in "looping the loop" of consciousness—his phrase (SS, 5)—he has allowed these techniques to remain wonderfully hospitable to the old—to Wordsworth, Hopkins, Hardy—not always in the parodic Ashberian way of knowing allusion, but often in the way of natural capacious memory. As Ford said in his Bradshaw interview—using a metaphor for tradition that might have surprised Eliot but not Wordsworth or Hopkins or Ashbery—"You scoop up a bucketful and enjoy as much as you can the various life-forms that happen to be in it."[13] We have the privilege of watching Ford scoop up, from the tide pools of both America and England, the life-forms and language-forms of our era. They are not tabulated by creed or system or ideology into any already known taxonomies of culture, but they group themselves happily in fleeting new convergences of the imagination.

In bringing Ashbery into the precincts of English verse, Ford has loosened the aspects of the English imagination that had remained within the stricter borders of Audenesque intellectuality, Movement dourness, and Larkinesque gloomy comedy. For a long time it seemed inconceivable to represent Englishness except within certain contained formal postures; the wilder postures belonged to the provinces, and were tacitly regarded as savage. With his irreproachable literary sophistication, Ashbery has out-Englished the English; but with his Whitmanian expansiveness he has introduced a loose-limbed provincial slouch into the drawing room of Wildean wit. Ford, with comparable parodic savoir faire, delights in the slippery and the farcical—those mischievous disruptions of the intellectual, the taciturn, the morose, and the well behaved. His cinema verité of contemporary English life accompanies his renditions of a postmodern and eclectic sensibility. Ford is at once a veteran of pop culture and a connoisseur of the desperation of high culture, an indoor reader of the past but also an outdoor breather of physically felt atmospheres. His generation of English poets is still in formation, but I believe Ford is to be one of its eventual definers, as Ashbery was crucial to postwar writing in the United States.

And in that defining of the contemporary human being, Ford agrees with Ashbery that everything amenable to experience is in perpetual circulation, that culture cannot come to any definitive stability. Yet what circulates, being human, is never merely small: what Ashbery calls the circulation of small largenesses is given its largeness by speculation, reflection, mockery, and irony; by a *dédoublement* in which one is at the same time an angel but misguided; a body, but a penumbra; a bleak connoisseur of facts but at the same time one who "re-marshalls" them into a rhyme that raises all the figures in the equation to a higher (that is, larger) power. Most of all, the contemporary awareness we find in Mark Ford is made large by the vigilant sense (mocked in the two-column scenes of "Then She Said She Had to Go") that any word can come usefully to hand as a particle or a wave, and that the consequent combinatorial potential of language guarantees its ability to represent everything from the sublime to the ridiculous. This is a largeness amply put into circulation by Ashbery, and one that survives translation into Mark Ford's England.

19

Wallace Stevens

Memory, Dead and Alive

I want to reflect on memory in Wallace Stevens—both memory seen as defective, whether it is the iterable memory of sense-experience or the nostalgic memory of one's emotional life, and memory seen as resurrective, as in "The Rock." My interest in memory in Stevens arose from my bafflement before a 1942 piece I admired, "Arcades of Philadelphia the Past."[1] Among Stevens's poems, "Arcades" is unusual in being more surreal than most, and its chief, and most shocking, surreal feature is the image of men holding their eyes in their hands (an image that recurs in "Page from a Tale"):

> There they sit, holding their eyes in their hands.
> · · · · ·
> They polish their eyes
> In their hands.

The eyes are no longer flesh; they have hardened to agate, and at the moment of the poem they are reflecting in their polished surface an image of lilac bushes, varying in color. In thinking about this poem, I was led to recall other Stevensian mentions of lilacs, not only in *Harmonium*'s "Last Looks at the Lilacs" (1923) but also in "Things of August" from *The Auroras of Autumn* (1950). Because of the problems raised by "Arcades of Philadelphia the Past" I also found myself looking across the page from it in the *Collected Poems,* and seeing "A Dish of Peaches in Russia." As these poems came together in my mind, I felt that one could say about Stevens what George Herbert said about Bible verses in "The H. Scriptures II":

Oh that I knew how all thy lights combine,
    And the configurations of their glorie!
    Seeing not onely how each verse doth shine,
But all the constellations of the storie.
This verse marks that, and both do make a motion
    Unto a third, that ten leaves off doth lie. . . . [2]

Stevens's constellations are mutually illuminating in this way, and propinquity within the *Collected Poems*—as with "Arcades" and "Peaches"—is often a sign of an imaginative relation between poems. Because memory is one of the oldest themes in lyric, and because Stevens's interest in memory evokes Wordsworth more than any other predecessor, I also hoped to see what was distinctive and non-Wordsworthian about Stevens's work with this time-honored idea.

In thinking about memory in Stevens, then, I begin with a non-Wordsworthian poem, "A Dish of Peaches in Russia" (LOA, 206), which, though it will ultimately concern itself with memory, begins with an ecstatic sense-experience in the present. The poem is spoken, in "naïve" couplets, by a Russian in exile who, confronted with a dish of peaches exactly like those of his native village, at first rejoices in the sense-stimuli offered him by the fruits, which are identical in color, smell, touch, and taste to the peaches of his former life. He comments on the peaches with the gratitude of a sensualist:

With my whole body I taste these peaches,
I touch them and smell them.

After an interposition—to which I will return—the excited sense-perception makes itself felt once again:

The peaches are large and round,

Ah! and red; and they have peach fuzz, ah!
They are full of juice and the skin is soft.

The senses of sight, taste, touch, and smell are fully satisfied by these peaches. But these fruits, in spite of their species-identity, are nonetheless not the peaches of the Russian's village. He is "that exile, for whom / The bells of the chapel pullulate sounds at / Heart," and the heart is an organ incommensurable with the organs of the senses. The verb "pullulate," originating from Latin *pullus* (young animal, young sprout, as in "pullet"), took on the metaphorical meaning "to teem, to germinate." It is the generative activity of sense-memory crossed with emotion that Stevens wishes to emphasize, since it is that which is lost when sense-response is present but human emotion is absent. Although the speaker attempts to assimilate the present peaches to the past ones in Russia, by saying of the present peaches, "They are full of the colors of my village," he cannot, finally, keep at arm's length a desperate disappointment:

> I did not know
>
> That such ferocities could tear
> One self from another, as these peaches do.

Past sense-memory—because it is embedded in past emotional experience—cannot be repeated or recovered, even if an identical sense-satisfaction is available in the present. The exile is torn in two precisely because the present peaches are, to the senses, absolutely indistinguishable from the past peaches. It is only to the heart that they are not comparable with the peaches of the vanished village. One part of the exile is dead and cannot be resuscitated by eating sense-simulacra in America. For this theoretical experiment, Stevens has kept one set of stimuli—those of the senses—constant in both memory and actuality, thus putting into relief the part of memory that frustratingly recalls the irrecoverably past gratification generated by the synesthesia of the Russian peaches and the sound of familiar bells.

When Stevens turns—in "Arcades of Philadelphia the Past" (LOA, 207)—to life-memory in general, he does not find it a rich and renovating source, as Wordsworth did in recalling his "spots of time." Rather, Stevens is taken aback by the poverty of memory. When we summon up the past, it is usually, he says, in the form of a set of visual images. We cannot—according to "Arcades"—hear the past or touch it or taste it or smell it. How odd it is that we can only *see* the past, that no other sense (in Stevens's view here) has the capacity to return and reproduce itself in memory. In "Arcades," the poet takes as axiomatic that the only people who are drawn to recalling the past are those who have riches (now lost) to remember. Those previous riches can be those of the senses (strawberries), of foreign travel (the Apennines), or of local region (Philadelphia):

> Only the rich remember the past,
> The strawberries once in the Apennines,
> Philadelphia that the spiders ate.

After this overture, Stevens describes for us the crowd of rememberers who populate "Arcades." He invokes, in picturing them, the Miltonic simile from *Paradise Lost* in which the fallen angels in hell are said to be thick as leaves in Vallombrosa, that shady valley high in the Apennines:

> He stood and call'd
> His legions, Angel Forms, who lay intrans'd
> Thick as Autumnal Leaves that strow the Brooks
> In *Vallombrosa*, where th' *Etrurian* shades
> High overarch't imbow'r. . . . [3]

Those attempting to remember the past, Stevens suggests, are themselves in a kind of hell, in which, although they can see the past as in a silent movie, they can no longer hear it, nor touch it, nor smell it, nor feel it:

> There they sit, holding their eyes in their hands.
> Queer, in this Vallombrosa of ears,
> That they never hear the past.
> . . . . .
>   Do they touch the thing they see,
> Feel the wind of it, smell the dust of it?
> They do not touch it. Sounds never rise
> Out of what they see. They polish their eyes
> In their hands.

In the midst of this catalogue of the deprivations of memory, the speaker inserts, almost parenthetically, what is to be alive in the present:

>   To see,
> To hear, to touch, to taste, to smell, that's now,
> That's this.

But he seems for some reason profoundly uninterested in pursuing the attractions of "now" and "this": for the moment, he is obsessed with the inadequacies of memory.

The next movement of the poem concerns lilac bushes, which come to be symbols of an erotic, but frustrated, romance, in which the love associated with lilacs and "the town" (presumably the Philadelphia of the title) never succeeded in their attempt to coalesce:

> The lilacs came long after.
> But the town and the fragrance were never one,
> Though the blue bushes bloomed—and bloom,
> Still bloom in the agate eyes, red blue,
> Red purple, never quite red itself.

The dead rememberers stare yearningly at the reflections of the lilacs in the agate eyes, which, peculiarly, mirror nothing of the past but the lilacs. However, the fluctuating colors of memory never quite approximate life itself—the unequivocal sun's red of the Stevensian real—but remain disappointing approximations of the vanished real, red blue, red purple. Nonetheless, the lilacs continue to bloom in those gazing-globes, the agate eyes, held in the palm of the commemorative hands. The preciousness of the visual lilac-memory means that the speaker can dismiss as worthless to the entombed dead all the other senses and end with a triumphant reiteration of the power of sight-memory:

> The tongue, the fingers, and the nose
> Are comic trash, the ears are dirt,
> But the eyes are men in the palm of the hand.

If, trying to remember the past, one cannot resuscitate the full sensory gamut of iterable stimuli—the dish of peaches—one can at least count on the persistence—if slightly discolored, slightly diminished—of sight.

But after this claim, the earlier slighting reference to the availability of full sense-experience in the now, the this, reasserts itself. We discover why the speaker avoids the now, the this:

> This? A man must be very poor
> With a single sense . . .
> . . . . .
> Of poorness as an earth. . . .

In the present speaker, his sense of metaphysical and all-extensive poverty, of almost total loss, has extirpated the potential pleasures of all the physical senses.

If he senses only poverty, everywhere he looks, everywhere he exercises his five usual senses, what good are the senses at all? He smells clouds, not fragrance; he redundantly *sees* the sea, not the vanished lilacs; when he finds a woman to touch, she is cadaverous; when he tries to taste foods, he finds "dry seconds and insipid thirds"; and when he tries to speak, he finds he cannot utter a word, though he eerily hears interiorly what he would want to say:

> This? A man must be very poor
> With a single sense, though he smells clouds,
> Or to see the sea on Sunday, or
> To touch a woman cadaverous,
> Of poorness as an earth, to taste
> Dry seconds and insipid thirds,
> To hear himself and not to speak.

I will return in a moment to Stevens's peculiar syntax in these ungrammatical lines. Having found the present so inadequate to desire, the speaker thinks to return to the riches of memory, only to find that to resummon those riches now—after having tasted actuality, however dry and insipid—is to render them ineffectual, artificial, damaged, inauthentic:

> The strawberries once in the Apennines . . .
> They seem a little painted, now.
> The mountains are scratched and used, clear fakes.

This three-line coda is devised to match the three-line overture, but while the genuineness of strawberries and mountains does not survive, the receding memorial arcades of Philadelphia the past remain unmentioned in this conclusion, are preserved from absolute dismissal. The town is spider-devoured, but its arcades still make an airy roof over the garden where the lilacs flowered; and the lilacs are still blooming in the agate eyes; and so the memorial part of the vanished city has not yet become "painted," or "scratched and used," or a "fake."

How to treat a romance that turned out badly is a question that preoccupied Stevens even in *Harmonium*, where he had announced, as early as the third poem, that "the lilacs wither in the Carolinas" (LOA, 4). In "Last Looks at the Lilacs," a lover perceives that his beloved, disappointed in him, has turned away from his embrace to dream of the ideal masculine lover of her imagination, the "Don John, / Who will embrace her before summer comes" (LOA, 39). The poem is savagely ironic, as the poet-speaker addresses himself as "caliper," the measurer of the embrace, and "poor buffo," the fool. He once loved the lavender lilacs; now they are to him nothing but trash. The "divine ingénue," his companion, turns her dissatisfaction with him into unreal dreams of a swaggering lover ("Well-booted, rugged, arrogantly male"), but the speaker, once he realizes her disaffection from his insufficiently masculine self, does not, on his part, dream of a better beloved to console him. He is too deep in loss and too skeptical for a new emotional adventure:

> Poor buffo! Look at the lavender
> And look your last and look still steadily,
> And say how it comes that you see
> Nothing but trash and that you no longer feel
> Her body quivering in the Floréal.[4]

The speaker's bitter denial in "Last Looks at the Lilacs," of value to the lilacs ("Nothing but trash"), and his assertion that he no longer feels desire for the beloved are both given the lie in "Arcades of Philadelphia the Past": the lilacs, in their changing spectrum of obsessively regarded but inconstant and imperfect colors, continue to bloom and bloom in the agate eyes of the reminiscent mind, preserved in the writerly hand. When Stevens realizes, as he later does in "Notes toward a Supreme Fiction VII," that the erotic and its souvenirs, however blighted, can be ultimately considered one of life's blessings, even after they have been lost, he recovers the smell of the lilacs and creates their synesthetic "purple odor," allowing in "Notes" a suffusion of recall more complete than that of "Arcades of Philadelphia the Past." But this memory in "Notes" "evok[es] nothing," is a Platonic "absolute," unattached to any past ingénue:

> Tonight the lilacs magnify
> The easy passion, the ever-ready love
> Of the lover that lies within us and we breathe
>
> An odor evoking nothing, absolute.
> We encounter in the dead middle of the night
> The purple odor, the abundant bloom.
> (LOA, 341)

Still later, in "Things of August, IV," Stevens has come to admit that the death of love, like any other death in nature, is natural. It is our mother the Earth, from whom we have derived our riches, who conceals always the fatal dagger she will one day direct at us. The smell of the lilacs survives their inhumation, but to the pure and detached odor no associations, whether of myth (Persephone) or of life ("the widow Dooley") can be attached:

> The sad smell of the lilacs—one remembered it,
> Not as the fragrance of Persephone,
> Nor of a widow Dooley,
> But as of an exhumation returned to earth,
>
> The rich earth, of its own self made rich. . . .
> . . . . .
>
> The sentiment of the fatal is a part
> Of filial love. Or is it the element, . . .
> . . . . .
> An arrogant dagger darting its arrogance,
>
> In the parent's hand, perhaps parental love?
> One wished that there had been a season,
> Longer and later, in which the lilacs opened
> And spread about them a warmer, rosier odor.
>
> (LOA, 419)

The phallic power of the imagined arrogant rival lover in "Last Looks at the Lilacs" has been transferred in "Things of August" to the maternal earth itself, as—out of love, perhaps—she sends the dagger of death from her hand to her children's hearts. Because the lilacs—here, as elsewhere, symbolic of sexual love—were originally exhumed from the earth, they have necessarily returned to the earth, like all living things. Although Stevens has come, like Whitman, to know—and to love—the earth as the death-principle as well as the life-principle, his embrace of the inevitable biological cycle does not mean he is without regret. Love had to die, but did it have to live so very briefly and so stintedly? Surely the season could have been longer and later, surely the lilacs might have been allowed to produce their most authentic odor, embodying the warmth and blush of sustained and sustaining love. A residual bitterness accompanies, but does not vitiate, the Stevensian erotic memory here; the defects of actual memory are supplied by a fantasy of what, under better circumstances, life under the fragrance of the lilacs might have become.

In "The Rock" (LOA, 445), the lilacs reappear for the last time, as Stevens offers a bleak picture of romantic love, so magical to the young, as merely an evolutionary biological phenomenon activated by "the sun's design of its own happiness." The young man advances to the end of his family's property as the young woman is making the same advance from her adjacent terrain: in the ordained moment, noon, at the height of the sexual warmth, they meet at the edge of the adjoining fields. The poet comments darkly:

> The meeting at noon at the edge of the field seems like
>
> An invention, an embrace between one desperate clod
> And another in a fantastic consciousness,
> In a queer assertion of humanity:
>
> A theorem proposed between the two—
> Two figures in a nature of the sun,
> In the sun's design of its own happiness.

Yet this intellectual assessment of the Darwinian imperative motivating sexual conjunction gives way to a recollection of how it really felt to be sexually and romantically alive, the moment of the blooming lilacs and the musk of desire: it was

> an illusion so desired
>
> That the green leaves came and covered the high rock,
> That the lilacs came and bloomed, like a blindness cleaned,
> Exclaiming bright sight, as it was satisfied,
>
> In a birth of sight. The blooming and the musk
> Were being alive, an incessant being alive,
> A particular of being, that gross universe.

This memory, actively recapturing the ecstatic emotions associated with the lilacs—the blooming and the sexual fragrance, the dazzling seeing and the humming aliveness—is more accurate to youthful experience than the wistful nostalgia of "Things of August," more complete than the merely visual memory encapsulated in the shifting lilac colors within the agate eyes, and much happier than the early self-loathing dismissals of "Last Looks at the Lilacs."

With all the earlier and later appearances of the lilacs in mind, we can now return to "Arcades of Philadelphia the Past," asking, this time, why it is composed as it is, and how the structure and language of the poem bear out its emotional freight, as Stevens reconsiders the deficiencies of memory. The overture has a tone, even if a sardonic one, of possible hope; one can at least, the speaker thinks, remember lost riches, even if one has no hope of reclaiming them: the spiders, after all, ate Philadelphia long ago. The coda, for its part, recognizes that the morose delectation described in the overture flattens very quickly into artifice. There is no nourishment in it; the strawberries are painted, now, like the deceptive grapes of Apelles; and memory is corrupted by repetition, like a record scratched and used. As for Philadelphia, except for its lilacs, it has been devoured.

The central part of "Arcades," between the prologue and the coda, oscillates between an irrecoverable "then" and "that" and a poverty-stricken "now" and "this." This oscillation puts the poem fully in a Wordsworthian genre, the poem of dual consciousness, in which the "now"—with a variety of emotions—looks back on the "then." But in entombing the past in the flesh-deprived and petrified agate eyes, Stevens refuses the "liveliness" of the evoked Wordsworthian past and consequently does not have to undergo the Wordsworthian "fall," classically phrased in "Tintern Abbey": "That time is past, / And all its aching joys are now no more, / And all its dizzy raptures." The shifting colors ("red blue, / Red purple, never quite red itself") that bloom in the agate eyes are asymptotic approaches to the first blooming of the erotic lilacs ("the blue bushes"), but they are identical neither to the blue actual lilacs nor to their "red" Platonic form of the real, and never can be.

To the Wordsworthian "then" of the actual past and the "now" of the actual present, Stevens has added a third, spatialized, moment, the "there" of the present spot of time of the dead, in which the men remember the past: "There they sit, holding their eyes in their hands." Because of the ironic detachment of the speaker intent on describing the "there"—as though he were not writing about himself—the body of the poem persists in its intellectualizing moments. The speaker has perceived that only the rich remember the past, that it is "queer" that the crowd of rememberers ("in this Vallombrosa of ears") possess sight but not hearing; he has decided firmly that all senses but sight are absolutely and always unattainable to remembrance ("Do they touch the thing they see [?] . . . / They do not touch it. Sounds never rise / Out of what they see"). His judgments on his "dead" self are final and devastating ("The tongue, the fingers, and the nose / Are comic trash, the ears are dirt").

In the midst of all this intellectualizing, perceiving, deciding, declaring, de-
riding, and judging sits the brief narrative of the lilac-blooming past. But even
here, a cool evaluation of the past intrudes: "the town and the fragrance were
never one." And although something that the men have lost is salvaged in the
present agate blooming of the lilacs, the past blooming was biological and real,
while the present is merely visually memorial, and approximate in coloring
at that.

The frigidity of the purely visual memory drives the speaker (who as a poet
is "polishing his eyes in his hands" as he writes down his memories) into the
unaccommodating present, the poverty-stricken "now" and "this." As I said
earlier, the elaborately accomplished diction of "Arcades" breaks down in this
third stanza. Since the poet has declared that to possess all the senses is a property of the living present ("To see, / To hear, to touch, to taste, to smell, that's
now, / That's this"), we are confused when he says "This? A man must be very
poor / With a single sense. . . ." We had thought that only the rememberers
had to get along with a single sense, their sense of sight. It is only as we continue reading that we see that the phrase "a single sense" is completed, three
lines later, by the complement "Of poorness as an earth. . . ." Apparently the
sense of poorness, a planetary poorness pervading the Earth, is enough to
wipe out the potential of all the normal senses.[5] The speaker makes a rhetorical concession—yes, the man does smell clouds, could see the sea on Sunday,
could taste food dry and savorless as dust, could touch an unappealing cadaverous woman—but who would want to? The poison of felt poorness, that
all-pervading single sense, invades and vitiates every other.

In this stanza of ultimate deprivation, the puzzle of syntax continues in the
peculiar infinitives. Normally, in Stevens, the infinitive is the sign of joyous possibility, as in "The Latest Freed Man":

> To be without a description of to be,
> For a moment on rising, at the edge of the bed, to be,
> . . . . .
>   to be changed
> From a doctor into an ox, before standing up,
> To know that the change and that the ox-like struggle
> Come from the strength that is the strength of the sun. . . .
> (LOA, 187)

But here, like broken phrases reduced from their original wholeness, we find
banal or repellent infinitives (with the archaic and therefore unsettling "or . . .

or" substituted for the modern "either . . . or") occurring within a broken syntax that must be rearranged to make sense:

A man [though he smells clouds] must be very poor
With a single sense [Of poorness as an earth]
Or to see the sea on Sunday, or
To touch a woman cadaverous . . .
                              [or] to taste
Dry seconds, [or]
To hear himself and not to speak.

How is it that the man encased in the oppressive poverty of "now" and "this" can smell clouds? This concession to sense-function and sense-presence works against the absolutism of the passage, in which the poet wants to argue that the sense of poorness annuls the normal working of the bodily senses. Poor though he be, the man cannot avoid smelling clouds, concedes the poet. The clouds in Stevens always have affinities with the blue of the sky and its connection to the imagination, but only invisible things—angels, Jove, the muse—inhabit Stevens's clouds. Clouds represent the realm of Ideas, where the Platonic paradigm of each thing exists in perpetuity, if in invisibility. "Smell" is an ethereal perception not attached to sight or hearing or taste or touch: no matter the speaker's sensual poverty, the Idea of Lilac-Fragrance, its Platonic odor, hovers in the clouds. To have no home but Plato may define the poorness of the poet when the body is entirely unmoved by normal sense-responsiveness.

It is Stevens's wish to enact his planetary sense of poorness that drives him to his conscious use of pictorial surrealism and to the trope of deliberate ungainliness of idiom. Sense-memory is easily summoned by language—"The strawberries once in the Apennines." Emotional memory—attempting to reenact the real lilacs of the past, the agate-blooming lilacs of the present, and the Platonic lilacs of pure fragrance—is harder to render and induces in Stevens the surrealism of the agate eyes, with their constantly unsatisfactory colors, held in the palms of the rememberers. Stevens was interested in the use of the surreal in rendering the unconscious, but was careful about its use. As he says in *Materia Poetica:*

The essential fault of surrealism is that it invents without discovering. To make a clam play an accordion is to invent not to discover. The observation of the unconscious, so far as it can be observed, should reveal things of which we have previously been unconscious. (LOA, 919)

From Stevens's observation of the unconscious, as it revealed to him the distinction between sense-memory and emotional memory, sprang the chilling surrealism of men—their eyes now turned to agate—contemplating the reflections blooming in those eyes extracted from their native skull and placed in the palms of the hands.

But if it is easy to render sense-memory, and possible—if only through surrealism—to render emotional memory, it seems impossible to render the paradoxical condition of activating all the bodily senses without enjoying them. Stevens must cross plenitude ("To see, / To hear, to touch, to taste, to smell, that's now, / That's this") with resistance to pleasure in these very activities. The exercise of the senses is usually considered involuntary: Wordsworth's Matthew, in "Expostulation and Reply," asserts:

> "The eye—it cannot choose but see;
> We cannot bid the ear be still;
> Our bodies feel, where'er they be,
> Against or with our will."

Wordsworth does not here dramatize what it would be to have one's body feel against one's will. But that is precisely what Stevens has to do in showing that his speaker's senses stream outward while his mind denigrates their potential for reward. The conflict between mind and sense results in the fractured syntax and the stilted ratiocination of what he might do with his senses ("or this, or that"); the same conflict generates the surrealism of smelling clouds and tasting seconds and thirds. We are shown the dispelling of desire by an anticlimactic postpositioned adverb ("on Sunday") or adjective ("cadaverous"). The standoff between mind and sense is summed up in the last paradox: "To hear himself and not to speak." In the mind, the speaker hears what he would say were he not so impoverished; but his power of expression feels itself so greatly sapped by his sense of poorness that he does not—though he could—speak. It is his *not speaking* that the very peculiar grammar, syntax, and diction of this stanza of the poem are contrived to communicate.

I return to Stevens's predicament in writing "Arcades of Philadelphia the Past." If, as he says in his *Materia Poetica*, "All poetry is experimental poetry" (LOA, 918), then this poem makes the experiment of disengaging from each other three states—the "then" of narrative memory (strawberries and Philadelphia), the "there" of emotional memory (agate eyes, shifting colors), and the "now" of the impoverishment of desire. "Then" is already codified for us in

Wordsworthian narrative; for "there," Stevens's imagination had to reach into a surreal realm for a strikingly physical symbolic equivalent—the eyes in the palm of the hands—of emotional memory deprived of all but a single visual recourse; for the "now" Stevens had to invent an experimental discourse so distorted, so hobbled, so uncontemporary that his third stanza will "resist the intelligence / Almost successfully" (LOA, 306). Allowing this peculiar against-the-will nowness to subside into intelligibility in his coda might have seemed a retreat from experiment had he not introduced into the coda the ultimate subsidence of preserved memory into artifice and fraud. The strawberries and the Apennines are fakes; the lilacs, however, at the moment of writing, still have authenticity. Remembered long enough, will they too become painted fakes, or a record scratched and used? This is the question Stevens leaves open; but in his later poems, as he accepts the sexual lilac-blooming as necessary and mortality as equally necessary, the lilacs are permitted to bloom fully again, more alive in "The Rock" than they were in *Parts of a World*.

It is in watching Stevens's self-revisions in the course of his writing that we construct a narrative about his predicaments as a poet. The making of a teleological evolutionary narrative out of Stevens's creations has been called an imposition of the desire of the critic on evidence.[6] If one believes, as I do, that it is necessary to construct such an explanatory narrative (if one has found successive phases, differently motivated, in Stevens's creative life), then the vicissitudes of the lilacs of memory, from *Harmonium* to *The Rock*, create one such story. As even the simple dish of peaches carries not only sense-memory but emotional freight for the exiled Russian, so the lilacs—as a recurrent symbol for sexual and romantic love—demand from Stevens stylistic and thematic reformulation, early and late.

There are many meditations on memory, personal and collective, in Stevens, and they are urgently connected, for him, to the quality of life. Insofar as we remember, we are alive; when the agate eyes cease to mirror the lilacs, it will be useless to polish them; their surfaces will reflect nothing. When the sound of bells no longer germinates within the taste of peaches, the peaches become, for all their lusciousness to the tongue, dry seconds and insipid thirds. Behind every access of memory—of peaches, of lilacs—lurks the possible blank of terminal emotional frigidity, when—as in the fade-out of death for the "Anglais Mort à Florence"—"the colors deepened and grew small" (LOA, 119). The emotional loss in "A Dish of Peaches in Russia," sudden and ferocious, becomes in "Arcades of Philadelphia the Past" an obsessive contemplation of lost romance, pervading everything. One might believe from "Arcades" that Stevens had fallen irrevocably into a view of memory as the locus of the petrified, the artificial, and the scratched and used, had he not allowed—against the sardonic and derisive drama of marriage in "The Rock"—the merciful influx of the living erotic musk and its lilac-fragrance, resurrected by memory in a form wholly alive. In his embers Stevens is the shaman of the past, not, like Wordsworth, closing on a nostalgia for "what was so fugitive," but rather resurrecting the fled past in language claiming its original fullness as a particular of being. When Stevens names being "that gross universe," he insists on the priority of physical responsiveness in the very idea of all existence. If memory is to be of any use, it must, as in "The Rock," recreate that living grossness, rather than mimic the elegiac Wordsworthian regret. It would be worthwhile, given the prevalence of the theme of memory in Stevens, to track his many descriptions and enactings of memory and its phases far more fully than I have done here; it would be a way both to ally him to his romantic predecessors and, I believe, distinguish him securely, in the end, from them.

20

Jorie Graham

The Moment of Excess

The breaking of style can occur on the largest scale, as when Hopkins invents a new rhythm distinguishing much of his later poetry from his earlier work; or it can occur, as in Heaney's writing, on the scale of a single poem, as the adjectival style called for by the poet's perplexity before the Grauballe Man is exchanged for the nominal style demanded by the trance of a memory-portent in "Deserted harbour stillness." Whereas a large-scale break in style like Hopkins's can scarcely be ignored by readers and critics, smaller breaks from poem to poem like Heaney's often go unnoticed, and the essential exposition through grammatical form of the thematics of the poem goes unremarked. When critics deprive a poem of its material body—which is constituted by its rhythm, its grammar, its lineation, or other such features—they constitute it as a mere cluster of ideas. Under such treatment, the poem loses its physical, and therefore its aesthetic, distinctness. Here, I want, in considering Jorie Graham's work, to look at the unit of the individual line, one of Graham's units of material variation.

Historically, the line has been the characteristic aspect distinguishing poetry from prose; it is the most sensitive barometer of the breath-units in which poetry is voiced. The very shortest way of composing a line is to isolate a single word (in Cummings and Berryman, even a single syllable or letter); the very longest invents a line that spills over into turnovers or, in a different move, suspends from its right margin an appended short line, what Hopkins called an "outride." When a poet ceases to write short lines and begins to write long lines, that change is a breaking of style almost more consequential, in its implications, than any other. Jorie Graham began as a writer of short poems in short lines, lines with a hesitant rhythm so seductive that one's heart, reproducing those poems, almost found a new way to beat. And then, with a burst of almost tidal energy, Graham began to publish long poems in long lines, poems that pressed toward an excess nearly uncontainable by the page. "Poetry," said Keats, "should surprise by a fine excess," and one form of that fine excess is the long line.[1] "In excess, continual, there is cure for sorrow," Stevens observed in "A Weeping Burgher," and one of those cures for world-sorrow is the independent, provocative, and exhilarating excess of voicing represented by the long line.[2] Graham's breaking of style, from short lines to long, invites us to consider these and other possible implications of her act. But before I come to Graham's recourse to the long line, it may be useful to say a word about the presence of the lengthened line in modern verse. There are two chief classical sources of the long line—the epic hexameter and the dithyrambic lyric: the first stands for heroic endeavor, the second for ecstatic utterance. When Hopkins compared "The Wreck of the Deutschland" to a Pindaric ode, he wanted to reclaim ecstatic and irregular form beyond what the classicizing eighteenth century had done; but it was chiefly in his sonnets, as we can see, that he pushed the regular English line to its utmost length, for both effortful and ecstatic reasons. Toward the end of his life, he wrote of his "herds-long" lines:

> My cries heave, herds-long; huddle in a main, a chief-
> Woe, wórld-sorrow; on an áge-old ánvil wince and síng—
> Then lull, then leave off.[3]

His several hexameter sonnets sometimes added outrides and even a coda; and finally, in the octameter lines of "Spelt from Sibyl's Leaves," Hopkins reached his breath-limit. Hopkins used the long line in several ways—as a container of heterogeneity, for instance, which could nonetheless rise to epic heroism: "Thís Jack, jóke, poor pótsherd, patch, | matchwood, immortal diamond / Is immortal diamond."[4] More interestingly, even, Hopkins used the long line to creep up on something by a chromatic series of words, each one melting ecstatically into the next by almost insensible half-steps: "Earnest, earthless, equal, attuneable, | vaulty, voluminous, . . . stupendous / Evening strains to be tíme's vást, | womb-of-all, home-of-all, hearse-of-all night."[5]

Like Hopkins, Whitman—who brought us the founding American free-verse line, deriving it from the Bible and Macpherson's *Ossian*—found the long line useful as a container for the heterogeneous; but he also used it to signify intellectual and speculative difficulties. It served Whitman, in its Hebraic co-ordinate form, for his ongoing repudiation of the old and embrace of the new: "I do not offer the old smooth prizes, but offer rough new prizes."[6] He also used it to signify spontaneity of speculation, and a ready turn to self-correction in ironic bewilderment, as in the poem "Of the Terrible Doubt of Appearances," where a single line (l. 9) says of appearances:

May-be [they are] seeming to me what they are (as doubtless they indeed but
    seem) as from my present point of view, and might prove (as of course they
    would) nought of what they appear, or nought anyhow, from entirely
    changed points of view.[7]

In spite of examples of length like those offered by Hopkins and Whitman, the English line tends stubbornly, when left to itself, to return to its more normative four- or five-beat length unless special heed is paid by the poet either toward shortening it—as Heaney deliberately did, for instance, in his volume *North* when he was seeking a more "Irish" music—or toward prolonging it, as Stevens did in a poem of Odyssean ongoingness called "Prologues to What Is Possible":

He belonged to the far-foreign departure of his vessel and was part of it,
Part of the speculum of fire on its prow, its symbol, whatever it was,
Part of the glass-like sides on which it glided over the salt-stained water,
As he traveled alone, like a man lured on by a syllable without any meaning.[8]

More could be said about the reasons why earlier poets such as Blake and "Ossian" and later ones such as Whitman, Hopkins, and Stevens were pressed toward lengthening the English line—lengthening it against prescription, against historical habit, almost (one could say) against nature. But I want to move on to Graham, and ask why this pressure arises in her, so that her poems sprawl across the page in ways that startle and unsettle us, even while we are enthralled by their urgency, their effort, and their power.

The body Graham first chose for herself in verse was one that above all rep-resented deliberation. Such deliberation could be seen—to invoke an organic metaphor she uses in the poem "Opulence" (from *Materialism*)—as a stalk which arises slowly, puts forth a leaf, matches that leaf with another leaf on the op-posite side of the stem, ascends a bit further, issues a branchlet, and then presses that branchlet to grow a twig. The poems in Graham's first two books, narrow on the page, grew by antiphonal lines—the first line flush left, the second indented, the third flush left, the fourth indented, and so on. Step by step, accreting individual perceptions, the verse descended the page, creating a parallel stairway (often of dimeter followed by monometer) for the reader. Here is a fragment of "Scirocco" from her second book, *Erosion* (1983):

> Outside his window
>> you can hear the scirocco
> working
>> the invisible.
> Every dry leaf of ivy
>> is fingered,
>
> refingered. Who is
>> the nervous spirit
> of this world
>> that must go over and over
> what it already knows,
>> what is it
>
> so hot and dry
>> that's looking through us,
> by us,
>> for its answer?[9]

We see in such lines, which owe much to Williams, the young poet's approach, increment by increment, to a mastery of the world. Most of the poems in *Erosion*, a book written in Graham's late twenties and early thirties, are composed in these stair-step short lines. They embody a process the poet at times calls erosion, at times dissection, in which something is crumbled, bit by bit, to dust; or something is opened, layer by layer, to view.

The process of step-by-step investigation of the world is itself defended in the central question, "How far is true?" posed by Graham's harrowing poem "At Luca Signorelli's Resurrection of the Body." The son of the painter Signorelli has died, and the father, reaching beyond his grief, dissects the body:

> [H]e cut
>> deeper,
> graduating slowly
>> from the symbolic

to the beautiful. How far
       is true?
. . . . .
       [W]ith beauty and care
       and technique
and judgement, [he] cut into
       shadow, cut
into bone and sinew and every
       pocket

in which the cold light
       pooled.
It took him days
       that deep
caress, cutting,
       unfastening,

until his mind
       could climb into
the open flesh and
       mend itself.

(E, 76–77)

This accomplished, steady, unflinching writing-in-short-lines (which deals
out the lines, group by group, in regular six-line stanzas) represents, we could
say, a faith in the power of the patience of mind; and with its deliberate respect
for the resistance of matter, it intimates the "beauty and care / and technique /
and judgment" that the mind must observe as it employs the precise investigative power of its various scalpels. The question "How far is true?" is left open-
ended, but that it is the poet's duty to take the symbolic through the beautiful
into the true is not in doubt.

Toward the end of *Erosion*, Graham includes a disturbing poem called
"Updraft," its title betraying a force which is the diametrical opposite of those
sequential, incremental, and orderly processes—whether natural ones like erosion or intellectual ones like dissection—which Graham's form had enacted.
The updraft, or convection current, of Graham's poem literally turns the atmosphere turbulently upside down in tumultuous irregular lines:

       all the blossoms ripped suddenly by one gust, one
updraft—mosaic

of dust and silks
by which we are all rising, turning, all
free.
(E, 70)

The movement chronicled by "Updraft" is the dissolution of meaning into unmeaning. The poet, now distrusting the closure of form, implores a Godlike
figure to let Eve, the mother of creation, symbol of the world of formed shapes,
slip back into the uncreated:

> so let her slip
>
> out of her heavy garment then, let her slip back
> into the rib, into Your dream, Your
> loneliness, back, deep into the undress. . . .
> (E, 71)

The undress exists "back / before Your needle leapt in Your fingers, meaning."
The "undress," then, that the poet longs for is what Kristeva calls by the Platonic name of the *chora:*—the presymbolic matrix of language, where rhythm
and syllable and semiosis have not yet coalesced into sign and meaning. But
since we cannot go backward to the *chora*, we must, in our resistance to closure, go forward, by entropy, into randomness and shapelessness.

The long line, therefore, is first generated by Graham as the formal equivalent of mortality, dissolution, and unmeaning. At this point in her writing, it is
set against the persuasions of shapely organic form, and against the intellectual intelligibility that is the result of careful deliberative investigation.
"The blood" says Graham in "Updraft," "smears itself against the mind," and
this contest, as suffering body disfigures questing spirit, is continued in all of
Graham's later books.

Erosion was followed by the volume uncompromisingly entitled *The End of
Beauty* (1987), which marks Graham's definitive break with short-lined lyric.
Though the old investigative antiphonies reappear once or twice ("Eschatological Prayer," "Noli MeTangere"), the preeminent move in the book is a
struggle against the intellectual and formal dénouement of shapely closure.
Rather, there is now in the poet an assent—voiced in a long-lined poem called
"Vertigo"—to uncertainty and unpredictability: this is the vertigo felt as one
abandons old and predetermined ways in favor of the pull of the unknown beyond the precipice of the new:

She leaned out. What is it pulls at one, she wondered,
what? That it has no shape but point of view?
That it cannot move to hold us?
Oh it has vibrancy, she thought, this emptiness, this intake just
                                                prior to
the start of a story, the mind trying to fasten
and fasten, the mind feeling it like a sickness this wanting
to snag, catch hold, begin, the mind crawling out to the edge of the cliff
and feeling the body as if for the first time—how it cannot
follow, cannot love.[10]

The dizzying extension of the mind, as it crawls out to the edge of the cliff of the conceptual, presses Graham to her long lines and to their "outrides"— small piece-lines dropping down at the right margin of their precursor-line. Graham's combination of indefinitely stretching right-edge horizontality with occasional right-edge vertical drops refuses both the model of step-by-step upward mental advance and the model of investigative penetration inward from the beautiful into the true. Rather, Graham redefines the human aim of verse as an earthly, terrain-oriented lateral search (which can reach even the epic dimensions of the Columbian voyage) rather than a vertical Signorelli-like descent into depth or, as in "Updraft," an ascent into prayer. Earthly desire itself is the thing allegorized by Graham's long horizontal line, desire always prolonging itself further and further over a gap it nonetheless does not wish to close. In this search by desire, mind will always outrun body. And the linear ongoingness necessitated by the continuation of desire means that the absence of shape, far from meaning dissolution and mortality, now stands for life itself.

In the poem "Pollock and Canvas," Graham, searching for a nontranscendent vertical which will be comparable to her earthly "desiring" horizontal, finds a metaphor for her line in the fluid drip of Pollock's paint between the body of the artist and his canvas spread on the ground. The line of paint, let down from the brush, is like a fishing line sinking without effort into the water: this cascading line is not epic, like the Odyssean one questingly covering distances toward a horizon; rather, it is ecstatic, living in the possible:

17
the line being fed out the line without shape before it lands without death
18
saying a good life is possible, still hissing, still unposited,

19

before it lands, without shape, without generation, or form that bright fruit.
(EB, 84–85)

At this moment, the long vertical line, "fed out," is pure middleness, the unposited, the possible, the "formless," the ethically indeterminate. It has not yet
tethered itself to shape, to ending, to decision; it has not yet plucked the apple
of the Fall.

To write a poetry of middleness, of suspension, is Graham's chief intellectual and emotional preoccupation in *The End of Beauty*. In that aim, she defers
closure in many poems by a series of ever-approaching asymptotic gestures,
each one of them numbered, and each advancing the plot by a micro-measure.
Her model for this halting use of the long line seems to be the cinematic freeze-
frame, by which an action sequence in film is divided, like the flight of Zeno's
arrow, into minutely brief "shots," or elements. To place each of her elements
into stop-time, Graham tries the experiment of numbering the freeze-frames
sequentially, so that the unfamiliar appearance of a number punctuates on the
page each quantum of perception delivered by a line or lines.

This experiment—affixing a number to each perception-packet—is tried in
only six of the twenty-six poems in *The End of Beauty*, but these six are the
dual self-portraits in which the volume finds its cohesion:

"Self-Portrait as the Gesture between Them"
"Self-Portrait as Both Parties"
"Self-Portrait as Apollo and Daphne"
"Self-Portrait as Hurry and Delay"
"Self-Portrait as Demeter and Persephone"
"Pollock and Canvas"

These poems have a collective importance beyond their mere number. Why,
we must ask, does this forcibly stopped numbered version of the long line pre-
dominate in the dual self-portraits (of which "Pollock and Canvas," despite its
title, is surely one)?

The self-portrait, as a visual genre, has always depended on some mirror-
strategy by which the painter can depict an object normally inaccessible to
vision: his or her own face. Not all self-portraits display the necessary mirror,
but even those that do not will prompt the viewer to some reflection on the difficulty of realization necessitated by a reproduction of one's own face. Some
self-portraits—Vermeer's of the artist in his studio, for instance—obliterate

the face of the artist, as Vermeer substitutes the inscrutable rear view with black hat as an index of that necessary but suppressed subjectivity of the painter that plays a role in every painting, no matter how "objective." Parmigianino, as Ashbery has reminded us, paints himself reflected in a convex mirror so as to emphasize the distortion inevitable in any stratagem for self-representation.

Graham's acknowledgment of the complex demands of her own dual self-portraits is articulated most visibly in her numerically interrupted frames. They say: "Look at yourself in a frozen moment; write it down. Gaze again; write it down. And now glance a third time; and write it down." The alternations of consciousness as the words succeed the gaze are not concealed; rather, they are inscribed on the page, number by advancing number. By "baring the device," as the Russian Formalists would say, Graham's self-portraits prevent an easy slide by the reader—or by the poet herself—into an introspection unconscious of problems of representation.

But what does the affixing of prefatory numbers have to do with Graham's break into the long line? The conventional view of the poetic line, as I have said, associates it with breath; and indeed, a good deal of theorizing about the material base of poetry links it to the inspiration and suspiration of the single breath as its measure. The physiological regulation of breathing makes natural breaths roughly isometric—in, out; in, out. And isometric breathing is a likely basis for regular lines, orderly and successive ones. But the gaze has no such isometric rhythm: a gaze can be prolonged at will, held for inspection, meditated on, and periodically interrupted. It is the gaze, rather than the breath, that seems to me Graham's fundamental measure in the numbered-line poems. By this choice of the gaze over the breath, as a governing principle, Graham redefines utterance; and what utterance becomes is the tracking of the gaze, quantum-percept by quantum-percept, bundle by bundle, rhythm by rhythm. In Graham's poetry, a trust in the vagaries of the perceptual comes to replace the earlier poetry's trust both in the physiologically regulated order of breath and in a teleologically regulated order of truth. Since the apotheosis of the perceptual is necessarily an apotheosis of the moment, Graham is as interested in the (numbered) interruptive pause as in the significant perception; and her sequestering of the pause as a good in itself can be seen most clearly in her freeze-frame lines in "Pollock and Canvas."

"Pollock and Canvas" is a poem in three Roman-numeraled parts, but only Part II affixes numbers to its lines. Part I is a conceptual summary (in the past tense) of Pollock's "drip" practice, linking him with the wounded King of *The Waste Land* and the Parsifal legends, a King suspended between life and death. The intermediate state of the King—alive but not life-giving, wounded but not

dead—is summed up in Pollock's question as he bends over his canvas, refusing to let the brush tip touch it: *"tell me then what will render / the body alive?"*
(EB, 82). Pollock, though accomplished in the conferring of shape, resolves to
keep his canvas safe from the death of final formal shape (*"his brush able to cut
a figure / on the blank and refusing"*).

I pass over, for the moment, the numbered Part II, to look at the way the
poem concludes. Pollock's Part I terror of the conclusiveness of final shape is
answered in Part III of "Pollock and Canvas," which envisages a way *out* of
formal shape. That formal shape (beauty, love, the figure), once it has been conferred on the canvas, permanently settles over a piece of life and determines it.
The only way out of the conclusiveness of that formal shape is the admission
into it of elements of chance; and Graham's figure for that possibility is God's
rest after He made the world, a point at which the unintended, the serpent, can
slip into Paradise:

> And then He rested, is that where the real
> making
>   begins—the now—Then He rested letting in chance letting in
> any wind any shadow quick with minutes, and whimsy,
>   through the light, letting the snake the turning
> in.
> (EB, 87)

Graham's conclusion is that the adventitious, the aleatory, the not-yet-true will
eventually, without God's intending it, become part of the Creation:

> Then things not yet true
>   which slip in
>
> are true,
>   aren't they?

The things which slip in are part of the Keatsian "fine excess" and, since they
are a "supplement" to what was intended, have their formal equivalent in whatever in the line seems arbitrary, unintended, added by chance, as though the
line had had to expand to take such things in.

In "Pollock and Canvas," long lines exist, it is true, in both the Amfortas-
suspension of Part I and the Jehovah-chance balance of Part III. But the quin-
tessence of the species "long line" in *The End of Beauty*—which I take to be

the long line intermitted by the long numbered pause—is achieved in Part II of "Pollock and Canvas," where, though Pollock cannot entirely avoid the forward pull of temporality, he attempts to spatialize time as much as possible by inserting between each gaze a pause, representing ecstatic being:

1

Here is the lake, the open, he calls it his day; fishing.

2

The lake, the middle movement, women's flesh, maya.

3

And here is the hook before it has landed, before it's deep in the current.

(EB, 82–83)

This pregnant section of the poem—enacting space, middleness, incarnation, illusion, suspension—speaks directly of what the double excess of the long line and the long pause mean to Graham: a way of representing the luxurious spread of experienced being, preanalytic and precontingent. This condition has Romantic affinities; but Graham does not want to be laid asleep in body to become a living soul. Rather, against Wordsworth, she almost wants to be laid asleep in mind to become a living body. Her *maya* contains no access to Wordsworthian transcendence; rather, she accepts its blessed stoppage in prolonged sensual illusion, that excess that is, in Stevens's terms, the cure of sorrow. The incarnation of this *maya* as it takes place "between the creator and the created" (EB, 83) is the Stevensian moment of credences of summer, of human existence without temporal entrance or exit, represented paradoxically by "of the graces the / 8 / most violent one, the one all gash, all description." This grace is the Muse of eternal process, who has replaced for Graham the meditated, investigative, and shaped Muse of product.

Graham's long line, representing being-in-process, continues, after *The End of Beauty*, into *Region of Unlikeness* (1991); but in the later, more autobiographical volume, the line drops its earlier partner, the open numbered space, which had represented being-in-pause. The gaze turns to the single autobiographical self-portrait (which replaces the mythological dual self-portrait), and the plot of narrative replaces bundled quanta of perception. Instead of dwelling on *Region of Unlikeness*, I will turn to Graham's *Materialism* (1993), because in it she combines the long line with its apparently ultimate narrative partner, the long sentence. Since the long horizontal line of extension in space toward the horizon is itself already formally effortful, it becomes even more epically taxing

when it is joined to the long sentence (together becoming the conventional equivalent of temporal and conceptual complexity). To the long horizontal axis of
the line is added the long vertical axis of the sentence. Graham had used long
sentences to good effect as early as *Erosion,* but there they were strung down
the page in very short lines. In *The End of Beauty,* the lines were longer, but
the long sentences appearing there were usually interspersed with shorter ones,
alleviating the effort of suspension. In *Materialism,* the combination of horizontal and vertical prolongation is carried out to the utmost degree, so that the
poems literally construct visual plane areas ("tarpaulins," to use Ashbery's word
from the poem of that name) in which words cover and spatialize being.

Total coverage is the ultimate effect toward which Graham has been
tending with her long lines ever since they first appeared. This area-effect has
affinities with other literary structures (the epic simile, the Miltonic verse-
paragraph, the Whitmanian catalogue, the Moore encyclopedia-page), since all
of these represent what Graham calls, in one of the titles of *Materialism,* "The
Dream of the Unified Field." In that dream (in Graham's version), the whole
world is extrapolated out from whatever center one chooses as origin. Stevens
conceived of this effect, in "The Man with the Blue Guitar," as one in which
the twang of the blue guitar would be "the reason in the storm," incorporating
the whole of the storm while giving it a focal point and intelligibility:

> I know my lazy, leaden twang
> Is like the reason in a storm;
>
> And yet it brings the storm to bear.
> I twang it out and leave it there.[11]

Against Stevens's brisk storm, we can put Graham's enveloping storm in
Materialism:

> The storm: I close my eyes and,
> standing in it, try to make it *mine.*
> . . . . .
> possession
> gripping down to form,
> wilderness brought deep into my clearing,
> out of the ooze of night,
> limbed, shouldered, necked, visaged, the white—

> now the clouds coming in (don't look up),
> now the Age behind the clouds, The Great Heights,
> all in there, reclining, eyes closed, huge,
> centuries and centuries long and wide,
> and underneath, barely attached but attached,
> like a runner, my body, my tiny piece of
> the century—minutes, houses going by—The Great
>   Heights—
> anchored by these footsteps, now and now,
> the footstepping—now and now—carrying its vast
> white sleeping geography—mapped—
> not a lease—*possession.*[12]

Graham compares this constant human desire for aesthetic possession of all space and time (the Great Heights, the long and wide centuries) to Columbus's desire to possess the New World; the hubristic dubiety of both enterprises is set against their spiritual ambition. Such undertakings are instinctive and unavoidable, Graham suggests, in creatures of mind and appetite. The human appetite desires metaphysical and intellectual, as much as material, gain. It is the limitlessness of the claims of intellect and of desire that inspire Graham's most ambitious poems; that limitlessness also appalls her.

The appetitiveness of the mind, and the infinity of the world's stimuli, generate the excess of Graham's long horizontal lines, which generate, in their turn, her long vertical sentences. Any given poetic idea begins to produce, in Graham, a version of an aesthetic Big Bang with its vertiginous perceptual expansion and its receding conceptual distances. We can see this happening in "The Turning."[13] The poem is about dawn in an Italian hill town, and it begins with several brief successive noticings (not quoted here). Each noticing creates a brief sentence, and then stops. Nothing can take wing. The poet cannot yet feel her way into the heterogeneity, simultaneity, chromatic change, spontaneity, and self-correction present in all acts of extended noticing. Eventually, the reason for the fizzling-out of each perception is formulated: there is either a war between the world and its perceiver, preventing their interpenetration; or else there is an indifference between them, making them remain on parallel tracks without intersection:

> There is a war.
> Two parallels that will not meet have formed
> a wall.

In spite of successive tries, the desired tarpaulin, area, square, updraft, thrown cloth has not yet been found. Not until inner feeling and outer perception begin to meld, and the poet's body becomes, kinesthetically, a form of the world's fluid body, can the world be re-created in language. The poet declares her creed: that the sun must come up in *her* before it can come up on her page; and it must come up on her page before it can come up for her reader:

> The sun revolves because of our revolving in
> the wall.

The wall is the poet's new perceptual blank sheet of paper. At the beginning of Graham's observation of the dawn, nothing is inscribed on her mental "wall" except Stevens's command to himself at the end of "Notes toward a Supreme Fiction," where he addresses the Earth, saying that poetry requires *"that I / should name you"*:

> Fat girl, terrestrial, my summer, my night,
> How is it I find you in difference, see you there
> In a moving contour, a change not quite completed?
>
> . . . this unprovoked sensation requires
>
> That I should name you flatly, waste no words,
> Check your evasions, hold you to yourself.
>
>   . . . You
> Become the soft-footed phantom, the irrational
>
> Distortion.[14]

Faced with her recollection of Stevens's command, Graham must name the "soft-footed phantom," the Earth as it presents itself on this Italian morning. But how is she to articulate the area, the cloth, the tarpaulin to be cast over this infinitely opening piece of reality without stiffening it into lifelessness?

It is within the moment of an unlooked-for chance event, when a single bird moves, that the poet finds she can rise unexpectedly with it into unimpeded voice, combining bird, soul, light, church bells, swallow-flocks, and human beings into a single long—almost unending—sentence which prolongs the second part of the poem (quoted here) from the words "Bright whites and citrines" to "I look down into the neighbor's garden":

Bright whites and citrines
gleaming forth,
layerings, syllables of
the most loud
invisible
that stick (no departure and no return) to their single
constantly revised
(I saw men yesterday, tuck-pointing, on their scaffold)
lecture on what
most matters: sun: now church bells breaking up
in twos and threes
the flock
which works across in
granular,
forked, suddenly cacophonic
undulation
(though at the level
of the inaudible) large differences of rustling, risings and lowerings,
swallowings of
silence where the wings
en masse lift off—and then the other (indecipherable) new
silence where
wings aren't
used and the flock floats in
unison—
a flying-in-formation sound which
I can see across the wall (as if loud)—shrapnel of
blacknesses
against the brightnesses—
fistfuls thrown (as if splattered) then growing fantastically
in size (also now
rising swiftly) as
they come—a stem of silence which blossoms suddenly
as it vanishes from the wall—(turning, the whole
flock
turning)—exfoliation of aural clottings where all wings open now
to break
and pump—vapor of accreting inaudible—

innermost sound scratchy with clawed and necked
                    and winged
indecipherables (a herald)—whole flock now rising highest just before it
turns to write the longest version yet against the whole
length of the wall where the churchbells
have begun to cease and
one name is called out (but low, down near the Roman
                           gate) and one
car from down there sputters
up—(the light brightest now, it almost
               true morning)—
these walls these streets the light the shadow in them
the throat of the thing—birds reassembling over the roof
in syncopated undulations of cooing as they settle. . . .
I look down into the neighbor's garden.

In order to maintain itself, this long-lined and outridered long sentence depends on several grammatical techniques of prolongation—present participles, appositions, relative clauses both adjectival and adverbial, parenthetical insertions, a colon, additive conjunctions like "and," negations, comparisons ("as if"), cotemporalities ("also"), successivities ("then" and "just before"), repetitions ("now . . . now"), qualifications, and nominal simultaneities ("these walls these streets the light the shadow in them / the throat of the thing").

It is only of course after the fact of reading that we can name these grammatical means accelerating the perceptual thrust of the sentence; during our actual stretched assimilation of this long cascade of words flung over a page we are, to put it imaginatively, participating in making the sun come up, the birds awaken, and the church bells ring. Such an epic sentence—as the town turns from night to morning—is a human, and therefore effortful, *Fiat lux*. It cannot have the concision and effortlessness of the divine illumination of chaos, because it is made from a sensing and concentrating body striving to comprehend a moment in one internalized physical and mental gestalt. And that human body is replicating *itself* in its aesthetic body of words, rather than replicating the outside world in a direct mimesis. The poet has to substitute, for the metaphysical divine will and the intellectual divine Logos, a frail human eye and an even frailer human will, which must concentrate fiercely, to translate into internal kinesthetic sense-response, "the most loud invisible" of the light and "the vapor of accreting inaudibles," the silent flocking of birds. The poet must translate these first into a consciousness of her own internal physical mimicry of the external stimuli, and then, in turn, she must translate that internal kinesthetic mimicry into the visible and audible signs of English, a language with its own internal constraints on expression. The order of linguistic signification, which succeeds the orders of perception and kinesthesis, is represented in the poem by the moment when "one name is called out." Every genuine poem, as Mallarmé insisted, aims at being "one name"—a single complex and indivisible unit of language proper to its moment and irreplaceable by any other. As the poet lifts the silent and the nonlinguistic and the nonpropositional from perceptual import to kinesthetic import into semiotic and rhythmic import, one form of suffering—seeing the day go by unregistered and unrecorded—is brought to an end.

The poet's subsidence into rest—after the epic but also ecstatic effort of turning dawn into words—is almost painfully brief: "I look down into the neighbor's garden." There are still things unheard, the poet reminds herself (the petal fall); there are still things her transcription has been unable to incorporate (the pine tree unincluded in the long central sentence):

> What if I could hear the sound of petals falling
> off the head that
> holds them
> when it's time?
> What if I could hear when something is suddenly
> complete?
> The pinetree marionette-like against the wall—but still,
> unused.
> Whose turn is it now? Whose?

A new sentence begins to brew in the poet's compelled heart: she has "done" one bit of morning, the turn from dark to light, from nested birds to flying flocks, from silence to church bells, from sleep to the crying of a single name—but "Whose turn is it now? Whose?"

The alternating rhythms of silence and naming become ever more anguishing in Graham's work, if only because each poem, at this point in her pursuit of the lyric, demands of her that she leave out nothing. This is a demand to which all serious artists eventually come—"O mother, what have I left out? O mother, what have I forgotten?" asks Ginsberg in "Kaddish"—and, implicitly, all readers test long lyrics by asking, "What *should* have been included here by way of observation, reflection, qualification, and conclusion, and was, to the detriment of the poem, left out?" (Even shorter lyrics must, to succeed, convince us of their completeness; they do it by a sort of Dickinsonian implosion, in which an implied prehistory of ignited totalization is condensed into charred post hoc indices of itself: "Ashes denote that fire was.")

At this moment in her writing, Graham chooses to show us her expanding universe by means of a slice of it in conic section. Graham's cosmological excess can be read as a corrective to the current lyric of personal circumscription. It is especially a corrective (in its descent from Dickinson at her most metaphysical and Moore at her most expansive) to the lack of grandeur in much contemporary American poetry. Just as the personal is always in danger of becoming petty, so of course the grand is always in danger of the grandiose; and the Great Heights (as Graham has called them) can, unchecked, become parodies of themselves. Graham's capacity to descend from the Great Heights to an unremarkable single dawn in an anonymous town suggests that she understands the Whitmanian sublimity of the ordinary as well as the Shelleyan sublimity of aspiration. She has shown, in still other poems, that she possesses self-irony and historical irony, both of them useful balances to the vaulting mind and the universalizing voice that impel her approach to the edge of the precipice of perception by means of her triple excess—her long lines, her long pauses, and her long sentences.

21

Attention, Shoppers

Where Shall I Wander, *by John Ashbery*

John Ashbery, in a youthful review of Marianne Moore, cited what he called the "almost satisfactory definition" of poetry given by the nineteenth-century French poet Banville: "[Poetry is] that magic which consists in awakening sensations with the help of a combination of sounds . . . that sorcery by which ideas are necessarily communicated to us, in a definite way, by words which nevertheless do not express them." Poetry expresses ideas, the poet claims, but not by means of propositional statements. Instead it relies upon an underlying "sorcery" dependent on a combination of sounds (arranged rhythmically, needless to say) that awaken sensations. If the sentences of the poem were written differently, the evoked ideas would disappear.[1]

Unlike many other "experimental" poets, Ashbery has resisted the notion that poetry need not communicate intelligibly; but he has also resisted tethering poetry to the expository flatness of the assertion of doctrine or ideology. Throughout his writing, he has taken risks to see how far he could go in transmitting, or even transferring, states of consciousness. "Poetry," he has remarked, "is not a stationary object but a kinetic act, in which something is transferred from somebody to somebody else" (SP, 211). Ashbery's magnificent book-length work *Three Poems* is written in prose, but it so powerfully summons up the waves of successive states in human life—early bewildered depression, the intoxication of recognizing one's identity, the further intoxication in the discovery of love, the feared subsidence of excitement, the return of dullness, the restorative insight into compensatory wisdom, the buoyant effect of a new love—that at the end the reader feels like an actor borne along on strange flowing and ebbing tides, a character in an abstract plot that is reticent as to time, place, or person, but convincingly "real" as the experience is undergone.

Ashbery's experiments have not always succeeded. Not everyone was convinced that the dual streams of consciousness (two separate columns running parallel down the page) of "Litany" could really be read as one, or remembered well enough to modify each other. Even so, that fascinating labyrinth of abstract autobiography, full of stunning writing, at least gestured toward the notion of the bicameral mind. In yet other risky ventures, Ashbery has based his writing on the oral roots of lyric in nursery rhymes, riddles, spells, doggerel, and popular song: all reminders that the primordial lyric emphasizes the play of sound and rhythm. The title of Ashbery's *Where Shall I Wander* is another such reminder: although it may sound Romantic, it comes in fact from one of Mother Goose's more sinisterly comic rhymes.[2] (I quote it here from Bartlett, although I learned the rhyme in childhood with Ashbery's American version of the second line):

> Goosey goosey gander,
> Whither shall I wander?
> Upstairs and downstairs,
> And in my lady's chamber;
> There I met an old man who wouldn't
>   say his prayers;
> I took him by the left leg
> And threw him down the stairs.

The persons, the actions, and the locales in the nursery rhyme do what the ingredients of Ashbery's poetry do: they make irregular jumps from person to person, action to action, place to place, nonsense to violence. See, for instance, the jumps in the poem called "Broken Tulips," which, originating in urban erotic life (but with absurd place-names taken from Marlowe), pauses to note the (temporary) suspension of terror while "the cave thing" hides itself; sketches an animated Easter rabbit cartoon of spring; echoes Hopkins on clouds ("Has wilder, wilful-wavier / Meal-drift moulded ever and melted across skies?"); and subsides into a comically tenacious defense of human storytelling. Although "Broken Tulips" (30) opens on the perplexities of sex, it leaps, in successive moves, to art:

> A is walking through the streets of B, frantic
> for C's touch but secretly relieved
> not to have it. At Tamerlane

and East Tamerlane, he pauses, judicious:
The cave thing hasn't been seen again,
schoolgirls are prattling, and the Easter rabbit
is charging down the street, under full sail
and a strong headwind. Was ever anything
so delectable floated across the crescent moon's
transparent bay? Here shall we sit
and, damnit, talk about our trip
until the sky is again cold and gray.

This hybrid language of literariness and contemporary pop culture is Ashbery's native speech (as it is ours, too, whether we like it or not). But in the second half of "Broken Tulips"—after an initial joke about the TV crawl and a paradox on unwelcome longevity—the poem darkens. God's promise that the deluge will not recur has been broken, like the titular tulips, and the menacing rifle-telescope of night warns us that it will not long comply with our wish to live:

Another's narrative supplants the crawling
stock-market quotes: Like all good things
life tends to go on too long, and when we smile
in mute annoyance, pauses for a moment.
Rains bathe the rainbow,
and the shape of night is an empty cylinder,
focused at us, urging its noncompliance
closer along the way we chose to go.

What is to be gained by writing this way? In answer, we need only imagine the poem done conventionally: a first-person narrator evokes his erotic anxiety, his sense of spring, his feeling of *taedium vitae*, his foreboding of a failure of spring, and his fear of death. These topics are so worn one can hardly think of writing about them—and yet what else stirs feeling in our hearts? "Make it new"— Pound's old command—is as talismanic as ever. Yet the trouble with superficial ways of making the new is that they leave out the old: Ashbery keeps the old in— through allusion, echo, and the revival of perennial topics—and therefore can "communicate ideas" after all. He does so best by his ingenious images—from the Easter rabbit to the empty cylinder and the rained-on rainbow—and (as a poet once remarked to me) by his ever-fresh sense of the seasons.

Where Shall I Wander is rich in grimly funny images of the dance of approaching death. He and his companion, in a form of Grand Guignol, are "walking the plank / of every good thing / toward the tank of carnivorous eels / singing, chiming as we go / into subtracted Totentanz"; farewell messages announce "sunflowers over and out, / ashes on the clapboard credenza"; and a man is "waiting to take tickets at the top / of the gangplank." "Novelty Love Trot" (51) ends with the poet's companion fixing an absurd gourmet meal while the poet dryly complains of his perpetual loneliness and his recalcitrant work:

> You are stuffing squash blossoms
> with porcini mushrooms. I am somewhere else, alone as usual.
>
> I must get back to my elegy.

Wonderful and sustaining as Ashbery's images are, tallying and making recognizable our own emotions, they are only one of the joys on offer in his poems. Outside of Lewis Carroll and Edward Lear, have there ever been comic opening lines like Ashbery's? The hands-down winner in *Where Shall I Wander* is: "Attention, shoppers" (36). The loudspeaker messages in Kmart are unavoidable subliminal tenants of our unconscious mind, but their grotesquerie is suddenly lifted into view by Ashbery's co-opting of them for his address to his readers. In a different but equally arresting vein, many of Ashbery's openings prophesy a coming catastrophe. The first line in *Where Shall I Wander* announces, "We were warned about spiders, and the occasional famine" (1); another asserts gloomily (but comically, too, given the Yeatsian echo) that "the passionate are immobilized" (46). These catastrophic bulletins are balanced by Ashbery's other preferred opening gambit, the ineffably bland beginning, often a joke on contemporary cult language.

> I enjoy biographies and bibliographies,
> and cultural studies. As for music, my tastes
> run to Liszt's Consolations, especially the flatter ones,
> though I've never been consoled
> by them. Well, once maybe.
> (50)

Ashbery's linguistic imagination draws him not only toward allusion and echo, but even more strongly toward parody of this kind. The title poem of *Where Shall I Wander* (75–81) is an extended prose poem parodying the diction of almost every American form of expression, oral or written—advertisements, manuals of instruction, bar talk, academese, the "poetic," children's verse, fashion babble. It is only by parody that the poet can make us really listen to what is bombarding us on every side, conceptually and verbally. Too long to be substantially quoted here, the poem glitters throughout its headlong progress with ridiculously incompatible linguistic adornments ("Heterophage, we come unblinking into the standing day"; "Wherever a tisket is available, substitute an item from column B, then return to the starting goal"; "Geez I don't know the answer, if I did, you—"). As the poem ends, the speaker—one of two hosts who have bade farewell to guests at the dispersal of a party—comments with complacent retrospection on the picture he and his companion made:

> You wore your cummerbund with the stars and stripes. I, kilted in
>   lime, held a stethoscope to the head of the parting guest. Together
>   we were a couple forever.

This closing tableau embodies the peculiar affection-within-satire that is Ashbery's characteristic touch. His comedy owes a good deal to old movies, and the poses of his characters often call up their visual equivalents: here, the freeze-frame gives us the cinematic united couple in evening dress, standing at their open door as their friends leave the house. The only way to see yourself accurately, Ashbery implies, is with the stereoscopic perspective of irony, to be aware always of the parodic potential of one's utterance and appearance.

Ashbery's remarks, in 1966, comparing the didactic intention of the "committed poets" of the time to the imaginative gaiety of Frank O'Hara are equally applicable to his own work. He says of O'Hara's poetry that it

> has no program and therefore cannot be joined. It does not advocate sex
> and dope as a panacea for the ills of modern society, it does not speak out
> against the war in Vietnam or in favor of civil rights; it does not paint gothic
> vignettes of the post-Atomic age: in a word, it does not attack the estab-
> lishment. It merely ignores its right to exist, and is thus a source of an-
> noyance for partisans of every stripe. (SP, 81)

Even more pointedly, Ashbery dismissed O'Hara's "committed" critics:

> It is not surprising that critics have found him self-indulgent . . . the poems
> are all about him and the people and images who wheel through his con-
> sciousness, and they seek no further justification. . . . Unlike the "mes-
> sage" of committed poetry, [O'Hara's work] incites one to all the programs

of commitment as well as to every other form of self-realization—
interpersonal, Dionysian, occult, or abstract. Such a program is absolutely new in poetry. (SP, 82)

This last phrase—"absolutely new"—is not entirely accurate: Whitman said
repeatedly that he was not preaching a program, but actively urging his readers
to find their own form of self-realization. Yet Whitman's messianic voice turned
his first readers into devotees rather than seekers of personal authenticity. What
is new in O'Hara and Ashbery is their refusal of an earnestly didactic tone. Describing O'Hara's poetry, Ashbery staked out his own territory as well—states
of consciousness, demotic language, a democratic inclusiveness of mention:

> Surrealism was after all limited to the unconscious and O'Hara throws
> in the conscious as well—doesn't it exist too? Why should our uncon-
> scious thoughts be more meaningful than our conscious ones . . . ? Here
> everything "belongs": unrefined autobiographical fragments, names of
> movie stars and operas, obscene interjections, quotations from letters—the
> élan of the poem is such that for the poet merely to mention something
> creates a place for it, ennobles it, makes us realize how important it has
> always been for us. (SP, 82)

This, too, is a Whitmanian program: mentioning something to create a place
for it is surely the justification of Whitman's catalogues. But the New York
postwar writers, from O'Hara to Koch to Schuyler to Ashbery, extended the
things mentioned beyond what Whitman had thought possible.

Enumerating his New York friends—Frank O'Hara, Barbara Guest, and James
Schuyler—Ashbery adds the explanation of their subsequent group title: "We
poets were dubbed, somewhat to our surprise, the New York School of Poets;
this was the idea of John Myers, whose gallery published our pamphlets and
who thought that the prestige of New York School painting might rub off on
'his' poets" (SP, 249). Many of the group—O'Hara, Koch, Schuyler—are now
dead; as Ashbery recalls that "school" he ironizes his nostalgic language with
the ridiculous eighteenth-century periphrasis for a school of fish:

> Must have
> been the time before this, when we all moved
> in schools, a finny tribe, and this way
> and that the caucus raised its din:

punctuation and quips, an "environment"
like a lovely shed.

Among the poets of the New York School, Ashbery has been the most influential in opening up new possibilities for the American lyric. He has done
this by enlivening the page with diction of a startling heterogeneity; by being
more broadly allusive than any other modern poet, including Eliot; by being
boyish and amusing while maintaining emotional depth; by finding a gorgeous-
ness of imagery rare since Stevens; and by taking headstrong risks that have
endangered whole books (notably *The Tennis Court Oath*), but which have paid
off in original forms of narrative and fable.

Ashbery was formed (after his education at Harvard and Columbia) not only
by his ten years in France speaking French and reading French literature; not
only by his many years as a writer of brilliant criticism of new painters and sculp-
tors and graphic artists; but also by the relatively marginalized poets that he
referred to in his Norton Lectures as the "other tradition," including John Clare,
Laura Riding, and Thomas Lovell Beddoes. The sentences of prose writers—not
only Proust but also Henry James and Gertrude Stein—have entered the rep-
ertoire of his sinuous syntactic style. And at its best it all adds up—when the
reader gets used to it—to something strange, exhilarating, cheeky, and moving.

All these qualities can be seen in "When I Saw the Invidious Flare" (37–38),
one of the many apocalyptic poems. In his seventies, the speaker wishes to
sum up, before the curtain falls, the life he has lived. The summary is voiced
(as is usual with Ashbery) in a mix of humorous plaintiveness, surrealist imagery, and giddy idiom. As a Stevensian "invidious flare" ("like a blaze of
summer straw, in winter's nick," in *The Auroras of Autumn*) lights up the evening
sky, the speaker reflects that he has had love, yes, but love has become tedious;
that life is, alas, more lonesome after choosing one's path than before; that he
has been devoted to learning, yes, but is about to be expelled—or worse, suspended in an afterlife—from the school of life; that (like Thomas Aquinas) he
may find at the end that all his learning seems but straw; that the vicissitudes
of life have turned his fellow Keatsian chameleons into coarse warthogs; and
that his style of writing is criticized from both left and right:

> When I saw the invidious flare
> and houses rising up over the horizon
> I called to my brother. "Brother," I called
> "why are these chameleons teasing us?

Is it that they are warthogs, and the gamekeeper is napping?
What I'd give for a pint of English bitter,
or anything, practically anything at all.
How lonesome it seems when you're choosing,
and then, when you have done so, it seems even more lonesome.
We should have got out more during the last fine days.
Now, love is but a lesson, and a tedious one at that.
Do they think they can expel me from this school, or worse,
suspend me? In which case all my learning will be as straw,
though there'll be a lot of it,
I can assure you."

Evening waves slap rudely at the pilings
and birds are more numerous than usual.
There are some who find me sloppy, others
for whom I seem too well-groomed. I'd like to strike
a happy medium, but style
is such a personal thing, an everlasting riddle.

This is the first part of the invidious evening, setting the stage of the Last Days, warthogs and all, and with nary a sedative in sight (not even the appropriately named English bitter). In the second half of the poem, even the invidious flare wants to be allowed to regress to its more dulcet youth, when it was merely a light at the end of a tunnel. The speaker reflects on the short time left before everything goes up in flames, before (in a linguistic skid to the ordinary) he reaches the end of the alphabet. Earlier decades were supported by knowledge attained from elders—but how many poems or paintings do we have telling us what it is like to live into our seventies or eighties? What will the looming letters W and Z threaten us with? But, he sententiously counters in a rapid drop into religion-speak and therapy-speak, the fair positives of our youth are, after all, not all there is to life; we need to know our negativity as well. The terminal flare (now a speaking part) opens the scene:

Then I saw the flare turn again.
Help, it said, I want to get out of this
even more than you do. I was once a fair twinkling light
at the end of a tunnel, then someone wished this on me.
Help me to put it behind me please.

> Turning from the blaze to the counterpane
> I saw how we are all great in our shortcomings, yea,
> greater because of them. There are letters in the alphabet
> we don't know yet, but when we've reached them
> we'll know the luster of unsupported things.
> Our negativity will have caught up with us
> and we'll be better for it.

But does old age have to be so brutal, so wasteful, so bestial, so destructive? Why, the speaker asks, are we behaving like the men whom Circe turned to swine, exhibiting our warthog selves? Nonetheless, because he must, he assents to the status quo, in a heaping-up of participles enacting the exaggerated theatricality of apocalypse:

>   Just
> keep turning on lights, wasting electricity,
> carousing with aardvarks, smashing the stemware.

The poem closes by surveying ending and beginning in one gaze: the comic scene of degradation is followed by an unexpectedly mild signing-off, since rhetorical tantrums, however authentic, cannot (at least not in Ashbery) last forever. There is, after all, something to be said for the Last Days:

> These apartments we live in are nicer
> than where we lived before, near the beginning.

I may be mistaken (I have been so before) in my synopses, since Ashbery—with his resolve against statement bearing the burden of a poem—would always rather present a symbolic whole than offer a propositional argument. Still, I have offered these synopses to show that Ashbery does make sense if we can tune our mind to his wavelength—something I am not always able to do, but which is exhilarating when that precarious harmony of minds is reached. Ashbery suggests; he does not assert. His readers are left to skate along the polished surfaces of his text, seeing images, bumping into pieces of diction, flashed at by paradoxes, speeding through tone after tone, as the atmosphere of the poem darkens or brightens.

   At the close, ideally, the kinetic transfusion has happened, and we feel its complex effect—in Stevens's terms, "an abstraction blooded, as a man by thought." For myself, I relish Ashbery's many spectacularly imagined versions of the promised end: its invidiousness, our futile thrashing under its glare, our elegiac mourning within ironic glimpses of ourselves participating in a parodic farce, heading toward that "tank of carnivorous eels." Most of all, I relish (in a poem called "Interesting People of Newfoundland") the poet's serene—and paradoxical, parodic, insouciant, and minatory—epitaph for his generation:

> we were a part of all that happened there, the evil and the good
> and all the shades in between, happy to pipe up at roll call
> or compete in the spelling bees. It was too much of a good thing
> but at least it's over now. They are making a pageant out of it,
> one of them told me. It's coming to a theater near you.
> (29)

I wish that all the poems in *Where Shall I Wander* were understandable to me immediately, because I trust Ashbery's power to give me a fresh look at life. But I remind myself that time brings about not only the fading of failed experiments but also the wonderful clarification of passages that were perplexing on first appearance. After all, sophomores now believe that they can read *The Waste Land*. And the sententiously reproachful American banalities about "accessibility" have been roundly refuted by Ashbery himself:

Critics of poetry tend to use the word as a club to beat the poets they don't like, [saying] that modern poetry is out of touch with its audience, and nobody reads poetry anymore because poets for some reason refuse to be accessible. Alas, the world is full of poets who are accessible in that definition and yet nobody reads them either. Could it be because they insist on telling the reader something he or she already knows? (SP, 267)

Whenever an undeniably original poet appears—Mallarmé, Eliot, Moore, Miłosz, Ashbery—no matter how alien the content, or how allusive the lines, readers flock to the poems. "Accessibility" needs to be dropped from the American vocabulary of aesthetic judgment if we are not to appear fools in the eyes of the world.

22

Seamus Heaney's "Sweeney Redivivus"

Its Plot and Its Poems

I want to attempt here a description and analysis of Seamus Heaney's sequence called "Sweeney Redivivus," which I'll consider in its 1998 fifteen-unit form (reduced from its original twenty units in the 1984 *Station Island*); the fifteen-unit sequence is the one printed by Heaney in his large selected poems called *Opened Ground.*[1] (The reduction tightens and improves the impact of the whole.) In looking at the sequence, I hope to illuminate not only aspects of the individual poems, but also the order in which Heaney arranged them in the 1998 revision (unchanged, except for the omission of five poems, from the original). But to speak about "Sweeney Redivivus" at all means revisiting its origin in Heaney's version of the Middle Irish work *Buile Suibhne,* known (in the Irish Texts Society version, edited by J. G. O'Keefe) as *The Frenzy of Sweeney.* For some years in the late 1970s, every time I met him, Heaney had in his briefcase a manuscript of his Sweeney translation, always under revision. Impatient for more poems from Heaney's own hand, and not knowing *The Frenzy of Sweeney,* I wondered at the time why he was returning, year after year, to this abstruse task. (Later, I came to understand the power of translation in extending Heaney's own style.) Eventually, in 1983, Heaney's version of the Middle Irish work—a tale told in prose with interspersed lyrics—appeared, somewhat cut from the original, more freely rendered than O'Keefe's translation, and bearing a new title: *Sweeney Astray.*[2]

Heaney's introduction to *Sweeney Astray* (ii–iii) orients his readers to the original story: Sweeney, a seventh-century Ulster warrior-king, angers the cleric Ronan by pitching his illuminated Psalter into a lake, and by killing one of Ronan's servants. At the battle of Moira, Ronan's curse transforms the formerly violent Sweeney into a migrant bird, enduring, for many years, homelessness and suffering among harsh elements, until, reconciled to religion by the kindness of another cleric, he repents and dies. Heaney's introduction offers some reasons for his attachment to the story: "My fundamental relation with Sweeney is topographical. . . . For over thirty years I lived on the verges of [Sweeney's] territory, in sight of some of Sweeney's places and in earshot of others." Heaney then adds other elements that drew his interest: that the work embodies "a tension between the newly dominant Christian ethos and the older, recalcitrant Celtic temperament"; that Sweeney "is also a figure of the artist, displaced, guilty, assuaging himself by his utterance." It is possible, Heaney continues, "to read the work as an aspect of the quarrel between free creative imagination and the constraints of religious, political, and domestic obligation."

Topography, cultural tension, and the difficulties of the artist are, then, some of the thematic concerns that spoke to Heaney, but another aspect, a technical one, strengthened the appeal of the Middle Irish poem: "The work," Heaney points out, "could be regarded as a primer of lyric genres—laments, dialogues, litanies, rhapsodies, curses"; it is also, in its original version, a display piece for many complex Middle Irish metrical forms (O'Keefe identifies them in his notes to the poems). Heaney confesses that he began by translating "the best lyric moments, points of poetic intensity." Yet, he concludes, "I gradually felt I had to earn the right to do the high points by undertaking the whole thing."

In "undertaking the whole thing," Heaney lived imaginatively for several years, regularly if intermittently, not only within Sweeney's literary voice but also within Sweeney's predicament as a poet wandering in exile. That predicament was a rich source for reflection. What is it to be cursed by authority and banned from the community? What is it to be hungry, thirsty, and shelterless in a strange territory? What is it like to be defeated, to lose your king and your comrades? What is it like to have wings and to survey human conflict from far above? And, finally, what is it to love a particular place, setting it higher than all others? In his lyrics, Sweeney exposes his reactions to his daily sufferings, but also sings the praises of his home, Glen Bolcain; he complains of bitter weather, but also—in his most famous lyric—makes a catalogue of his intimate reactions to many different sorts of trees. Misery and praise alternate with each other in his psyche; vituperation against his enemies and laments over his condition are neighbors to dreams of the past and anxious visions of the future. The interminable consequences of Saint Ronan's curse evoke lengthy comparisons of the normal past to the afflicted present.

As Heaney revoices the Irish verses, he freshens the archaic language of O'Keefe and finds metaphorical inventions, creating new poems in English.

Sweeney's "thin" stanzas encouraged Heaney to continue that thinner, more "Northern" music begun in *Wintering Out,* where Heaney experimented with changing the earlier broad and laden manner of his first book, *Death of a Naturalist.* But the best result of Heaney's long labor of translation was to turn Heaney into Sweeney, or vice versa, generating in "Sweeney Redivivus" a new set of tones for Heaney—caustic, dry, mocking. Some of the units in this sequence refer directly to aspects of the original Irish *Sweeney Astray:* the protagonist is sometimes a bird; he makes hostile remarks about the cleric who has invaded his territory; he is exiled from his normal terrain. But the protagonist is often not a bird, and does not always reflect the Sweeney story: the mask of Sweeney simply liberates Heaney into becoming someone more acerbic and ironic (especially about his own past) than the Heaney of the earlier volumes. Although the speaker of the sequence (whom, for convenience, I will call Heaney) begins autobiographically (in poems 1 through 5), he begins a severe extrication of himself (in poems 6 through 8) from his earlier terrain. He directs his attention in the third group of poems (9 through 12) to aesthetic principles; and, finally, in the last group (poems 13 to 15), he addresses the ultimate topic— that of personal salvation. "What must I do to be saved?" is the query to which the whole sequence is made to tend.

Let me describe the four groups of poems in more detail. Much of the first, autobiographical, part of "Sweeney Redivivus" is poetry of recapitulation, a genre inescapable in middle age. The titles of the first set of five poems (with the exception of "In the Beech") suggest a retrospective look at crucial aspects of the past, treated chronologically: "The First Gloss," "Sweeney Redivivus," "The First Kingdom," and "The First Flight." However, as we read on, we see that toward the end of the sequence there appear other units retrospective of youth, notably "The Old Icons" and "In Illo Tempore." Why, we wonder, were these not placed among the earlier poems? (As we shall see, their late arrival tells us that the sequence is not solely chronological; they form part of the fourth group of poems, those dealing with salvation.) The second group of poems ("Drifting Off," "The Cleric," and "The Hermit") reflect on the alienation of the artist as he leaves, or severs himself from, his native ground: Was he ousted? Did he desert? How is he to make a fresh start? How much of his past does he need to extirpate? Are his feelings solely elegiac, or has his departure brought a compensatory gain?

The third group of poems examines aesthetic questions both negatively ("The Scribes") and positively (in "The Master" and "An Artist," two poems about exemplary models, a poet and a painter, neither named but identifiable as

Czesław Miłosz and Paul Cézanne). These lyrics on aesthetic principles (which include a fourth poem, "Holly"), seem to have nothing to do with Sweeney or his story, and we need to ask why Heaney placed them in the sequence. The last three poems have to do with the sacred: they first examine the forsaken sacred of the past, how it is both preserved ("The Old Icons") and repudiated ("In Illo Tempore"). The last poem, "On the Road," envisages a pilgrimage in bird-form to something that might be held sacred in the present. This sublime closing poem, though it could not have been conceived without the notion of the transmutation of a human being into a bird, has left the plot of Sweeney's adventures far behind. But the voice in the majority of the poems of "Sweeney Redivivus" has a stubborn outlaw quality encouraged by the story of Sweeney the migrant, Sweeney no longer on the field of battle but hovering over it, Sweeney the rebel, Sweeney the unsparing judge of his enemies, and Sweeney experiencing exhaustion and even despair.

I must pause for a moment to point out Heaney's formal means in the original twenty poems of "Sweeney Redivivus." The poems exhibit various prosodic structures, some metrical, some free. Seven of the twenty are composed in tercets, two in couplets, three in quatrains, the other eight in regular stanzas (for example, ones of five lines) or stanzas of irregular lengths. Two of the original poems ("Sweeney Redivivus" and "In the Chestnut Tree") have fourteen lines and could be construed by some as informal sonnets. The first units composed may be the many tercet poems, several of which are closest to the material of *Sweeney Astray*. Although there are intermittent appearances of rhyme and internal rhyme, they are not regularized, and this absence of predictable rhyme keeps the poems "truthful," as though no end-words have been lodged there chiefly for aural reasons (reasons normally so important to Heaney). The same can be said for the metrical freedom Heaney gives himself in the less regular poems to vary between longer and shorter lines: this practice, too, means no lines can be thought of as having been "stretched" or "shrunken" into a pre-existing metrical template. In some of the units having stanzas, stanza lengths within the same poem vary, as if to confirm that each subtopic could have its say without stanzaic coercion of its shape. A certain "unpoeticalness" is thus conferred on the sequence by such freedom and outlawry—appropriate, needless to say, to the errant Sweeney and to the terse and often satiric nature of the poems. Although tercets, couplets, quatrains and cinquains (in the poems employing them) betoken a measure of formal control, the more irregular poems must seek their stylistic effects by means other than visible stanzaic form or recurrent rhyme.

I return, now, to the fifteen-unit reduced sequence. The first group of five poems, as I have said, is ordered chronologically, and concerns Heaney's youth. In "The First Gloss" (247), the scribe-speaker urges himself to muster the courage to grasp the "shaft" of his instrument (the pen that we recall from "Digging") and use it no longer to inscribe but rather to subscribe to an independent action—to go outside the law of the margin (and to "gloss" the original story of Sweeney, as Heaney's note in *Station Island* remarks). The poet will no longer copy the model: rather, he will comment on it:

> Take hold of the shaft of the pen.
> Subscribe to the first step taken
> from a justified line
> into the margin.

The speaker's fellows in the scriptorium faithfully reproduce the "justified" script of socially sanctioned religious prose; in becoming a writer of independent opinion, the scribe steps firmly over the right margin into the "unjustified" irregular line of verse, confirming his alienation from his peers. Here, as often in the sequence, there is an order visible under the freedom: a linking *"n"* passes from "pe*n*" to "take*n*" to "li*n*e" before wandering into "margi*n*," never losing its cursive connection. This brief quatrain-epigram inaugurates the vow of independence of mind that the rest of the sequence will keep and, in its emphasis on transgressive originality, prophesies the poems on aesthetic principles that will form the third part of the sequence.

The next poem of the first group, "Sweeney Redivivus" (248), from which the sequence borrows its title, appears to be a symbolic account of Heaney's arrival in California in 1970, a displacement preceding his move to the Republic. The Ireland of his youth has receded into absence, and the thin scribal penwork has metamorphosed into lost hedges:

> The old trees were nowhere,
> the hedges thin as penwork
> and the whole enclosure lost
> under hard paths and sharp-ridged houses.

The earlier Heaney would not have been so categorical: nostalgia and piety would have forbidden the curt statement that the past was "nowhere," the "whole enclosure" suddenly "lost." But the strangeness of arrival in a new country lets the poet's mind, "dense with soakage" of his country of origin, begin to "un-wind," serving as a clue to the labyrinth of self. Among foreigners, far from the environment where he was known to all, Heaney warns himself against be-coming the tale of himself:

> And there I was, incredible to myself,
> among people far too eager to believe me
> and my story, even if it happened to be true.

This wary and ironic Heaney, learning from his displacement, can satirically picture himself from the outside, "my head like a ball of wet twine." The auto-biographical impulse of lyric survives, but in an atmosphere of unfamiliarity:

> Another smell
> was blowing off the river.

If the idea of Sweeney contributes to this poem, it is in the tone of hard sur-veying of the foreign place, and a terse gathering of forces to enter a new life, with a stern refusal of homesickness for the nowhere that has vanished. The comic contrast between the Latinity of the title and the head dense from soakage suggests further ironies to come.

The twine of the mind unwinds as far as adolescence in the next poem, "In the Beech" (249), when Heaney recalls that it was in that tree that he began his first conscious seeking of solitude, privacy, and independence. In the high con-cealment of the beech, "the school-leaver discovered peace to touch himself." Attendant on sexual privacy is the first stirring of poetry, when the young boy begins to attempt an accurate description of his environment. Was the tree trunk a natural "bole" or would it be better described metaphorically as an architec-tural form, a "column"? "Was it bark or masonry?" What would be the right comparison for a chimney arising nearby? Could its slender form be called "its stamen"? And are the steeplejacks rightly seen as "flies against the mountain"? These attempts at verbal approximations to the impressions of the mind are not the thoughts common to the boy's fellow adolescents or to his family members—nor, certainly, to the Ireland-based American soldiers in the nearby road, rehearsing in tanks and planes for World War II. The young poet-to-be winces at the "imperium refreshed" in the tracks of the tanks, but can do nothing but remain in his "airy listening post." "In the Beech" is a poem of love for the sequestered peace and beauty available in the "boundary tree," but also one of sexual anxiety as the boy flinches from the emblems of rough masculinity below. The bird-boy in the tree is narrowly constrained between the life of the soldiers and the life of the farm, between "the concrete road" and "the bullocks' covert." Neither offers him a congenial future; and so he remains in stasis, not moving from his "tree of knowledge," keeping his watch as "a lookout posted and forgotten." The poem cannot advance, ending in the tree where it began, since its protagonist is as yet uncertain of his future place in the world.

The stasis of "In the Beech" is dryly, even angrily, broken in "The First Kingdom" (250) by a satirically reductive reevaluation of "home," emphasizing the medieval routines and concerns of farm life, and scorning the elders' timid social acquiescence in their minority status, a resignation driven by their piety. The child's youthful fantasy of royal birth is rudely and comically overturned in the opening tableau describing the local terrain, the mother at milking, and the cattle-dealing father-nobles:

> The royal roads were cow paths.
> The queen mother hunkered on a stool
> and played the harpstrings of milk
> into a wooden pail.
> With seasoned sticks the nobles
> lorded it over the hindquarters of cattle.

Nowhere else is Heaney so hard on his earlier romanticizing of Mossbawn. It is not that he has forgotten the harpstrings plucked there; one can hear them in the liquid sounds of "royal," "stool," "milk," "pail," "nobles," "lorded," and "cattle." But the persistent de-idealizing, though comic, is fierce; and in the middle of "The First Kingdom" the limited language and provincial concerns of the family become anticlimactic "unwinding" and "backward" satire:

> Units of measurement were pondered
> by the cartful, barrowful and bucketful.
> Time was a backward rote of names and mishaps,
> bad harvests, fires, unfair settlements.
> deaths in floods, murders and miscarriages.

Heaney, as the oldest son, would be the normal heir to the farm. But—he asks in his repudiatory mood—was that inheritance worth having? He ends by applying a harsh set of adjectives to the Catholic minority in Northern Ireland:

And if my rights to it all came only
by their acclamation, what was it worth?
I blew hot and blew cold.
They were two-faced and accommodating,
and seed, breed and generation still
they are holding on, every bit
as pious and exacting and demeaned.

"The First Kingdom" is incised in steel: tableau; linguistic denigration; final judgment. The object of its derision is at least as much the poet himself as his family and the minority to which they belong: What was he thinking of when he created his past sentimental idealizations? Why did he ever pay heed to the family's cautious measurements, their interminable family narratives? Why did he vacillate, blowing hot and cold in judging them? Does he admire their tenacity or hate their accommodation to their demeaned status? The poem is so distinctive, in its three icy parts, that it freezes into place in the memory. Since Sweeney is not revived here, what could the figure of Sweeney have had to do with the composition of such a piece? He enabled, I think, the view from above, foretold perhaps by the boy's observations in the beech. Nobody still within the house could judge "the first kingdom" from this distance.

The envisaging of self-removal from native ground enables the action of "The First Flight" (251–252), taken while its protagonist is still on home territory. The unstable tercets of the poem are gathered, sentence by sentence, into uneasy units: two tercets for the first sentence; then three; then two; then four. The bird-speaker withdraws from other poets, but they, wary of his "empty place," try to persuade him back from his tree to their hostile camp, even when libeling him to others. "Sweeney's" response is to fly high enough to judge them, to "survey out of reach" their conspiracies and recruitings, their timid and defensive poetry. The last, almost unpunctuated, sentence is the longest, with its devastating description of Sweeney's arrogant and cowardly companions:

I was mired in attachment
until they began to pronounce me
a feeder off battlefields

so I mastered new rungs of the air
to survey out of reach
their bonfires on hills, their hosting

and fasting, the levies from Scotland
as always, and the people of art
diverting their rhythmical chants

to fend off the onslaught of winds
I would welcome and climb
to the top of my bent.

Surveyor and judge, the airborne "Sweeney," formerly "mired in attachment," welcomes the winds of conflict, and masters "new rungs of the air." This aggressive and enterprising Heaney exults in his newly discovered powers; but we already sense, I think, that he will not be able to maintain forever his alienated position. In the martial advancing tercets of this first flight, however, he is still exhilarated by his new freedom.

With "Drifting Off" (253), which continues the tercets of "The First Flight," we begin the second group of poems, those treating the protagonist's definitive departure and his extirpation of former attachments. Sweeney Redivivus has to find, somewhat too programmatically perhaps (this is a list-poem), his place and role among other birds. The lyric becomes an examination (sometimes a critical one) of the character of others: Sweeney envies the birds stronger than he in body or mind, and, as he learns which birds to distrust, he overrates some and

too often cave[s] in
to the pathos of waterhens
and panicky corncrakes.

At times, he seems ready to catch the beautiful birds as Hopkins caught the windhover:

But when the goldfinch or kingfisher rent
the veil of the usual,
pinions whispered and braced

as I stooped unwieldy
and brimming,
my spurs at the ready.

In the next tercet poem, "The Cleric" (254), Sweeney voices his rage against the priest who has usurped his lands. Christianity has triumphed in Ireland and has excluded the lamenting pagan Sweeney:

> History that planted its standards
> on his gables and spires
> ousted me to the marches
>
> of skulking and whingeing.

Sweeney the excommunicate, "ousted," is the victim in this self-pitying version of the story. But the irony suffusing this sequence prompts Sweeney to turn on himself, as he immediately proposes an alternate story: "Or did I desert?" He decides that his banishment by the cleric was in the end a gain:

> Give him his due, in the end
>
> he opened my path to a kingdom
> of such scope and neuter allegiance
> my emptiness reigns at its whim.

This closing tercet, containing the most powerful lines of self-recognition in the sequence, replaces the "first kingdom" with a second one. The small measure of the farm is far exceeded by the scope of the kingdom of the air; the familial allegiance of the home is surpassed by the freedom from political allegiance in the second kingdom; the social commitments of the earlier kingdom are nonchalantly exchanged for the license of "whim" in the second; and the piety of the first opens to a new potential within the "emptiness" of the second. "Sweeney" now has a personal kingdom in which he—or his alienated emptiness—"reigns." This extraordinary victory over familial, religious, and political claims cannot yet be phrased, however, in anything but colorless terms: "neuter," "emptiness," "whim." It has not yet discovered what its positive content will be; it has arisen from a negation, whether the poet terms it "ousting" or "desertion." But what a set of lines these are, declaring possession of a new realm of "such scope" that it confers kingship.

"Neuter allegiance" is a phrase conveying a clearing of the ground; before any new bonds can be forged, neutrality toward former passionate loyalties must be won, acre by acre. Heaney does not want to repudiate in scorn the things he has loved; rather, he wants to free himself from their hitherto unrecognized power over his affections, thoughts, and deeds. The hermit, in Heaney's poem of that name (255), clears his ground, tercet by tercet, in a single effortful sentence, sparing not one "stump of affection." His vocation requires that he detach himself mentally, by brute force if necessary, from his former life and its earlier claims. The hermit is analogous to Sweeney in his removal from society, but he has not been "ousted," has not "deserted" some group, is neither mad nor cursed. As the hermit clears his field with "the blade of choice," he becomes one tense arc of physical exertion, and we see that there is a strict proportion between effort and reward:

> The more brutal the pull
> and the drive, the deeper
> and quieter the work of refreshment.

The hermit's work of detachment needs (in Heaney's metaphor) both the drive of the ploughshare and the pull of the horses; and what is envisaged after this creation of a "whole field of force" is a ground cleared of the past, every "stump of affection" uprooted. Surprisingly, what follows on the strenuous effort or detachment is a spiritual sweetness, a deep and quiet "work of refreshment" as the asceticism of vocation is fulfilled. We are meant to feel, I think, that the eventual flow of joy is entirely unexpected by the straining hermit himself, and that its appearance means that the severing of self from former attachments has been completed. This completion opens the way for Heaney to meditate on the commitments to which he will subscribe in the new life.

The third set of poems in "Sweeney Redivivus"—"The Master," "The Scribes," "Holly," and "An Artist"—meditate on aesthetic principles. The first of these, "The Master" (256), relates the story of the apprentice-poet learning his craft, instructed by an elder. Heaney once said that it was Czesław Miłosz whom he had in mind as the poet who

> dwelt in himself
> like a rook in an unroofed tower.

Miłosz, when Heaney was at Berkeley, was living up on Grizzly Bear Peak. In this ordeal-poem, the speaker has to climb up, without flinching, to the master's "coign of seclusion." He is indeed rewarded with maxims from the master, but

> it was nothing
> arcane, just the old rules
> we all had inscribed on our slates.
> . . . . .
>
> *Tell the truth. Do not be afraid.*

Heaney added the maxims after the first printing of "Sweeney Redivivus" in *Station Island*. To make the lesson credible, the poet must demonstrate how, when the "old rules" arrive rewritten by the master, they take on weight and gravity. He does this in two ways. The rules, as copied on slates by pupils, seem unimportant. But the master's presentation honors the rules by inscribing them on parchment in carefully worked illuminator's lettering until they seem to take on "volume" and "space":

> Each character blocked on the parchment secure
> in its volume and measure.
> Each maxim given its space.

From the majestic distribution and shape of Miłosz's words of poetry, the young poet takes his first lesson. A second lesson arises from the inference the pupil draws concerning the tools necessary to write undeterred by circumstance: the old rules are

> Durable, obstinate notions,
> like quarrymen's hammers and wedges.

From his further reflection on the tools, that they are "proofed by intransigent service," the apprentice learns that there is a higher motive for art than self-expression. The tools and their service are the illustrations of the writer's obligations to his conscience; but they are, at last, followed by a fourth, unexpected, lesson about the "old rules": if obeyed, they miraculously change from prescription to refreshment,

> Like coping stones where you rest
> in the balm of the wellspring.

Once the lessons have been learned, the apprentice (now refreshed, like the hermit) can bring his ordeal to an end. Nonetheless, as he begins his climb down from the tower, he still feels "flimsy"—like a structure not yet built of stone, a person not yet acclimated to tower-life. His wings are not full-grown like those of the master, nor does he feel the master's certainty:

> How flimsy I felt climbing down
> the unrailed stairs on the wall,

hearing the purpose and venture
in a wingflap above me.

The allegory of a "climb up deserted ramparts" to be instructed, and then of a risky climb down "unrailed stairs" back to earth, omits the crucial moment of the pupil's actual audience with the master. However, we know that the master has told the apprentice (as we can deduce from the pupil's similes of quarrymen's tools) how to search out and shape stone for his own future tower, and has promised him (in the culminating simile of "coping stones") the refreshment of the completed work. Heaney withholds that balm to the very end of the audience with the master so that the ordeal may be repeatedly emphasized before the poem is allowed to relent in hope that the lesson may be a strengthening one. And although the apprentice must leave the presence of the master—and may never encounter him again—he will be able to recall the strong wingflap from above, reminding him that the exemplary master does not cease from "purpose and venture." Miłosz's extraordinary lyric self-revelation and political courage warrant his appearance as Heaney's master, and remind us of Heaney's awareness of the poetry of Eastern Europe, testified to by *The Haw Lantern*.

At the beginning of "Sweeney Redivivus," the speaker, awakening in a new place, had felt he needed only to "unwind" the past to find understanding and detachment. "The master" sets a higher goal: an ambition to undertake "intransigent service," to tell the truth and not be afraid. Having left the master, the young scribe joined in the work of the scriptorium (prophesied in "The First Gloss"), but he was scandalized by what he found there: a set of older scribes psychologically maimed by their crabbed profession, who jealously slandered the speaker after his exile. We see in "The Scribes" (257) a negative example (by contrast with the positive aesthetic principles of "The Master") of what the life of a writer might produce. Heaney associates the scribes' disordered souls with their clogged pens:

In the hush of the scriptorium
a black pearl kept gathering in them
like the old dry glut inside their quills.
In the margin of texts of praise
they scratched and clawed.

This stanza makes us look back to "The First Gloss," as we learn that these scribes, too, let their pens wander into the margin. Their glosses, however, are not new creations but polemics against fellow commentators. The margin becomes a field of mean-spirited dispute, contaminating by proximity the joyous texts the scribes have been sent to copy. Their emotions of anger and resentment corrupt even their creation of single letters:

> Under the rumps of lettering
> they herded myopic angers.
> Resentment seeded in the uncurling
> fernheads of their capitals.

In the battle of words, the outlaw-scribe will outlast his jealous fellows, as he intimates by the almost liturgical Latinate periphrasis with which he closes "The Scribes":

> Let them remember this not inconsiderable
> Contribution to their jealous art.

Writing in the persona of a learned scribe, Heaney is free to put into this poem all his eloquence of diction, from the demotic "scratched and clawed" to the mixed metaphors of rumps and of lettering and seeded resentments to closing Latinity.

The three opening sentences of "The Scribes" alternate between the speaker's "I" and the third-person "they," imitating the conflict the poem describes:

> I never warmed to them.
> If they were excellent they were petulant
> and jaggy as the holly tree
> they rendered down for ink.
> And if I never belonged among them,
> they could never deny me my place.

In the following twelve lines, however, the poet abandons this oppositional dance of grammatical subjects: his sheer fascination with delineating the warped nature of the scribes takes over the lyric. And by the close of the poem, though the pronominal structure of conflict resumes, it does so in distanced and intermittent fashion, with the outlaw retaining firm possession of the subject-position: "I started up . . . and [I] saw . . . and [I] felt."

Now and again I started up
Miles away and saw in my absence
The sloped cursive of each back and felt them
Perfect themselves against me page by page.

In his final warning—"Let them remember"—the outlaw has vanished into his art. He refers to "this contribution" rather than "my contribution" because significance lies in what is written, not in the person who wrote it. What will be preserved of the scribes in the end is their exiled fellow's description of their hostile maneuvering and their defacing—with their marginal scratchings—ancient and beautiful texts of praise.

The third of the poems of aesthetic principles, "Holly" (258), begins in childhood disappointment: "It rained when it should have snowed." Nonetheless, the family went hunting for holly through wet ditches, and brought home sprigs which, though berryless, gleamed "like smashed bottle-glass." Now the poet, with no effort, can have holly in the house, but it is too easily come by:

Now here I am, in a room that is decked
with the red-berried, waxy-leafed stuff,

and I almost forget what it's like
to be wet to the skin or longing for snow.

I reach for a book like a doubter
and want it to flare round my hand,

a black-letter bush, a glittering shield-wall
cutting as holly and ice.

The aesthetic principle here is the risk and longing necessary for the creation of passionate work, so that a book will ultimately contain, locked within itself for the reader to receive, a flare, a burning bush, a shield, a jagged force. Holly was used by the scribes to make their ink; now the poet will render from it his own "black-letter" work, reclaiming the keen sensations of childhood.

The atmosphere of intransigence that suffused "The Master" reappears in the fourth and last poem on aesthetic principles, "An Artist" (259), Heaney's homage to (the unnamed) Cézanne. The painter is praised for "anger," for "obstinacy," for "fortitude"—qualities the formerly mild Heaney, taking example from Sweeney, is attempting to allow himself to exhibit. The poet is taking a stand against his own "complaisant pith" ("Granite Chip"), since compliance is as dangerous to art as

> the vulgarity of expecting ever
> gratitude or admiration.

The obstinate independence of Cézanne had its costs, undeniably, for his inner life, as Heaney implies by the circularity of the sentences revealing it:

> The way he was a dog barking
> at the image of himself barking.
> And his hatred of his own embrace
> of working as the only thing that worked.

The recipe for artistic integrity is simply another "old rule"—not to falsify one's capacities:

> his fortitude held and hardened
> because he did what he knew.

A ghost of an aural and metrical chiasmus fortifies this formulation: "fortitude: held: hardened: what he knew." Heaney's manner in "An Artist" is unrelenting. One "hard" word follows another, and even when an image from nature— "green apples"—is allowed entrance, it is pressed into the "hardness"; "I love," says Heaney of Cézanne,

> his coercion
> of the substance from green apples.

Usually the subjects of Heaney's frequent "I love" are images full of warmth, but here what is loved is the artist's stern will, his coercion of the real into displaying its essential substance. Heaney, who was the "flimsy" youth in "The Master," is lashing himself now into stoicism, tenacity, indifference to the opinions of others, and even self-hostility ("barking at himself barking")—all in order to surmount cultural temptations to piety and obedience. Earlier in the sequence, Heaney had permitted himself the balm of refreshment after acceding to the rules of conscience taught by the master, but here there is no mention of rest and relief: instead, the result of aesthetic fortitude is a terrifying feeling of being "hurled" by some unknown force into the next venture. Cézanne has painted the green apples; he has painted the Mont Sainte Victoire again and again; now, once more, the surface of a fresh unpainted canvas both attracts and challenges him, until his unleashed purpose carries his mind, like a directed missile, through and beyond the canvas's blankness:

> His forehead like a hurled *boule*
> travelling unpainted space
> behind the apple and behind the mountain.

The steel and resolve within himself must be liberated, Heaney knows, from the political and religious training that taught him to "know [his] place," be "biddable and forthcoming" ("Station Island," IX, 239–241). The outlaw role of Sweeney permits Heaney to assume the mask of an alienated warrior, of a wilful temperament (that of Miłosz, that of Cézanne) in many ways unlike his own. The assumption of a persona cannot, of course, be a permanent solution to the problematic aspects of one's own personality and culture ("As if the eddy could reform the pool"—"Station Island," 241), but in resorting to the masks of Miłosz and Cézanne, Heaney can glimpse further authentic extensions of his own imagination. After all, if Sweeney must invent a new song at every vicissitude, so must his re-creator.

The last three poems in the fifteen-poem version of "Sweeney Redivivus"— "The Old Icons," "In Illo Tempore," and "On the Road"—concern salvation. The first two deal with those "stumps of affection" that the hermit had attempted to eradicate. "In Illo Tempore" (261), with its Latin title "At that time" alluding to a familiar opening of gospel narrative, allows the poet to look back once again to his youth, and to repudiate a past passivity: "At that time," when he and his companions attended Mass, they were commanded by group ritual, not by individual commitment:

> Intransitively we would assist,
> confess, receive. The verbs
> assumed us. We adored.

Heaney's massing of verbs which could well be transitive, but in the context of preknown ritual are not, turns slightly surreal: "The verbs assumed us"—caught us up, but were also confident of our summoned presence, converted us into themselves. Even in the context of ritual, however, the future poet had an eye for the aesthetic and etymological vibrations of sacred words, which in his young mind took on sensuous color:

> And we lifted to our eyes to the nouns.
> Altar-stone was dawn and monstrance noon,
> the word "rubric" itself a bloodshot sunset.

In this "then and now" poem, the sacred "illud tempus" has occupied the first three tercets; in the closing, the last two tercets ask where conviction is now to be found:

> Now I live by a famous strand
> where seabirds cry in the small hours
> like incredible souls.

Ritual and its aesthetic scenery have faded into nonexistence in the poet's adult life, yet his religious upbringing will not be extirpated from his language even as he impugns the belief it proclaims: seabirds cry on the Joycean strand, he says, "like incredible souls." And try though he may to find credibility in the indubitable solidity of the physical world, that world fails him even as it failed Wordsworth:

> and even the range wall of the promenade
> that I press down on for conviction
> hardly tempts me to credit it.

The desolation succeeding the loss of childhood beliefs is assuaged in part by the poet's retaining, even as an adult, icons of deep significance. In "The Old Icons" (260), the second of the poems on salvation, Heaney asks why, "when it was all over," did he still keep certain pictures on his wall? As he contemplates them, he replants those stumps of affection that he had earlier so purposefully, even puritanically, cleared away. He realizes now that the "old icons" have been kept because they testify to a residuum of values, values that are still affirmable. In the etching of Robert Emmet he sees fidelity; in the oleograph of the outdoor Mass in penal times he sees courage; and in the engraving of the 1798 patriots he sees the passion for political liberty, even though their cause was lost through betrayal. I have identified the icons (which Heaney identified in conversation with me), but the poet leaves them anonymous, perhaps letting his Irish audience's presumed familiarity with them obviate any need for naming. For other readers, the anonymity of the icons makes the poem a wholly inward one, in which the poet's abbreviated descriptions denote his long acquaintance with these "old icons" of his youth. The first two icons are unproblematic in their purity of representation: an etching of a single young patriot facing death; an oleograph of a religious community still at worship though under ban and threat. Each of these icons fits neatly into its tercet, following Heaney's one lone self-querying cry:

> Why, when it was all over, did I hold on to them?

> A patriot with folded arms in a shaft of light;
> the barred cell window and his sentenced face
> are the only bright spots in the little etching.

> An oleograph of snowy hills, the outlawed priest's
> red vestments, with the redcoats toiling closer
> and the lookout coming like a fox across the gaps.

These first two icons appear grammatically in unchanging nominal form: a patriot in a shaft of light, the priest and the approaching redcoats. They hang on the wall as recorded single elements of history, the first a static standing form, the second a suspended moment, the redcoats forever toiling, the lookout forever coming.

But the third icon, representing a committee of patriots from the unsuccessful 1798 rebellion, overspills its expected space. Rather than a single tercet, three tercets are needed to unfold its significance. Unlike its two predecessors, it brings time, causation, and devastating results into Heaney's gripping poem. A fellow-patriot turned spy brings down the uprising of 1798; the icon reveals the unawareness, on the part of the patriots, of the betrayer in their midst, who has handed over to the authorities a list of their names. As he approaches this icon, the poet admits that his earlier sacred images of an executed patriot and tenacious worshippers cannot keep the evils of the world at bay. All values can be undone by treachery:

> And the old committee of the sedition-mongers,
> so well turned out in their clasped brogues and waistcoats,
> the legend of their names an informer's list

prepared by neat-cuffs, third from left, at rear,
more compelling than the rest of them,
pivoting an action that was his rack

and others' ruin, the very rhythm of his name
a register of dear-bought treacheries
grown transparent now, and inestimable.

The idea represented by this third icon is neither the stable fidelity of patriotism nor the eternal tension between Empire and its subjects, redcoats and red vestments. It is the idea of causation, voiced in the verb "pivoting." The chain of cause-and-event embedded in this description begins with the "turning" of one of the patriots who becomes a spy for the government;[3] we see in the engraving proper the meeting of the betrayed rebels; we learn that the action of the patriot-turned-informer "was his rack and others' ruin." The ever-expanding vortex of consequence extending into the future is, literally, unable to be estimated. Although history eventually makes "transparent" who the traitor was, it cannot record all the damage, family by family, generation by generation, caused by the executions following on the betrayal.

Although there is no overt reference to Sweeney in "The Old Icons," in *Sweeney Astray* Sweeney betrays an agreement ratified by his warriors. The troops arrayed for battle at Moira have agreed to confine their fighting to set hours, but Sweeney the outlaw breaks faith: "Sweeney, however, would continually violate every peace and truce . . . slaying a man each day before the sides were engaged and slaying another each evening when the combat was finished" (6). Sweeney's violation of his promise is not explained: he merely will not be bound by the group's rules. Within any group, the informer (a classic figure in Irish literature) may be found; and who is to say who it will be? In holding on to the icon of betrayal and tragedy, with its inestimable results unspooling through generations, Heaney reminds himself of the "black and grainèd spots" (*Hamlet* 3.4) of political existence. The three pictures, held on to unselfconsciously until this moment of adult scrutiny, persuade Heaney that representations once honored in naïveté can retain a set of implicit values—fidelity, tenacity, commitment—still ratified by his adult self. In that sense, the icons of the past restore to the present the possibility of sacredness.

In ending "Sweeney Redivivus" with a poem far milder than those recommending intransigence and obstinacy as aesthetic principles, Heaney returns to his own voice, no longer combative but yearning for an idea of salvation as powerful to his conscience as the Christian one once was. It is exhaustion he writes from in his pilgrimage-poem "On the Road" (262–264), But there are no pilgrimages in the secular world, nor shrines; and transport is by car, not by foot; where can the pilgrim seek "the balm of the wellspring"? Heaney begins his bewildered pilgrimage-without-a-destination in a "trance of driving" that makes all roads one. Visited by a guide in the form of a bird (Sweeney, one might say, watching over his translator), the poet lifts himself by imagination into a bird-form, flies (like the ousted Sweeney) to a cleft in a churchyard wall, and then, in optative mood, wishes to migrate into a place that would antedate Christian belief. "I would migrate," he says, into a cave with walls covered by the paintings and carvings of prehistoric masters. In "the deepest chamber" of that cave, the poet would find, and meditate on, the "incised outline" of a deer bending to drink, whose predicament resembles his own:

> the incised outline
> curves to a strained
> expectant muzzle
> and a nostril flared
>
> at a dried-up source.

This is a poem to match George Herbert's "The Pilgrimage": when Herbert arrives at the summit where he expects his reward, he finds only "a lake of brackish water." Exhausted, he cries out, "Can both the way and end be tears?" At the end of *Buile Suibhne*, Sweeney is reconciled to the church by a kindly cleric, but Heaney, though able to imagine taking brief shelter in a cleft in a churchyard, cannot remain there. There is no help to be found in the unresponsive icons of the church, where, for generations,

> hand after hand
> keeps wearing away
> at the cold, hard-breasted
> votive granite.

In summarizing Heaney's journey, first in the car and then as an imagined bird, I have omitted the words that keep ringing in Heaney's mind, interrupting his narrative:

> *Master, what must I*
> *do to be saved?* . . .

Sell all you have
and give to the poor.

And follow me.

This exchange between the rich young man and Jesus appeared earlier in Heaney's work. In "The King of the Ditchbacks" (221–223), Heaney remembers being taken as a boy on a pigeon-shoot, camouflaged with a headgear made of twigs woven through a fishnet, "so my vision was a bird's / at the heart of a thicket." Because no pigeons appear, he is invited to return in the autumn, at harvest: he even imagines himself at that moment, but realizes he will not be there, because he is vowed to other things:

> And I saw myself
> rising to move in that dissimulation,
>
> top-knotted, masked in sheaves, noting
> the fall of birds: a rich young man
>
> leaving everything he had
> for a migrant solitude.

Now, in middle age, Heaney puts the young man's question again and meditates the Biblical answer: *"Follow me"*—yes, but where? And if the churchyard cleft and the votive granite are no longer the possible end (as they were in youth when, "drunk and happy," the poet climbed up "on a chapel gable"), where can an alternative path to salvation be found? In "On the Road," Heaney compares himself to "Noah's dove / a panicked shadow" because his searches for stable ground have so far been frustrated. When he does think of a piece of salvation beyond a temporary "slab of exile," he finds, like Noah's dove, a piece of high land:

> I would migrate
> through a high cave mouth
> into an oaten, sun-warmed cliff,

but it is not until he penetrates to "the deepest chamber" of the cave that he finds the prehistoric image of the deer "at a dried-up source." The cave becomes a legitimate place of devotion where, the poet affirms (continuing his optative mood), he would "meditate / that stone-faced vigil" until his "long dumbfounded spirit" could recover itself and once more beat its wings, in the "font" of a second baptism—

> until the long dumbfounded
> spirit broke cover
> to raise a dust
> in the font of exhaustion.

It is only in this final quatrain that Heaney reveals what his state had been when the poem opened with its directionless driving. A long time had passed (we now understand) since the poet had had a glimpse of his spirit, so long that the only quotation of adequate desperation that arose in his mind was "What must I do to be saved?" At the moment of asking such a question one feels one-self to be among those excluded from salvation. And the demand cannot be answered solely in obedience to the aesthetic rules of the masters: *Tell the truth. Do not be afraid. Coerce the substance of the earth into art.* The final plea of "Sweeney Redivivus" concerns the whole of life rather than the creation of poetry. When past spiritual resources have lost their power and comfort, where is one to turn?

Invoking prehistoric art as the locus of potential regeneration, Heaney returns to a moment when the sacred and the aesthetic seem to have been one. In the cave can be found the earliest evidence of human desire for the representation of life by some mimetic act—carving, painting. Some person incised a deer after carefully finding the right surface, where wall-contour could suggest haunch and neck; and that prehistoric artist worked with such psychological sympathy that the curve of the outline carries the strain of expectation and the flare of desiring nostril. It is Heaney who, projecting his own parched state onto the wall-deer, decides that its drinking place has no water. The long centuries of the thirsty deer's endurance make Heaney able to decide for endurance too; he will meditate his version of the I Ching—"my book of changes"—until his wings flutter again, even if it is only to "raise a dust" in his dried-up font. The "thin" dimeter quatrains of "On the Road" mimic the stages of the poet's on-going journey until, at last, they reach the coming-to-life implied by the warm-vowelled words inspired by the entrance into prehistory—*oaten, sun-warmed, soft-nubbed.* The ease of this bird-flight into "the deepest chamber" casts a new light on the early ordeal of the climb up to the master's tower. Both the arduousness of that ascent and the swiftness of this cave-flight are true to Heaney's dual sense of his calling: that it is difficult and that it is natural. In "The Master," the young poet could merely listen for the monitory "wingflap" above him; but when the bird-poet enters the cliff-cave, we hear his own "wingflap" as he migrates downward through history to the place where human beings first made art. There is as yet no water in the "font of exhaustion"—nor in the font of type—but the spirit has rebegun its efforts to live in the light of a possible salvation. The deer is iconic within Christian representation because of the words of Psalm 42: "As a hart panteth for the water brooks, so my soul panteth for thee, O God." By carrying the Christian symbol back to its pre-Christian presence in the prehistoric cave, Heaney affirms for himself the truth that a natural symbol has always preceded an institutional one.

Heaney's venture into "Sweeney Redivivus" was of course enabled by the poet's inhabiting of Sweeney's tale and songs as he translated *Buile Suibhne* into his *Sweeney Astray*. But the sequence goes far beyond its origin. Sweeney's plight, it is true, gave Heaney a model for hardness, purpose, and venture, for the courage of alienation, even of outlawry. Sweeney's legendary adventures enabled some of Heaney's allegories in "Sweeney Redivivus": allegories of kingdoms and scribes, flight and vengeance, anger and self-examination. Yet as we read "Sweeney Redivivus," we see that it has decided on a four-part order of its own, with its own logic and its own pursuits, advancing from childhood to severance from the birth community, from severance to aesthetic principles, from aesthetic principles to the ultimate question of a secular salvation. That order is not declared as such by Heaney, but it certainly governs his fifteen-poem version—now, I believe, the canonical one—of "Sweeney Redivivus." As a sequence, "Sweeney Redivivus" is a notable companion to Heaney's other brilliant ventures into the sequence form, from the autobiographical "Station Island" to the spectral "Squarings." And, in reviving *Buile Suibhne* for contemporary attention and relish, "Sweeney Redivivus" gives more than its memorable self to the literary world.

23

The Democratic Eye

A Worldly Country, *by John Ashbery*

John Ashbery's *A Worldly Country* offers another installment of the strange diaries regularly appearing from the poet over fifty years. (Ashbery has had the good luck to retain the capacity to write his decades into poetry.) I think of Ashbery's shorter poems as "diaries" because so many of them have the dailiness, the occasional inconsequentiality, the fragmentary quality, the confiding candor, and the obliquity we associate with the diary form. The diarist, careless of communication (since he already has all the information necessary for the decoding of his own private pages), may remain indifferent to explicitness, to "message," to "statement," to "meaning." The diary has, at its off-the-cuff best, a kind of intriguing charm: its vicissitudes (digressions, interruptions, unexplained allusions) keep later annotators busy; the elliptical text can end up occupying less space than its commentaries.

Much as the historian must explore, by research, the brief entries of a diary (think of Laurel Ulrich's expansion into a chronicle of the diary of a New England midwife), so the reader must intuit by association the psychic history implicit in Ashbery's metaphors. And in spite of our attempts, much in Ashbery remains uncertain. I was once (not recognizing an allusion to the Finnish epic the *Kalevala*) dead wrong in thinking that an Ashbery poem was about awaiting Death. Ashbery told me, with bemused sympathy for my misapprehension, that it was really about awaiting love. I suppose one could still say it was about awaiting, and that that was what mattered.

Not all of Ashbery's poems are diary-like: his long poems (at least those that are extended autobiographies in abstract form) usually have an intermittent purposeful coherence, while the diary-lyrics allow a more whimsical, wayward, teasing progression that has been, to his readers, by turns annoying, provoca-

tive, and enchanting. Over the years, Ashbery has been claimed by many special interest groups: the Francophiles (citing his formative years in Paris as
a young man); the avant-garde (pointing to such experiments of his as the
"cut-up" poem and the double-column poem); artists (finding in his work a
corollary to abstract painting); and the young (delighting in his fondness for
movies, cartoons, pop culture, and the transient lingo of the day). Followers
of his career can admire his searching range of observation and his murmuring
continuity with the entire tradition of Western poetry, from doggerel to divine poems, not to speak of his fondness for haiku. Ashbery himself is at pains
to declare, in "The Loneliness," that he writes for everybody:

> "Bound and determined" one writes a letter
> to the street, in demotic, hoping a friend
> will find, keep it, and analyze it.[1]

The letter is not always found; or if found, not kept; or if kept, not analyzed;
and the poet reproaches himself for the failure to reach others, which "leav[es]
you brackish, untried." And so he compulsively starts up again, hoping for a
more amiable effect, "peaceful, this time":

> It's as though a message
> remained to be harvested, paperwork from me to you.

(The turnover from the Romantic "harvest" to the bureaucratic "paper-
work" is characteristic of Ashbery's restlessly contemporary imagination.)
Even when he writes his difficult long poems, Ashbery thinks of them not as
esoteric investigations but as public spectacles, "long, loose-skeined parades"
deploying themselves along ordinary "service routes." And when he addresses
his audience, in "Litanies" (10), it is to say, with a childish glee in mock
vengeance,

> You ask me what I'm doing here.
> Do you expect me to actually read this?
> If so, I've got a surprise for you—
> I'm going to read it to everybody.

Like all lyric poets, Ashbery is convinced that his musical invention can
rescue, from the tinny clang of contemporary noise, those universally felt

surges of emotion and flexings of language in which readers can recognize themselves.

A Worldly Country understandably concerns itself, in part, with emotions attendant on old age: the pangs of memory, the menace of boredom, the fear of impending catastrophe. (It should be added that all of these feelings have appeared in Ashbery before, and are not restricted to the old.) *A Worldly Country* is satiric as well as elegiac, often funny, sometimes sardonic. And in spite of its lacunae and its opacities (points of continuity with the poet's early work, points of honor, almost), it continually implies the existence of narratives retrievable from under its impressionistic surfaces. The captivating illusion of romance, for instance, the pastoral of "idle spring," pervades Ashbery's more nostalgic pages, even if spring's romance is only a "poor excuse for summer"—that season of ideal warm love that disappoints even as it is pursued. Although summer has long been known to be impossible, one languishes even in age for its innocent harbinger, spring. The longing for romance forms a continuous background to thought—but Ashbery puts that truth more wittily; even when there is no romance in the air, when age has "mislaid" it, "it's here even when it's not here":

> Spring is the most important of the seasons.
> It's here even when it's not here.
> All the other seasons are an excuse for it.
> Spring, idle spring,
> you poor excuse for summer—
> Did they tell you where they mislaid you,
> on which arterial road piercing the city,
> fast and faster like breath?
> (10)

The speeding up of arterial time—"fast and faster like breath"—is felt throughout *A Worldly Country* in the form of clicking clocks and hovering dooms. In the title poem, Ashbery waves aside the uncertain epistemological status of autobiography—"If it occurred / in real time, it was OK, and if it was time in a novel / that was OK too" (1)—so that the metaphors of his stream of consciousness can proceed unbothered by any demands for consistency: "The directorate / had other, hidden goals. To proclaim logic / a casualty of truth was one" (46). As the poet proceeds on his "Via Negativa," he admits that language, in tracking the contour of life, reaches at best an approximation, but he is compelled nonetheless (in the poem "Feverfew") to art's self-frustrating pursuit:

> Road rage had burst its flanks;
> all was uncertain on the Via Negativa
> except the certainty of return, return
> to the approximate.
> (5)

As "Feverfew" continues its narrative of the past, we are told of a horn, sounding at night and at morning, that introduces beginnings, sexual discovery, romance, uncertainty, threat. (In the horn's contrastive summons to prayer or pleasure, Ashbery may be recalling Baudelaire's "Recueillement," in which night brings diverse gifts, "Aux uns portant la paix, aux autres le souci.") Those seeking pleasure exhale not sighs (as in Eliot) but jests, take up the midnight song and turn it to Edenic dream, transform the river of hellish woe to a pastoral heaven:

> Night and morning a horn sounded,
> summoning the faithful to prayer, the unfaithful to pleasure.
> In that unseemly alley I first exhaled
> a jest to your comic, crumb-crusted lips:
> What if we are all ignorant of all that has happened to us,
> the song starting up at midnight,
> the dream later, of lamb's lettuce and moss
> near where Acheron used to flow?

The intrusion of universal doubt—"What if we are all ignorant of all that has happened to us?"—is a recurrent feature in *A Worldly Country* as in Ashbery's other collections, and motivates a reexamination of the past that ceaselessly generates narratives describing once again something already written about. It is no accident that one of the best poems in the book is entitled, punningly, "Lacrimae Rerun" (33): the tears of things, a second showing ("Rerun" in lieu of the original "Rerum"). It recounts a couple's life that used to be, says Ashbery, a novel, a nursery rhyme, even music (a catch, a glee), but has now descended into a grim sermon, while its characters are reduced to beggars asking for scraps:

> We had our season together.
> Operatic in the city, we shifted mightily
> the stress to other fulcra as they became available.

We never knew what prompted us to smile
or to embrace. That was part of the city's dynamic,
deep under the pavements. We dreamed of philosophy sometimes
in restaurants or beside a chattering brook.

All our resources are being trained
on this critical juncture in our fates' history.
It's no longer a novel or nursery rhyme,

a catch or glee, but a sermon grinding on continuously.
They come to the back door these days,
asking for a piece of meat, anything.

The sudden brutality here of "a piece of meat, anything," is repeated elsewhere in Ashbery's "cool" narratives, justifying the conclusion of "Lacrimae Rerun": "Was ever anything / crosshatched so ripe with despair?"

Not all of Ashbery's narratives are so transparent, but generally somewhere in their unfolding a recognizable crisis breaks out. Here are some such revelations:

                          Now when ribald toasts
sail round a table too fair laid out, why the consequences
are only dust, disease and old age. . . .
(46)

Imagine that you can have this time any way it comes
easily, that a doctor wrote you a prescription
for savage joy and they say they can fill it
if you'll wait a moment. What springs to mind?
Do you turn and walk out of the drugstore . . . ?
(48)

Oh hell everything is that way,
this way, that way, twisted in the sun
of endurance—
(74)

Reading an Ashbery narrative, centering it around one or the other of its crises, entails some unsupported guessing: the reader's imagination is lit up by its own energy of interpretation, as the Möbius strip constructed by the words of the poem exhibits its delusive twist. "Still hungry?" says the poet chattily in the midst of his longest narrative: "Read on" (28). Seeking out poetry is a distinct hunger, one that famishes as it satisfies: Ashbery-Scheherazade never really winds up his skein of tales, merely suspending us from night to night, from page to turning page.

In reclaiming the centrality of narrative moments within short poems (while avoiding "stories" such as those of Crabbe, Browning, or Frost), Ashbery enlarges the purview of the lyric (more usually given to meditation). He continues the efforts of those American writers—from Whitman to Pound to Crane to Ginsberg to Merrill to Ammons—who have given importance in lyric to the narrative vignette. (But he also retains the abstraction learned in part from painting, in part from Gertrude Stein, in part from Auden.)

The most moving and elaborate narrative of the ecstasies and desolations of the inner life in twentieth-century America was given us by Ashbery in his 1972 *Three Poems*, but this sort of expansive narrative does not appear in *A Worldly Country*. Rather, the recent lyrics insist on the brevity of narrative glimpses, as a life unfolds in time. "I see by glimpses now," Wordsworth said, "when age comes on, / May scarcely see at all" (*Prelude* XI, lines 338–339). Ashbery's coarser "glimpses" of life among the implacable routines of old age forcibly revise the Wordsworthian lament. "The Inchcape Rock" (named after the dangerous rock off the coast of Scotland that sank the ship of the pirate who had destroyed its warning bell) begins its glimpse of the day's duties with derisive self-irony, followed by desperation:

> Prop up the "meaning,"
> take the trash out, the dog for a walk,
> give the old balls a scratch, apologize for three things
> by Friday—oh quiet noumenon
> of my soul, this is it, right?
>
> (32)

Another glimpse, this time one of pain, announces that "the bruise will stop by later":

> For now, pain pauses in its round,
> notes the time of day, the patient's temperature,
> leaves a memo for the surrogate: What the *hell*
> did you think you were doing?
>
> (60)

The poet's work—perpetuating the present in language that will remain alive in the future—is ecstatic in success, laborious in process, and (the poet reflects) for the most part unthanked. Under Ashbery's comically up-to-date textures any number of literary threads can be seen unobtrusively glistening, tethering his poetry to that of his predecessors. As I wandered through *A Worldly Country,* I jotted down—just to see which past authors gave the quality of bas-relief to the allusive Ashberian map of words—the names of Stevens, Baudelaire, Emerson, Keats, Arnold, Eliot, Pater, Williams, Bishop, Shakespeare, Southey, Byron, Verlaine, Trollope, Dickinson, Lowell, Whitman, and Milton (and I may have missed many more). But in spite of Ashbery's canonical piety (quizzical as often as not), his language mostly comes from all quarters, low and high, of the twentieth century. We find in his pages the movies (with mention of "reaction shots" and "process shots" and an elegy for the early movie star Helen Twelvetrees), astronomy ("eclipse," "axis"), computers ("pop-ups"), bands ("back-up"), business ("profit-taking"), comics ("Daddy Warbucks"), politics ("Litmus Tale"), poetry/music (Verlaine/Fauré, "La Bonne Chanson"), war ("the fresh troops that needed freshening up"), theatre ("casting call"), hotels (where an eclipse is "checking in"), and so on.

Besides the literary and the contemporary, there are in the Ashberian lexicon occasional archaisms: words such as "filigrane" and "theorbo." (Even these pieces of remoteness are sometimes subterraneanly linked to modernity: if Wallace Stevens writes a poem called "Asides on the Oboe," Ashbery will reply with one called "Asides on the Theorbo"—a double-necked archaic lute.) "The mind is so hospitable," Ashbery wrote in "Houseboat Days," "taking in boarders."

In perpetually creating and undoing his mini-narratives, Ashbery is hospitably admitting—in tones of gravity, jeering, regret, impatience, and erotic reminiscence—everything from rabbits to Acheron. "The Recipe," for instance, seems to be a set of instructions for continuing a relationship, but its first tone is nostalgic, as it harks back to a shared past:

> Lie in that grass. It's what we came for.
> Nothing could ever be that velvety again,
> so close to the ground. My gaze fathoms whiskers.
> . . . . .
> The recipe vectored a long-ago collision by a pier
> in and out of fins of sun,
> now labeled and put away, with much else,

and too little of what was needed
that particular afternoon
close to the source of warmth and confusion.

(52)

"The Recipe" then closes its narrative with a comic and camp proposal (of marriage, of the future, of the audience) which does not vitiate the warm pastoral
that preceded it:

I'll post the banns, send out invitations, polish toenails,
describe moot situations to the skeptical. You rest the same.

(53)

Ashbery has staked his poetic wager on our recognition of his lexical and
tonal hospitality, and on what it enables him to say about the circumstances—
mechanical, physical, and emotional—of modern living. Above all, he has
staked his reputation on restoring to the lyric the tones—impatient, jocular,
slangy, fragmented—of everyday conversation. He asks if his wager was the
right one:

What were the rights and the right ways?
Did we invest our strength in the kind grains
of conversation that blew across our page, and out?

(7)

"The kind grains / of conversation" are a sort of manna, refreshing the traveler as he slogs through the desert of exhausted language.

In several of the poems of *A Worldly Country* Ashbery casts a retrospective glance
at his life's work. The title of one of these poems, "The Gallant Needful" (58),
alludes to the most famous biblical defense of the contemplative life, Jesus's words
to Martha (Luke 10):

[She] said "Lord, dost thou not care that my sister hath left me to serve
alone? Bid her therefore that she help me." And Jesus answered and said
unto her, "Martha, Martha, thou art careful and troubled about many
things: But one thing is needful: and Mary hath chosen that good part,
which shall not be taken away from her."

"Gallant" (in the title "The Gallant Needful") brings an air of insouciant chivalry to the otherwise earnest allusion. Ashbery, with a nod to Herbert's "The Forerunners," bids farewell here to his poems ("Farewell nightmares, simulacra"), and represents his life-work as an attempt to design and wear new clothes. But the clothes of aesthetic taste, like all others, become out of date— they turn into those "robes surannées" worn by the "défuntes Années" ("Recueillement" again). Nowhere is Ashbery's commitment to the conversational narrative better seen than in his *dégagé* renewal, in "The Gallant Needful," of the conventional metaphor of clothes (flickering through literature from Saint Paul to Shakespeare to Carlyle). Shakespeare's version arrives as Prospero, preparing to leave his isle, proposes to lay down his magic robes and resume the clothes of Milan: "I will discase me." Ashbery, in his demotic version, imagines his style, its era now over, being recycled into the Lincolnesque Americana of a stovepipe hat with shawls tied around it:

The Gallant Needful

The hat hasn't worn too well. Nor, come to think
of it, have the pants. The shirt and cap are negligible.
As for the drawers . . .
                   So it went. Time was running
downhill while the clothes gave out. No one
wanted to wear them any more, which was
understandable, given that clothes are a going concern
to many. Mended with gay stuffs, they'll serve
another time, tied like shawls around
a stovepipe.
          Farewell nightmares, simulacra.
All the time a little is growing. As soup is to stew,
so the sea to bubbling chasms that prop up the "meaning."
Nice is nice enough. Just don't expect thanks.

The one thing needful—to have created, by contemplation and research and originality, a new style—is followed by the poet's rueful observation of that very style's descent into obsolescence. The bubbling style-chasms of emotion that support statement, message, "meaning," will give rise to poems by others in the future; for the moment, it is enough to have made something "nice"—a typical Ashberian understatement. His farewells infuse an astringent mockery into the intrinsic mournfulness of elegy.

Over and over Ashbery rinses the palate of style, cleansing from it, with his brisk narratives, the sickly aftertaste of imitative verse. Rewriting the title of Katharine Lee Bates's pious anthem as "America the Lovely," he satirizes aesthetic desire:

> If it's loveliness you want, here, take some,
> hissed the black fairy.
>
> . . . . .
>   Only be careful what you ask for,
> she warned. Here in hither Tartarus we have names
> for jerks like you.
> (59)

A passage such as this takes us first by its comedy, but we have only to rewrite it slightly to see how much it also takes us by its hearable cadences and its sibilant sounds. Imagine it phrased otherwise, becoming more clunky, less peremptory, its language closer to the simplicities of the fairy tales it stems from:

> If what you're seeking is loveliness, I have some for you,
> the black fairy said.
>   Only think first about your wish,
> she continued. Here in the first chamber of Tartarus we know the nature
> of people of your sort.

It is always hard to talk about the way rhythms, sounds, and syntactic articulations fall on the ear, but the one thing needful in a poem is that its rhythms should somehow be seductive. Ashbery's almost always are, and it is those rhythms of utterance that propel us through his strange narratives:

> The clock was on the verge of striking. And you know something,
>
> it never did! Not while I was there, anyway.
> There were shouts, always the same, unusable shouts
> and an angry wind starting up in the hedges
> but unable to articulate, like me and the other guests.
> Again it was time to flee. . . .
> (57)

We may not know the story behind the chaos, but we know that the poet, like us, has met it before. Yet every time it comes (says this poem tellingly entitled "And Other Stories") the chaos needs a different articulation:

> This had been foreseen,
> but like a migration, took on another sense
> as it unfolded, the sky Royal Worcester by now,
> a narrative that will endure for many years,
> even if no one reads it. . . .
>
> (57)

With that envoi, Ashbery commits his endlessly unfolding narrative to the printer, counting on its intrinsic worth to preserve it, at least for a time.

What difference has it made to American poetry to have had Ashbery within its precincts for many decades? In one sense, hardly any: any number of poets go on writing bad blank verse, bad rhymed verse, bad short lines, bad long lines—all stiffly talking, all tugging their forelock to some predecessor utterly unlike themselves whose language they find "poetic." With not a stanza of interesting syntax, with not a line of beguiling rhythm, with not a glance at the contemporary language buzzing about their ears, with not a spark of intellectual originality, the self-styled poets nonetheless find publication somewhere, somehow. If they stay around long enough, they even get prizes. And it has always been this way (witness the dim poets laureate of England, and the feeble best-selling women poets of the nineteenth century). Keats himself raged that it should be so. In *The Fall of Hyperion*, he called upon the sun god Apollo (in his role as sender of plagues) to slay all the bad poets. He is even glad to die himself if he can see them destroyed:

> Apollo! faded, far-flown Apollo!
> Where is thy misty pestilence to creep
> Into the dwellings, through the door crannies,
> Of all mock lyrists, large self-worshippers
> And careless hectorers in proud bad verse.
> Though I breathe death with them it will be life
> To see them sprawl before me into graves.
>
> (lines 204–210)

No one can say what effect the work of good poets may have on others. But just as in Ashbery's lines there hover the voices of the past, so in future lines by another original poet will hover the voice of Ashbery. That voice—tender and funny, full of gaiety and gloom, perpetuating the century's lexicon as it mockingly delineates its follies—is entering the ears of the talented, who will follow its lead not by imitating its inimitable elations but by having learned from its tuning-fork accuracy. Ashbery's own comment on the bewildering enterprise of making sense of one's journey through the world looks haplessly to the consolations of the poems of the past, petrified in their "stone books":

> We're leaving again of our own volition
> for bogus-patterned plains, shreds of maps recurring
> like waves on a beach, each unimaginable
> and likely to go on being so.
>
> But sometimes they get, you know, confused,
> and change their vows or the ground rules
> that sustain all of us. It's cheery, then, to reflect on the past
> and what it brought us. To take stone books down
>
> from the shelf. It is good, in fact,
> to let the present pass without commentary
> for what it says about the future.
> There was nothing carnal in the way omens became portents.
>
> (70)

"The wraparound flux we intuit as time," Ashbery continues, "has other claims on our inventiveness" besides the creation of poetry, adding wryly, "A lot of retail figures in it." Ashbery has always been agreeably conscious of all that life offers besides literature, retail included. It is for that reason that his poems seem to stretch over our contemporary consciousness without strain: nothing in ordinary life is alien to his democratic and comprehensive and indulgent eye, nor does the omnipresence of the ordinary make him forget the equal omnipresence, on another plane, of Satie or Fauré or Parmigianino. It is a fraternal sensibility that animates these Ashberian pages, puzzling though they can be, for as we encounter Ashbery's omens and portents, they oddly and satisfactorily take on for us the sheen of our own.

24

Losing the Marbles

James Merrill on Greece

Greece was won and lost and won again in the life and work of the American poet James Merrill (1926–1995). His poems about Greece can serve as an index to several of his aesthetic modes and, in a larger sense, can be viewed as a life-long evaluation of what Greece, and the poetry of Cavafy, might mean to a modern American poet.

As a well-educated young man—trained at St. Bernard's School and Law-renceville School, and then at Amherst College, where he studied both Latin and ancient Greek—Merrill absorbed the Greek myths, not only from English prose retellings, from Ovid, and from Greek drama, but also from the English poets, especially Keats. But there were nonliterary influences, too: Merrill's first lover, the Amherst College professor Kimon Friar (a son of Greek immigrants and a translator of Greek poetry), made modern Greece a permanent part of the young poet's consciousness. Merrill's first poem on Greece, "Beginner's Greek," written in 1946 when he was twenty, locates in things Greek a passion he longs for, but flinches from. Characterizing himself as a person who shuts his eyes to the sun, fears the presence of music, and refuses to observe anything but technique in paintings, the young poet concludes that to cry unashamedly, "This is what I / Love, what I cherish!" is fraught with danger: "What is be-yond analysis / Is perilous . . . Be wary of such / Intensity."[1] In this first, naive equation, Greece becomes the physical haunt of Eros as well as the literary land of myth.

In 1950, Merrill made his first visit to Greece, but it was not until 1964, when he and his partner David Jackson bought a house in Athens, at the foot of Mount Lycabettus, that Greece began to play a major part in his poetry. For two de-cades Merrill and Jackson spent a part of every year in Athens, and in that pe-riod, every volume of Merrill's verse had a Greek component. Even later volumes contain reminiscent pieces, and I will come to those in the course of this chapter. In the 1966 volume, *Nights and Days,* Merrill made his first forays into Greek myth, retelling, for instance, the story of Cupid and Psyche in the long poem "From the Cupola," a modern setting of a love looked on askance by Psyche's two unsympathetic sisters. In the end, Psyche, distressed, is comforted by her poet, "James," who exonerates her of shame for her secret trysts:

> Psyche, hush. This is me, James.
> Writing lest he think
> Of the reasons why he writes—
> Boredom, fear, mixed vanities and shames;
> Also love. . . .
>
> All our pyrotechnic flights
> Miss the sleeper in the pitch-dark breast.
> He is love:
> He is everyone's blind spot.
> We see according to our lights.

(214)

Eros in Greece gave permission for love still illegal in the United States. Over the years, Merrill learned modern Greek, made Greek friends (notably Maria Mitsotáki), and took a Greek lover, named Strato Mouflouzélis. He translated a few Greek poems (including three by Cavafy) and appropriated Cavafy's title, "Days of . . ." for five of his own poems.[2] The Greek landscape, Greek art, Greek acquaintances, and the Greek language infiltrated Merrill's verse.[3]

Eventually, disillusion set in. Athens became somewhat polluted; Strato aged into a money-hungry gambler; there was a fire in Merrill's house; and the charm of the new country and the new language wore off. The Greek house was sold, and Key West replaced Athens as Merrill's and Jackson's winter residence. A new tone was adopted toward Greece—a more ironic, less erotic one. A distanced comedy pervades the later poems, about a return to the former house (rented from its new owners for a short stay), about Strato, about the nine lives of the adopted kitten. Yet there are surges of warmth in which Greece, now seen without rose-colored glasses, is loved with a familiarity that surpasses in value—because of its veracity—the ignorant idolatry of youth.

There are some Greek poems that fail—notably, two dramatic monologues spoken by Greek men ("Kostas Tympakianákis" and "Manos Karostefanís"), phrased in an uneasy demotic, and the rather slack, late poem "Days of 1994," which has little of Cavafy about it, except the adapted title. But on the whole, Greece was markedly useful to the enlargement of Merrill's verse, and I want to speak about four modes in which he rose well to the challenge of writing about, and within, a culture so unlike his own.

The first mode is a worldly, Jamesian one. Here, Merrill the American visitor is the wry observer of social detail, and also the converted son who finds both love and affection in his alternate home: my examples are "Days of 1964" (1966) and "After the Fire" (1972). Merrill's second mode is a rhapsodic one, in which the poet is the impersonal celebrant of something Greek, but at the same time its symbolic counterpart: my examples are "The Power Station" (1959) and "Samos" (1980). The third mode is a cultural one, for which my example is "Losing the Marbles" (1988); and the fourth is a mythical one: my examples are "Violent Pastoral" (1966) and one of Merrill's last poems, "Minotaur" (1994).

The Jamesian mode is the familiar one of the innocent abroad and is thematically not original; but Merrill used it astringently to demystify both Eros and Greek family life. In "Days of 1964" (220–222) the plot is simple: Merrill and his new lover, in their intoxicated first days of lovemaking, employ a middle-aged housekeeper named Kleo. To them she seems maternal and frumpy:

> Her legs hurt. She wore brown, was fat, past fifty,
> And looked like a Palmyra matron
> Copied in lard and horsehair. How she loved
> You, me, loved us all, the bird, the cat!

Kleo's maternal love is gratifying to the poet: "She lived nearby with her pious mother / And wastrel son. She called me her real son." But one day, as Merrill goes out of the house to market, he sees Kleo beginning to climb up the nearby hill: "Poor old Kleo, her aching legs, / Trudging into the pines." He calls her, calls again, again. Finally she reluctantly turns, and he sees, astonished and repelled, that she is en route to a sexual encounter.

> Above a tight, skyblue sweater, her face
> Was painted. Yes. Her face was painted
> Clown-white, white of the moon by daylight,
> Lidded with pearl, mouth a poinsettia leaf,
> *Eat me, pay me*—the erotic mask
> Worn the world over by illusion
> To weddings of itself and simple need.

The sight sends the poet into a vertiginous reevaluation of his own sexual life: "If that was illusion, I wanted it to last long; / . . . I hoped it would climb when it needed to the heights / Even of degradation." But between the spoiling of the idyllic beginning by the revelation of sexual compromise, and the defiant statement just quoted, the poem finds its symbolic image of erotic exchange in the local marketplace (vegetables, chickens, pottery) where all the buyers and sellers are wary hagglers:

> hagglers each at heart
> Leery lest he be taken, plucked,
> The bird, the flower of that November mildness,
> Self lost up soft clay paths, or found, foothold,
> Where the bud throbs awake
> The better to be nipped, self on its knees in mud—

And the voice breaks off in contradiction and anguish. This poem becomes un-Jamesian, not only in its fluster and headlong confusion, but also in its cascading rush of successive, and suggestive, images. In the middle of its social observation of the lovers, the hill, Kleo, and the market, the Merrill poem "loses itself," recording the upsetting of narrative control by emotional response.

Another, more detailed Jamesian narrative occurs in the 1972 poem "After the Fire" (296–298), when Merrill—returning to set things right after the fire in his Athens house—is told there by Kleo that her now-senile mother, the *yiayia* (grandmother), has taken to screaming to the street that Kleo's son, Panayióti, is "a *Thieving Faggot!*" and that Kleo is "a *Whore!*" Merrill reacts silently:

> I press Kleo's cold hand and wonder
> What could the poor yiayia have done
> To deserve this terrible gift of hindsight,
> These visions that possess her of a past
> When Kleo really was a buxom armful
> And "Noti" cruised the Naval Hospital.

The next day, visiting Kleo's household, Merrill finds everything changed by time: the fever-ridden *yiayia* no longer recognizes him, and various objects, once Merrill's own—his robe, his slippers—are being worn by Panayióti:

> (It strikes me now, as happily it did not
> The insurance company, that P caused the fire.

> Kleo's key borrowed for a rendezvous,
> A cigarette left burning . . . Never mind.)
> Life like the bandit Somethingopoulos
> Gives to others what it takes from us.
>
> Some of those embers can't be handled yet.

Greece has become a pyre of incinerated loves, its remnants "taken from us" by the bandit Time. Just at this moment of distress, however, "Jimmy" sees sanity return to the *yiayia:*

> I mean to ask whose feast it is today
> But the room brightens, the yiayia shrieks my name—
> It's Tzimi! He's returned!
> —And with that she returns to human form,
> The snuffed-out candle-ends grow tall and shine,
> Dead flames encircle us, which cannot harm,
> The table's spread, she croons, and I
> Am kneeling pressed to her old burning frame.

The Proustian magic of his uttered name allows the returned poet's sense of Greece to end in nostalgia, rather than in the embers of love-embittered irony. He is too far away, in this later commentary, for the fire of Eros to trouble the cultivated speech of the poem, as it had done in "Days of 1964." There is no passage in "After the Fire" of a present struggle between the repression of, and acknowledgment of, the mercenary side of Eros. "My heart leaps," says the poet, as his doorbell rings at the opening of "After the Fire," but immediately adds "out of habit," as the primitive erotic response is quenched as soon as it is experienced:

> Everything changes; nothing does. I am back,
> The doorbell rings, my heart leaps out of habit,
> But it is only Kleo—how thin, how old!
> Trying to smile, lips chill as the fallen dusk.

The prose of the present has replaced the poetry of the past. And though both poems are largely unrhymed, in "Days of 1964," the loose texture of the recurrent words "love," "pain," "climb," "flowers," "illusion," and "mask" suddenly—when the poet addresses his lover at the end—becomes more closely woven, transforming the hitherto linear narrative shape into the unity of lyric:

> If that was illusion, I wanted it to last long;
> To dwell, for its daily pittance, with us there,
> Cleaning and watering, sighing with love or pain.
> I hoped it would climb when it needed to the heights
> Even of degradation, as I for one
> Seemed, those days, to be always climbing
> Into a world of wild
> Flowers, feasting, tears—or was I falling, legs
> Buckling, heights, depths,
> Into a pool, of each night's rain?
> But you were everywhere beside me, masked,
> As who was not, in laughter, pain, and love.

No such inclusive gathering informs the nostalgic, final embrace of the *yiayia* in "After the Fire." The poet, for all his final moment of emotion, remains the spectator of himself: "And I / Am kneeling pressed to her old burning frame." His ironic detachment cannot be shaken off. These poems, which I have called "Jamesian," arise out of Greek incidents—Kleo's sordid tryst, Panayióti's trespassing, arson, and thieving, the *yiayia*'s paranoia and family betrayal—that in some way shock Merrill, destroying his idealized image of love and the Greek spirit. These worldly, narrative poems represent the first, autobiographical stratum of Merrill's Greek experience; they are less transformed than the Greek poems in the other modes, and belong as much to the larger category of travel literature as to the genre of lyric.

Merrill's second, rhapsodic mode is more impersonal, as I have said; and yet, somewhere within it there beats a personal, a lyric, desire. An early example, called "The Power Station," dates from 1959: Merrill has visited Greece but has not yet put down roots there. The poem, describing the oracle at Delphi, is spoken (as Cavafy might have satirically arranged it) by a Christian, complacent in his belief that his "sane God" has now replaced the irrational, chthonic deity who expressed himself through the oracle. Yet somewhere (as in a Yeatsian second coming), a new post-Christian oracle is stirring; the depths are demanding voice once more. The poem is written in an adaptation of the "heroic" quatrain (pentameters rhyming alternately), a form normally employed for poems on lofty philosophical or political matters. Merrill alters the model, perhaps to suggest the restlessness of the oracle, making his openings more lyric by substituting a modest trimeter for a pentameter in the first line of each quatrain, while expanding the third line into a "Greek" hexameter (a double trimeter). The poem contains no personal, lyric "I": its speaker—representing collective Christianity—refers to "our" sane God:

> Think back now to that cleft
> In the live rock. A deep voice filled the cave,
> Raving up out of cells each time in some way left
> Huger and vaguer. There was a kind of nave
>
> Strewn with potsherd and bone.
> The tribe's offspring, converted now, rejoice
> In our sane god. But two or three hours south, not known
> To them, the charges of the other's voice
>
> Break into light and churn
> Through evening fields. Soon a first town is lit,
> Is lived in. Grounded. Green. A truth fit to unlearn
> The blind delirium that still utters it.
>
> (114)

The tame Christian speaker of "The Power Station" is eclipsed by the two descriptions—of the past Delphic oracle and the anticipated new oracle—that bracket his declaration of religious sanity. In predicting a recurrence of "the blind delirium" of the unconscious that utters truth, the speaker appears to accept the pendulum-swing from Delphi to a "sane" god, and thence to the "charges" of another electric voice, a Dionysian nuclear "power station" of culture, lighting first one town then the next. These are the liberating associations that Merrill as rhapsode, scarcely acquainted as yet with Greece, will worship in it: its primitiveness, its raving oracle, its huge and vague representations of the unconscious, its blind delirium of libido, defying rationality. The notion of ancient urges from the depths that, if vanquished in one arena, reappear in another, is impersonally voiced here. Yet, stern though it may seem in its utterance, the poem is romantic in the poet's assumption of truth generated from delirium; in its respect for primitive devotions performed within a "nave / Strewn with potsherd and bone"; and, above all, in its personal subtext—that of a young poet seeking inspiration from Delphi, and a young homosexual seeking justification for sexual expression.

Later, in a 1980 lyric called "Samos,"[4] Merrill will again worship Greek elements, now not in predictable rhymed quatrains, but in a sestina-like form representing variability within the predictable. He knows Greece so well that he
has perceived its five essential and elemental nouns: "sense," "light," "land,"
"fire," and "water." ("Sense" is that human, physical faculty which perceives
the four elements of water, earth, air, and fire; and in Merrill's adaptation of
these ancient four, "light" stands in for "air" as "land" stands in for "earth.")
Each of the five twelve-line stanzas of "Samos" concerns one of the five elemental nouns but also cites the others; these stanzas are followed by a five-line
envoi, one line per essential noun. Merrill rings changes on the elemental words,
which in a poem are also sounds: in the second stanza, "light" rhymes with
itself, but also with "chrysolite," "daylight," "alight," and "leit- / Motif." This
quasi-sestina, arising from a nightlong ferry ride to Samos, imagines Greece
as a series of oceanic, semantic waves, presenting a resemblance which is
never an identity. The poem, though it derives from two others—Valéry's "Le
Cimetière Marin" and Stevens's "Sea Surface Full of Clouds"—has an atmosphere of its own, since the fundamentally absurd requirement that each of its
sixty-five lines must end in one of five sounds makes for sentences that are, in
a way, scarcely English. The erotic couple of the poem, as they explore Samos,
desire elemental immersion:

> Know nothing, now, but Earth, Air, Water, Fire!
> For once out of the frying pan to land
> Within their timeless, everlasting fire!
> Blood's least red monocle, O magnifier
> Of the great Eye that sees by its own light
> More pictures in "the world's enchanted fire"
> Than come and go in any shrewd crossfire
> Upon the page, of syllable and sense,
> We want unwilled excursions and ascents,
> Crave the upward-rippling rungs of fire,
> The outward-rippling rings (enough!) of water . . .
> (Now some details—how else will this hold water?)

The personal lyric desire of the poet is still for inspiration's "unwilled excursions and ascents," but the *basso ostinato* of the recurrent end-words keeps
the poem from "taking off" into the spontaneity that enacts the elemental, while
the ironic parenthetical remarks—often self-deprecatory ones—prevent any

rapturous annihilation in the sublime. The last question of the poem—"Do things that fade especially make sense?"—frames the poem as elegy, even while the lyric utterance frames itself thematically as rhapsody. "Samos" is not, to my mind, one of Merrill's better poems, but it shows his persistent desire to raise Greece to the level of a power station, to an elemental sublime. As he had said in the 1962 poem, "After Greece," "I want / Essentials: salt, wine, olive, the light, the scream." By the time he writes "Samos," in 1980, there remains of the earlier five essentials only light: the colorless word "land" has come to stand for salt, wine, and olive, and the libidinal scream from the power station has been sublimated to unearthly fire.

More interesting to me than the Jamesian narratives and the worshipper's rhapsodies are Merrill's poems stimulated by some element of our Western inheritance of Greek culture. The most remarkable of these poems is a 1988 sequence called "Losing the Marbles" (572–579). Its punning title refers not only to Greek attempts to regain the Elgin Marbles (Merrill later mentions "the Athens press, / Breathing fire to get the marbles back"), but also to the extent to which these fragments of archaic statuary have come to stand for "Greece" in the Anglophone community, ever since they were admired by Keats, Haydon, and others. Keats, writing his sonnet on the Elgin Marbles, finds them daunting. Even though, as he recognizes, they are merely "the shadow" of "a [former] magnitude," the magnitude that he extrapolates backward from the marble fragments intimidates him: "My spirit is too weak," he cries out, feeling that he can never equal the Greek sublime. By now, Merrill too has acknowledged that "Greece" is largely a made-up cultural signifier, constructed out of fragments that are never complete enough to guarantee the meanings we make of them.

The poet's figure for the incompleteness of the past is the incompleteness of the manuscript remains of, say, Sappho. (Though he does not name her, Sappho's status as the founder of Greek poetry suggests that her papyrus fragments provide the paradigm of the incomplete text to which, as we shall see, his own poem has been reduced.) The title, "Losing the Marbles," also refers to the loss of memory feared by the poet as he passes sixty: "he has lost his marbles," we say colloquially. "Another marble gone," says Merrill, as he loses his calendar and forgets what he talked about at lunch.

The precipitating event of "Losing the Marbles" is a rainstorm in part 3 of the sequence: the poem that Merrill has been writing, left on his desk and rained on through an open window, has lost many of its words in places where the ink has run. The ruined lines of verse now present themselves as a conundrum that he—and we—are asked to reconstruct, "come evening, to sit / Feverishly restoring the papyrus." The ruined lines look like this—and they are Sapphic enough in appearance:

body, favorite
gleaned,   at the
vital
frenzy—

act and moonshaft, peaks
stiffening
Unutter[able]
the beloved's

slowly
stained in the deep   fixed
summer nights
or,

scornful   Ch[arm]ides,
decrepitude
Now, however, that
figures also

body everywhere
plunders and
what we cannot—from the hut's lintel
flawed

white as
the field's brow.

sliced turnip
our old
wanderings

home   palace, temple,
having   of those blue foothills
no further   clear
fancy[.]

Does the poem have a form? We do not know. Does it have a theme? We are not sure, except that the still-legible words indicate the presence of a body and a be-loved, decrepitude and plunder and flaws. The fragment seems to end with the word "fancy." There is an "act"; something is "stained." Our reconstruction might take almost any form, just as our "Greece," as we deduce it from literary and artistic vestiges, might assume almost any shape. Before reconstructing—or reinventing—his lost poem, Merrill pauses to meditate in heroic couplets on the modern admiration for the unfinished, the fragmentary, the blank passage on the canvas—modernity's reverence for artworks in which the void is integral to creation. He, however, suspects that marble remains unsatisfactory to the flesh:

> My illustration? The Cézanne oil sketch
> Whose tracts of raw, uncharted canvas fetch
> As much per square inch as the fruit our cloyed
> Taste prizes for its bearing on the void . . .
> Ah, not for long will marble school the blood
> Against the warbling sirens of the flood.

For all the resistant firmness of marble's ethical resolve, the Homeric warbling sirens will lead every listener to the erotic maelstrom.

And so we come to the restored poem. Merrill has perhaps reconstructed the original, perhaps created a new object from the inky ruin on the page. Its subject is the inexpressibility in words of the body: first, that of the solitary, auto-erotic youth; next, the "unutterable" body of the beloved, his "fair, slowly / turned head"; and then the groupings of youthful bodies, all "scornful . . . of decrepitude." But now, the speaker's body and that of his friend, "Charmides," no longer belong to gilded youth; the body has declined into adult "peasant shrewdness," making do in ways repugnant to former aesthetes. We read the newly assembled poem with some humiliation:

> The body, favorite trope of our youthful poets . . .
>   With it they gleaned, as at the sibyl's tripod,
>   insight too prompt and vital for words.
>   Her sleepless frenzy—
>
> cataract and moonshaft, peaks of sheer fire at dawn,
>   dung-dusted violets, the stiffening dew—
>   said it best. Unutterable too
>   was the beloved's
>
> save through the index of refraction a fair, slowly
>   turned head sustained in the deep look that fixed him.

From then on veining summer nights with
    flickering ichor,

he had joined an elite scornful—as were, Charmides,
    your first, chiseled verses—of decrepitude
        in any form. Now, however, that
            their figures also

begin to slip the mind—while the body everywhere
    with peasant shrewdness plunders and puts to use
        what we cannot—from the hut's lintel
            gleams one flawed image;

another, cast up by frost or earthquake, shines white as
    sliced turnip from a furrow on the field's brow.
        Humbly our old poets knew to make
            wanderings into

homecomings of a sort—harbor, palace, temple, all
    having been quarried out of those blue foothills
        no further off, these last clear autumn
            days, than infancy.

The reinvented poem presents a shape we could not have suspected from the rain-blurred draft—a four-line Sapphic stanza, slanting downward to the right. Its "act" turns out to be a "cataract"; its "stained" is really "sustained"; its "or" an "ichor"; and its "fancy" an "infancy." We were wrong about almost everything; we blush for our assumptions. The topic of the completed poem turns out to be the haunting power of remembered fragments to stand—in the mind of a poet in late life—for the absent whole. Young, the poet scorned "decrepitude" (that Yeatsian concept) "in any form." Now, as memory falters, a single "flawed image," gleaming from the lintel of a hut, or another, revealed in a geological upheaval, can turn "wanderings" into "homecomings of a sort." The images of infancy are transferable almost anywhere, because they are Types: "harbor, palace, temple." If we have reconstructed Greece into types of our own longing, the revelations it offers may be true precisely for that reason.

"Losing the Marbles" ends in comedy, almost. Merrill's young lover has given him, as a joking present to restore the "marbles" that the aging poet fears he is losing, a bag of large decorative children's marbles, which the poet has now embedded in the deck slats around the pool at his Key West house. The marbles become domestic stars, arranged around the pool's "oubliette," forming "a kind of heaven / To sit in, talking, largely mindless of / The risen, cloudy brilliances above." The fateful stars above—descendants of Keats's "huge, cloudy symbols of a high romance"—can almost be forgotten among the microcosmic marble-stars below. Acknowledging that the true "Greece" will always hover unattainably above our individual "Greece," that we can invent only the tokens of the Types, Merrill can now abandon the positivist idea of finding out "the truth" of the past, together with the nostalgia for that presumed truth. He had first tried to fix "Greece" as the signifier of the erotic, the primitive, and the inspired; but then he found himself ironizing it as the fallen travesty of that once-idolized concept—as the gay bar "The Metro" (in the poem of that name) has become a bank.

Life is more fluid and more complex than either the idealized or the disillusioned version of itself; and the act of creating now must have as its object the co-presence of the ruined and the perfect. No longer is the archetypal Greek work of art the Charioteer of Delphi, as in Merrill's 1959 poem admiring him. Now it is the strong, male bronzes found off Riace, which in the 1985 poem, "Bronze" (454–455), speak reprovingly to the poet, opposing their masculinity (with its hormonal power) to his effeminacy. "We are," they say,

> Not tea-gowned ephebes like the driver
> At Delphi, but men in their prime
> With the endocrine clout so rebarbative
> To the eternally boyish
> Of whichever sex.

These statues reprove all rhetorical postures directed to pleasing an audience, whether the political "hot line" of Communist propaganda, or the erotic "hot line" of Hart Crane; the masculine bronzes also refuse to be vehicles for the sort of epiphany Rilke experienced before the archaic torso of Apollo. The bronzes speak, repudiating romanticism:

> Rhetorical
> Postures, the hot line direct
> To the Kremlin or out of Hart Crane,
> Leave us cold. It's for you to defuse them.
> For us, in our Dämmerung swarming

With gawkers, what trials of mettle
Remain? . . .

Go. Expect no
Epiphany such as the torso
In Paris provided for Rilke. Quit
Dreaming of change. It is happening
Whether you like it or not,
So get on with your lives. We have done.

Thus speak the sternly paternal bronzes to the "eternally boyish" Merrill, their terse lines framed within a long Jamesian narrative sequence ending, rather sinisterly, with the bronze sculpture of the head of Merrill himself, at the age of six, done by a sculptor who was, later, murdered by his two sons. "I too exist in bronze," reflects the rueful poet, speaking of himself as a person almost posthumous. The molten ardors of the flesh—its "ire and yearning"—stiffen, yes, into cast metal; but whatever becomes fixed in that way is always a cast-off self. Merrill is no longer six; change is happening, the bronzes say, "whether you like it or not." In such poems as "Losing the Marbles" and "Bronze," we see that Greece has entered Merrill's poetry as something both ruined and alive, a changing culture, not an immobile object of reverence.

I come, finally, to Merrill's most daring appropriation of Greek materials—his rewriting of myth. There are many poems of this sort that come to mind, and had I not written on it elsewhere, I would have chosen to look again at the marvelously inventive "Syrinx" of 1972 (355–356), too complex to be described briefly. It ends with Merrill's poignant compass rose of the erotic:

> Nought
> Waste   Eased
> Sought

Or one could cite the accomplished early sonnet of 1959, "Marsyas" (96), which is spoken posthumously by the poet Marsyas, after he has been flayed and hanged for offending Apollo. As Marsyas (updated to a popular poet, famous in nightclubs) sat with his friends, disparaging Apollo's "stiff rhythms, gorgeous rhymes," he was suddenly confronted by the god himself with his "gold archaic lion's look." Marsyas admits that he heard, in Apollo's music, "the plucked nerve's elemental twang" and a manner so divine that it eclipsed matter:

> They found me dangling where his golden wind
> Inflicted so much music on the lyre
> That no one could have told you what he sang.

But instead of "Syrinx" or "Marsyas," I will cite two poems about erotic submission. The first, an early one—"Violent Pastoral," published in 1966 (190)—is based on the myth that Jove, in the form of an eagle, abducted Ganymede, holding the youth in his talons as he soared aloft. In "Violent Pastoral," Merrill forsakes the clear narrative line of the "Jamesian" mode for something far more Yeatsian: we feel the influence of "Leda and the Swan," with its initial "sudden blow." Merrill's oxymoronic title wishes to ravish pastoral away from its level glades and purling streams, to drag it upward into the sexual sublime, "Beyond Arcadia at last," as an eagle "mounts with the lamb in his clutch: / Two wings, four hooves." The poem is strung on a set of infinitives—"to feel," "to be," "to link," "to be"—and on recurrent present participles and participial adjectives in "-ing"—"pounding," "pounding," "aching," "bleating," "making," "looking." Even "lightnings" appears to be a near-sibling of the "-ing" verbals:

> Against a thunderhead's
> Blue marble, the eagle
> Mounts with the lamb in his clutch:
> Two wings, four hooves,
>
> One pulse pounding, pounding,
> So little time being given
> To feel the earth shrunken,
> Gong-tilt of waters,
>
> To be at once helplessly
> Aching talon and bleating
> Weight, both,
> Lest the pact break,
>
> To link the rut in dust
> When the rope shortens
> Between foreleg and stake
> With the harder spiral of making
>
> For a nest wrapped in lightnings
> And quilted with their beaks who not yet,

As with their bones who no longer,
Are wholly brothers;

Beyond Arcadia at last,
Wing, hoof, one oriented creature,
Snake-scream of pride
And bowels of fright

Lost in the rainbow, to be one
Even with the shepherd
Still looking up, who understood
And was not turned to stone.

(190)

The seven quatrains of "Violent Pastoral" make up a single sentence, mimicking the effort of staying aloft on a sexual surge, until two become "one oriented creature," when "Snake-scream of pride / And bowels of fright / [Are] Lost in the rainbow." The poem would end at that rainbow phrase, if sexual success were its only aim; but there is a last "to be":

           to be one
Even with the shepherd
Still looking up, who understood
And was not turned to stone.

This Merrillian shepherd, emblem of gentle pastoral, or of the virginal adolescent wanting love, can (in this double-exposure poem, showing youth contemplating sadomasochistic intercourse) view the violent union of eagle and lamb without construing the entwined bodies as a Gorgonian monster.

Many of Merrill's stanzas in "Violent Pastoral" exhibit a predominance of "feminine endings" (rhythmically speaking, trochees) in the lines' end-words. We hear only "eagle" in the first and "bleating" in the third; we find only "creature" and "shepherd" in the last two stanzas; but all the other stanzas emphasize words of this trochaic falling cadence, by featuring more than one in the end-position: after the initial "eagle," we hear "pounding," "given," "shrunken," "waters," "bleating," "shortens," "making," "lightnings," "longer," "brothers," "creature," "shepherd." By the very cadence of his trochaic name, "shepherd," the shepherd is brought into conjunction with this sexual pulse of the poem. The physicality of the poem's rendering of the myth ("To be at once helplessly /

Aching talon and bleating / Weight, both") is attended by the metaphysicality of aspiration to the divine, as the poem links "the rut in dust" of the tethered animal "with the harder spiral of making / For a nest wrapped in lightnings." The metaphysical, Jovian nest is the place where the present engenders the future on the leavings of the past: the nest is "quilted with their beaks who not yet, / As with their bones who no longer, / Are wholly brothers." As in Yeats's "Leda," the myth implies that the divine cannot engender without a lower body as partner, but that the lower body—at first incapable (in its lamb-shepherdness) of imagining a sexuality pervaded by violence—must be overpowered into discovering its own true chimerical nature as "Wing, hoof, one oriented creature." The revelation of selfhood reflected here is a Blakean one. Just as we might say that Blake's lamb turns in adolescence into a tiger, and wonders at the revelation of its own violent and fiery self—"Did he who made the lamb make thee?"—so Merrill's shepherd undergoes his own burning sublimation in the person of his ravished lamb. We remember the rape of Ganymede as we read, but we feel Merrill is not so much retelling the myth as remaking it.

Merrill remakes the myth of the Minotaur as well, in a poem written in the last year of his life. He is dying of AIDS, contracted ten years earlier, and the labyrinth awaits him. As if to forestall ending, Merrill forswears the use of periods in "Minotaur" (854–855): sentences begin with capital letters, but end in air. Amazingly, the Minotaur turns out to be the erotic, blue-eyed youth of one's dreams, though sinisterly clad in a cloak resembling fur, "dense with soft black spines." The aging speaker and other old human beings (not, as in the myth, the young), willingly follow the Minotaur into the maze, wanting (they are so oppressed by life) to become tribute and die. There is an obscure "sacrifice," glancingly rendered in synecdoche. Did we live through it? "Depends who tells the tale." The conflagration of sex, as the old thirst after the young lover, can be recounted from two points of view: the young Minotaur has his version of what went on, the old theirs. Monster though he is, the Minotaur does only what the old implore him to: "*Devour my life* each prays."

Though Merrill retells the myth in narrative order, it is told imaginatively rather than narratively, in free indirect discourse. One of the old, who has penetrated to the open center of the maze, looks on in surprise as the terrifying Minotaur lifts off his Halloween mask—"His father's terrible head"—revealing the beauty of his features, his earring, his sun-crimsoned black locks, his blue eyes. "Who would have thought that the Minotaur—the agent of death—would be a young beauty?" wonders the speaker, as we overhear his thoughts (irregularly rhyming "nougat" with "nugget," "portico" with "Cocteau," "head" with "red"):

> A young one who'd have thought
> dreaming in late light
> before a portico
> pinker than nougat
> His father's terrible head
> laid aside uncovers
> an ink sketch by Cocteau
> The earlobe's cunning nugget
> Colors of Crete   Sun washing
> black locks blood-red

Two more ten-line stanzas follow, ending with the old speaker's prayer to be devoured:

> Pale ankle firm as cactus
> escaping from his cloak
> dense with soft black spines
> To see not quite a threat
> to touch not quite a joke
> A vital rivulet
> pulsing along his throat
> he looks up   Shafts of blue
> fatally attract us
> Drawn two by two

> after him through the maze
> we've come as tribute Ten
> old women ten old men
> This youngster is expected
> to feed on what we are
> or were   Mind's meat heart's blood
> all that we've seen and known
> treasured up rejected
> will now become his body
> *Devour my life* each prays

The meter is the trimeter that Yeats reinvented for the twentieth century; the pause after each line (a musical "rest" in lieu of the expected fourth beat) offers a natural space for thought, for query, for additions. So we might comment as we read:

> This youngster is expected [to *do what?*]
> to feed on what we are [*or?*]
> or were   Mind's meat heart's blood [*and?*]
> all that we've seen and known [*and yet more: all that we've*]
> treasured up rejected [*will?*]
> will now become his body [*why? Because*]
> *Devour my life* each prays

Sexual intimacy in old age with a young lover is so unexpected that one reacts in the hyperboles of the last stanza, overcoming even the chill and bruise of death:

> Amazement   Golden beeline
> for greenest dark   Strong fusion
> of grape and cardamom
> As for the "sacrifice"
> one lightning-fleet contusion
> sparklers of ice
> farewell's euphoric hail
> It must have been benign
> if we lived through it   *Did* we
> Depends who tells the tale
> (854–855)

In this paradoxical green darkness, with juice of grape and smell of cardamom for the seeking bee, the "sacrifice" is unimportant. The *frater ave atque vale* uttered here is "farewell's euphoric hail." And if the Minotaur of AIDS is one's young love, is one's quasi-posthumous life after the "contusion" and "ice" of the diagnosis nonetheless benign—lived, as it is, in his company? Comedy or tragedy? The victim's tale or the Minotaur's? The end is a riddle.

It is not surprising that a poet living in the shadow of AIDS should be reminded of the sinister tribute of the young to the Minotaur—perhaps deriving the Minotaur's uncanonical, youthful son from the unknown person who was

the source of Merrill's infection and death. But Merrill's originality in recon-
ceiving the Minotaur as, in some sense, a life-giving presence to the aged men
and women arriving as tribute, springs from a sense of Greece (and Greek
myth), which was for him always—even in its more violent forms, even when
revised, as here—a life-giving source. The simplicity of the mythic diction in
"Minotaur" contrasts strongly with the more ornate diction of "Marsyas" and
"Syrinx," and its wondering calm contrasts even more strongly with the pro-
pulsive force of "Violent Pastoral." Merrill is almost seventy as he enters the
labyrinth, and his mode is a transparent and meditative one, although broken
in each stanza by one or two violent phrases. "His father's terrible head" reminds us of the monstrous lineage of the Minotaur; the "soft black spines" are
unnatural forms of fabric; "Mind's meat heart's blood" foretells the ultimate
sacrifice; "contusion" is the visual understatement of the killing blow. Around
these stanzaic contusions are the ballad-like simplicities: "a portico pinker
than nougat"; "Shafts of blue"; "Ten / old women ten old men"; "sparklers of
ice." The sophisticated poet of travel has become the reteller of folktale. Spun
into archetype, the thread of love and betrayal is once more followed into the
labyrinth.

As he extends his acquaintance with Greek myth, Merrill becomes almost a
Greek poet. It is not inconceivable that a contemporary Greek poet could have
written poems like "Violent Pastoral" or "Minotaur." In them, Merrill is least
the American. In his Jamesian observations, in his traveler's rhapsodies, in his
reflections on our necessarily mistaken construction of the ancient past, he had
remained the visitor from abroad. Uttering myth, he speaks from within the
Greek power station itself.

It would offend this poet's spirit to end on a solemn note, so I append Merrill's mocking rendition, in "Two Double Dactyls" (814), of Greeks repudiating their colonization by Americans. It is entitled "Neo-Classic," and is written
in double dactyls, a comic contemporary form, always beginning with the line
"Higgledy-piggledy."

> Higgledy-piggledy
> Jacqueline Kennedy
> Went back to Hydra and
> Found it a mess—
>
> Neon lights, discotheques . . .
> "Landlord, what's *hap*pening?"

"Ἀνθρωτηστήκαμε,
Go home, U.S."

(The Greek word is glossed by Merrill's editors as "We have become human beings.")

Merrill went home, but his Muse did not; one of his last-written poems was entitled, in imitation of Cavafy, "Days of 1994."

25

Mark Ford

Intriguing, Funny, Prophetic

In 1992, a book—*Landlocked*—was published in England that contained remarkable and immensely likable poems by Mark Ford.[1] I wanted to write on it,
but the journal I was writing for wouldn't review a book not published in
America. Frustrated, I wrote to its unknown author instead, so that my delight
at the book would reach him at least privately, if not publicly. The poems in
Landlocked were neither decorous (in conventional lyric ways), nor tightly tacit
(Philip Larkin), nor historical (Geoffrey Hill), nor demotic (Tony Harrison),
nor sensual (Seamus Heaney). They were idiosyncratic and wildly imaginative, and—to use Ford's own words—"funny peculiar."

The author was able to do without the long sigh for the European past that had
animated modern poetry after World War I; he did not imitate the theatrical tones
of Berryman and Plath; he prized (for all his outrageous comedy) a linguistic
equanimity both intellectual and fine-grained. Ford is not nostalgic for a lost
England, nor does he lament contemporary morals. Instead, he simply acknowledges the modern situation as the inescapable form of life; it is what we are living,
and he describes it with dark comedy. Modern existence in modern circumstances
cannot be argued with; it simply is, as in the poem "Funny Peculiar":

> I sit down here drinking hemlock
> While terrible things go on upstairs.
>
> Sweat creeps like moss outward to the palms,
> And time itself seems a strange, gauze-like medium.
>
> Sleep will leave still newer scars each night, or,
> Infuriatingly, is a curtain that refuses to close.

On the horizon, bizarre consolations make themselves
Known—a full fridge, a silent telephone,

The television quiet in its corner.
Everything and nothing have become a circular

Geometrical figure, seamlessly joined,
To be wrestled innocently this way and that

Into the most peculiar almost whimsical shapes.
(L, 44)

The opening is dégagé in the Frank O'Hara manner—"I do this, I do that"—but sardonic, not joyful. The baffled imagination is charged to include "everything" and "nothing," objects equally impregnable, seamlessly joined in a perfect figure offering no point of entrance. Yet the resistant circular contour vaguely hovering in the writer's mind demands to be "wrestled" into new topological forms, the agon of wrestling countered only by the happy whim of making.

The "I" of a poem such as "Funny Peculiar" is a cartoon creation, with his hemlock in hand, and his wrestling in prospect. However, his speech is adult, and intriguing, and funny. (Poetic form is silently present, declaring itself not by rhyme but by resemblances in syntax or rhetoric or sound.) After several other accounts of his circumstances, all in the present tense, the insomniac speaker generates a prophetic imperative: the enigmatic "circular / Geometrical figure" is to be forced, against its own resistance, into peculiar shapes. True of writing, the obligation is as true of life; the genetically given must be insistently wrestled into a self. This is a more athletic conception of "soul-making" than Keats's claim that the Intelligence is "schooled" into a Soul by "a world of pains and troubles," but Ford is a latter-day Keats in his certainty that "pains and troubles" are the sure subjects of art and life.

Because Ford's poems are almost all undergirded by a narrative (however surreal), they need to be quoted whole, in full spate—a difficulty here, where excerpts from their inspired stories will have to do in most cases. In some of the autobiographical narratives, Ford's cosmopolitan past flickers on the page. He was born in Nairobi where his father, a BOAC executive, was temporarily posted; other postings took the family to Sri Lanka, Canada, and the United States. As Ford puts it in "Signs of the Times":

We

Were born in the forward-
Thinking sixties, and grew up in various capital cities in Africa
And Asia—wherever, that is, the British Overseas Airways Corporation
(BOAC, for short) saw fit.[2]

And although Ford was sent back to England at the age of eight for schooling, the family travel made his "Englishness" uneasy ("After Africa, Surbiton"). He went to Oxford, gained a First, was a Kennedy Fellow at Harvard, and taught for two years at the University of Kyoto before returning to England, where he wrote his DPhil dissertation on the poetry of John Ashbery. He is now Professor of English at University College, London. Unlike most poets, he has had a sustained career as a critic (essays collected in two volumes), biographer (of Raymond Roussel, the French Surrealist), translator (of Roussel's forbidding *Nouvelles Impressions d'Afrique*), editor (of John Ashbery's poems in the Library of America), and anthologist *(London: A History in Verse)*.

Ford's *Selected Poems* includes (along with some new work) poems from Ford's three previous volumes—*Landlocked, Soft Sift,* and *Six Children.*[3] Deeply literary and teasingly allusive, the poems can yet be read with pleasure by readers unaware of the references, because Ford bases his work on seductive instances of everyday happenings, however fanciful or surreal.

Ford's restlessness in experimentation, evident in his resort to taxing forms (the sestina, the pantoum), is less patent, but more ingenious, in the internal structures of the poems. He presents the new poem "In Loco Parentis" (SP, 139) in two halves, in itself not an unusual arrangement: the first half shows him as a child in an English public school, with unlovable people (to say the least) serving *in loco parentis,* as the phrase goes. As Ford begins with realistic images of the "creepy" staff, the title seeps into the first line:

In Loco Parentis

    were some quite creepy men—one
    used to lie down
    on the dayroom floor, then get us all
    to pile on top of him—and a basilisk-
    eyed matron in a blue uniform with a watch
    dangling
    beneath her right

collarbone. *Thump thump*
thump went her footsteps, making
the asbestos ceiling tiles shiver, and me
want to hide, or run like a rabbit
in a fire . . .

The poet's will to render the school is not satisfied with this "realistic" first half, in which we have indeed seen the pile-up of the boys summarized in the pile-up of the opening four lines, and have equally glimpsed the watch of the matron in its imitative one-word vertical "dangling."

For Ford, the poem must not only describe the repellent dramatis personae of the school; it must also invent a symbolic equivalent for the feeling and the tone of the child's sense of impotence. And so Ford does the poem over again in the second half, this time as a symbolic Lewis Carroll chess game in which malice, "a minor / devil," forces the boys into ignorant moves in complex games they cannot possibly understand or win: the chess pieces, under devilish command, "levitate / and hover, flourishing swords, in midair." As an adult, the child wishes he could replay the game, this time to win, but the childhood loss is permanent. In Ford's symbolic reprise, the creepy man becomes "the stealthy / knight," the intimidating matron "the all- / knowing queen":

What we lost, we lost
forever. A minor
devil played at chess
with us, forcing
the pieces to levitate
and hover, flourishing swords, in midair. I'd grasp
them now, the orotund bishop, the stealthy
knight, the all-
knowing queen,
but they dissolve
in my fingers, refuse
to return to the board, to their squares.

The evaporation of the threatening ogres of childhood means that one cannot ever be revenged on them, and Ford's tense drama replays, in its brief enjambed lines, the frightened boys' forward-halting rhythms in the failed encounter.

Wordsworth perfected the sort of poem in which a childhood "then" is reflected upon in the adult "now," but Ford's school game-war offers no Wordsworthian compensation for the child's suffering. In Ford's "now," which denies any consolatory wish fulfillment by present conquest, the puppets of the symbolic imagination refuse the will of their own conceiver as they dissolve into thin air. The game pieces are not to be retrieved; the game itself has become unplayable. And although traditional reprises usually retain the same setting as the original one, and end on an upward curve, Ford's move from dormitory to chessboard abandons the realistic sketch of the school and replaces it with chess, the better to convey, by abstraction, the universality of adult oppression of children.

Poets of any era feel they must imagine, and make palpable in feeling, what the age needs to hear: in Ford's case, his colonial childhood leads his poetry into postcolonial reconsideration. What feelings will a colonial childhood such as his own call up in a retrospective scan? Nostalgia? Anti-imperial sentiment? Guilt? All of these, and more: But how is the poet to embody them without becoming sententious or maudlin or pious? An ambitious recent poem, "World Enough" (SP, 142–143), offers Ford's childhood house as a microcosm of colonial life; it pictures an incident in which a native servant, dismissed for cause, returns to the house, humiliated and "red- / eyed, to retrieve a cushion / he'd forgotten." Ford begins "World Enough" in his satiric vein, jeering at late colonialism as a form of piracy:

> The Empire
> was flummoxed, and dissolving
> fast when we
> set sail on the Seven Seas, late, late
> buccaneers in quest
> of whatever booty
> remained. . . .

The "booty" sequestered by the colonizers consisted of "a retinue of 'bearers,'" a gardener, a chauffeur, and drinks on the veranda. So far, a cliché of colonial complacency. But "real life" suddenly and chillingly intrudes upon the life of the booty-amassing colonials (the ellipses below are Ford's):

> my sister
> wept when "David," an aging, impassive servant

> dismissed for getting "filthy drunk"
> on arak, returned, red-
> eyed, to retrieve a cushion
> he'd forgotten . . . I watched
> him adjust
> his bundle, rise, then stagger off again, his wispy
> gray hair coming loose
> from its bun . . .

The servant "David" had, among his duties, the dusting, one by one, of the family's ever-accumulating hoard of souvenirs. These are inventoried in the last brilliant movement of Ford's narrative. How, poets must often ask, is a long list to be fitted stylistically into a poem without boring the reader? With "David" gone, says the speaker, there will be

>   no more
> dusting of ebony heads
> from Nigeria, onyx elephants, sphinxes carved
> out of soapstone; our gaudy, bug-eyed
> demon masks, or the glass
> protecting seven
> saffron-robed Masai warriors leaning
> on their spears in a clearing
> at midnight; a moon-
> landing souvenir mug, a slab
> of agate on a Chinese chest, my pen-
> holder made
> from the hide
> of a lion.

At first glance the list reads innocently enough, but on inquiry it breaks down into repellent and redundant multiples of objects and materials: heads, elephants, sphinxes, masks; ebony, onyx, soapstone, something "gaudy." "David" unwillingly dusts these herds of things, but he then turns to dust a different sort of object, a framed photograph, on which the poem surprisingly pauses for five lines. To "David," the photograph of the Masai, unlike the commercial knick-knacks, represents something real, familiar, and authentic.

After that pause, the list explodes into a pointless heterogeneity—moon-mug, slab of agate, Chinese chest, pen-holder—exemplifying the indiscriminate gluttony of the family for the "exotic." Ford closes the list on his boyhood lion-hide pen-holder because it brings into view a different sort of "booty": the lions shot for sport by the "civilized" colonials. The king of beasts is commercially diminished to a child's ornamental possession, in the past no doubt a source of pride (it is the climax of the list), but now a source of guilt. Yet the repudiation of the family collection is not strident, not audience-directed, as in too many "protest poems"; it remains, convincingly, an inward and personal shame, dryly proffered.

A list in a poem must be bound together by something other than the categories of its contents; it must (said Yeats) "articulate sweet sounds together." In Ford's list, the words "masks," "glass," "seven," "saffron," "spears," and "clearing" make up a characteristic sound chain linked by alliteration, internal vowels, and final consonants. There are several other such chains: "midnight," "moon," "mug," for example, or "protecting," "leaning," "clearing," "landing." Ford's unobtrusive but careful tending to his sound chains—audible everywhere in these poems—makes his lines cohere, attract each other magnetically, no matter their content. Again, as in the items of his list, Ford is unobtrusive, avoiding the virtuoso sound links of Hopkins or Thomas or Heaney; his articulations lurk, do not dominate.

What can Ford do besides find good subjects—the unnerving boarding school; the colonial discourse exemplified in the reference to a servant as "filthy drunk"; the acquisitive amassing of "booty"? Ford said, in an off-the-cuff interview, that he writes two kinds of poems, the "concept poem" and the rest:

> I divide poems up when I'm writing into concept poems, which have a kind of donnée or a concept like "Hart Crane's alive" or "Whitman had six children." . . . You get a concept poem like that and they're very appealing because they're easy to do whereas the other poems are a lot more agonising to write for me, they're a bit like spinning it all out in your insides like a spider and inching from—not even line to line but from word to word—you're making it all up out of nothing. Recently these poems have taken me months and months, even a year, to get them.[4]

The "concept poem" plays variations on some aspect of culture recognizable to any reader. The most giddy one in the *Selected Poems* takes its inspiration from a recent phenomenon—the mendacious letter or e-mail from a foreign place announcing that the writer desperately needs money. Ford's five absurd variations in the new poem "Adrift" (SP, 138) imagine the scamming requests arriving (always from malign dictators' female associates) via every contemporary means of communication:

> Colonel Muammar Gaddafi's wife, or rather
> widow, recently wrote to me asking for help in transferring
> some important financial assets from a secret location: only I,
> she insisted, had the expertise to perform this complex operation.
>
> Is there a more ferocious texter than General Pinochet's
> daughter? . . .
>
> A minor ex-mistress of Laurent Gbagbo's tweets practically
> every day. . . .
>
> I'm just too tired to think of replying to this e-mail
> inviting me to go trekking in the Himalayas with a distant "cousin"
> of Perez Musharraf. . . .
>
> "You have reached 0207 . . ." my machine was intoning. . . .

To write, to text, to tweet, to e-mail, to phone: as this ironic testimony of progress provokes a "What next?" after the answering machine, we drift into imagining the scam-by-quantum-motions, the scam-by-telepathy. . . .

In his "concept poems" Ford also likes curiosa: one poem, "John Hall" (SP, 87), arises from Hall's sixteenth-century compendium *Select Observations on English Bodies*. That book seems at first to consist only of outlandish remedies recommended by Hall:

> He cured, he records, Michael Drayton of a tertian
>> Fever with a spoonful of syrup of violets, and his own
>
> Hemorrhoids with a pigeon he cut open alive, then
>> Applied to his feet. . . .

Only toward the end of the grotesquerie do we learn that John Hall was Shakespeare's son-in-law. But "None of the cases . . . mentions his father-in-law's afflictions // Or demise"—the very facts we yearn to know.

In spite of the humorous appeal of such "concept poems" it is the webs spun out of the poet's insides, those pieces composed out of nothing but the ear's instinct and the heart's imagination, that are Ford's most rewarding successes, finding, as

they unerringly do, unusual language for the usual. The autobiographical poems
are of that sort, but so are some of the allegorical pieces. Of those, my favorite is
still "The Long Man" (SP, 51). In it Ford becomes "The Long Man of Wilmington," an outline in white of a 227-foot-tall male figure cut into the grass of a
hill in East Sussex, and first credibly mentioned in the seventeenth century. And
how does the insomniac Long Man feel out on his damp hill?

The Long Man

of Wilmington winces with the dawn; he has just
endured yet another mythical, pointless, starry
vigil. His ankles ache, and the weather looks
irksome and moody. . . .
                    Across the damp fields a distant
siren pleads for attention; he cannot
move, nor, like a martyr, disprove the lie of the land.

This is the aubade of a poet who has drunk the dangerous potion of his native language and literature, and finds in consequence "a stream of curious tags
and sayings" flowing through his veins. The giant Long Man wakes to the dis-
consolate weather of England:

I woke up feeling cold and distended,
my feet pointing east, my head in low-hanging
clouds. A stream of curious tags and sayings
flowed like a potion through my veins.

He is disoriented, floating among "invisible obstacles," attempting to create a
self out of nothing: a bewildering and paradoxical exercise but necessary, since
to create selfhood by imitating traditional literary precedents is to collapse into
cliché. The poet is furious at his predicament:

The alarmed
senses struggled to respond, then bewailed
the absence of detailed, all-powerful
precedents.

There is nothing to do but to investigate and explore, yet again, the huge if psychologically repetitive dimensions of one's own origins and existence:

> I kept picturing someone tracing
> a figure on the turf, and wearing this outline
> into a path by walking and walking around
> the hollow head, immobile limbs, and cavernous torso.

In an interview, Ford mentioned something once said to him by his friend the poet Mick Imlah (who is recalled in a touching elegy, "Ravished," in the *Selected Poems*):

> I remember talking with Mick and him saying that [the unity of one's poetry] takes care of itself, in that your psychological flaws or configurations emerge again and again. So in terms of finding a unity, your own problems surface in poem after poem, just in different styles. It's like putting together a bit of music, just getting a thing so that it works.[5]

Ford's poems, elaborated from a witty and sinister imagination, "work" in that instinctual way, allowing details to rise into salient being and beautiful formal shape for the reader as for the poet.

In the *Selected Poems*, Ford includes several translations from the Latin (Tacitus, Apuleius, Lucretius, Catullus, and Pliny the Elder), rescuing electrifying stories and scenes (the castration of Attis, the death of Petronius) from the translatorese of earlier versions. All are worth reading for Ford's vigorous and idiomatic staging as he keeps ancient "spots of time" alive in our Latinless age.

26

Notes from the Trepidarium

Stay, Illusion, *by Lucie Brock-Broido*

Lucie Brock-Broido's *Stay, Illusion*[1]—a finalist for the 2013 National Book Award and the 2014 National Book Critics Circle Award—follows three dazzling earlier volumes: *A Hunger* (1988), *The Master Letters* (1995), and *Trouble in Mind* (2004). Brock-Broido is now the director of Poetry and professor in the School of the Arts at Columbia; I have followed her work since 1988, when she became my colleague as a five-year Briggs-Copeland Lecturer at Harvard. Her books amount to a highly original contemporary autobiography.

Brock-Broido's writing is imaginative beyond the usual notions of that word; unlike the many dull poems, domestic or disarticulated, that proliferate on page and web, her poems have power. The personal narrative subtending the poems occasionally breaks through: we hear of youthful anorexia and hospitalization; parents (a mother dying; a father and a stepfather, both dead); three sisters; occasional travel; love affairs; the death of friends. In the first poem of her first book, *A Hunger*, Brock-Broido mocks the restricted identities of identity-politics, offering instead the multiple cartoon-identities that populate, as she says, "this work of mine":

> It's peopled by Wizards, the Forlorn,
> The Awkward, the Blinkers, the Spoon-Fingered, Agnostic Lispers,
> Stutterers of Prayer, the Flatulent, the Closet Weepers,
> The Charlatans. I am one of those.[2]

The poems in *A Hunger* were sometimes spoken by persons regenerated from bizarre news clippings (Baby Jessica, who had fallen into a well; Birdie Africa, the child survivor of the Move police bombing in Philadelphia), but even in such "fact-based" poems the invented child-voice possesses—in an individualized form—all the perverse energy of Brock-Broido's eccentric language. To read her is to become tutored in alternative versions of English. She has plucked and inserted into her poems the English of prison guards, of insane twins, of "the Glasgow Coma Scale," and other such outliers of discourse, while compiling a personal lexicon part real, part dislocated. In her recent elegy for the poet Liam Rector, a beloved friend in declining health who shot himself, expressions of grief are interrupted by the medical language of the autopsy record, its impersonal chill confronting personal desolation:

> Winter then, the body is cold to the touch, unplunderable,
>   Kept in its drawer of old-world harrowing.
>
> Teeth in fair repair. Will you be buried where; nowhere.
> . . . . .
> The eyes have hazel irides and the conjunctivae are pale,
>
> With hemorrhaging.
> (SI, 6)

Brock-Broido's titles resemble no one else's: among the more extravagant ones in *Stay, Illusion* are "You Have Harnessed Yourself Ridiculously to This World"; "Pax Arcana"; "Father, in Drawer"; "Notes from the Trepidarium"; "Scarinish, Minginish, Griminish"; and "Carpe Demon." (There are conventional titles, too, but not many.) The title once absorbed, the first line of the poem once again stops the eye. Punning on a poet-recluse and the recluse-spider, Brock-Broido opens *Stay, Illusion* with an icon both immobile and mobile: "Silk spool of the recluse as she confects her eventual mythomania" (SI, 3). Other first lines are equally unexpected: "Don't do that when you're dead like this, I said" (SI, 12); "There should be one spectacular of ruin, red, mid-tragedy" (SI, 48). The titles and verses alike prevent paraphrase by their ornamental fictive language. They are eerie, they resist interpretation, they abound in odd similes, yet their strange idiolect transmits the complicated shadings of feeling essential to lyric.

Deviations in language, though not rare in poetry, awaken mixed reactions. Ben Jonson, repelled by Spenser's archaisms, said "Spenser, by affecting the Ancients, writ no language," and yet a few lines later allowed for the attraction of unfamiliar words:

> Words borrow'd of Antiquity, doe lend a kind of Majesty to style, and
>   are not without their delight sometimes. For they have the Authority

of yeares, and out of their intermission doe win to themselves a kind
of grace-like newnesse.[3]

Deformations and deviations, generations later, become less peculiar; nobody
flinches now at Dickinson's subjunctive grammar and metaphoric definitions
("Hope is the thing with feathers"); nobody finds Dylan Thomas's "a grief ago"
strange; and even the words of "Jabberwocky" have entered the common sphere.
The constant refreshment of language (not necessarily by deviation—think of
George Herbert) is the stressful obligation experienced by poets. In one of his
Dream Songs (#67), Berryman explains the oddity of his own linguistic performance: "I am obliged to perform in complete darkness / operations of great deli-
cacy / on my self." Brock-Broido's "operations," like Berryman's, often emerge
from a darkness (of bewilderment, of pain, of loss), and produce linguistic distor-
tions peculiar to the necessities of each poem, spells for enchantment.

Brock-Broido's first two spell-casting books conceived of imagination as a
form of magic—chiefly a magic that could hold off catastrophe. The baby Jessica trapped in the well is, astonishingly, saved by a cohort of rescuers who
urge her to speech to preserve her alertness. She describes their efforts and her
responses:

> And: *How does a kitten go?*
> And I go like a kitten goes, on
>
> & on in that throaty liquid lewd bowlegged
> voice like kittens make.
> Then shut these big ole eyes.
>
> (AH, 25)

The Creole of baby Jessica—baby talk and sexual vocabulary crossed with
regional dialect—is one of many mixed languages issuing from the unlikely
protagonists of *A Hunger*. Even when the poet speaks in her "own" voice, she
is alive in an imagined time and place, "listening for secrets":

> I am the medieval child in the basket, rocking.
> Feigning sleep, up all night listening for secrets:
> why there are punishments,
> what news bad weather brings,
> how things get winnowed out.
>
> (AH, 8)

Once the "secrets" of disaster are understood, the world will be intelligible—
or so goes the magical thinking of *A Hunger*. "What I want is to sleep away an
epoch, / wake up as a girl with another kind of heart" (AH 8).

Brock-Broido's second book, *The Master Letters*, abandoned the arias of invented personae, and was possessed by the daimon of Dickinson the letter-
writer. Engendered by the three abject "Master Letters" written by Dickinson
to an unknown recipient, Brock-Broido's half-ventriloquized, half-personal
poems assume some of Dickinson's stylizations, among them a disjointed syntax.
Dickinson's "Master Letters" (says Brock-Broido's "Preamble") "maintain the
lyric density, the celestial stir, the high-pitched cadences, her odd Unfathom-
able systems of capitalization, the peculiar swooning syntax, the fluid stutter
of her verse."[4] Some of the pieces in *The Master Letters* are highly artificial
prose poems, but others are lineated verse: the poet says archly that in her
fourteen-line poems she is writing in the form of "the Old World sonnet—but
American & cracked, the odd marriage between hysteria and haiku" (ML, vii).
As for the unattainable Master himself, he is "a composite portrait, police-artist
sketch. Editor, mentor, my aloof proportion, the father, the critic, beloved, the
wizard" (ML, viii). But even the wizard, in after years, cannot perpetuate the
magic protecting *A Hunger*.

Brock-Broido's own Master Letters—Ingénue to Wizard—strike notes of resentment, yearning, confusion, candor, remoteness, apology, and sorrow. She is
forced to suspect that love, no matter how powerful, cannot compel satisfaction:
"There are no sorcerers left, only mechanics to fix things as they break down"
(ML, 37). (Things can at least still be "fixed.") Brock-Broido's excellent satiric
eye exposes America's ersatz repairs: "I am invited, with religious frequency in
parking lots, to be Saved, to convene, to partake in redemptive ritual, to come
back to the small circle of prayers" (ML, 37). Instead, the poet settles for a
"glooming peace" (Shakespeare, *Romeo and Juliet*) in which winter draws in and
dramas diminish, in which a strict self-definition is imposed to circumscribe the
steely passions of the will. The poet asks whether her attachment to the Master is
a form of desire, or the enacting of a compulsion. As magic wanes, the poet becomes expert in grim self-analysis, watching herself freeze into the Dickinsonian
stupor of "letting go" as the Master dissipates into phantasm and specter:

> The sedative of frost composes
> Its infinity of dormant melodramas
>
> On the glass. It consoles one,
> The solstice of the hour's no

Apparent motion, standing still.
It contents one, the solace of

Form & phantasm, of sieve
& specter, root & disposition.

The difference between desire & compulsion
Is that one is wanting, one is warding off.

(ML, 41)

Joining the long tradition of winter poems (Keats's "In drear-nighted December," Melville's "Monody," Dickinson's "After great pain," Stevens's "The Snow Man"), Brock-Broido's impeccable poem of the oncoming of emotional winter is worthy to stand with those predecessors. It locks its words into fixed relation: a solstice is a solace; what consoles one contents one; as form and phantasm click their alliterative identities, wanting and warding off become the painful time-keeping functions of the heart. Ironic melodrama is a congenial mode to Brock-Broido: she monitors its vagaries (hysteria, dormancy) under the formal demands and constraints of art.

By the end of *The Master Letters*, the power of the will to direct the course of a life is no longer efficacious. "Long ago . . . druidry // Was my first dream," she confesses in "How Can It Be I Am No Longer I," the poem banishing the druidic will to power: "soon / My little book of incantation // Will be done. It was a magical. And it is nothing that I want" (ML, 63). The poems recall an earlier self—"dryadic, gothic, fanatic against / The vanishing—" and then announce that deaths have erased that girl-self: "I will not speak to you again" (ML, 74).

A changed self requires a changed style, and a reader may mourn the poet's sacrifice of linguistic girlishness and gaiety. "We begin to live," said Yeats in a hard piece of wisdom, "when we conceive of life as tragedy." Brock-Broido's third book, *Trouble in Mind*, declares a moratorium on embellishment and fantasy, as the unignorable cruelties of human life impose themselves on the eyes and mind. Early innocence, the poet says, has been discovered to be finite:

As finite as the grade school teacher in Sierra Leone

Whose arms were axed off only at the hand, first left
And then the right, and then his mouth as he was making noise

And should be shut.[5]

She adds an aphorism: "Wisdom is experience bundled, with prosthetic wrists." This poem, titled "The One Theme of Which Everything Else Is a Variation," is the manifesto of the poet in her second, experienced stage:

> I cannot master anymore the surgical or magical,
> I do not know how the specific punishments or amputations are so
>
> Meted out. When you delete a wing or limb
> From a creature's form, it will inevitably cry out against this
>
> Taking, but in the end it will become grievously docile,
> Shut; far gone old god, you have been plain.
> (TIM, 9)

Against the stoic and Christian doctrine of compensation, which asserts that suffering strengthens and improves the soul, Brock-Broido proposes a cruel corrective: that suffering weakens and tames the formerly independent creature. To oppose the injustice of the "far gone old god," the poet will be as plain as he:

> If I am lucky in this life, here, I will go on
> Being whole, and speak again old god, I will be plain.
> (TIM, 9)

Trouble in Mind, in being "plain," includes bitter and sardonic poems about a love affair; the poet no longer idealizes a lover, but instead exposes his heavy and "gluey" being to derision (TIM, 59).

The disavowal of magical power is reiterated in "Soul Keeping Company," Brock-Broido's elegy for her mother. The legend that "The hours between washing and the well / Of burial are the soul's most troubled time" prompts the vigil by the corpse between death and burial:

> I sat with her in keeping company
> All through the affliction of the night, keeping
>
> Soul constant, a second self. Earth is heavy
> And I made no wish, save being
>
> Merely magical. I am magical
> No more.
> (TIM, 26)

The heart resents its impotence, and lashes out at those who have urged compliance with "reality":

> The New Realism
> Will be a bovine one with widened eyes.

But the poet succumbs to fact, urging her own reform. The New Realism to which she must concede requires a new heart, material not magical, animal, not narcissistic:

> Heart be strong as a burden beast,
> Common, clumsy, sunlit, oxish, kind.
>
> (TIM, 47)

As usual in Brock-Broido, the words are laden, but the double or triple meanings do not exclude each other. *Common:* is it "held in common" or "frequently encountered" or "low"? *Clumsy*—in what aspect: physically, emotionally, verbally, imaginatively? And then the wholly unexpected and beautiful *sunlit:* the darkness generating wizards and druids must lift. *Oxish* reorders the resentment of *bovine*, voicing the quality as natural, not debased. The sustaining end-word, *kind*, is a comment on the mutual needs of daily life—a quality not acknowledged by those self-endowed with magical powers.

Trouble in Mind had reprised the earlier deaths of both parents and a stepfather:

> First, my father died. Then my mother
> Did. My father died again.
>
> After the strange storm they were ruined down
> From the boughs.
>
> There were apples everywhere.
>
> (TIM, 4)

Those deaths are rapidly succeeded by later ones in an accelerating pace; elegies in *Stay, Illusion* commemorate not only Liam Rector but also the writer Lucy Grealy, dead of an overdose; the writer Jason Shinder, extinguished by cancer; Brock-Broido's mentor, Stanley Kunitz; and an unnamed friend who killed herself by drinking antifreeze. The poet is unwilling to return to ordinary life after each death; she does not want to enact the myth of Psyche and be re-born a butterfly. In "Pyrrhic Victory," she resists the successive metamorphoses of self demanded by the scale of loss: "Some grief is larger than my body is." "I do not want to be a chrysalis again"—but she is in her chrysalis already:

> How long will I have to live here quickened in
>
> My finespun case, like a folded pilgrim, blushing,
>   Till I am moth.
>
> (TIM, 62)

The will is defeated not merely in its inability to stave off mortality, but even more in a new helplessness, the inability to command its own passions, as its erotic vertigo returns. "Pamphlet on Ravening," spoken from "the prison of the Post-Hellenic world," is uncompromising in admitting the continued strength of the erotic, not manipulable by will:

> You cannot will intoxication, vertigo, a ravening or wild
>   Love.
>
> (TIM, 67)

Because in the unmagical everyday "it's against the law to harbor wonder," the poet finds herself, satirically, "On the slower barge / Up the River Hubris in the post-curiouser world" (TIM, 67). *Trouble in Mind*, in one of its excursions, borrows from Wallace Stevens's notebook a few of the titles for which he never wrote the intended poems. Brock-Broido takes the occasion to write a new poem under each Stevensian title. In one of these, "The Halo That Would Not Light," childhood is violently rethought, as the poet borrows from (and contradicts) Wordsworth. In Brock-Broido's myth, from its obscure pre-existence among raptors, the tiny body of the child is dropped into life and (temporarily) deposited in a deceptive softness: now, to end childhood, a raptor-wind is "hover-hunting," looking to pluck the child back, killed, into the dark raptor-world, "And the spectacular catastrophe / Of your endless childhood // Is done" (TIM, 3). The death knell of innocence sounds again.

Brock-Broido's first three books record the inner life of a poet passing from childhood through adolescence through maturity: "I was little; I am middle. Will I not // Grow old, not final / As the broken pleated falcon's wing?" (TIM, 4). And then *Stay, Illusion* appeared, its title citing Horatio's address to Hamlet's father's ghost: summoned by his son, the ghost returns, suggesting that the wish to retain illusion never vanishes. Time is now told in girlhoods lost, as "A Girl Ago" is followed by "Two Girls Ago." The first says, "I was sixteen for twenty years," and the second, referring to anthologies that append dates of birth and death to the poets' names, ventures "In the table of contents I'm not dead yet." The plainness vowed in *Trouble in Mind* lives on in these pages: "If it is written down, you can't rescind it" (SI, 3). The sway between wishing and rescinding governs *Stay, Illusion*. Comedy, tragedy, and irony are no longer discrete effects. In "You Have Harnessed Yourself Ridiculously to This World," the effect on the polar bear of the melting of the arctic ice cap, retold in the sentimentally anthropomorphic words of *Animal Planet*, coexists with the poet's mordant self-portrait mocking her diminished animal grandeur as she divests herself from primacy, changing from Great Ape to a murmuring marmoset:

> Too far gone to halt the Arctic Cap's catastrophe, big beautiful
> Blubbery white bears each clinging to his one last hunk of ice.
> . . . . .
>
>   We have come to terms with our Self
> Like a marmoset getting out of her Great Ape suit.
> (SI, 7)

In between these two comic bookends is the devastating question of the denuded heart: "For whom left am I first?" (SI, 7).

In *Stay, Illusion*, Brock-Broido's lyric habitats take on invented Latin names never free of self-irony: she dwells in the Trepidarium, or the Abandonarium, anatomizing fears or loneliness in her third person "case history" of the self:

> Case history: wistful, woke most every afternoon
>   In the green rooms of the Abandonarium.
>   Beautiful cage, asylum in.
>
> . . . . .
> Her single subject the idea that every single thing she loves
>   Will (perhaps tomorrow) die.
> (SI, 29)

Pathos is surrounded by harsher moments: in "Contributor's Note," which forces the conventional genre into emotional exposure, the poet reproaches herself in her autumn poetry-making for not making full use of the material that life has given her (in this case a mythical horse, resembling those in the prehistoric caves, mentioned elsewhere in the poetry):

> How dare you come home from your factory
> Of autumns, your slaughterhouse, weathered
> And incurious, with your hair bound
> Loosely, not making use
> Of every single part of the horse
> That was given you. What of his hooves.
> His mane. His heart his gait his cello tail
> His joy in finding apples fallen
> As he built his coat for winter every year.
>
> (SI, 22–23)

"The wise man avenges by building his city in snow," said Stevens,[6] and the poet's stoic horse, every year, builds his coat in snow. He lives not in anticipation of spring, but in preparation for another winter. The stoicism of the helpless recurs in *Stay, Illusion:* in "The Death-Watch Log," illiterate prison guards record an illiterate condemned man's docile and deluded wish for a last meal: "koolaid, cherry & he said, for later—/ pecan pie for just after when he would went to sleep" (SI, 55). There is stoicism, too, in the poet's own existence among her ghosts: "How is it you can explain their living here with me . . . / In my single-person tax-bracket of one alive, there are more / Living here with me not alive // Than are" (SI, 66). Brock-Broido finds stoic epigrams in her silent world: "There is no thou to speak of" (SI, 71). (Expecting "speak to," we experience the sudden mortal wrench as second-person speech becomes third-person reference.)

The pity that animates the pictures of suffering—of people, of animals—in Brock-Broido's work is balanced against the pictures of incarceration, of infidelities, of illness, of deformation: "The animals are ironed, docile now, flat at my feet" (SI, 94). The poet's Gothic, so indispensable to her early work, has become "plain" in her flattened menagerie, in her taciturn journeys ("The train passed slowly through every belt we know: Prayer, Tornado, Bible, Grain," SI, 64), in her description of a mummified bird placed in its owner's purse "circa 1892" and hidden behind the chimney bricks in the Dumas Brothel Museum: "In your glass case now, canary, . . . // You are beautiful, grotesque" (SI, 60). The poet constructs a single Gordian knot of the beautiful, the pathetic, the grotesque, and the plain, entangled in provocative language boldly ascending into precarious regions. With her fourth book, so original and so candid, Brock-Broido awakes in her readers an appetite for future lyrics of pity, satire, grief, comedy, and epigram. Uncontainable in any single category of women's verse, she is autobiographer and ventriloquist, domestic and urban, melancholy and sparkling, contemporary and archaic, plain and wizardly, American and European. She memorializes moments at once unforgettable and inconspicuous. Of all the vignettes of her childhood tucked into the poems, my favorite remains the one recounting the absurd safety procedures in the "bomb shelters" of elementary schools. The world was still "warm inside," when the innocence of childhood was as yet unacquainted with death's cold:

> Before the Iron Curtain, before the sadder
> Century, the one I was born into as
> A little Cosmonaut, creeping in bomb shelters
> With Mr. White, the school custodian
> Who shoveled the coal while I occupied the alcove
> Of my ways, it was so warm inside.
> (SI, 87)

"Medieval Warm Time" is the title of this snapshot of childhood. The chill that has succeeded it gives *Stay, Illusion* its prevailing climate, but Brock-Broido does not sacrifice her comic edge to the gloom of elegy. What is artifice, after all, but the wry recognition of comic distance in every representation?

27

Pried Open for All the World to See

Berryman the Poet

On October 25, 1914, the remarkable poet John Berryman was born in McAlester, Oklahoma. To mark the hundredth year since Berryman's birth, Farrar, Straus and Giroux offered *The Heart Is Strange: New Selected Poems* and reissued *The Dream Songs*, *77 Dream Songs*, and *Berryman's Sonnets*. The title of the peculiar *Selected Poems* obscures the fact that the selection includes not a single poem from Berryman's most famous work, *The Dream Songs*. (The publicity notice for the *Selected* promises "a generous selection from across Berryman's varied career" and claims to celebrate "the whole Berryman.") A reader ordering the book online might well expect that a rational *Selected* would devote a substantial number of its pages to *The Dream Songs*, and would feel deceived when the book arrived. (The far more comprehensive *John Berryman: Selected Poems* from the Library of America finds room for sixty-one Dream Songs.) What we really need, of course, is a *Complete Poems*, but that is not forthcoming from any quarter.

Berryman's life, as related in John Haffenden's detailed 1982 biography, makes for excruciating reading. The maladies from which Berryman suffered—bipolar illness and severe alcoholism—ruined his abused body and shook his excellent mind. Since the medicine of his era could do little for these illnesses, his life became marred by successive hospitalizations, attempts at rehabilitation, divorces, the loss of at least one job, and desperate remedies (including a late return to his childhood Roman Catholicism just before his suicide at fifty-seven). His physical state in middle age brings to mind Whitman's "A Hand Mirror":

> Hold it up sternly! See this it sends back! (Who is it? Is it you?)
> . . . . .

No more a flashing eye, no more a sonorous voice or springy step,
   Now some slave's eye, voice, hands, step,
. . . . .
No brain, no heart left—no magnetism of sex;
Such, from one look in this looking-glass ere you go hence,
Such a result so soon—and from such a beginning!

When Berryman was eleven, his financially unsuccessful (and unfaithful) father, John Allyn Smith, shot himself in Tampa (where the Smiths had moved when they left Oklahoma). The poet's formidable and overbearing mother shortly afterward married their landlord (who had apparently been her lover before her husband's suicide). She then made it the principal business of her life to establish a fusion of identities with her elder child; as her intrusive and incessant letters reveal, she never relaxed her tentacular grip on her son. The young John Smith, adopted by his stepfather, was known thenceforward as John Berryman, inaugurating a strange duality of identity that was to influence both his poetic themes and his stylistic inventions. The Berrymans moved from Florida to Connecticut, and John was sent to the South Kent School, an Episcopal establishment where he found adolescent devotion serving as an acolyte at morning Mass.

When Berryman went off to Columbia, he began to reap the rewards of his enormous ambition and omnivorous reading; he attracted close friends who prized his wit and emotional abandon, and he was encouraged by his teacher Mark Van Doren, who understood his literary powers. On the Columbia Kellett Fellowship, Berryman went off to Clare College, Cambridge:

O a young American poet, not yet good,
Off to the strange Old World to pick their brains
& visit by hook or crook with W. B. Yeats.[1]

(He indeed managed to visit Yeats, who remained his poetic hero.) At Cambridge, Berryman won the prize for the best Shakespeare essay, and developed an interest in Shakespeare that evolved into a lifelong torment as he struggled with various Shakespearean projects (including a never-completed edition of *King Lear*). While grant after grant supported the work on Shakespeare, grant after grant was undermined not only by the poet's ever-worsening alcoholism but also by a heart-rending set of guilts, humiliations, infidelities, embarrassments, and failures.

Like most young poets, Berryman began with serial imitation—of Hopkins, of Yeats, of Auden, and eventually of Shakespeare, writing when he was thirty-three 157 Petrarchan sonnets to "Lise," a young married woman at Princeton. When finally published by Berryman, the sonnets were prefaced by a poem in which the fifty-six-year-old poet plays the ironic spectator of his own folly at thirty-three, referring to "Lise" as "an Excellent lady, wif whom he was in wuv."[2] That mocking line is both a parody of the poet's own longing and a parody of the European sonnet tradition. Berryman learned irony from the Shakespeare of the *Sonnets*, and that irony becomes the eventual Muse of *The Dream Songs*. In an acute remark on his own poetry, Berryman announces that his Muse, though beginning as "a nymphet," in time "grew taller" and finally "manifested, well, a sense of humour / fatal to bardic pretension" (HS, 96). Before *The Dream Songs*, Berryman was unable to leap from colloquial humor to bardic aspiration: it is precisely the triumph of the best *Dream Songs* to perform tragedy and comedy simultaneously.

In his Introduction to *The Heart Is Strange*, Daniel Swift understandably wishes to urge—against the sorrows teeming in *The Dream Songs*—the poet's comedy, "a joy of voices, antic and alive . . . the pull toward life" (HS, xxxv). Swift also proposes—less convincingly—that Berryman's late "devotional" poems also serve as a counterweight to the tragic sense:

> His last two collections each include a cycle of devotional verse. . . . Like all devotional verse—and Berryman here sounds at times like George Herbert, perhaps the greatest devotional poet of all—these poems contemplate the limits of the self, and human life. (HS, xxxiii)

The "devotional" poems have none of the aesthetic élan of the tragicomic ones, and never in them does the histrionic Berryman sound at all like the subtle and fine-grained Herbert. He tries out different religious genres, imitating in his "Opus Dei," for instance, Auden's *Horae Canonicae*, a sequence marking the liturgical hours (Matins, Prime, Terce, etc.). Like Berryman's other religious poems, these "Hours" are a strained mélange of the prophets, the Psalms, the liturgy, and various manners of prayer, interspersed with badly integrated outbursts of anxiety, resentment, and penitence. Here is a sample of the late religious Berryman: at fifty-five, he wildly assumes the persona of King David, summing up his life in "King David Dances," a poem that ends with an impossible exclamation:

revolted sons, a pierced son, bound to bear,
mid hypocrites amongst idolaters,
mockt in abysm by one shallow wife,
with the ponder both of priesthood & of State
heavy upon me, yea,
all the black same I dance my blue head off!

(HS, 154)

Berryman being Berryman, there are flashes of intellectual or emotional fire even in his weaker poems, but those moments are insufficient to bear the weight of the whole. Berryman's life as a poet ends unhappily in bathos and aesthetic uncertainty, awkwardly imitating devotional predecessors at the close just as he had awkwardly imitated predecessor-poets at the beginning. In January 1972, he killed himself by jumping off a Minneapolis bridge spanning the frozen Mississippi.

But if both beginning and end are radically imperfect, the center is remarkable. Berryman's originality had first been acknowledged when he published the 1953 "Homage to Mistress Bradstreet," a daring poem of fifty-seven stanzas taking its origin from the life and work of America's first woman poet, Anne Bradstreet. A passenger on *The Arbella* in 1630, Anne had, at sixteen, been married to Simon Bradstreet, to whom she eventually bore eight children. In spite of pregnancies and household duties, Anne continued doggedly to write her poems, which were published in England in 1650 as *The Tenth Muse Lately Sprung up in America*. In his "Homage," Berryman experiments with forms of narration: partly, he retells Anne Bradstreet's life in historical terms, partly engages in dialogue with her, partly allows Anne to speak for herself as his own voice recedes, and, increasingly, as the poem progresses, fuses his own identity with hers. In a bravura passage at the climax of the poem she gives birth, addressing the poet who suffers her pangs as he ventriloquizes her voice. Fearing in her pain that she is in the grip of the devil, she dramatically banishes, and then recalls, her poet:

So squeezed, wince you I scream? I love you & hate
off with you. Ages! *Useless.* Below my waist
he has me in Hell's vise.
Stalling. He let go. Come back: brace
me somewhere. No. No. Yes! everything down

hardens I press with horrible joy down
my back cracks like a wrist
shame I am voiding oh behind it is too late

(HS, 55)

In the Age of Eliot, such violence of language (learned principally from Hopkins) made the poetry-reading public take notice. Daniel Swift says unequivocally that "Homage to Mistress Bradstreet" is Berryman's "masterpiece, in the old-fashioned sense of the word—the early work that proves an apprentice is now a master of his chosen form" (HS, xiii). Yet in the light of what was to come in *The Dream Songs*, there is something stiff and willed in Berryman's historical pastiche. Archives, histories, and poems supply Anne's potted *récit* of life in Andover:

Food endless, people few, all to be done.
As pippins roast, the question of the wolves
turns & turns.
Fangs of a wolf will keep, the neck
round of a child, that child brave. I remember who
in meeting smiled & was punisht, and I know who
whispered & was stockt.
We lead a thoughtful life. But Boston's cage we shun.

(HS, 54)

The invented hermaphroditic self of Bradstreet/Berryman and the simultaneous co-presence of the seventeenth and the twentieth centuries woke up the reviewers, and Berryman's fame began.

What was missing in "Homage to Mistress Bradstreet," in spite of Berryman's years of labor on the poem, was his humor—an intrinsic part of his personality but not yet of his style. The voltage of the later Berryman style surged up a decade later in *77 Dream Songs* (1964), a volume that still gives transcendent pleasure. Michael Hofmann praises "that whinny; those initially baffling, then canny and eventually unforgettable rearrangements of words; that irresistible flow of thoughts and nonthoughts."[3] It is true that *The Dream Songs* had been preceded in 1948 by the poet's three "Nervous Songs," which—Daniel Swift says inaccurately—were "each in the same stanzaic form as the later Dream Songs" (HS, xix)—except that they weren't. Each of the "Nervous Songs" does consist of three stanzas of six lines each, but their "stanzaic form" differs in instantly apparent ways from that of *The Dream Songs*. (*The Dream Songs* rhyme loosely, and lines 3 and 6 of each stanza are normally trimeters, whereas the stanzas of "The Nervous Songs"—most in successive pentameters and tightly rhymed—have none of the insouciant lilt of song.)

In the first Dream Song, Berryman introduces Henry; "Henry" was the nickname given him by his wife Eileen Simpson. Henry is a comic and stylized Id, on whose behavior the poet comments in both his own voice and that of an unnamed Interlocutor (who resembles in his dry remarks a taciturn but kind psychoanalyst). Henry's petulant observation are often relayed in indirect discourse: "It was the thought that they thought / they could *do* it"—where the "it" is never specified, the "they" perpetrating "it" equally unnamed, but the paranoia patent:

> Huffy Henry hid   the day,
> unappeasable Henry sulked.
> I see his point,—a trying to put things over.
> It was the thought that they thought
> they could *do* it made Henry wicked & away.
> But he should have come out and talked.
>
> All the world like a woolen lover
> once did seem on Henry's side.
> Then came a departure.
> Thereafter nothing fell out as it might or ought.
> I don't see how Henry, pried
> Open for all the world to see, survived.[4]

We can't see how Henry survived, either. But survive he does, through all the illiterate glory of the Songs, jaunty with their adventitious rhymes, aghast at the turns of fortune.

The relation between the narrator and Henry is clarified by the dialogue between Henry and—as Berryman adopts the convention of a minstrel show—his Interlocutor, the other nameless "end man" who intervenes in the role of Henry's conscience, and who sometimes addresses Henry as "Mr. Bones" ("bones" being slang for gaming dice). In a minstrel show, while the stage curtain was down between vaudeville acts, the "end men"—white stand-up comics in blackface—entertained the audience with jokes in coarse Negro dialect. Berryman was perfectly well aware of the political incorrectness of the minstrel show; that was the point. Just as the traditional end men pretended to be black while mocking "their own" black speech and offering crude jokes of black life, so the Interlocutor mocks Henry's resentful wish to live outside the usual moral and intellectual codes. Henry is a dashing imaginative invention, not merely in concept (although a walking, talking, Id is a fine idea) but in language. As occasion requires, Henry can be somber or fantastic, rueful or angry, funny or speculative, awed or contemptuous, and his sentences, especially his opening sentences, are a spectacle in themselves. Sometimes the openings are blunt: "Henry hates the world" (DS, 81). Sometimes they are puzzling: "The taxi makes the vegetables fly" (DS, 80). And sometimes they are painful: "He lay in the middle of the world, and twitcht" (DS, 53). As for the conclusions of the Songs, they are often nightmarish, rife with obscure threats:

> —Are you radioactive, Pal?—Pal, radioactive.
> —Has you the night sweats & the day sweats, pal?
> —Pal, I do.
> —Did your gal leave you?—What do *you* think, pal?
> —Is that thing on the front of your head what it seems to be, pal?
> —Yes, pal.
> (DS, 55)

After publishing the breathtaking *77 Dream Songs*, one of the permanent volumes of twentieth-century American poetry, Berryman went on compulsively to write still more. By the time of *His Toy, His Dream, His Rest* (1968), the number mounts to 385 (and he left behind, when he died, both finished and unfinished Songs, together with boxes and boxes of manuscript notebooks, dream analysis, and letters). While it's true that after the first 77, the vivacity and humor of the Songs diminished, there are still numberless sardonic remarks and comic scenes to entertain the reader: "Three limbs, three seasons smashed; well, one to go" begins one of the hospital sequences:

> His friends alas went all about their ways
> intact. Couldn't William break at least a collar-bone?
> (DS, 183)

Deaths begin to crowd out gaiety, and the Songs increasingly become dirges. And still the Songs pursue their thorny way, tirelessly pursuing possibilities of utterance, elaborate and spare, hit-and-miss or mad:

O formal & elaborate I choose you

but I love too the spare, the hit-or-miss,
the mad, I sometimes can't   always tell them apart.
(DS, 284)

Berryman inherits his bold stylistic inclusiveness from Whitman's *Song of Myself:*

I find I incorporate gneiss, coal, long-threaded moss, fruits, grains,
    esculent roots,
And am stucco'd with quadrupeds and birds all over.

But Berryman differs from Whitman in his willingness to be deliberately illiterate; even Whitman was not prepared to operate outside of grammatical
norms. Whitman is full of humor, but it is not syntactic or grammatical humor,
on the contrary; his ornately parallel syntax, his fluid grammar, do not risk
outraging literacy itself, no matter how heterodox his themes. Influenced by
Hopkins's wrenching of syntax, Berryman adopted grammatical and syntactic
illiteracy as his stylistic signature, wronging syntax in a mode beyond even that
of Hopkins. Although Berryman has been criticized for "appropriating" the
"black English" of the minstrel show end men, his aim is not transcriptive but
again, as always, stylistic: he invents a freedom from standard English not
by writing poems in authentic dialect—as both black and white poets had
done—but by confecting an intermediate form of speech—half dialect, half
sophisticated—that never existed in "real life." Berryman makes up his own
weird form of incorrectness, exaggerating the hybrid diction of the white man
in blackface. Berryman's grave Interlocutor, too, is a stage presence, not a
person, and the Songs' parade of idiosyncratic models, from Hopkins to folk-
song, is Berryman's Dickinsonian "menagerie," his Yeatsian "circus animals."
    Everyone has a repertoire of favorite Dream Songs. Michael Hofmann (in
Where Have You Been?) says that in his youth, intoxicated by Berryman's language, he could, if cued merely by number, have recited many of the Songs: say
"14" and he could flash back "Life, friends, is boring." To read the Songs as
Hofmann did is to find (on one page or another) one's own life, simultaneously
jeered at and sympathized with. In "Dream Song 134" (the song for university
lecturers), Henry-as-academic is at once bedraggled and heroic: sick with a
hangover, his digestion deranged, he wakes at dawn not only to vomiting and
depression but also to a grim sense of the avid narcissism of his students:

Sick at 6 & sick again at 9
was Henry's gloomy Monday morning oh.
Still he had to lecture.
They waited, his little children, for stricken Henry
to rise up yet once more again and come oh.
They figured he was a fixture,

nuts to their bolts, keys to their bloody locks
. . . . .
He had smoked a pack of cigarettes by 10
& was ready to go. Peace to his ashes then,
poor Henry,
with all this gas & shit blowing through it
four times in 2 hours, his tail ached.
He arose, benign, & performed.

(DS, 151)

The words "benign" (exalted by bracketing commas) and "performed" (reflecting on the lecturer's meta-role as actor) pull readers up short. On such a
morning, with such a hangover, who could rise to being "benign" and at the
same time possess the detachment to watch himself "perform"? After Berryman's
theatrical fireworks, some midcentury poets could seem buttoned up, inhib-
ited, careful of the proprieties, in thrall to a filtered conception of life. Plath and
Lowell and Ginsberg, however, cooperated in the postwar performance of the
improper. In "The Creations of Sound," Stevens remarks that "Speech is not
dirty silence / Clarified. It is silence made still dirtier."[5] Berryman would have
understood those lines.

Untold pages have already been written on Berryman. The old questions—
the existential status of Henry (a persona? an alter ego?) and the Interlocutor
(a caricature? a guardian angel?)—have been well aired, even to excess: after
all, representation of a person in the fictive brevity of lyric could hardly be
anything but a stylized sketch, with none of the "roundness" of novelistic
character. What remains true is that *The Dream Songs* find a thrilling way of
creating a protagonist far more winning in his failure and sadness and rage than
the archaic troubadour of *Berryman's Sonnets* or the stiff Mistress Bradstreet's
symbiotic poet. *The Dream Songs* dramatizes a history of indignities and humiliations expressed with a striking candor that Berryman learned, it seems to
me, from Shakespeare's tragedies. Shakespeare's is a candor both plain ("No

cause, no cause": *Lear*) and baroque ("If it be now, 'tis not to come; if it be not to come, it will be now; if it be not now, yet it will come": *Hamlet*). And Henry's dramatic inventories of explicit misery draw on those that Shakespeare poured out in *Lear:*

> Poor naked wretches, wheresoe'er you are,
> That bide the pelting of this pitiless storm,
> How shall your houseless heads and unfed sides,
> Your loop'd and window'd raggedness, defend you
> From seasons such as these?

Berryman's candor is medical ("More Sparine for Pelides"; DS, 60); physical ("Three limbs, three seasons smashed; well, one to go"; DS, 183); sorrowful ("There sat down once on Henry's heart a thing / só heavy"; DS, 33); comic ("what wonders is she sitting on, over there?"; DS, 6); intellectual ("I am heavy bored"; DS, 16); marital ("It is a true error to marry with poets"; DS, 206); social ("The doomed young envy the old, the doomed old the dead young"; DS, 209); legal ("He had a court case / he was bound to lose"; DS, 233); and interrogative ("Why then did he make, at such cost, *cra\\;y* sounds?"; DS, 290). The reader is arrested by the bristling or plangent candor of Song after Song. In the Songs, Berryman is an orchestra all by himself, in which one instrument after another prevails. In a single stanza, an insistent percussion ("need need need") suddenly pivots into the silent writing-voices of a dismembered body:

> Hunger was constitutional with him,
> women, cigarettes, liquor, need need need
> until he went to pieces.
> The pieces sat up & wrote. They did not heed
> their piecedom but kept very quietly on
> among the chaos.
> (DS, 333)

In the Songs, it is, in Prufrock's words, "as if a magic lantern threw the nerves in patterns on a screen." Whenever a complex problem demands attention— health, family, despair, God, art, reputation—restless modulations thrust themselves forward on the screen, frustrated in turn by their own vacillations.

Berryman's quest for fame (in his more abject and therefore flamboyant moments) led him to measure himself constantly against famous poets of his century; curiously, among these Stevens stands out as the real challenger. Berryman's elegy "So Long? Stevens" (DS, 238), in its reluctant and envious judgment, memorably flouts Stevensian sublimity. It begins in comedy, proceeds to a self-deprecating definition of poetry as a "mutter," and then comments, baffled, on the impression of "something . . . something . . . not there in [Stevens's] flourishing art." In mid-stanza Henry addresses himself apologetically to Stevens ("O veteran of death") and then cannot decide whether Stevens's extended meditations are "monotonous" or "ever-fresh": "It sticks / in Henry's throat to judge—brilliant, he seethe; / better than us; less wide" (DS, 238). Berryman knows very well the cost of relinquishing a Stevensian stoicism in favor of the world's broad social comedy, but he makes that choice, all the while doubting its value. He suspects, in fact, that the minimalism and pessimism of an author such as Beckett are fully warranted, and rebuke his own comedy. Questioned whether it is the artist's duty to express "human affirmation," Berryman replies:

> Well, I don't know. I am *incredibly doubtful*. All you have to do is to think about Samuel Beckett: a mind so dark that it makes you wonder *if the Renaissance really took place!*[6]

The "Dark Ages," in short, never ended: and what, the example of Beckett sarcastically asks, is there to "affirm"?

Berryman was twelve when he wrote his first long work, a science fiction novel.[7] Henry, and his stern Interlocutor as well, are like characters in science fiction: programmatic, single-functioned, allegorical: the Id and the Conscience. Within the encounters of this nonrealistic pair, Berryman inserts the imperfect, grandiose, inebriated, wry, grieving, guilt-ridden existence of a greatly gifted poet possessed by the devils of mania, depression, and drunkenness. *The Dream Songs*, flawed as they are, remain infinitely quotable—the witty lament of a singular man with the courage to exhibit himself in shame, indignity, and exuberant speech. Nothing else in Berryman equals them.

Notes

Introduction

1. This essay was originally given as the 2001 annual ACLS Charles Homer Haskins Lecture for the series "A Life of Learning," and was published as "Occasional Paper No. 50" by the ACLS.

1. The Ocean, the Bird, and the Scholar

1. Wallace Stevens, *Letters of Wallace Stevens,* ed. Holly Stevens (Berkeley: University of California Press, 1996), 73.

2. Wallace Stevens, *Collected Poetry and Prose* (New York: Library of America, 1997), 269; henceforth cited in the text with parenthetical page references.

2. Fin-de-Siècle Lyric

1. W. B. Yeats, *Collected Poems* (New York: Macmillan, 1956), 67. Page numbers for all subsequent quotations from Yeats refer to this volume and are cited parenthetically.

2. Jorie Graham, *Region of Unlikeness* (New York: Ecco, 1991). Page numbers for all subsequent quotations from Graham refer to this volume and are cited parenthetically.

3. Wallace Stevens, *Collected Poetry and Prose* (New York: Library of America, 1997), 311.

4. Ibid., 218.

3. The Unweary Blues

1. Langston Hughes, *The Collected Poems of Langston Hughes,* ed. Arnold Rampersad and David Roessel (New York: Alfred A. Knopf, 1994), 143; henceforth cited in the text with parenthetical page references.

4. The Nothing That Is

1. Charles Wright, *Hard Freight* (Middletown: Wesleyan University Press, 1973), 19.

2. Charles Wright, *Chickamauga* (New York: Farrar, Straus and Giroux, 1995), 47; henceforth cited in the text with parenthetical page references.

3. Charles Wright, *The World of the Ten Thousand Things: Poems 1980–1990* (New York: Farrar, Straus and Giroux, 1990), 33.

5. American X-Rays

1. Czesław Miłosz, "To Allen Ginsberg," *New and Collected Poems, 1931–2001* (New York: HarperCollins, 2001), 612.

2. Allen Ginsberg, *Collected Poems, 1947–1997* (New York: HarperCollins, 2006), 134–136; henceforth cited in the text with parenthetical page references.

7. *The Snow Poems* and *Garbage*

1. A. R. Ammons, *The Snow Poems* (New York: W. W. Norton, 1977); henceforth cited in the text as SP with parenthetical page references.

2. A. R. Ammons, *Set in Motion: Essays, Interviews, Dialogues*, ed. Zofia Burr (Ann Arbor: University of Michigan Press, 1996), 5; henceforth cited in the text as SM with parenthetical page references.

3. A. R. Ammons, *Garbage* (New York: W. W. Norton, 1993), 13; henceforth cited in the text as G with parenthetical page references.

8. All Her Nomads

1. Mary Jo Salter, foreword to *The Collected Poems* by Amy Clampitt (New York: Alfred A. Knopf, 1997), xviii; henceforth cited in the text as F with parenthetical page references.

2. Amy Clampitt, interview with Emily B. Todd, *Verse* 10, no. 3 (1993): 5; henceforth cited in the text as V with parenthetical page references.

3. Amy Clampitt, *The Collected Poems* (New York: Alfred A. Knopf, 1997), 143; henceforth cited in the text as CP with parenthetical page references.

9. Seamus Heaney and the *Oresteia*

1. This essay was originally read at a meeting of the American Philosophical Society on May 26, 1998.

2. Seamus Heaney, "The Art of Poetry No. 75," *Paris Review* 144 (Fall 1997): 136–137.

3. Seamus Heaney, "Mycenae Lookout," *The Spirit Level* (London: Faber and Faber, 1996), 34; henceforth cited in the text with parenthetical page references.

4. Seamus Heaney, "Further Language," *Studies in the Literary Imagination* 30 (Fall 1997): 12.

5. Aeschylus, *The Oresteia*, trans. Robert Fagles (New York: Penguin, 1979), 104.

6. Ibid., 153.

7. Wallace Stevens, "Thirteen Ways of Looking at a Blackbird," *Collected Poetry and Prose* (New York: Library of America, 1997), 74.

8. Czesław Miłosz, *Collected Poems, 1931–1987* (New York: Ecco Press, 1988), 60.

9. Heaney, "Art of Poetry," 136.

10. Melville

1. Herman Melville, *Collected Poems of Herman Melville*, ed. Howard P. Vincent (Chicago: Packard and Company, 1947), 102; henceforth cited in the text with parenthetical page references.

2. The last line of "The March into Virginia" is quoted from the original publication of *Battle-Pieces*.

3. Stanton Garner, *The Civil War World of Herman Melville* (Lawrence: University Press of Kansas, 1993), 349–351.

11. Lowell's Persistence

1. Robert Lowell, *Collected Poems* (New York: Farrar, Straus and Giroux, 2003); henceforth cited in the text with parenthetical page references.

2. Robert Lowell, *Collected Prose* (New York: Farrar, Straus and Giroux, 1987), 287; henceforth cited in the text as CP with parenthetical page references.

12. Wallace Stevens

1. Wallace Stevens, *Collected Poetry and Prose* (New York: Library of America, 1997), 30; henceforth cited in the text with parenthetical page references.

2. Cited from Wallace Stevens's notebook *From Pieces of Paper*, in George Lensing, *Wallace Stevens: A Poet's Growth* (Baton Rouge: Louisiana State University Press, 1986), 183.

3. Gottfried Benn, *Prose, Essays, Poems*, ed. Volkmar Sander (New York: Bloomsbury Academic, 1987), 33.

4. Ibid., 183.

5. Dates cited for individual poems in this essay follow those given in Holly Stevens, ed., *Wallace Stevens: The Palm at the End of the Mind* (New York: Vintage Books, 1990), ix–xv.

13. Ardor and Artifice

1. James Merrill, *Collected Prose* (New York: Alfred A. Knopf, 2004), 143; henceforth cited in the text as CP with parenthetical page references.

2. James Merrill, *Collected Poems*, ed. J. D. McClatchy and S. Yenser (New York: Alfred A. Knopf, 2001), 600–601; henceforth cited in the text with parenthetical page references.

14. The Titles

1. The titles here were published by W. W. Norton, with the following exceptions: *Ommateum* (Dorrance); *Expressions of Sea Level* (Ohio State University Press); *Corsons Inlet* (Cornell University Press); *Tape for the Turn of the Year* (Cornell University Press); *Northfield Poems* (Cornell University Press); *The North Carolina Poems* (North Carolina Wesleyan College Press).

2. *Bosh and Flapdoodle* was published posthumously.

3. A. R. Ammons, *Set in Motion: Essays, Interviews, and Dialogues,* ed. Zofia Burr (Ann Arbor: University of Michigan Press, 1996). The foreword was originally published in *Ommateum, with Doxology* (Philadelphia: Dorrance, 1955).

4. A. R. Ammons, *Corsons Inlet* (Ithaca: Cornell University Press, 1996), 8.

5. "The Art of Poetry: LXXIII," interview with David Lehman, *The Paris Review,* no. 139 (Summer 1996): 62–91.

6. A. R. Ammons, *Expressions of Sea Level* (Columbus: Ohio State University Press, 1963), 23.

7. A. R. Ammons, *Collected Poems* (New York: W. W. Norton, 1972), 1.

8. A. R. Ammons, *Brink Road* (New York: W. W. Norton, 1996), 153.

9. Ibid., 106.

10. A. R. Ammons, *Glare* (New York: W. W. Norton, 1998), 94.

11. A. R. Ammons, *A Coast of Trees* (New York: W. W. Norton, 1981), 19.

12. A. R. Ammons, *Bosh and Flapdoodle* (New York: W. W. Norton, 2005), 14; henceforth cited in the text with parenthetical page references.

15. Poetry and the Mediation of Value

1. This essay was prepared for the Tanner Lectures on Human Values, delivered at the University of Michigan, October 29–30, 1999.

2. Walt Whitman, *Leaves of Grass and Other Writings* (New York: W. W. Norton, 2002), 276–283; henceforth cited in the text with parenthetical page references.

3. Walt Whitman, *Prose Works 1892: Collect and Other Prose,* vol. 2, ed. Floyd Stovall (New York: New York University Press, 1964), 521; henceforth cited in the text as PW with parenthetical page references.

16. "Long Pig"

1. Elizabeth Bishop, *The Complete Poems, 1927–1979* (New York: Farrar, Straus and Giroux, 1983), 159; henceforth cited in the text with parenthetical page references.

2. W. B. Yeats, *The Collected Poems of W. B. Yeats* (New York: Macmillan, 1956), 244.

17. Stevens and Keats's "To Autumn"

1. Wallace Stevens, *Collected Poetry and Prose* (New York: Library of America, 1997), 912; henceforth cited in the text with parenthetical page references.

18. "The Circulation of Small Largenesses"

1. Mark Ford, *Landlocked* (London: Chatto and Windus, 1992); henceforth cited in the text as L with parenthetical page references.

2. Mark Ford, *Soft Sift* (London: Faber and Faber, 2001); henceforth cited in the text as SS with parenthetical page references.

3. John Ashbery, *As We Know* (New York: Viking, 1979), 93.

4. John Ashbery, *Selected Poems* (New York: Viking Penguin, 1985), 175; henceforth cited in the text as SP with parenthetical page references.

5. Ezra Pound, *The Cantos* (London: Faber and Faber, 1987), 178.

6. Transcript of a letter to Helen Vendler from Ford, January 31, 1998.

7. John Ashbery, *Wakefulness* (New York: Farrar, Straus and Giroux, 1998), 40–41.

8. Mark Ford, *Times Literary Supplement*, August 29, 1997, 26.

9. Mark Ford, *New Republic*, May 26, 1997, 39.

10. Mark Ford, *Times Literary Supplement*, September 19, 1997, 27.

11. Michael Hofmann, *Times Literary Supplement*, March 6, 1992, 23.

12. Mark Ford talking to Graham Bradshaw, in *Talking Verse*, ed. Robert Crawford, Henry Hart, David Kinloch, and Richard Price (St. Andrews and Williamsburg: Verse, 1995), 54–58, especially 57.

13. Ford, *Talking Verse*, 58.

19. Wallace Stevens

1. Wallace Stevens, *Collected Poetry and Prose* (New York: Library of America, 1997), 207; henceforth cited in the text as LOA with parenthetical page references.

2. George Herbert, *The Works of George Herbert*, ed. F. E. Hutchinson (Oxford: Clarendon, 1964), 58.

3. John Milton, *Paradise Lost*, Book 1: 300–304, in *Complete Poems and Major Prose*, ed. Merritt Y. Hughes (New York: Odyssey, 1957).

4. There were in Stevens's day hotels by this name in Lille and Vence; Stevens no doubt uses the name generically, as one suitable to a honeymoon hotel. Later, in "Arcades of Philadelphia the Past," he puts Parisian arcades into his American town. His early reading in French poetry (see *Souvenirs and Prophecies*, passim) pervades his poems to the end. "French and English," as he says in his *Adagia*, "constitute a single language" (LOA, 914).

5. The word we would expect to find, one used elsewhere by Stevens, is "poverty." But "poverty" is a concept, and "poorness" is a quality, as we are made to realize when the unexpected

word "poorness" makes us examine its difference from the conventionally used "poverty." The richness of "poorness" can be seen by examining its meanings as listed by the *OED*. The first, listed as obsolete, is "want of wealth or possessions; indigence (now replaced by POVERTY)." The others are, in succession: "Deficiency in some good constituent; unproductiveness; leanness or want of vigour caused by ill feeding; thinness, scantiness, insufficiency. Deficiency in some desirable quality; smallness of worth; inferiority, paltriness, meanness. Want of spirit or courage; paltriness or meanness of character or conduct." Stevens's "poorness," which stems from sexual rejection and describes the absence of an emotional life in the present, partakes of all these qualities, both material and characterological. I imagine Stevens scanning the *OED* after thinking of "poorness" and being pleased with what he found.

6. Here is what Bart Eeckhout says: "The reason that Vendler interprets the poem's syntax as unequivocally as she does is that she wants 'The Motive for Metaphor' to corroborate a teleological narrative according to which Stevens passes from an embryonic stage in *Harmonium* through a more complex but not yet fully realized middle period (evidenced by 'The Motive for Metaphor'), to the final culmination of his late work, where extremes of complexity and awareness are reached." Bart Eeckhout, *Wallace Stevens and the Limits of Reading and Writing* (Columbia: University of Missouri Press, 2002), 248n39.

I do not believe I have ever referred to the stage of Stevens's writing in *Harmonium* as "embryonic." To the contrary: Stevens was never more sophisticated, "aware," and "complex" than he was in certain poems in *Harmonium*. To point out change, and continuous self-revision, is not to point out a "teleological" advance in "complexity" and "awareness." However, the issues of old age are not those of youth or middle age; and Stevens's awareness of new issues in his life and culture, with a consequent opening up of such issues in language and structure, is one of the features of his poetry.

20. Jorie Graham

1. John Keats, *Letters*, ed. Hyder Rollins, 2 vols. (Cambridge, MA: Harvard University Press, 1958), 2:238.

2. Wallace Stevens, *Collected Poetry and Prose* (New York: Library of America, 1997), 48.

3. Gerard Manley Hopkins, *Poetical Works*, ed. Norman H. Mackenzie (Oxford: Clarendon, 1990), 182.

4. Ibid., 198.

5. Ibid., 190.

6. Walt Whitman, *Leaves of Grass*, ed. Michael Moon (New York: W. W. Norton, 2002), 103.

7. Ibid.

8. Stevens, *Collected Poetry*, 437.

9. Jorie Graham, *Erosion* (Princeton: Princeton University Press, 1983), 8–9; henceforth cited in the text as E with parenthetical page references.

10. Jorie Graham, *The End of Beauty* (New York: Ecco, 1987), 67; henceforth cited in the text as EB with parenthetical page references.

11. Stevens, *Collected Poetry*, 138.

12. Jorie Graham, *Materialism* (New York: Ecco, 1993), 85–86.

13. Jorie Graham, *The Errancy* (New York: Ecco, 1999), 103–106.

14. Stevens, *Collected Poetry*, 351.

21. Attention, Shoppers

1. John Ashbery, *Selected Prose*, ed. Eugene Richie (Ann Arbor: University of Michigan Press, 2004), 112; henceforth cited in the text as SP with parenthetical page references.

2. John Ashbery, *Where Shall I Wander* (New York: Ecco, 2005); henceforth cited in the text with parenthetical page references.

22. Seamus Heaney's "Sweeney Redivivus"

1. Seamus Heaney, *Opened Ground* (New York: Farrar, Straus and Giroux, 1998); henceforth cited in the text with parenthetical page references. The poems omitted from "Sweeney Redivivus" in the 1998 *Opened Ground* are only tenuously allied to the story of Sweeney (with the exception of "Sweeney Returns," in which Sweeney sees his wife domiciled with another man). The five omitted poems (with their numbered place in the sequence) are as follows: "Unwinding" (no. 3), "Alerted" (no. 8), "A Waking Dream" (no. 13), "In the Chestnut Tree" (no. 14), and "Sweeney's Returns" (no. 15).

2. *Sweeney Astray* (New York: Farrar, Strauss and Giroux, 1984). The original 1983 publication was by the Field Day Theatre Company, Derry, Ireland.

3. Heaney said that the traitor referred to here is Leonard McNally. McNally is not actually represented in the engraving described in "The Old Icons," though Heaney, at the time of writing, thought he was included in the group depicted. (Conversation with Helen Vendler.)

23. The Democratic Eye

1. John Ashbery, *A Worldly Country: New Poems* (New York: Ecco, 2008), 64; henceforth cited in the text with parenthetical page references.

24. Losing the Marbles

1. James Merrill, *Collected Poems*, ed. J. D. McClatchy and S. Yenser (New York: Alfred A. Knopf, 2001), 809; henceforth cited in the text with parenthetical page references.

2. These are "Days of 1964," "Days of 1935," "Days of 1971," "Days of 1941 and '44," and "Days of 1994."

3. For Merrill's interest in, and use of, the Greek language, see Rachel Hadas, "From Stage Set to Heirloom: Greece in the Work of James Merrill," *Arion* 6, no. 3 (Winter 1999): 51–68.

4. James Merrill, *The Changing Light at Sandover* (New York: Alfred A. Knopf, 1982), 369–370.

25. Mark Ford

1. Mark Ford, *Landlocked* (London: Chatto and Windus, 1992); henceforth cited in the text as L with parenthetical page references.

2. Mark Ford, *Selected Poems* (Minneapolis: Coffee House Press, 2014), 96; henceforth cited in the text as SP with parenthetical page references.

3. Mark Ford, *Soft Sift* (London: Faber and Faber, 2001); Mark Ford, *Six Children* (London: Faber and Faber, 2011).

4. Personal letter to Helen Vendler.

5. "Out of Nothing—Mark Ford," interview with Kit Toda, *The Literateur*, July 10, 2009, http://literateur.com/out-of-nothing-mark-ford/.

26. Notes from the Trepidarium

1. Lucie Brock-Broido, *Stay, Illusion* (New York: Alfred A. Knopf, 2013); henceforth cited in the text as SI with parenthetical page references.

2. Lucie Brock-Broido, *A Hunger* (New York: Alfred A. Knopf, 1997), 3; henceforth cited in the text as AH with parenthetical page references.

3. http://spenserians.cath.vt.edu/TextRecord.php?textsid=33407, accessed June 30, 2014.

4. Lucie Brock-Broido, *The Master Letters* (New York: Alfred A. Knopf, 1995), vii; henceforth cited in the text as ML with parenthetical page references.

5. Lucie Brock-Broido, *Trouble in Mind* (New York: Alfred A. Knopf, 2004), 9; henceforth cited in the text as TIM with parenthetical page references.

6. Wallace Stevens, *Collected Poetry and Prose* (New York: Library of America, 1997), 128.

27. Pried Open for All the World to See

1. John Berryman, *The Heart Is Strange: New Selected Poems* (New York: Farrar, Straus and Giroux, 2014), 105; henceforth cited in the text as HS with parenthetical page references.

2. John Berryman, *Berryman's Sonnets* (New York: Farrar, Straus and Giroux, 2014), xxxii.

3. Michael Hofmann, *Where Have You Been?* (New York: Farrar, Straus and Giroux, 2014), 29.

4. John Berryman, *The Dream Songs* (New York: Farrar, Straus and Giroux, 2014), 3; henceforth cited in the text as DS with parenthetical page references.

5. Wallace Stevens, *Collected Poetry and Prose* (New York: Library of America, 1997), 274.

6. William Heyen, "A Memoir and an Interview," *Ohio Review* 10 (Winter 1974): 61.

7. Ibid., 57.

Credits

Acknowledgments

I am grateful to all the editors who commissioned these essays, especially Leon Wieseltier, Robert Silvers, Mary-Kay Wilmers, John Serio, Andrew Hoyem, and the editors of other journals and collections, cited in the Notes, in which the essays were published. I thank the institutions that invited me to give the lectures printed here: the National Endowment for the Humanities (The Jefferson Lecture, "The Ocean, the Bird, and the Scholar"); the British Academy ("Wallace Stevens: Hypotheses and Contradictions"); Emory University (The Ellmann Lecture, "Jorie Graham and the Moment of Excess"); the University of Utah (the Tanner Lecture, "Poetry and the Mediation of Value: Walt Whitman"); the American Philosophical Society ("Seamus Heaney and the Oresteia"); and the American Council of Learned Societies (The Haskins Lecture, "A Life of Learning"). Harvard University has given me welcome research support from both the University Professors' Fund and the Dean's Fund. John Kulka, editor at Harvard University Press, proposed this collection and sponsored it generously. At the Press, I also wish to thank the admirable designer Annamarie Why and the production staff. Finally, I appreciate the invaluable help of my assistant Lea Sabatini, who overcame the problems of optical scanning and entered multiple corrections into electronic files.

Index